Rediscovering Irregular Warfare

CAMPAIGNS & COMMANDERS

GREGORY J. W. URWIN, SERIES EDITOR

CAMPAIGNS AND COMMANDERS

GENERAL EDITOR
Gregory J. W. Urwin, *Temple University, Philadelphia, Pennsylvania*

ADVISORY BOARD
Lawrence E. Babits, *Greenville, North Carolina*
James C. Bradford, *Texas A&M University, College Station*
Robert M. Epstein, *U.S. Army School of Advanced Military Studies, Fort Leavenworth, Kansas (retired)*
David M. Glantz, *Carlisle, Pennsylvania*
Jerome A. Greene, *Denver, Colorado*
Victor Davis Hanson, *Hoover Institution of Stanford University, Stanford*
Herman Hattaway, *Leawood, Kansas*
J. A. Houlding, *Rückersdorf, Germany*
Eugenia C. Kiesling, *U.S. Military Academy, West Point, New York*
Timothy K. Nenninger, *National Archives, Washington, D.C.*
Bruce Vandervort, *Virginia Military Institute, Lexington*

Rediscovering Irregular Warfare

Colin Gubbins and the Origins of Britain's Special Operations Executive

A. R. B. Linderman

University of Oklahoma Press | Norman

Some material in chapter 3 was published in an earlier version in Aaron Linderman, "Afrikaner Influence on the IRA and SOE," in *Securing Africa*, edited by Toyin Falola and Charles Thomas, 33–63 (New York: Routledge, 2014).

Excerpts from the private papers of Major General Sir Colin M. Gubbins, KCMG, DSO, MC, are held in the Imperial War Museum, London, and are reprinted here with permission.

Library of Congress Cataloging-in-Publication Data

Linderman, A. R. B., 1983–
  Rediscovering irregular warfare : Colin Gubbins and the origins of Britain's Special Operations Executive / A. R. B. Linderman.
    pages cm. — (Campaigns and commanders volume 52) Includes bibliographical references and index.
  ISBN 978-0-8061-5167-0 (hardcover) ISBN 978-0-8061-9400-4 (paper)
  1. Gubbins, Colin, Sir, 1896–1976. 2. Great Britain. Special Operations Executive—History. 3. Military doctrine—Great Britain—History—20th century. 4. Irregular warfare—Great Britain—History—20th century. 5. World War, 1939–1945—Secret service—Great Britain. 6. Intelligence officers—Great Britain—Biography. I. Title. II. Title: Colin Gubbins and the origins of Britain's Special Operations Executive.
  D810.S7L483 2015
  940.54′8641092—dc23
  [B]
                        2015024753

Rediscovering Irregular Warfare: Colin Gubbins and the Origins of Britain's Special Operations Executive is Volume 52 in the Campaigns and Commanders series.

The paper in this book meets the guidelines for permanence and durability of the Committee on Production Guidelines for Book Longevity of the Council on Library Resources, Inc. ∞

Copyright © 2016 by the University of Oklahoma Press, Norman, Publishing Division of the University. Paperback published 2024. Manufactured in the U.S.A.

All rights reserved. No part of this publication may be reproduced, stored in a retrieval system, or transmitted, in any form or by any means, electronic, mechanical, photocopying, recording, or otherwise—except as permitted under Section 107 or 108 of the United States Copyright Act—without the prior written permission of the University of Oklahoma Press. To request permission to reproduce selections from this book, write to Permissions, University of Oklahoma Press, 2800 Venture Drive, Norman, Okla. 73069, or e-mail rights.oupress@ou.edu.

*To Lazarus Innocent Linderman. Please pray for us.
And to Glynnis.*

Contents

Acknowledgments	ix
Acronyms	xi
1. Introduction	3
2. Baptism by Fire	12
3. Formulating a Doctrine: Learning from the Past	39
4. Formulating a Doctrine: Contemporary Examples	72
5. Gestation of Gubbins's Thinking and the Creation of SOE	102
6. SOE Training	124
7. Operations and Assessment	150
Epilogue	178
Notes	181
Bibliography	247
Index	259

Acknowledgments

Countless people contributed in one way or another to the completion of this work and deserve recognition. I regret that I can only draw attention to a few. The members of my doctoral committee, Arnold Krammer, Jason Parker, James Burk, and James Olson, provided a variety of comments and assistance. Special thanks go to my committee chairman, R. J. Q. Adams, who supported me and this project in every way imaginable. It is a better work of history for having passed through his hands, and I am the scholar I have become largely through his guidance.

The staff at Texas A&M's Sterling C. Evans Library and Cushing Memorial Library & Archives worked wonders on more than one occasion; particular thanks are deserved by the interlibrary loan staff there and at libraries around the world who made my research possible. The administrative staff of the Texas A&M History Department, especially Rita Walker and Barbara Dawson, cut through several Gordian knots of paperwork on my behalf. David Hudson deserves far more credit than I can give for his many labors in the service of the department's graduate students. Many people at Texas A&M and elsewhere read drafts or shared their expertise: Col. William Collopy, USMC (Ret.), Francis Grice (King's College, London), Eunan O'Halpin (Trinity College), Andrew L. Hargreaves, Brian Hilton (Wiley College), Brian M. Linn, Jill Russell (King's College, London), and Micah Wright, as well as anonymous reviewers and various conference participants. Two colleagues in particular, Nathaniel Weber and Blake Whitaker, suffered through years of commentary about SOE and OSS, with good humor, keen insights, and unfailing friendship. Paul and Alicia Fraser provided friendly accommodations for all my visits to Kew.

The staffs at the Bodleian Library, the Imperial War Museum, and the National Archives in Kew and College Park were always helpful. Rosalie Spire assisted me with documents at Kew. The Gubbins family has my thanks for permission to quote from Sir Colin's papers. I am indebted to all those who helped fund my research: the Texas A&M History Department, the Melbern G. Glasscock Center for Humanities Research, the Smith Richardson Foundation, and Florence and Bookman Peters. Gregory Urwin and Charles Rankin believed in this project enough to print it, while Stephanie Evans sheperded it through the editorial process, and Susan Harris graciously labored to resolve my inveterate overcapitalization, idiosyncratic punctuation, and convoluted tenses. Chris Dodge assembled the index.

Finally, Boniface, Clare, Thomas, and Thomas have my eternal thanks for assistance I can only begin to appreciate.

Acronyms

ADC	Aide-de-camp
AGW	*The Art of Guerilla Warfare*
BSC	British Security Coordination
CIGS	Chief of the Imperial General Staff
COI	Coordinator of Information
CS	Alternative name for Electra House
DCIGS	Deputy Chief of the Imperial General Staff
DDMI	Deputy Director of Military Intelligence
DMI	Director of Military Intelligence
DMO	Director of Military Operations
EH	Electra House
FANY	First Aid Nursing Yeomanry
FSR	*Field Service Regulations*
GSO2	General Staff Officer, Grade 2
GSO3	General Staff Officer, Grade 3
GS(R)	General Staff (Research)
IRA	Irish Republican Army
IWM	Imperial War Museum
MEW	Ministry of Economic Warfare
MI3(a)	France/Spain section of the Military Intelligence Directorate
MI3(c)	Soviet section of the Military Intelligence Directorate
MI5	Alternative name for the Security Service
MI6	Alternative name for the Secret Intelligence Service
MI9	War Office's escape and evasion service
MI(R)	Military Intelligence (Research)
MT1	Planning section of the Military Training Directorate
NCO	Noncommissioned officer
NKVD	Soviet People's Commissariat for Internal Affairs
OG	Operational Group

OSS	Office of Strategic Services
OWI	Office of War Information
PLH	*The Partisan Leader's Handbook*
PRO	Public Record Office
PWE	Political Warfare Executive
RA	Royal Artillery
RA5D	Royal Artillery, 5th Division
RADD	Royal Artillery, Dublin District
RAF	Royal Air Force
RFA	Royal Field Artillery
SA/B	Secret Intelligence Branch of OSS
SA/G	Special Operations Branch of OSS
SHAEF	Supreme Headquarters, Allied Expeditionary Force
SIS	Secret Intelligence Service
SMP	Shanghai Municipal Police
SNS	Special Night Squads
SO1	Propaganda branch of SOE
SO2	Operations branch of SOE
SO3	Research and planning branch of SOE
SOE	Special Operations Executive
SS	*Schutzstaffel*
S&T	Schools and Training
TA	Territorial Army
TNA	The National Archives

Rediscovering Irregular Warfare

CHAPTER 1

Introduction

Speaking to a group of Danes after World War II, Sir Colin McV. Gubbins, former director of Britain's Special Operations Executive (SOE), commented that "it is all very well to 'decree' an organization, but then someone has to create it."[1] This work examines the processes whereby SOE was created, including how its doctrine was formulated and subsequently disseminated, both to its own agents and to its American counterpart, the Office of Strategic Services (OSS). This book approaches the topic of irregular warfare from the perspective of intellectual history, seeking to understand how ideas in various times and places influenced later thoughts and actions.

The question of precedents has received some attention—if only in passing—in the scholarship of SOE. A lecture detailing the organization's history may be taken as representative of a common view: "When war broke out the art of underground warfare was unknown in England. There was nothing to build on, no past experience and no precedents."[2] While such a narrative makes all the more glorious the subsequent successes of SOE and its colleagues in OSS and the various resistance movements, it also plays to certain stereotypes of the British amateur jack-of-all-trades gentleman. This book argues that that narrative is wrong, however engaging it may be. There *were* precedents upon which SOE could, and *did*, draw. It was not created ex nihilo. Gubbins and his colleagues consciously looked to past and contemporary examples for their inspiration. In some respects, this is unsurprising. As historian Andrew Hargreaves explains:

> Britain entered the Second World War with a military that was conducive toward the development and exploitation of irregular means: the country had both a small and decentralized military well experienced in the rigors of colonial warfare and a strategic culture that placed a premium on surprise, maneuver, and peripheral attack. . . . The prominent vein of irregular actions occurring throughout British military history ensured that by the outbreak of the Second World War the British "way in warfare" was inherently amenable to the creation and employment of specialist formations.[3]

3

Such a disposition, though perhaps necessary, is not sufficient for the creation and large-scale operation of an organization such as SOE. The achievement of Gubbins and those who worked with him was taking the general idea of irregular warfare, distilling it into a manageable number of principles, and turning those principles into action in the field.

This work relies heavily on the pioneering research of M. R. D. Foot and the impressive work of Peter Wilkinson and Joan Bright Astley. Journalists sometimes claim to write the first draft of history; in the case of SOE, however, there was no such journalistic account. As a secret organization, it had very little meaningful history available to the public before Foot's *SOE in France*, published in 1966. Thus, he, Wilkinson, Astley, and other members of the first generation of SOE historians have had to do the difficult but very necessary task of accurately establishing basic facts: who did what, when, and where. Their work has not only added to the historical record but has done so with insightful comment, lively writing, and patriotism of the truest sort, a patriotism that is not blinded by pride but that rejoices in its service of fellow man.[4]

With the broad outlines of SOE's history already traced, we now have the luxury to step back and ask more analytical questions. Who were the men and women of SOE? Where did they come from? What ideas underlay their strategy and tactics? How did they learn to do the things they did? These questions, which may appear deceptively simple at first glance, point us toward more intellectually complex questions: What was SOE's doctrine and where did it come from?

SOE was created by the merger of two earlier organizations, Section D, a branch of the Secret Intelligence Service (SIS or MI6) and General Staff (Research) (GS[R]), a branch of the War Office. As historian Simon Anglim observes, "The historians of SOE, William Mackenzie, M. R. D. Foot and Mark Seaman, all discuss [GS(R)] summarily and in terms of its input into SOE."[5] The story of these agencies and their leading light, Colin Gubbins, must be told in its own right. This book follows Gubbins's career from 1914 onward, examining his experience of irregular warfare, first in the Allied intervention in Russia (1919), most importantly in Ireland during the Irish Revolution (1919–22),[6] and then, to a much lesser extent, in British India (1923–30). To this personal experience he added the insights of colleagues who served in these same places and also in Iraq. Gubbins's knowledge of irregular warfare was further augmented by study of several other conflicts: the Second Anglo-Boer War, the Arab Revolt led by T. E. Lawrence, the German guerrilla war in East Africa, the Revolt in Palestine between the World Wars, the Spanish Civil War, and the Second Sino-Japanese War.

With this knowledge at his disposal, in 1939 Gubbins authored two brief guides, The *Art of Guerilla Warfare (AGW)* and *The Partisan Leader's Handbook (PLH)*.[7] The approach in each is pragmatic, only venturing into theory when necessary. Gubbins wanted to create "how-to guides," works "intended for the actual fighting partisans, tactical and not strategic."[8] One writer describes the *AGW* as "the first synthesis of British unconventional warfare doctrine, or at any rate the first codification of irregular experience. The work is bold, original and arguably unique; an incisive summary of lessons learned from Russia, Ireland, Arabia and elsewhere."[9]

The lessons of the various conflicts that Gubbins studied may be found throughout these two works: the centrality of the local population; the collection, protection, and use of intelligence; the necessity of cooperating with conventional forces; and the use of speed, surprise, and escape in carrying out ambush operations. The historian Józef Garliński, who fought with the Polish Resistance, argues that "before the outbreak of war, before mobilization, when no one knew what turn events would take or how the Germans would overrun Europe, preparations were already in hand for underground warfare in territories that might fall under their control. In this field, Britain was better prepared for war than any other country."[10] That preparation was the result of early planning by Gubbins and a handful of colleagues.

Once formulated, these ideas were given time to germinate while Gubbins liaised with the Poles in 1939, commanded troops in Norway in 1940, and made plans for the use of guerrillas in Britain itself, should it be invaded by the Germans. Though of some significance, none of these actions would have earned the place that Gubbins deserves in history; that came in 1940, when he was invited by Minister Hugh Dalton to join the new Special Operations Executive, an organization within the Ministry of Economic Warfare tasked with supporting resistance and subversive activities in Nazi-occupied Europe. Upon Gubbins's arrival at SOE, he was given charge of not only operations but also training. Thus, it was his ideas that shaped SOE's new agents and formed their thinking on irregular warfare. Moreover, the United States turned to Britain for training in intelligence and sabotage, even before its official entry into the war.

SOE played a significant role in this training process, which rapidly blossomed after the Japanese attack on Pearl Harbor. As the British lent instructors and their training syllabus to the Americans, Gubbins's ideas were propagated even further. The Americans had their own sources of inspiration to draw upon when formulating ideas about irregular warfare, but SOE and Gubbins's doctrines played a key role. As he was promoted to deputy director and then director of SOE, the significance of Gubbins's thinking—and the many years of irregular conflict that informed it—only became more acute. In 1942 Lord Selborne, then minister of Economic Warfare, explained to Prime Minister Winston Churchill: "There is perhaps no officer . . . who is more vital to the continuance of the work of this organisation than Brigadier Gubbins. He has seen the growth of S.O.E. from its early beginnings, and . . . has acquired a technique, a knowledge and experience which are really irreplaceable."[11] If the story of SOE's doctrinal origins is to be told, Gubbins must be its central character.

Writing about SOE

On 7 November 1949, Gubbins visited the Foreign Office to discuss the possibility of writing a book about his experiences during World War II. The following month he received a letter from a Foreign Office official, William Strange. "The proposal has now been fully discussed by all the authorities concerned," Strange explained. "The publication even of such a sober and balanced review as you would write would be undesirable on security grounds. . . . The technique of organising resistance movements does not alter greatly with the passage of time and we could not be sure that your book might not give valuable assistance to a future enemy."[12] But following the publication of a series of unauthorized memoirs and Foot's authorized *SOE in France* in 1966, the climate began to shift. By 1970, Robin Brook—who had served in SOE's Western Europe section and went on to become a director of the Bank of England—explained to the Foreign Secretary that "the techniques of subversion and sabotage have been so largely transformed since SOE's day that a mild office censorship on the final text [of a new book on SOE] could exclude anything in the least harmful."[13] With the passage of time, many of SOE's secrets lost their deadly associations.

If security was no longer a major concern when writing about SOE, there remained the problem of sources. It has been suggested that a fire in early 1946 destroyed a significant quantity of documents relating to SOE.[14] Gubbins strenuously denied this, explaining,

> The suggestion of a fire in the small remaining office in Baker Street in January 1946 destroying any important files is absolutely wide of the mark. I returned from the Far East ... about the end of December, 1945 to find nothing remained of S.O.E. except this little remnant. Everything else ... had been transferred to "C" [the director of the Secret Intelligence Service] including all operational files. . . . There have been suggestions ever since the War, rather nasty ones, that S.O.E. destroyed material that would have incriminated itself. This is absolutely false, as the Historical Section was formed long before the end of the War, and worked independently under the War Cabinet Historical Section, over which neither I nor any other Offices in S.O.E. had any control.[15]

In spite of this insistence, a number of writers have commented on the famous fire of February 1946. C. B. Townshend, the first professional archivist to attempt an organization of the SOE papers after the war, notes that the fire "destroyed an unknown quantity of records the subject of which it has been impossible to trace."[16] Duncan Stuart, former SOE advisor at the Foreign and Commonwealth Office, observed that several independent sources of evidence confirm the damage to the Belgian files, which still bear the burn marks.[17]

Apart from the state of the SOE archives generally, there is the problem of sources regarding its earliest days. Section D, one of SOE's two predecessor agencies, belonged to the Secret Intelligence Service, which as a rule does not release documents. Likewise, Gubbins himself noted that "there are no records that I know of on the matter" of GS(R), the other predecessor.[18] In spite of the fact that GS(R) kept a war diary, it has not survived among the SOE papers held in Britain's National Archives.[19] This paucity of sources is not entirely the product of secrecy. Section D and GS(R) were both quite small when compared to SOE at its wartime height; thus, the number of documents produced by SOE dwarfs that of either of its predecessor agencies. Moreover, as is the case with any wartime organization, records from the end of the war are simply more plentiful, due to the common practice of throwing out old papers in a bid to save space.

Finally, when discussing SOE, one is bound to run into the question posed by Foot: "Was SOE any good?" There are certainly critics who insist it was not. Military historian John Keegan concludes that SOE was costly, misguided, and pointless.[20] In contrast, Foot argues that SOE did a great deal of good, providing considerable support to the Allied war effort at a relatively low cost.[21] The overall value of SOE and irregular warfare will be considered in the conclusion of this work. However, this ongoing debate about SOE's success or failure can sometimes obscure other questions about what SOE and OSS actually did and why they did it. Should sabotage officers work alone or in conjunction with local populations? How closely should their activities be coordinated with military operations? And how much should be expected from them? Gubbins engaged these questions as he sifted the experience of four decades of irregular warfare, concluding that it was a tool of great potential, though one that needed to work in concert with other elements of war.

Colin Gubbins

Colin McVean Gubbins was born on 2 July 1896 in Tokyo. His father, John Gubbins, attended Harrow and spent thirty years in the Consular Service at the British Legation in Tokyo. His grandfather, Martin Gubbins, was a member of the Bengal Civil Service, was present at Lucknow when it was besieged in 1857 during the Indian Mutiny, and later became a judge of the Supreme Court in Agra. Colin's mother, Helen McVean (known to all as Nonie), was born in India but grew up on the Isle of Mull in Scotland. Colin too grew up there, from the age of four onward; while his father served abroad, Colin was raised by his maternal grandparents from whom he acquired a love of nature and a fierce sense of Highland identity. It was a family of imperial civil servants: two uncles were in the Indian Army, another worked for the Hudson's Bay Company, and one of Colin's aunts was a nurse in the Second Anglo-Boer War. Gubbins attended Cheltenham College, in Gloucestershire, and although he commented, "I felt all the time that I was in prison," the school served its intended purpose, securing him a place at the Royal Military Academy at Woolwich.[22]

In appearance, Gubbins was "shortish, [a] dark man with clipped speech, clipped moustache and brisk movements."[23] Gubbins's one-time secretary, Joan Bright Astley, described him as "quiet-mannered, quiet-spoken, energetic, efficient and charming. A 'still waters running deep' sort of man, he had just enough of the buccaneer in him to make lesser men underrate his gifts of leadership, courage and integrity."[24] In studying Gubbins, one is struck by his incredible balance. He was a man of creativity and intellectual power; after the war he occupied much of his time visiting art galleries, reading novels, and watching ballet.[25] However, he never attended a university. His writing always remained accessible to the common man, even if it contained a few romantic flourishes. Gubbins possessed considerable belief in the importance of ungentlemanly warfare; his zeal for his work made him "the driving force behind SOE."[26] But Gubbins was no wild-eyed fanatic. When in the mid-1950s the future historian M. R. D. Foot and a group of fellow Oxford students decided to attack a railway bridge in Hungary, in support of that country's anti-Soviet aspirations, Foot looked up Gubbins's address in *Who's Who* and wrote to him for advice. Gubbbins prudently suggested they abandon the idea.[27]

Gubbins was certainly hard working and proud in his way. Leo Marks, an SOE cryptographer, described Gubbins as an intense and sometimes inscrutable man of great intelligence and exacting standards.[28] Lord Selborne acknowledged after the war that "Gubbins is not universally popular in all other Departments, and I believe he has his critics in some parts also of the War Office." However, he insisted "that no Minister was served more loyally by a subordinate than I was by him, and that when a strong man is fighting to create a new Organisation, which is to be carved out of the three Services and other Departments, it is not unnatural that he sometimes trod rather badly on people's toes."[29] Sir Frank Nelson, Gubbins's first boss at SOE, echoed these sentiments, describing him as a man who provided "ever genial, calm and brilliant help, loyalty and support."[30]

Rediscovering Irregular Warfare in Context

This book is part biography, part intellectual history, and part organizational history; SOE cannot be understood apart from the ideas that animated it, nor can those ideas be understood apart from the life of Colin Gubbins, who did so much to shape them. Moreover, Gubbins embodies a pattern typical of his era, in which men—and, to a lesser extent, women—gained a variety of experiences around the world, often in the British Empire, before employing their knowledge in creative and asymmetric ways during World War II. Arguably, other individuals might also stand in as incarnations of this process. William E. Fairbairn, discussed in chapter 6, had more than his share of high adventure abroad and certainly molded a great many individual agents. At the doctrinal and organizational level, however, it becomes harder to assess his influence. Other men with imperial experience, among them Ralph A. Bagnold and Dudley Clarke, who were instrumental in the creation of the Long Range Desert Group and the Commandos, respectively, served as intellectual conduits to their organizations. But with regard to SOE itself, Gubbins's influence was unrivaled. His role in SOE has been written about elsewhere, but this book brings to the fore his personal contribution to its corpus of ideas, to an extent that has never been done before. Nevertheless, while its three threads—the biographical, the intellectual, and the organizational—are here woven together, in some parts of the story one or another predominates. This should come as no surprise: in the natural course of life, sometimes individuals are of the utmost importance, at other times organizations; in some moments, deliberation predominates, in others, action.

Several features make SOE an interesting organization to study within the larger field of special operations. SOE was created within weeks of Britain's Commandos and the Long Range Desert Group. Moreover, its two predecessor organizations, GS(R) and Section D, trace their origins even earlier. Thus, SOE can legitimately claim to have been one of the earliest special operations organizations in the English-speaking world. But for all its innovation, SOE emerged squarely from the context of early twentieth-century warfare, with many of its central tenets drawn from the lessons of imperial small wars. Thus, an examination of SOE and its origins invites consideration of how modern special operations relate to other forms of warfare, not only other contemporary forms, such as maneuver warfare or terrorism, but also historical forms, such as imperial policing.

Moreover, SOE reminds us that influence is not always direct. Gubbins and his colleagues learned from the example of the Boers in South Africa, but they also studied the Irish Republican Army (IRA) and the German colonial *Schutztruppe* (SS), which were themselves influenced by the Boers. Nor is influence always linear. Many of the lessons the SOE applied were first learned when British soldiers acted not as insurgents but counterinsurgents; only later were those lessons turned on their heads.

Finally, one of the striking things about SOE was its focus. In their broadest sense, special forces conduct four major tasks: intelligence collection, offensive action, training and organization, and psychological operations.[31] While offensive action receives the lion's share of both popular and scholarly attention, SOE placed its emphasis on training and organization, empowering resistance movements to carry out the other tasks, particularly offensive action, on their own. Thus, renewed scholarship on SOE offers the possibility of broadening the discussion of special operations, recalling the full breadth of tasks that specialized military or paramilitary units may conduct.

Although this work focuses on SOE, its import is far wider. To the field of special operations scholarship, this examination of Colin Gubbins's ideas offers a new approach that might be applied profitably elsewhere. Although histories of special operations units often trace their lineage, this is frequently done with broad gestures toward earlier examples that do not fully explore their ties or with a focus upon continuity of organizations or personnel rather than ideas.[32] Scholarship on insurgency and counterinsurgency doctrine has proliferated in the last decade, as have histories of operations and doctrine.[33] This book aims to further those efforts by tracing not simply how dominant doctrines have changed but how conflicts decades in the past could influence one organization and its doctrine. Recent scholarship on the British Empire has examined interactions among the empire, the home islands, and other parts of the world, particularly nonpolitical dimensions.[34] This study not only highlights some of the clandestine and military aspects of those interactions but also connects the era of colonial small wars with Britain's own support for insurgencies and resistance.

CHAPTER 2

BAPTISM BY FIRE

In 1914 Colin Gubbins was introduced to the life of a soldier. Many of his experiences in the years that followed were unexceptional. His time in India, for example, was characterized more by sports than battles, and his experience of the Raj was not substantially different from that of thousands of other officers across the decades. His combat experience on the Western Front, though considerably more violent than his time in India, was also shared with thousands of other soldiers. More unusual than typical soldiers' experiences, Gubbins participated in irregular conflicts in Russia and Ireland, providing his first introduction and the germ seeds of his later thinking. Although his experiences in France and India were less significant with respect to SOE's doctrine, they should not be neglected entirely. The massive scale, imprecise use of force, and tremendous costs of the Western Front are a foil for the small, focused, and economical operations that Gubbins later advocated. Moreover, SOE achieved success because Gubbins not only possessed good ideas but transformed them into action. His various assignments and experiences prior to the 1930s provided him with the skills and credentials to work alongside conventional military forces, even when he was organizing unconventional forces. Finally, it was on the Western Front that Gubbins first made the acquaintance of Adrian Carton de Wiart, with whom he would collaborate again at the outbreak of the Second World War.

World War I

In the summer of 1914, Gubbins, a cadet at the Royal Military Academy at Woolwich, was innocently trying to study in Heidelberg. Having shown "a certain inherited predilection for foreign language, it occurred to my father that it might give me a leg-up if I learnt German."[1] Instead, his plans were cut short by the advent of the Great War. He quickly made his way back to Britain, arriving in Dover on

3 August, the day before the British declaration of war. Three other Woolwich cadets had been in Germany at the time; all three were arrested and interned for the duration of the conflict.[2]

Although only halfway through his course of studies at Woolwich, Gubbins was commissioned a second lieutenant on 15 September 1914 and posted to the 126th Battery, XXIX Brigade, arriving in France in early November 1914.[3] Gubbins and his brigade participated in the Second Battle of Ypres in April and May 1915, and in June he was promoted to lieutenant. His brigade saw action in the Battle of the Somme, in which Gubbins was awarded a Military Cross "for conspicuous gallantry. When one of his guns and its detachment were blown up by a heavy shell, he organised a rescue party and personally helped to dig out the wounded while shells were falling all round."[4] In August (about a month after his twentieth birthday) he was made an acting captain and served for a short time on the staff of the General Officer Commanding, Fourth Army; this would be the first of several stints of staff work.[5] "Refus[ing] to stay at GHQ when the battery came into action" again at the Somme, Gubbins rejoined his unit and was wounded on 7 October 1916.[6] Discharged from the hospital after eleven days, Gubbins commanded the battery while his major was on leave in January 1917, was sent to a battery commander's course at Larkhill in February, and attended an aircraft course at Arras, France, in March.[7] The future looked bright as young Gubbins's career advanced apace.

At the Battle of Arras, which lasted for most of April and into May 1917, Gubbins met Adrian Carton de Wiart, whose infantry brigade Gubbins's battery supported. Gubbins was sent as liaison to Carton de Wiart, a man with a reputation. Wounded seven times in the course of the war—having already lost an eye in Somaliland—Carton de Wiart won a Victoria Cross in the summer of 1916. "After three other battalion Commanders had become casualties, he controlled their commands, and ensured that the ground won was maintained at all costs. He frequently exposed himself in the organisation of positions and of supplies, passing unflinchingly through fire barrage of the most intense nature. His gallantry was inspiring to all."[8] Reflecting on his experience afterward, Carton de Wiart commented, "Frankly I had enjoyed the war."[9] Gubbins recalled, "He was already a legendary figure with his Victoria Cross, his black eye patch, his stump of an arm and his formidable bearing. When the divisional orders for next day's attack reached him—long and voluminous—he read these through twice, questioned me on one or two gunner matters, then deliberately tore up the orders and sent for his battalion commanders; a ten-minute conference; a few clear verbal orders from him; and it was all over."[10] In the summer of 1939 their paths would cross again, this time in Poland.

On 1 November 1917 Gubbins was made an acting major with temporary command of the 125th Battery and then two other batteries within the brigade.[11] That same autumn he was gassed "but fortunately not badly."[12] The XXIX Brigade participated in the Battle of Cambrai, where tanks made their first significant appearance, with limited success. On 12 February 1918 Gubbins was promoted to substantive captain and given command of the 126th Battery.[13] When the Germans launched the Spring Offensive in March 1918, Gubbins's brigade was in the thick of it.[14] After "handling his battery with skill and authority," Gubbins contracted trench fever and was evacuated to England in May.[15] Thus ended his single large conventional experience in an otherwise unconventional career. He had served with distinction, was decorated, and received numerous promotions and additional training. After recuperating he served as an instructor at the Royal Artillery (RA) Officer Cadet School in Weedon and attended courses at the School of Education at Oxford and the School of Instructors at Bockhampstead.[16]

Russia

Background

In April 1918 a small body of British Royal Marines landed at Murmansk, followed on 23 June 1918 by a mixed force of Royal Marines and Canadian, Australian, and American soldiers. This force intended to secure the stores at the port of Archangel and defend the rail line to Murmansk, which was then being threatened by a Finnish-German offensive. However, the Bolshevik Revolution and the Treaty of Brest-Litovsk caused many Russian soldiers to abandon the fight against the Germans; moreover, Czech troops who had once fought alongside Russian forces now had nowhere to go. Thus the Allied force at Archangel hoped to meet up with, train, and equip those Czech soldiers, while also recruiting and training local Russian citizens to continue the fight against the German troops.[17] In this way, the project was originally conceived as part of the broader campaign against Imperial Germany, but when Germany agreed to an armistice on 11 November 1918, the Allied forces did not leave Russia.

The politics of Archangel were difficult, to say the least. Shortly before the Allied troops arrived, Capt. Georgi Chaplin staged a coup in the port city and reorganized the local administration. When he decided the new government was not to his liking, he staged a second coup, backed by tsarist officers.[18] Gen. Frederick Poole, the British commander at Archangel, was sacked for his passive participation in the coup and replaced with Maj. Gen. Edmund Ironside.[19] Matters were further complicated by the fact that, on his arrival, "Ironside . . . found a disturbing number of his British officers openly sympathetic with the most reactionary monarchists among their Russian counterparts."[20]

There were other political considerations as well. At one point Ironside records that Russian and American troops at Shenkursk— an Allied outpost nearly two hundred miles south of Archangel— "were, from a military point of view, too far advanced, but it was decided for political reasons to maintain them there during the winter."[21] Elders in one village outside Archangel did not even know of the White Russian Provisional Government there and could not understand why the British wanted them to join the conflict against the Bolsheviks.[22] In spite of Ironside's efforts at accommodating the local politics—and he had no inconsiderable political ability—an American observed: "There was a sad failure to realize that an expedition of this sort is bound to run into social and political problems that are quite as important, perhaps more so, than mere military practice."[23] Such problems were not unique to the British forces, however; Ironside notes that "the Archangel officials were . . . completely out of touch with the people they were controlling." As a corrective, Ironside records, "I urged them to get civilian officers out into the country at once, to get into touch with the people."[24]

Gubbins's Experience in Russia

On 22 February 1919, Gubbins was appointed as aide-de-camp (ADC) to General Ironside.[25] Ironside commanded a mixed force of British, French, American, Italian, Polish, and Russian troops, now actively aiding the White Russians against the Bolsheviks.[26] Ironside spoke several European languages, including Russian, and had previously operated with Canadian forces, an advantage when commanding a multinational force. He possessed considerable energy and was keen on details and meeting his men. But his most notable quality was his overwhelming size: he was six foot four and weighed nearly 280 pounds, requiring two sleeping bags sewn together since he could not fit in an ordinary bag.[27] His nickname was "Tiny."[28]

Gubbins served with Ironside until 6 October 1919. We know little about what precisely Gubbins did in his six months as ADC, except that he obtained a passing knowledge of the Russian language, the Order of Saint Stanislaus (third class), and "a deep hatred of Communism and all it stood for."[29] In one episode he is remembered as safeguarding the kitchen on Ironside's private river steamer, fairly mundane work.[30] More interestingly, he likely saw many of the reports coming to and going from Ironside's office. We know that the ADCs of Lord Rawlinson, who assumed overarching command of both Archangel and Murmansk in August 1919, "were always busy collecting the necessary material for his reports."[31] Gubbins likely did similar things for Ironside. In any case, Gubbins later reflected that "to anyone who had studied the Russian revolution... the crippling effect of subversive and para-military warfare on regular forces was obvious."[32] Gubbins complained, however, that the Russian Revolution was "not studied at any of the higher colleges of War—[it was] 'Irregular' and not deemed worthy of serious attention."[33] It was, however, one of a handful of case studies he cited as an example upon which he drew when building SOE.[34]

There was no continuous front in Russia, as there had been in France; instead, the Allies occupied only certain strongpoints, while vast stretches of terrain were left unoccupied.[35] The conflict was one characterized by espionage and propaganda, where events behind the lines occupied leaders as much as the enemy before them.[36] Ironside complained, "It is extremely hard to know whom to employ as Head Russian Agent because, as soon as I have chosen someone, the secret service come and tell me that he is a German spy.... Everyone distrusts everyone else and denouncements are taking place every day."[37] An Anglo-Polish-Russian attack on the village of Kuliga, for example, was spoiled when a Bolshevik spy apparently warned the defenders of the impending attack.[38] But two could play at this game: Ironside used his intelligence personnel to send false information to the enemy and thereby deceive them about impending operations.[39]

The Allies also had to contend with sophisticated Bolshevik propaganda.[40] Long after the war, Ironside confidently recalled that "propaganda . . . is a very difficult [weapon] to employ, especially against troops on active service. It is a long-term weapon and like advertising it must be repeated over and over again to produce any effect. No soldier picks up a pamphlet and at once becomes infected by it."[41] However, his wartime correspondence was less confident, recording that "the most active propaganda was carried out amongst the rank and file of all the Allied Contingents by the enemy, and [as a result] discontent showed itself in many places."[42] In particular he worried about the impact of Bolshevik propaganda on Russian-speaking American troops, many of them recruited from Detroit.[43] Enemy propaganda distribution was virtually impossible to control, since "there was no continuous line of defence between the enemy and ourselves which could prevent the passage of individuals, and we had not sufficient police or troops to patrol the crowded town in a proper manner."[44]

Finally, recruitment and discipline were constant problems, extending even to mutiny. Complex politics meant that virtually every group in the Archangel area had one quibble or another with the local Allied-backed government, which struggled to enlist soldiers.[45] Meanwhile, Ironside complained that he could not find leaders willing to command an anti-Bolshevik force.[46] The Russian officers feared their men, discipline in the barracks was poor, morale was weak, and Ironside doubted the Russian forces could stand on their own, even with British training.[47] Between December 1918 and July 1919 the Allied force faced no fewer than six mutinies from Russian, French, and British forces, with some of the mutineers deserting to the Bolsheviks and others becoming international fugitives.[48] Ironside complained that one episode highlighted how "one propagandist can make [the Russians] do anything."[49] If Captain Gubbins harbored romantic notions about the quality of local forces, such events probably dashed them. Yet all was not gloom; one British report noted, "Force Commanders have been unanimous in their appreciation of the energy, loyalty and adaptability of the Russian Engineer units, which have not only gained credit by the speed and thoroughness with which the men, many of them old soldiers, have performed their work, but also by the high stamp and powers of leadership displayed by many of the officers."[50] Gubbins may have also learned that, under the right conditions, local forces can be very effective.

Ironside and Calwell's Small Wars

On Ironside's arrival in Russia, he found that neither he nor the Russian officers with whom he worked knew much about North Russia or river or forest fighting. However, Ironside was happily able to turn to "the old and well-tried textbook, 'Small Wars,' which was found an infallible guide."[51] Col. Charles E. Callwell's *Small Wars: Their Principles and Practice*, was first published in 1896 and revised and republished in 1899 and again in 1906. Callwell's experience was typical of officers serving the British Empire: having been educated at Haileybury, he fought in the Second Anglo-Afghan War (1880), the First Anglo-Boer War (1881), the Greco-Turkish War (1897), and the Second Anglo-Boer War (1899–1902) and also served in the intelligence branch of the War Office (1886–91).[52]

Ironside would have found much in *Small Wars* that paralleled his experience in Russia. Battling the Russian winter as often as the Bolsheviks, Ironside would have appreciated Callwell's comment that "it is perhaps the most distinguishing characteristic of small wars . . . that they are in the main campaigns against nature."[53] In words that could describe the Archangel Expedition, Callwell observes that in campaigns against insurrections, "the regular army has to cope not with determinate but with indeterminate forces. . . . Such campaigns are most difficult to bring to a satisfactory conclusion, and are always most trying to the troops."[54] One of the greatest burdens the Allied forces faced was settling on a clear objective. What were they trying to conquer? Who were they supposed to fight? Callwell notes, "When there is no king to conquer, no capital to seize, no organized army to overthrow, and when there are no celebrated strongholds to capture, and no great centres of population to occupy, the objective is not so easy to select. It is then that the regular troops are forced to resort to cattle lifting and village burning and that the war assumes an aspect which may shock the humanitarian."[55]

Though Ironside does not write of cattle lifting or village burning in his memoirs, he does observe that "a blow in the air would yield us nothing."[56] Advancing into empty space was virtually useless; the Allies had to wait for the enemy to coalesce before they could strike a meaningful blow. But victory on the battlefield was not the only matter at hand. Though Allied defeats were few, the withdrawal from Archangel on 27 September 1919 was followed by the collapse of the Provisional Government in February 1920.[57]

Politics, in the British cabinet and across Russia, were as important as military might. Or, as Callwell puts it, "The beating of the hostile armies is not necessarily the main object even if such armies exist. ... Moral effect is often far more important than material success."[58] It was, perhaps, the bitterest lesson.

There are parallels between Callwell's *Small Wars* and Gubbins's thinking regarding intelligence, logistics, and guerrilla tactics that deserve consideration; Gubbins may have read Callwell while in Ironside's service or may have encountered it at another time in his career. As Andrew Hargreaves notes, "Upon the shelves of many an interwar staff college or officers' mess bookshelf one could have likely found well-thumbed copies of the likes of C. E. Callwell's seminal appraisal of colonial low-intensity operations."[59] Nevertheless, no evidence has yet been found that Gubbins read Callwell in Russia or elsewhere, so any parallels must be viewed with circumspection.

Judging Callwell's opinion of guerrillas is often difficult. On the one hand, his writing regularly displays the condescension common in nineteenth-century imperialism; on the other hand, that irregular forces merited a handbook of over five hundred pages suggests the power Callwell believed they could wield. Indeed, he warned that guerrillas are "very troublesome" to regular troops, since they avoid direct conflict and favor "protracted, toilsome war."[60] Gubbins, later considering the possibilities of fielding or supporting guerrillas, would have found this assessment affirming.

Callwell and Gubbins agree that guerrillas can possess an advantage by fighting on terrain they know well. Callwell notes that "the enemy [i.e., the guerrilla force] is generally operating in a theatre of war with which he is familiar."[61] This increases the guerrillas' intelligence collection and deprives the counterguerrilla force of the possibility of surprise.[62] Following a similar line, Gubbins demands in the *PLH* that leaders be intimately familiar with their area of operations and observes that "the advantage of superior information is the guerillas' greatest asset."[63]

Callwell observes that collecting intelligence on guerrillas can be very difficult. "It may . . . be accepted as a general rule—and the reason why this is so needs no demonstration—that the less organized the forces of the enemy are, the more difficult is it to form any estimate of their strength or their quality."[64] But what to Callwell was a vice was a virtue to Gubbins: "The organization of guerillas must not be of a higher degree than circumstances will, with reasonable safety, and a view to efficiency, permit. The factor of 'safety' concerns possible enemy counteraction; the closer and higher the organization, the more easily can it be broken up and become ineffective."[65]

Callwell, discussing how guerrillas may be defeated, contends that "it is not a question of merely maintaining the initiative, but of compelling the enemy to see at every turn that he has lost it and to recognize that the forces of civilization are dominant and not to be denied."[66] Elsewhere he writes that counterguerrilla forces must appear in total control of the war's direction, never showing weakness, but instead causing the guerrillas to lose heart.[67] It is precisely this kind of strategy that Gubbins knew his guerrillas must defeat, and therefore he emphasizes morale and the human spirit. He notes in the *AGW* that "the immunity of partisans from enemy action is a most valuable moral factor; to inflict damage and death on the enemy and to escape scot-free has an irritant and depressing effect on the enemy's spirit, and a correspondingly encouraging effect on the morale, not only of the guerillas but of the local inhabitants, a matter of considerable moment; in this sphere of action nothing succeeds like success."[68] Thus, guerrilla actions must have not only a military dimension but also a moral one; remaining in the field proves that antiguerrilla forces, however successful elsewhere, have not yet defeated the people of the occupied nation.[69]

Callwell admits that complex organization, extensive armament, and excessive equipment hinder regular troops.[70] In contrast, Gubbins encourages his guerrillas, observing that they should enjoy superior mobility due to local knowledge and lighter equipment.[71] Callwell further admits that antiguerrilla forces are limited by their supply lines. In contrast, "the adversaries with whom the regular troops . . . have to cope depend on no base and have no fixed system of supply. They are operating in their own country. . . . [The enemy] does not need communications as a channel for replenishing food or warlike stores."[72] Gubbins insists that guerrillas recognize and protect this strength. He encourages them to avoid "wild [areas], with little cultivation or pasture land for carrying stock or feeding the guerillas' animals, [where] supplies would have to be brought in specially. At once the guerillas would begin to be dependent on communications, a situation cramping their mobility and exactly opposed to the characteristic which constitutes their chief military value."[73] Freedom from a supply train is one of the defining characteristics of a guerrilla. The absence of such freedom is one of the weaknesses of regular forces that guerrillas can exploit. Callwell observes that long lines of communication are exposed to guerrilla attacks, while "their protection absorbs a large proportion of the forces in the theatre of war."[74] Gubbins too recognizes that extended communications create opportunities to "strike at many points ... in order to harass the enemy and keep him always on the alert."[75] Like Callwell, Gubbins perceives such attacks compel the enemy to spread thin his forces to guard a variety of potential targets.[76] Even if such a tactic, alone, cannot win a war, it can change the number of regular troops available for offensive operations.

The battlefield superiority of regular troops makes avoiding pitched battles crucial for guerrillas. "On the battlefield the advantage passes over to the regular army," notes Callwell. "Superior armament, the force of discipline, a definite and acknowledged chain of responsibility, esprit de corps, the moral force of civilization, all these work together to give the trained and organized army an incontestable advantage from the point of view of tactics."[77] Thus, regulars actively seek battle against guerrillas.[78] Gubbins, recognizing this reality, insists that partisans avoid prolonged battles.[79] Lest they be crushed in the kind of battle Callwell hoped for, Gubbins advises partisans to "break off the action when it becomes too risky to continue."[80]

Callwell devotes several pages to the discussion of flying columns, which he sees as a key part of a counterguerrilla strategy.[81] If Gubbins read Callwell, he may have taken this to heart, assuming as he does in the *AGW* that flying columns will be part of any antiguerrilla action.[82] But like most of the matters discussed in *Small Wars*, flying columns were a regular feature of the Irish Revolution, in which Gubbins fought shortly after leaving Russia. He may have been influenced by Callwell, by his own experiences in Ireland, or by both. This is one of the difficulties of attempting an intellectual history of SOE or any other topic: ideas rarely come in neat linear patterns of diffusion. An individual's interest in a topic may come from one source, but his method of thinking about that topic from another. An individual may be exposed to a set of ideas for years without any conscious result, while a single experience or source of information later produces an epiphany. An individual's sources of inspiration may themselves have been variously influenced by one another or by other sources entirely. In such complex circumstances, often only dimly captured in historical records, how is influence to be ascribed? The answers are rarely tidy or final. In weighing Gubbins's personal experience against his possible reading of Callwell, it seems likely his lived experience had greater effect than *Small Wars*, whose popularity was beginning to wane by 1919, but we cannot know for certain.

In any event, it is somewhat curious that this is the only occasion on which Callwell's *Small Wars* intersects with Gubbins's story. As historian Simon Anglim explains, "This work seems to have influenced not only at least two generations of colonial soldiers . . . but also approved Army 'doctrine': it formed part of the curriculum of the Army Staff Colleges and the RAF [Royal Air Force] Staff College at Andover, and the chapter on 'Warfare in Undeveloped and Semi-Civilised Countries' in the 1929 edition of *FSR* [*Field Service Regulations*], appears to be an unattributed summary of Chapters VI–VIII of the 1906 edition of Callwell."[83] Put simply, *Small Wars* was almost omnipresent. If Gubbins did not encounter it while in Ironside's service, one would expect him to have seen it in his time in Ireland, at Staff College, with GS(R), or elsewhere. But Gubbins never mentions *Small Wars*, nor do any of the leading historians of SOE. The most likely explanation for this lacuna is three-fold. In the first place, as Callwell himself admits, "the subject [is] discussed merely from the point of view of the regular troops," not from that of the partisans.[84] This alone, however, could be overcome with a small dose of imagination. Indeed, some passages, such as those on ambushes, would seem to be directly useful to guerrillas.[85] On closer examination, however, we discover a second problem that makes these extracts inappropriate for use by Gubbins's prospective partisans. The ambushing forces are often large in size and usually include both cavalry and infantry. While the Boers on the veldt could field horsemen, most twentieth-century guerrillas—particularly those Gubbins imagined in Europe—would not include cavalry forces.

But the third and deepest problem with *Small Wars* is that it fails to engage with the inner workings of guerrilla movements. It treats the symptoms but not the disease itself. As Douglas Porch explains, "A primary weakness of *Small Wars* . . . is its overreliance on operational solutions to political problems."[86] Rightly or wrongly, the star of *Small Wars* began to wane as T. E. Lawrence's began to rise; whereas Callwell had argued that guerrillas and rebels could be put down, Lawrence seemed to have proved their success.[87]

Ireland

Gubbins's Experience

After leaving Russia, Gubbins reported for duty in Ireland in late 1919. Here he was involved in many of the diverse aspects of the conflict, including its political and intelligence dimensions. The war was, in historian David Fitzpatrick's words, one involving "flying columns, raids, ambushes, slaughter of 'informers,' cutting of communications, destruction of property, looting ('requisitioning'), and bullying of opponents."[88] In retrospect these elements may appear common, but at the time they were quite disorienting to the British Army. Gubbins complained that he was "shot at from behind hedges by men in trilbys and mackintoshes and not allowed to shoot back!"[89] But rather than despairing at the disarray into which this well-organized guerrilla resistance threw the British troops, he drew from this experience valuable lessons about irregular warfare and its handmaiden, intelligence.[90]

Peter Wilkinson and Joan Bright Astley, authors of the most complete account of Gubbins's life, comment that "there is no open page relating to Gubbins' sojourn in Ireland."[91] While there is indeed less readily available information about this period of his life than other periods, a good deal more can be said than the two pages Wilkinson and Astley devote to Gubbins's service in Ireland. It is essential to understand what we can of this period if we are to properly understand the context in which Gubbins's doctrine of irregular warfare germinated.

Gubbins was initially posted to the 47th Battery at Kildare, one of the artillery elements of the 5th Division, the unit responsible for much of central and western Ireland.[92] He was in Kildare for two years before assuming temporary duties as brigade major at division headquarters at the Curragh in November 1921. He briefly rejoined the 47th Battery from January until March 1922 but returned to division headquarters as temporary brigade major, remaining in this position even as headquarters moved to Dublin at the end of April 1922.[93] On 30 September 1922 Headquarters Royal Artillery, Dublin District, was dissolved and its last remaining personnel withdrawn to Britain.[94]

At first glance one might wonder how much of the messy guerrilla war an artilleryman actually saw. Though artillery hardly played the role in Ireland that it had on the Western Front, it would be misleading to think of Gubbins's service as strictly related to artillery, for it was much more diverse than that. Gubbins sent artillerymen to act as guards of both military supplies and soldiers' families at such sensitive Dublin locations as the shell factory, the Newbridge Train Station, and the magazine fort in Phoenix Park.[95] With the exception of a short hiatus in early 1922, the 30th and 36th Brigades—the bulk of 5th Division's artillery—were organized as Royal Artillery Mounted Rifles or Composite Batteries combining infantry and artillery.[96] Similarly, the 1st Brigade Royal Horse Artillery was reorganized into Royal Artillery Mounted Rifles.[97] In the spring of 1922, plans were drawn up to convert *all* of 5th Division's dismounted artillery units to infantry, "should urgent evacuation be ordered."[98] By June 1922 one artillery unit, 33rd Brigade, Royal Field Artillery (RFA), was operating armed cars and foot patrols but no artillery at all.[99]

William Cassidy claims Gubbins also served as an intelligence officer in Ireland, and Wilkinson and Astley confirm that he "had all the instincts of a good 'I' officer" who "set out to learn all he could about . . . intelligence," though they do not explicitly state that he served as such, nor has Cassidy's claim been confirmed elsewhere.[100] Indeed, Peter Hart observes that many regiments, unwilling to part with good officers, assigned the expendable to intelligence duties.[101] Thus, the quality of Gubbins's "instincts" may not have been relevant to his assignment. Nevertheless, even if Gubbins was never an intelligence officer per se, in his role as brigade major he certainly saw intelligence.

The guerrilla war in Ireland was especially complex due to its political dimensions. In early 1920 the army had the rebels on the run, utilizing police information, captured documents, and Irish informers. However, a hunger strike by captured Irish Republican Army (IRA) leaders caused the British administration at Dublin Castle to capitulate and release them. Such releases of the enemy for political reasons were a recurring feature of the conflict, happening almost annually from 1916 to 1920.[102] Gubbins noted in the 5th Division artillery's war diary that "all internees in Ireland were released" on 8 December 1921, just two days after the Anglo-Irish Treaty was signed.[103] Gubbins's reaction to this event is not recorded, though his entry indicates his awareness of one of the many ways in which political and military policy intersected in Ireland. Such intersection was likely not something Gubbins saw with frequency on the Western Front, though he would experience or study numerous other examples by the time of the Second World War.

Although much of Gubbins's time as brigade major came after the signing of the Anglo-Irish Treaty in December 1921 and all of it after the suspension of hostilities between British forces and the Irish rebels on 11 July 1921, this state of truce should not be confused with peace. In early 1921 Gubbins received intelligence stating that rebels "intended to attack troops while evacuation was proceeding"; all officers were warned "to be prepared to defend themselves against sudden attacks."[104] In February Lt. J. H. Wogan Browne, RFA, was killed in broad daylight, while returning to his barracks in Kildare, Gubbins's old post. In a separate incident three more soldiers were wounded in Kildare the same evening. Two days later the evacuation of British troops from the 5th Division was temporarily suspended for two weeks.[105] In May Gubbins wrote about "uncertainty as to the nature and duration of operations," and June saw another attack on his artillerymen, as well as reports of further threats.[106] That same month he issued contingency plans for the defense of Phoenix Park in Dublin in the event of major trouble: "All ranks must be prepared against a sudden outbreak of hostilities without warning." That these plans included measures for aerial resupply by the RAF indicates how dangerous Gubbins thought the situation.[107] Into August the War Office was still holding units in Britain in readiness should the situation in Ireland deteriorate.[108] With succinct understatement, the *Record of the Rebellion in Ireland* describes the conflict as "a curious mixture of peace and war."[109]

In early 1922 Gubbins began dealing with the security implications of the fall-out between the protreaty and antitreaty factions of the IRA. In March he was warned that "attempts would probably be made by mutineers [i.e., antitreaty forces] to steal or buy arms"; before the end of the month the "mutinous IRA" were disrupting traffic on the Naas–Dublin road, had stolen the private car of the General Officer Commanding, 5th Division, and opened fire on a group of artillery officers.[110] By April Gubbins had reports that "the mutinous IRA intended to attack British soldiers" in the near future.[111] On 22 June Field Marshall Sir Henry Wilson was assassinated and troops in Ireland confined to their barracks as a result.[112]

Meanwhile, the antitreaty-ite Rory O'Connor's occupation of the Four Courts in Dublin was undermining the new protreaty Free State government, and Gubbins found himself drawn into the matter. On 27 June Gubbins notes that at 11:59 A.M. "two 18-pdrs of 17th Battery RFA and 20 rounds of ammunition [were] handed over to the Provisional Government." The following day at 4:00 A.M. "P.G. Troops commenced the attack on the Four Courts. Two more 18 pdrs of 17th Bty RFA & 20 rounds of ammunition handed over to the Provisional Government."[113] Gubbins watched the action from just across the River Liffey, as Michael Collins's Free State forces pounded the antitreaty forces.[114] On the second day of the battle, fearing that the situation might deteriorate further, British forces halted the withdrawal of their artillery from Ireland. On 30 July, O'Connor gave himself up unconditionally,[115] though Britain's potential role in the emerging civil war was not ended. On 1 July 1922, Collinstown Camp was attacked by "irregulars," likely antitreaty forces trying to draw Britain back into the conflict as a means of uniting the two republican factions.[116] On 22 August, less than two months after his victory at the Four Courts, Michael Collins was killed in an ambush by antitreaty forces. Three days later, "6 Horses of 17th Bty RFA were lent to PG for funeral of Michael Collins" and returned on 4 September.[117] "I did not like . . . having to provide a gun carriage and six black horses for the funeral," notes Gubbins.[118]

As Peter Wilkinson, later explained, Gubbins "experienced at first hand the disadvantage felt by regular troops when attacked by well organised terrorists and guerrillas."[119] His service was certainly not peaceful, nor was it limited strictly to irrelevant artillery duties; he made use of intelligence reports, navigated political issues, such as prisoner releases and the split in the IRA, and coordinated with law enforcement, such as the Royal Irish Constabulary. Finally, it is worth noting that the removal of British forces from Ireland, in which Gubbins played a major role, was an operation of considerable logistical difficulty. His ability to carry out both unconventional and conventional functions appeared throughout his life and may account for his general success in the field as well as in the meeting room.[120]

The Doctrinal Significance of Ireland

Of all the conflicts that inspired Gubbins's thinking on unconventional warfare, his experience in Ireland was likely most influential, for several reasons. Firstly, we know that lessons from the Irish conflict were collected and disseminated while it was still going on, likely aiding Gubbins's own process of study. Secondly, the parallels between the Irish conflict and Gubbins's writings are many. Thirdly, Gubbins and his colleagues explicitly stated that they were inspired by the Irish example, even if they did not elaborate in detail which particular aspects they considered most noteworthy.

The Guerrilla Warfare Class at 5th Division, to which Gubbins belonged, is a concrete instance of the collection and dissemination of irregular warfare knowledge in the Irish context. Conceived in October 1920, the three-day course was designed "to enable [officers and NCOs] to deal with the peculiar type of guerrilla warfare in which they were becoming more and more engaged."[121] Though designed to teach *counter*guerrilla tactics, the course included "practical tactical exercises carried out *by the class itself* in ambushes on lorry parties and cyclist patrols."[122] This is an important psychological shift, moving from the mind-set of a status-quo imperial power to that of a revisionist insurgent. If Gubbins attended the course, this may have been his first introduction to the idea of playing the role of the guerrilla rather than the occupier. But did he attend? Sadly, records are insufficient to answer that question. However, even if Gubbins did not personally attend, the lessons from these classes were printed and distributed to every unit of the 5th Division, as well as to the Royal Irish Constabulary, the Auxiliaries, and to other divisions as well.[123] In the initial ten iterations of the course, 280 officers and NCOs were trained, and when reinforcements began arriving in Ireland in January 1921, all officers and NCOs of arriving battalions underwent the course. Thus, the question of his attendance may be moot: if Gubbins himself never attended the Guerrilla Warfare Class, he most probably would have read its lessons and frequently interacted—particularly when serving as brigade major at the Curragh—with men who had attended. Such speculation is not unfounded; the many parallels between Gubbins's writings and the Irish conflict confirm its strong influence on his thinking.

SOURCES OF INTELLIGENCE. In Ireland, British intelligence officers relied on informers and captured documents for information.[124] The *Notes on Guerrilla Warfare in Ireland*, the printed lessons learned from the Guerrilla Warfare Class, detail nine different places to check a man for concealed documents.[125] Gubbins later warns that letters and other documents seized from guerrillas pose one of the gravest threats to an insurgent cause.[126] He observes that "it has been proved over and over again in guerilla warfare that it is the capture of guerilla documents that has helped the enemy the most in his counter-measures," while also noting that "lack of communications" should be seen by guerrillas as an "inherent advantage."[127] He advises that messages should be verbal whenever possible and that the level of documentation should not exceed guerrillas' ability to ensure its security.[128] Nevertheless, if written messages must be used, Gubbins observes that "it is often better to use women and children who are less suspect and probably could enjoy greater immunity from search."[129] Likewise, Gubbins took informers no less seriously than documents: "The most stringent and ruthless measures must at all times be used against informers," he explains. "Immediately on proof of guilt they must be killed, and, if possible, a note pinned on the body stating that the man was an informer."[130]

The *Notes* also observe that "the leakage of information in Ireland is very great, and it may be generally accepted that no inhabitant or civilian employee is to be trusted."[131] Nearly three decades later, Gubbins the guerrilla organizer advocated utilizing the local population as the best source of information, since occupying troops must necessarily brush elbows with the inhabitants. Locals, Gubbins says, may passively obtain information by keeping an open ear, or more actively by questioning soldiers and "purloining letters."[132] He lists people who might make suitable agents: waitresses, domestic servants, priests, doctors, barbers, telephone and telegraph operators, postmen, "camp followers," and so on.[133] Such people, he insists, must be trained to know what sort of information will be valuable and to keep an eye out for traitors in their midst.[134]

LIMITED ENGAGEMENTS. An IRA memorandum from September 1920, captured and quoted in the *Record of the Rebellion in Ireland*, argues that "our troops must not be drawn into an operation or into a general engagement with large bodies of military." The *Record* goes on to quote a similar piece of advice from the commandant of the Mid-Clare Brigade, IRA, from February 1921: "A little action wisely and well done must be our motto at present."[135] Likewise, the *Notes* dismissively explain that "the rebels [have] small stomach for fighting at close quarters or suffering heavy casualties."[136] Gubbins's writings echo the tactics advocated by the IRA. In the *AGW* he admonished partisans to "avoid prolonged engagements" or "being pinned down," instead "break[ing] off the action when it becomes too risky to continue."[137] The *PLH* expresses the same sentiments, arguing that partisans should not fight pitched battles but disengage when risks become too great.[138] Ambushing marked the epitome of such limited engagements. The *Notes* explain that "these ambushes are dependent on secrecy, which is easily obtainable owing to the fact that they are dressed as civilians and move amongst a population of sympathizers similarly attired. These ambushes are dependent for their success on surprise. . . . Individuals cutting peat in a bog may not be as harmless as they appear."[139] Here we see three themes, all of which can be found in Gubbins's writings: the centrality of the ambush, the importance of secrecy and surprise, and the role of the local population. Ambushing appears in both the *AGW* and *PLH*, the latter of which includes an appendix each on road and rail ambushes.[140] With regard to secrecy and surprise, Gubbins explains that surprise has two components, "finding out the enemy's plans and concealing your own intentions and movements,"[141] while elsewhere he insists: "Surprise is the most important thing in everything you undertake."[142] The local population helps ensure such secrecy. Thus, partisans should work hard not to aggravate the people but instead to foster their hatred of the enemy and their sense of resistance.[143] The population's cooperation may be active—"providing information for the guerrillas"—or passive—"withholding it from the enemy."[144]

Whether Gubbins personally attended the Guerrilla Warfare Class or simply read about it, many of his recommendations to guerrillas correspond to its prescriptions. The *Notes* insist that counterguerrilla forces fighting off an ambush should always attack the enemy's flank and rear,[145] but Gubbins responds by insisting that sentries be posted to prevent guerrillas waiting in ambush from becoming the ambushed.[146] ("Women and children, who are less likely to be suspected," may be utilized in this role.[147]) The *Notes* observe that most rebels, being poorly trained, are likely to break if their line of retreat is threatened; Gubbins answers that a "*secure* line of retreat," which "will give all the men a safe and sure way of escape," is essential for any ambush position.[148] The *Notes* point out that successful searches and raids require surprise; in response, Gubbins advises guerrillas that fostering the local population as intelligence gatherers "will ensure that the guerillas are kept au fait with the enemy's movements and intentions, whereas their own are hidden from him."[149]

AVOIDING COUNTERMEASURES. The IRA was hit hard by the British counteroffensive that followed the violence of 21 November 1920, remembered as Bloody Sunday. As historian Peter Hart explains, "Activists still at large went on the run, . . . arms were moved and better hidden, [and] larger and more vulnerable flying columns were broken up."[150] Gubbins's comments to partisans in 1939 could have been descriptions of Ireland: "Searches, raids, . . . curfew, passport and other regulations" will eventually force guerrillas to abandon their homes and "go on the run," that is, "live as a band in some suitable areas where the nature of the country enables them to be relatively secure."[151] Likewise, he recommends that guerrilla parties be kept small, to improve mobility and secrecy, and that supply of weapons be given very careful consideration.[152] Many of the more military countermeasures Gubbins expected guerrillas to encounter are found in the *Notes* as well: raids, lorry patrols, armoured cars, and so on.[153]

THE IMPORTANCE OF PLANNING. The *Notes on Guerrilla Warfare in Ireland* insist that no party should ever leave barracks without a precise plan and that officers and NCOs should practice giving orders before conducting an operation.[154] This emphasis on sound preparation, always important in the chaos of war, but particularly so in the confusions of irregular warfare, is also found in Gubbins's writings, such as the *PLH*'s comment that "every operation must be planned with the greatest care."[155]

These strong parallels suggest that Gubbins drew heavily from his experience and the official British descriptions of the war in Ireland, though such parallels, by themselves, offer only circumstantial evidence. However, we can say with confidence that Gubbins's time in Ireland influenced his thinking because he and so many of his colleagues said just that. In a memo describing the requirements for the *AGW* and the *PLH*, Gubbins's superior at GS(R), J. C. F. Holland, explained that "there is little doubt that the Irish made guerrilla warfare into a science, which has been followed since. . . . *It is proposed to base this present study on such information as can be obtained of Irish principles* and their application by other revolutionaries subsequently."[156] Likewise, when describing his writings decades later, Gubbins commented that "we had only our own experience to go upon . . . in Ireland 1919–1922 and . . . in North Russia at the end of the First World War."[157] These are not romanticized accounts of SOE's origins but honest assessments that are borne out by a careful consideration of the strategy and tactics in question.

Eunan O'Halpin, one of the few authors to comment on the IRA-SOE connection at any length, contends that the influence was minimal. He acknowledges that Gubbins and his colleagues studied the IRA, but highlights the fact that other conflicts—including the Boer War, the Russian Revolution, and the Arab Revolt in Palestine (1936-39)—were also studied. Moreover, he contends that "the Chinese and Spanish [civil] wars provided more recent and larger scale examples of the use of irregular warfare."[158] O'Halpin is right to insist that Ireland be placed alongside other sources of inspiration (see chapters 3 and 4), but this does not ipso facto mean that Ireland was insignificant. While China and Spain provided recent examples, neither Gubbins nor Holland participated in or directly observed either conflict. Both men, however, fought in Ireland, where Gubbins served far longer than he had served in Russia. In terms of personal contact, at least, the Irish experience remains preeminent. O'Halpin further contends that there is no evidence Section D, one of SOE's two progenitors, looked to Ireland.[159] True though this may be, it does not affect Gubbins's own work at GS(R). His time spent in Ireland, coupled with the strong parallels between the Irish experience and his later writings, argues strongly in favor of the contention that Ireland played a crucial role in the formation of Gubbins's thinking. Finally, O'Halpin observes that one knowledgeable figure, Guy Liddell, claimed that Gubbins's organization was modelled not on the IRA but on the Arab Bureau that supported the Arab Revolt of 1916-18.[160] Although Liddell may have known a great deal about both Ireland and intelligence, his position was with the Security Service (MI5), not with SOE or any of its predecessors. Nevertheless, a useful distinction can be made here: Gubbins saw himself supporting foreign guerrillas rather than becoming a guerrilla himself. Thus the Arab Bureau may have been a major inspiration with regard to the concept of advising, while the IRA or other partisans were probably the preeminent model of guerrilla tactics to be taught. Unfortunately the documentary evidence of Gubbins's thinking is often too thin to substantiate such fine distinctions.

India

In 1921, Gubbins earned an interpretership in French; in early 1923 he took a Russian course at King's College London and earned a second interpretership. That spring, Gubbins was posted to British India. Although his seven years there included experiences and education relating to such topics as tribal warfare, subversion, intelligence, and politics, the absence of major combat operations likely explains the limited influence that India had on Gubbins's irregular warfare doctrine, far less than the influence of Ireland or even Russia. Nevertheless, Gubbins's time in the British Raj merits discussion for two reasons. Firstly, it likely broadened and reinforced many of the lessons he learned in earlier conflicts. Secondly, his service in India allowed him to reach several important career milestones, including attendance at Staff College and service in formal intelligence positions. Thus, when Gubbins returned to Britain in 1930, he did so with a well-rounded résumé and a growing knowledge of staff duties, attributes that, in future years, would help him to mediate between the military establishment and irregular formations.

The 1920s were an interesting time to be in India: Mohandas Gandhi was leading a growing resistance movement to British rule, Japanese agents were active in South and Southeast Asia, the Bolsheviks had designs on India, and the Afghans had invaded as recently as 1919.[161] Although the invasion had been quickly defeated, it caught the British by surprise, was an embarrassment to local intelligence, and was followed by tribal revolts, which were not so easily put down.[162] Into this context, Gubbins was posted to the 15th Battery, RFA, in Lucknow, northern India. After nearly a year, he was appointed officiating general staff officer, 3rd grade (GSO3) for intelligence at Mhow in the Central Provinces District.[163] Though this new appointment is tantalizing with respect to his future work in clandestine warfare, little is known of this period, except that "here he was able to indulge his passion for mounted sport."[164] After eight months as GSO3 (intelligence), he returned to the 15th Battery, now at Jubbulpore.[165]

In January 1925 he was appointed adjutant to the XXIII Field Brigade, RA, in Nowshera, just outside Peshawar near the eastern end of the Khyber Pass.[166] Not long after he arrived there the RAF began a series of operations a couple hundred miles southwest in South Waziristan. These strafing runs against Mahsud tribesmen became known as Pink's War, after their architect, Wing Commander R. C. M. Pink. This conflict may have shaped Gubbins's thoughts on airpower (see below), but it certainly did not destroy his confidence in the abilities of guerrillas. He later commented that "it is undeniable that in certain campaigns in the past the activities of guerillas have had a marked influence on the operations of regular armies." Among the examples he cites are "the continual small wars on the North West Frontier of India."[167] He was not alone in his observation of irregular warfare on the North-West Frontier; historian Chaz Bowyer calls the locals "the finest guerilla fighters in the world."[168]

Gubbins did not stay in Nowshera long, attending the Northern Command's annual intelligence course in Murree, also near Peshawar, from May to June 1925.[169] Col. Reginald Hillyard recommended Gubbins in the strongest terms, noting that he "worked with the greatest keenness throughout the class and is suited in every way for Intelligence work especially in the Far East."[170] That year Gubbins, ever the linguist, also passed a preliminary Urdu exam.[171] From October 1925 to February 1928 he served as GSO3 (intelligence) at the army headquarters at Simla, the summer capital of the British Raj. There he spent much of his time reading and translating secret Soviet communications, making use of his facility in Russian.[172]

Soviet premier V. I. Lenin made no secret of his hatred for the British Empire, annulling the Anglo-Russian Convention of 1907, which had ended the Great Game, the nineteenth-century struggle for mastery of Central Asia.[173] In 1920, Lenin declared that "England is our greatest enemy. It is in India that we must strike them hardest."[174] This open hostility must have lent a certain edge to the intelligence work of Gubbins, a man who already loathed Communism from his first-hand experience in Russia. Historian Peter Hopkirk notes that "from remote listening-posts far beyond India's frontiers, British Indian intelligence officers monitored every Bolshevik move against India and reported these back to their chiefs in Delhi and London." Within India itself, the British carried out "the discreet reading of suspects' mail, the interception and decoding of Bolshevik wireless messages, and the penetration of Indian nationalist groups suspected of having links to Moscow."[175] Such wireless intercepts were enabled by the fact that, "from 1920 to 1927 [the British] were able regularly and extensively to read Soviet codes, including those of the Comintern, ... [gaining] detailed insights into Soviet policy at the highest levels."[176] When Gubbins wrote in 1939 that "ALL [guerrilla] MESSAGES IN WIRELESS MUST BE IN CODE OR CIPHER," he wrote from a personal experience of just how vulnerable signals could be.[177] (He also knew, however, the potential usefulness of wireless in a "whispering" campaign aimed at galvanizing discontent among an enemy population.[178]) SOE was not an intelligence agency per se; its mission was sabotage and subversion. However, like the traditional practitioners of intelligence, SOE depended upon secrecy, utilized intelligence information, and relied upon encoded communications. Thus, Gubbins's study and practice of intelligence, particularly signals intelligence, in India can be viewed as part of his preparation to craft SOE doctrine and subsequently lead the organization.[179]

From Simla, Gubbins went to Staff College at Quetta, a course he completed in December 1929. There he studied various topics including military history, airpower, joint operations with the Royal Navy, signals intelligence, and the political and military challenges of frontier warfare.[180] Among Gubbins's colleagues at Quetta was Frederick William "Nick" Nicholls, who had managed to establish wireless communications with the British Embassy in Kabul during the Third Anglo-Afghan War. During World War II, Nicholls would serve under Gubbins as director of signals at SOE. Gubbins was often awake until 2:30 or 3:00 A.M., laboring over his studies.[181] "The one ambition of all the students now," he wrote to his cousin Helen, "is not to get a 1st class report but just to get thro' safely and get it over."[182] Gubbins finished fourth in the class, with his commander, Field Marshal Sir Ian Birdwood, commending him for "an excellent performance."[183] Having completed his studies, Gubbins was back in Britain by the end of January 1930.[184]

Airpower

Gubbins came of age as a soldier at the same time that airpower matured as a tool of war. The precise origins of his thoughts on the role of airpower in guerrilla warfare are unknown, though he had various experiences of airpower prior to drafting his guerrilla doctrine and lived in an environment where the emerging use of airpower was often discussed. In all likelihood, it was Britain's own use of aircraft against irregular forces in the British Empire that led Gubbins to recognize the grave danger posed by aircraft to guerrillas.

Gubbins first saw combat in the first conflict to feature any significant use of airpower, the Great War, and he attended the aircraft course in 1917. The Archangel Expeditionary Force made the first air-supported landing in world history, covered by biplanes from HMS *Nairana*.[185] The RAF contingent of the Archangel Force also brought eleven planes of various kinds and, on arrival, discovered additional aircraft among the supplies that had been sent to Russia. Just as important, the RAF discovered twenty-seven veterans of the Russian Flying Corps, to add to the thirty pilots and observers they had brought.[186] Gubbins's presence alongside General Ironside meant he likely brushed elbows with some of the RAF personnel, among whom Ironside praised Lt. Col. Robin Grey "for his direction of the Royal Air Force and for his courage and determination."[187] In Ireland the RAF dropped propaganda leaflets, conducted reconnaissance, escorted convoys to deter and detect ambushes, and carried out both bomb and strafing attacks against IRA guerrillas.[188] In May 1921 the Republican newspaper *an t-Ólgach* explained that "enemy aircraft were a factor which our troops had to give serious attention"; retreating guerrillas had to worry about "keeping in cover from the aircraft" since "the most dangerous thing was being observed by [British] aircraft."[189] In India, the air force headquarters were located in Simla, alongside the army headquarters, where Gubbins was stationed, and among the topics he studied at the Staff College in Quetta was the role of airpower.[190] Thus, although Gubbins records in his SOE Record of Service that he flew an aeroplane "only once!" he had considerable familiarity with aircraft and had numerous occasions on which to consider their role in guerrilla warfare.[191]

Why do Gubbins's writings display a considerable fear of airpower? Although airpower played roles in Russia and Ireland, in neither theater could it be called decisive. Gubbins was certainly aware of airpower in the Chinese and Spanish Civil Wars, both raging as he wrote the *AGW* and the *PLH* (see chapter 3). However, the most unambiguous uses of airpower in the interwar period involved Britain's own RAF, at work in the empire. In 1919, the RAF deployed to Somaliland to end the rebellion of Mohammed bin Abdullah Hassan, known to the British as the "Mad Mullah." In addition to bombing rebel strongholds—very nearly killing the rebel leader—the RAF also performed reconnaissance and communications functions.[192] Contemporary assessments of the air operations in Somaliland were quite positive, concluding, in the words of the governor that "threats from the air offer the surest guarantee of peace and order."[193]

In 1919 a series of rebellions broke out in Mesopotamia and the RAF again conducted ground attack and communications operations, as well as dropping propaganda leaflets, attacking Turkish incursions into Mesopotamia, and engaging in aerial mapping. As the regional situation worsened in the coming years, overall command in the recently renamed Iraq was invested in an RAF officer, while "air control" of certain territories was substituted for army control.[194] Conflict, much of it centered on Sheikh Mahmud's rebellion, continued until 1932, the same year Iraq officially received independence. In spite of more than a decade of insurgency, many viewed the RAF's experiment in air control as a success; upon Sheikh Mahmud's surrender in 1931, he described the RAF as "the people who have broken my spirit."[195]

As the Arab Revolt broke out in Palestine in 1936 (see chapter 4), the RAF coordinated with police and army forces, once more conducting reconnaissance, distributing propaganda, and carrying out strafing and light bombing against Arab mobs, criminal gangs, and Arab and Jewish terrorist groups. It was in Palestine that the RAF began the tactic of "air cordons," in which entire villages or cities—such as Jerusalem on 18 October 1936—were surrounded by aircraft flying around the perimeter to prevent anyone from entering or leaving, while the army then searched the location for rebels or arms caches.[196]

Gubbins would have only learned about the above conflicts at a remove, but India was also a significant scene of air operations against irregular forces. In the tribal rebellion in Waziristan, which followed the Afghan invasion, the RAF engaged in both close air support and independent bombing, often at great peril.[197] Its work was praised by the official historian of the conflict, who argued that "officers of the land forces would find their labour well repaid if they undertook the study of this important auxiliary to the art of tactics."[198] But the most striking use of airpower came during Pink's War, operations against a few tribes on the North-West Frontier that chose not to accept the British terms, as their neighbors had, but launched a fresh rebellion in 1925. These operations—by both day and night—were not simply led by the RAF, as was the case in Iraq or the earlier conflict in Waziristan, but were exclusively conducted from the air. When the rebels were foolish enough to move through open country, considerable casualties were inflicted from the air. Perhaps more importantly, neighboring tribes began refusing the rebels sanctuary, having been warned by the RAF that their villages and flocks would be bombed if they cooperated with the rebels. That the rebellious tribes came to terms after only fifty-four days of RAF operations suggests the stunning possibilities of airpower against unconventional forces.[199]

Gubbins advises in the *AGW* that "partisan leaders must impress on all their men that the surest way of attaining success in their operations is by remaining undetected, and that detection will always be followed by enemy action against them." Such detection could come with very little warning from the air. Thus, "concealment from aircraft is of the greatest importance, and men must be trained to take cover quickly, to lie face downwards, and to remain absolutely still until the aeroplane has passed."[200] Elsewhere in the *AGW* he observes that of "the various weapons that the enemy may employ . . . the most dangerous to the partisans is the aeroplane."[201] Drives and other actions of enemy mobile detachments are made more dangerous by the fact that "aeroplanes are certain to co-operate."[202] In addition to simply posing a direct danger, aircraft also imposed limits on partisans, forcing them to organize bands of twenty-five men or fewer; anything larger could not be concealed.[203] Because of the danger of being spotted from the air, Gubbins advises partisans to "move as much as you can by night."[204] When preparing an ambush site, arrangements were never to be of the sort that could be spotted from the air.[205] Gubbins was keen to see that his men did not suffer the same fates as the Mad Mullah and Sheikh Mahmud.

Conclusion

By the dawn of the 1930s, Gubbins had seen conventional warfare on the Western Front, where he served with distinction. He had participated in irregular conflict, first in Russia and then in Ireland, and had spent several years in India, where problems of intelligence, subversion, and the irregular warfare of the North-West Frontier occupied much of his time. Moreover, he had occasion to reflect on guerrilla warfare, its methods and qualities, and how it intersected with intelligence, airpower, and larger strategy. He had certainly considered some of these matters during the intelligence course and at Staff College in India; he likely considered them in the light of the *Notes on Guerrilla Warfare in Ireland* and may have also examined them with reference to Callwell's *Small Wars*. Nevertheless, an overly teleological view should be avoided; although Gubbins had considerable experience with irregular warfare, he did not yet see it as his particular vocation, nor did he single-mindedly seek it out, as if somehow consciously preparing himself for his future leadership of SOE. Further turns of events were required before Gubbins became irrevocably devoted to irregular warfare.

CHAPTER 3

Formulating a Doctrine

Learning from the Past

Gubbins returned to Britain in early 1930. He spent two years at the War Office, where he worked in intelligence against the Soviets, and was an observer at the Czechoslovak withdrawal from the Sudetenland. For the most part, however, the nine years that followed his return from India were filled with unexceptional staff and training duties. Yet even these, arguably, helped prepare Gubbins for his future work at SOE, where he routinely interacted with senior staff elements and developed a course of training for British and foreign partisans. All the while, senior leaders in the British military wrestled with the fundamental problem of inadequate resources to defend the empire and simultaneously deal with rising dangers in Europe. Several organizations explored the use of irregular warfare to meet Britain's security demands within the context of limited resources. Gubbins was attached to one of these organizations, GS(R), in April 1939.

Gubbins was chosen for this position in part on the basis of his experience with irregular warfare in Russia and Ireland. To supplement this personal experience, he undertook a program of study examining both historical and contemporary conflicts. From the Second Anglo-Boer War, the exploits of T. E. Lawrence, and the German guerrilla campaign in East Africa, he learned many of the basic principles of guerrilla warfare regarding organization, intelligence, operations, and leadership. However, he departed from some of his models by demanding coherent strategic vision, integration with conventional military efforts, and a reasonable probability of success.

The 1930s

Gubbins's Return to Britain

Upon Gubbins's return from India, he spent nearly a year with 5 Light Brigade at Ewshot, Hampshire, and then reported to MI3(c), the Soviet section of Military Intelligence.[1] Although Gubbins had read intercepted Soviet communications in India, the new cipher pads adopted by the Soviets in 1927 proved much harder to crack and so he spent much of his time culling the Russian press for useful information. This posting was Gubbins's first at the War Office, and he enjoyed the cosmopolitan atmosphere there, a welcome break from the sometimes drab world of regular soldiering.[2]

In April 1933, Gubbins left MI3(c) and was appointed brigade major, RA to the 4th Division in Colchester.[3] Here he was responsible for training artilleryman from the Territorial Army (TA), Britain's reserve force. Like his experience with MI3(c), Gubbins appreciated the wide variety of enthusiastic men the TA provided, as well as the constructive criticism they brought to military practices. While many soldiers, skeptical of civilians, might have discouraged such comments, Gubbins encouraged them.[4]

His work in training continued when, in October 1935, he was appointed to the policy-making branch of the Military Training Directorate, MT1, where he served as head of the artillery section. While there, he also doubled as personal staff officer to Maj. Gen. Alan Brooke, inspector of artillery and soon-to-be director of military training.[5] Brooke would later become General Officer Commanding-in-Chief Home Army and Chief of the Imperial General Staff (CIGS), at which time his friendship proved valuable to Gubbins.

In October 1938 Gubbins was among the British military observers who watched the withdrawal of Czechoslovak forces from the Sudetenland. He considered Czechoslovakia "a thoroughly decent democratic little nation" and disapproved of the Munich Agreement, which he saw as a prelude to the war Hitler desired.[6] Ever after, Gubbins was ashamed that the Czechoslovaks had fallen victim to the Nazis by virtue of what he judged to be British and French weakness.[7]

British Military Policy in the Interwar Period

A great deal has been written about the course of British military policy following the First World War and in the lead-up to the Second World War, often focusing on whether a more robust policy of rearmament and modernization might have deterred or more quickly defeated Germany. There were, however, sound reasons for the British government to limit its military preparation. Following the horrors of the First World War, a spirit of "never again!" pervaded much of British society. Arguing for more and better weapons was unlikely to win a favorable hearing. Moreover, having faced war debts and economic depression, the British government sought a return to balanced budgets and economic growth. Finally, Britain's military preoccupations were primarily with the empire, not with Europe, resulting in installations and capabilities of use in the former but not necessarily the latter.[8]

As a result, limited military spending followed the Great War and the army often fared worst of the three services.[9] The Royal Navy and RAF were, the argument went, defensive services, which could be used to protect Britain itself against aggression, whereas the army was an offensive service, used to project power onto the European continent.[10] The damage done to the army was not merely financial, but also psychological: pessimism set in among the officers, particularly those who were progressive-minded, the very reformers Britain needed in order to prepare for the next war.[11]

Throughout the 1930s, British policy makers considered deploying an expeditionary force to the European continent, in the event of a general war. Military planners complained, however, that the resources given them were inadequate for the task. Historian Brian Bond has argued that, by 1933, the British Army could not, in a reasonable amount of time, field an expeditionary force that could stand up to even a second-class opponent.[12] The Chiefs of Staff concluded as much when they wrote in 1933 that "should war break out in Europe . . . we should be able to do little more than hold the frontiers and outposts of the Empire."[13] But the empire was not the only consideration distracting from the army's ability to conduct operations in Europe. Gubbins's former superior, General Ironside, noted in his diary in 1938 that "the Air Defence of Great Britain is absorbing all the money which was intended for the Field Force."[14] Even after the Munich Crisis of September 1938, the cabinet refused to increase the army's funds and, as late as December 1938, the army received only £277 million of a total defense budget of £2 billion.[15]

Thus the British Army was left with an imbalance between resources for the proposed expeditionary force and the requirements it might face. One proposed remedy was to turn to the Dominions for help. But when Britain asked for troops to garrison Mesopotamia in 1920, only a single New Zealand battalion was offered; the Chanak crisis two years later demonstrated even more clearly that Britain could not count on Dominion aid for problems in Europe.[16] Another solution was to lobby for increased resources. Yet in 1935 the Defence Requirements Committee concluded that all three services were so deficient that, even with a £200 million loan, the military would struggle to be ready for a European war by 1942.[17] Likewise, Gen. Sir John Burnett-Stuart, a leading commander of the time, recalled in his memoirs, "I was convinced that to send the British Army to a Continental War in its then condition would be to condemn it to disaster."[18] In addition to financial constraints, any talk of conscription was out of the question.[19]

If adequate resources were simply unavailable, commitment to continental action could be curtailed. This was the approach that occupied most contemporary debates. Alternatively, B. H. Liddell Hart argued that limited resources must be prioritized. In modern warfare, particularly on the continent, he contended, dismounted infantry divisions would be of little use and so the British Army should prioritize motorized and armored forces.[20] A third approach suggested that, if resources were insufficient for a conventional war, Britain should consider unconventional methods. This was a natu-ral conclusion, since the British Army spent the decades between the World Wars engaged in colonial conflicts. Indeed, many soldiers considered the Great War an aberration, the exception to the rule of imperial small wars.[21] Moreover, employment of unconventional means offered to avoid not only the slaughter of the trenches but also the harsh realities of the government budget. This was the con-clusion reached by several different people. They did not all agree with one another or even know of each other's existence. Their efforts were ad hoc at first, but they grew, by fits and starts, into Britain's irregular warfare capability, including SOE.

That such clandestine efforts began as tiny organizations, employing sometimes amateurish methods, should not be a surprise. In the 1930s generally, and 1938 and 1939 in particular, Britain made extensive use of reporting supplied by private citizens. In some cases this intelligence was passed to the Foreign Office; in other cases it went directly to various officials in Whitehall, with little respect paid to proper organizational protocols. In this way, some officials were able to build unofficial private networks of informants.[22] SOE's predecessor organizations enjoyed official recognition, but their informality was quite in keeping with practices of the times.

Electra House

As the British government faced the possibility of a European war, the Committee of Imperial Defence set up a small organization called the Department of Propaganda in Enemy Countries—known as EH (after its headquarters, the Electra House on the Thames) or CS (after its head, Sir Campbell Stuart)—with the purpose of influencing German opinion. Stuart, a Canadian, had been deputy head of Crewe House, Britain's propaganda machine in the First World War, and was now chairman of the Imperial Communications Committee, whose offices were at Electra House.[23] Electra House was placed under the authority of the Ministry of Information, then the Foreign Office, and back again several times during 1939 and 1940. It eventually became the Political Warfare Executive (PWE), an independent wartime propaganda agency, but before such independence it would pass through the hands of SOE.[24]

Section D

In April 1938, a month after the German annexation of Austria and around the time EH was proposed, the Secret Intelligence Service (SIS) established Section D to study unconventional warfare or—in the words of the SIS chief—"to cogitate upon the possibilities of sabotage."[25] Maj. Laurence Douglas Grand, of the Royal Engineers, led the new organization. He was tall and lean, described by one colleague as having "all the paraphernalia of the 'spy master' of popular fiction": civilian clothes (always with a red carnation in the buttonhole), a black homburg hat, dark glasses, and a tapered cigarette holder in his mouth.[26] Further matching the stereotypes of fiction, Section D had an "obsession with security."[27] Grand commanded great loyalty but was short on tact.[28] He got off to a quick start, moving Section D from the SIS basement to a new location a couple hundred yards away on Caxton Street, where its offices connected by passageways to St. Ermin's Hotel.[29]

Section D's first objects of study were the transportation of key raw materials to Germany: iron ore from Sweden and oil from Romania. The section also considered groups that might carry out sabotage, including Jews, Catholics, and Communists. Like SOE, into which it developed, Section D aimed to use anti-Nazi organizations already in Europe. It recommended deploying agents to countries bordering Germany, both to intercept imports and to supply resisters within Germany. However, Section D recognized that such deployments would be too provocative in peacetime. Until the outbreak of war, it limited itself to research and preliminary organization, with a one-time appropriation of £20,000.[30]

In May 1938 Grand submitted a list of likely targets and methods of sabotage. Other sections of SIS commented that the ideas were ambitious to the point of being impractical.[31] Grand nevertheless pressed ahead. In the autumn of 1938 he traveled to Czechoslovakia, meeting with the Czechoslovak General Staff and considering the possibilities of sabotaging the Skoda Armaments works, should it fall into German hands. Grand even organized a network within the main Skoda factories themselves, to carry out such sabotage, although it never happened.[32]

Since Section D's original field of operations included "moral sabotage," it overlapped with EH's propaganda.[33] Open broadcasts from Britain were unequivocally the BBC's responsibility, but Grand planned for extensive propaganda against Germany via neutral countries and was also interested in "black" radio, broadcasts claiming to come from within Germany, while really originating elsewhere. Out of Section D's secret allocation he funded the Joint Broadcasting Committee, which carried out both black and white (avowed) broadcasts.[34]

With the outbreak of war, Section D began running operations, particularly in the Balkans. The Ploeşti oilfield in Romania supplied Germany with 20 percent of its oil; Section D attempted attacks on both the oilfield itself and the means of transport, but all efforts failed.[35] Unsurprisingly, the British diplomats of the region were squeamish about these clandestine operations, about which they knew little and over which they had no control.[36] Nevertheless, the failures themselves may have proved something to the diplomats: denying Britain's (unacknowledged) saboteurs the support of the (official) diplomatic staff only increased the likelihood of embarrassing failures. Cooperation, it appeared, might be mutually beneficial.[37]

At the same time, Section D established contact with Jewish, Catholic, labor, émigré, and other anti-Nazi organizations. Its relationships extended to international groups with a presence in Britain but also to organizations in Germany, Austria, Hungary, Romania, Italy, Yugoslavia, Bulgaria, Greece, Turkey, Palestine, and Egypt. Although Section D was not an intelligence organization per se, it was an extension of SIS, and so the various intelligence data that came from these sources—including a secret index of the Nazi hierarchy provided by a German émigré—was passed along in course. A few cases of explosives were distributed to would-be saboteurs in Germany, but the results were minimal: the reported destruction of a single munitions dump.[38]

In the four weeks leading up to the outbreak of war, Section D delivered more than two tons of propaganda to Germany, Austria, and Czechoslovakia, by way of courier lines through neutral countries. As 1939 drew to a close, some lines were shut down, but even more new lines were opened.[39] By the beginning of 1940, radio broadcasts could be heard in fourteen countries, with negotiations underway for broadcasts in several others. Hundreds of recordings and thousands of individual phonograph records —including special records that could be hidden inside rolled newspapers—were produced each month.[40] Little, however, came of these efforts, in part because commercial radio stations in neutral countries would only broadcast material too mild to be effective.[41]

In addition to examining external possibilities for sabotage and subversion against Britain's enemies, Section D also worried about the use of sabotage and subversion against Britain. It produced directions for antisabotage precautions that were approved by MI5 and circulated not only in Britain but also throughout the empire. Moreover, Section D also documented the allegedly pro-Nazi activities of the "Oxford Group" and studied the potential value of secret censorship (i.e., reading mail, not censoring the press).[42]

General Staff (Research)

In 1936, the Imperial General Staff set up a small section in the War Office called General Staff (Research), or GS(R), reporting directly to the deputy chief of the Imperial General Staff (DCIGS). This section was really more of a fellowship, extended to a single officer for one year, in which he would "research . . . problems of tactics and organisation" and "liaison with other branches of the War Office and with Commands in order to collect new ideas on these subjects."[43] Put simply, the fellowship holder could study any topic of interest, so long as the DCIGS approved. The first holder of the office considered army education; the second examined military medicine.[44] Nevertheless, GS(R)'s clandestine potential was suggested by the DCIGS from the beginning: "This section must be small, almost anonymous, go where they like, talk to whom they like."[45]

In 1938 the position passed to Lt. Col. J. C. F. Holland, a Royal Engineer who had attended Woolwich in the class behind Gubbins. In 1916, Holland was attached to the Royal Flying Corps and served in the Balkans, for which he was awarded the Distinguished Flying Cross.[46] Holland also served on the North-West Frontier of India and during the postwar fighting in Ireland, where—according to Foot—he befriended Gubbins.[47] Holland was intelligent, imaginative, and practical, loathing pretense.[48] He was "completely unselfish . . . [and] had no intention of building an empire for himself," Gubbins explained.[49] Holland's secretary described him as a hardworking chain smoker with a fiery temper ("I can feel now the quick downward movement by which I ducked the impact of a book flung at my head one day on opening the door of his office"), a man both feared and loved.[50]

In March 1937 Prime Minister Neville Chamberlain declared, "I am quite sure we shall never again send to the Continent an Army on the scale of that which we put into the field in the Great War."[51] The General Staff was told to plan accordingly. Holland, impressed by the hit-and-run tactics of irregular forces in China and Spain, took guerrilla warfare as his topic of study, officially seeking lessons for British colonial operations. In secret, however, the DCIGS ordered Holland to examine ways in which Britain might support guerrillas in Nazi-occupied Eastern Europe.[52]

In January 1939, on the strength of a preliminary report, Holland received authorization to expand GS(R) by adding two general staff officers, second grade (GSO2), one a demolitions expert, the other in charge of organization, recruitment, and training. For the demolitions post he selected Millis Jefferis, another Royal Engineer, described by Joan Bright Astley as "an inventive genius."[53] For the position overseeing organization, recruitment, and training, Holland chose Colin Gubbins, at least in part because of his service in Russia and Ireland.

On 4 April 1939 Gubbins joined Holland's operation and that spring they authored various papers on the theory and practice of guerrilla warfare.⁵⁴ Their source material came from the conflicts in which they had fought—the Russian Civil War and the Irish Revolution—as well as from the earlier Anglo-Boer Wars, the guerrilla campaign of Paul von Lettow-Vorbeck in East Africa, T. E. Lawrence's exploits in Arabia, and such recent affairs as the Spanish Civil War, the Sino-Japanese Wars, and the Arab Revolt in Palestine.⁵⁵

In addition to the officers, Holland also had a secretary typist, Joan Bright (later Astley). She was a genuine Miss Moneypenny, holding together the office with diligent work and keen wit.⁵⁶ She was born in Argentina and served as a typist with the British delegation in Mexico.⁵⁷ After the war Gubbins described her as professional and a "great personal friend."⁵⁸ Of these early members of GS(R), Dennis Wheatley writes, "It would have been difficult to find . . . people better qualified to run such a 'free-lance' department with vigour and imagination."⁵⁹

Though struggling to meet the growing threats in Europe with inadequate resources, the creations of GS(R), Section D, and Electra House are proof that the British foreign policy in the 1930s was not simply inactive but considered creative ways to prepare for future conflict. From these small and diverse elements, SOE would be forged, though early relations between them were often confusing and not always amicable.

Development of and Relationship between Section D and GS(R)

In March 1939, Section D and GS(R) began a series of interactions that would ultimately see their merger. On 20 March Grand submitted a joint paper to W. E. van Cutsem, deputy director of Military Intelligence (DDMI).⁶⁰ Mackenzie comments that "the basic ideas of this paper are recognizably those of Colonel Holland; its style and its unquenchable optimism are certainly Colonel Grand's."⁶¹ The report emphasized lessons from "experiences which we have had in India, Irak, Ireland and Russia." With regard to applications of guerrilla warfare, it advocated the following:

a. Creating the maximum of insecurity to occupying troops and occupying Gestapo;
b. Creating the maximum of insecurity on the lines of communication;
c. Encouragement of local desire for independence;
d. Making any fresh adventure, and the most recent in Czecho-Slovakia and Austria, as expensive as possible.⁶²

The report proposed fomenting insurrection in Italian Libya and Italian-occupied Abyssinia and fostering Romanian, Danish, Dutch, and Polish guerrillas for possible future resistance. The Czechoslovaks too were to be armed and encouraged "to commence operations on the lines of the Irish Terror in 1920–21." To do all this, Grand requested a staff of twenty-six officers, including Holland, and a budget of half a million pounds.[63]

On 22 March, Good Friday of that year, the CIGS, Viscount Gort, was briefed on the proposals, along with R. H. Dewing, the director of Military Operations (DMO); DDMI van Cutsem was again present.[64] The next day the foreign secretary, Lord Halifax; the permanent undersecretary of the Foreign Office, Sir Alexander Cadogan; the acting SIS chief, Sir Stewart Menzies; Gort; and Grand met to discuss the paper of 20 March. Halifax was concerned about funding a sabotage organization that might be traced back to His Majesty's Government; Grand convinced him that plausible deniability could be maintained. Someone else asked why the paper proposed only to tell the prime minister and foreign secretary about subversive operations; why was the chancellor left off? Grand explained that fewer people reduced the chance of leaks. Halifax said he understood but pointed out that it would be hard to obtain funding while the chancellor was in the dark. Thus, the assembled leaders agreed that, with Prime Minister Chamberlain's approval, some preparatory work could be done by Section D, with an emphasis on counteracting the Nazis in the small countries Germany was threatening.[65] Holland, in turn, secured Gort's approval for the expansion of GS(R)'s work, though the new funds came from the SIS budget.[66]

As part of the change, GS(R) was redesignated "D/M Section."[67] Although authorized to expand, efforts to limit costs and attention meant that D/M Section received only a handful of regular officers; most of its new staff were reserve.[68] Holland's small outfit moved from the War Office to Section D's offices on Caxton Street in April 1939, since Section D was making similar plans and could more easily divert the treasury's prying eyes.[69] In June 1939 D/M Section was moved from the DCIG's jurisdiction and placed under the director of Military Intelligence (DMI), Gen. Frederick George Beaumont-Nesbitt, and again renamed, initially MI.1(R), though MI(R) is the name that stuck.[70]

In retrospect, the dynamic relationship between MI(R) and Section D was confusing and at times unclear; the same was true for the participants then. Peter Fleming, having been recruited by MI(R), recorded his confusion with a biblical turn: "I seem to be under but not of the War Office."[71] Likewise, Joan Bright Astley records that in April 1939 she joined "Section 'D/MI(R),'" though all the superiors she lists were from the MI(R) side.[72] This confusion regarding the relationship between the two organizations is only heightened by later attempts to establish the primacy of one or the other in the historiography. An internal SOE history, likely authored by a veteran of Section D or by someone utilizing documents from it, claims that "M.I.R. [was] an organisation . . . initiated by Colonel Grand."[73] While Grand may have shepherded its development into a guerrilla agency, its existence as a kind of research fellowship undeniably antedates the creation of Section D or Grand's arrival on the scene.

Attempts by historians to identify a division of labor between the two organizations have been inconclusive. Mark Seaman contends that Section D provided wartime contingency plans, while the more "visionary" MI(R) contributed "thoughtful development of the theory and practice of guerrilla warfare."[74] However, Foot appears to contradict this directly, noting that Holland "seems to have believed [Section D's] head to be too visionary and impractical to suit the exigencies of the war that both he himself and Gubbins regarded as imminent."[75] On 11 February 1940, DMI Beaumont-Nesbitt attempted to delineate the boundary between the two organizations: activities that could be publicly acknowledged by the British government would be handled by MI(R); those that could not, by Section D.[76] Perhaps the best distinction comes from a memorandum of 4 September 1939, in which MI(R) clarified that Section D would focus on "action [which] must be sub-terranean, i.e., in countries which are in effective occupation," while MI(R) would focus on "action [which] is a matter of military missions, whether regular or irregular."[77]

The parallels between MI(R) and Section D are considerable: Holland, like Grand, was an engineer; both, like Gubbins, studied at the Royal Military Academy, Woolwich. Grand and Gubbins both served in France, Russia, and India, though Grand also served in Iraq. Just as his counterparts at MI(R) looked to the IRA, the experience in Russia, and the experience of imperial policing for lessons, so too did Grand.[78] That Grand, Holland, and Gubbins all had similar experiences and ended up in subversive warfare in the late 1930s attests to the fact that there existed a circle of men who had cut their teeth on the same irregular conflicts in the interwar period and were drawn to similar problems prior to the Second World War.

In spite of the similarities, there was a basic difference in temperament between the two organizations, a difference that explained Gubbins's mixed feelings toward Section D. As seen during his experiences with military intelligence and military training, Gubbins opposed bureaucratic thinking and appreciated alternative views, particularly from civilians. In Section D he encountered risk-taking businessmen and generous budgets to finance innovative ideas. However, he was aghast at some of Section D's more grandiose projects and the amateurish way they were executed.[79] MI(R) was creative, but it also remained realistic.[80] Holland explained in April 1939, for example, that MI(R) would focus on defending countries that remained unoccupied. Those that had already fallen to the Germans were beyond its modest abilities.[81] Holland's decision was simple, clear, practical, and quite unlike the empire-building often found within bureaucracies.

From June 1939 onward, the tone at MI(R) changed, as Holland explained in a memo to his subordinates: "From now until the middle of August we must aim primarily at getting anything ready that we can in the time."[82] Under orders from the DCIGS, MI(R) operated "on the assumption that war might occur in August/September."[83] For the time being, however, MI(R) remained in the same building as Section D, in spite of the concerns of Holland and Gubbins that Section D might be too impractical for the coming conflict.[84]

As part of the new growth that attended MI(R)'s establishment, it was permitted to earmark and train British personnel for work in sabotage and guerrilla warfare. When necessary, they could be commissioned in the Officers' Emergency Reserve.[85] If, up to this point, there had continued to be a pretext of broad research at GS(R), it was dropped. Holland focused on producing reports on irregular warfare and Gubbins prepared a syllabus for three MI(R) training courses in the elementary theory of guerrilla warfare, held in late June at Caxton Hall, just two doors down from MI(R) headquarters. For these courses he recruited explorers, linguists, international businessmen, and regular officers with special skills.[86] Classes were kept small for security; everyone, civilians and officers alike, wore civilian dress.[87] Holland hoped these men could accompany future military missions sent abroad, making "contact with any elements that might be able to operate behind the Germans."[88]

Meanwhile, Gubbins traveled abroad to connect Britain's potential agents with potential guerrillas abroad. In May he visited Poland, the three Baltic republics, and Romania, meeting with the British military attachés in each country. He concluded that the Poles possessed a "natural aptitude . . . for guerilla activities . . . fostered by the national spirit during a century of oppression by Russia and Germany."[89] The British ambassador in Warsaw informed Gubbins that the Polish General Staff had been very frank; the ambassador insisted that the Poles "could be trusted to the hilt" and hoped that MI(R) would match their candor.[90] On two later trips to Poland, the Baltic, and the Balkans, he contacted the Polish General Staff and its intelligence service and again met with the British military attachés.[91] In his meetings with the Poles, Gubbins discussed guerrilla warfare only generally, without making any joint plans, though he met Col. Stanislav Gano of Polish military intelligence at this time and the two subsequently became friends.[92] However, very little is known of these travels, since, as Gubbins himself admitted years later, they "were so secret that even the D.M.I. was not informed and was very angry when he discovered."[93]

In addition to the information and relationships Gubbins acquired in Poland, he also brought home a device called a "time-pencil," a time-delay fuse capable of detonating plastic explosives up to thirty hours after activation. It had been invented by the Germans during World War I and was improved by the Poles; SOE would subsequently improve the device further and manufacture it in the millions.[94]

The Art of Guerilla Warfare and *The Partisan Leader's Handbook*

In April 1939 Holland sent a memo to his subordinates, explaining that the organization had permission to act on three items:

a. To study guerilla methods and produce a guerilla "F.S.R" [Field Service Regulations], incorporating detailed tactical and technical instructions, applying to each of several countries.
b. To evolve destructive devices for delaying and suitable for use by guerillas, and capable of production and distribution on a wide enough scale to be effective.
c. To evolve procedure and machinery for operating guerilla activities, if it should be decided to do so subsequently.[95]

Holland envisioned an easily translated pamphlet to explain the general principles of guerrilla operations, "followed by chapters or sections dealing with the detailed application to each country."[96] Gubbins answered this call, completing in May two brief but significant pamphlets: the *PLH* and the *AGW*.[97] (Gubbins also coauthored with Jefferis a third work, *How to Use High Explosives*.[98]) The *AGW*, though completed second, is logically primary, since it covers "the organisation of guerilla warfare generally," while the *PLH*, as the name implies, is "of the 'Section Leading' type, for the leaders of partisan parties."[99]

These two guides, although not extensive, are the essential links in the intellectual history of SOE's doctrine. They represent the culmination of MI(R)'s research and the codification of lessons learned from personal experience, case studies from the past, and contemporary conflicts. They also represent an early and clear articulation of the theory and practice of the irregular warfare to be conducted by SOE. For unknown reasons, Gubbins's works are general guides and not country specific; as a result, they are some of the broadest doctrinal statements of the war, focused not on a particular aspect or location but irregular warfare writ large.

These short guides range from the overarching objectives of guerrilla warfare—"to harass the enemy in every way possible"—to the details of conducting a road or rail ambush.[100] The *AGW* covers such organizational problems as partisan leadership, training, and relations with a supporting "Guerilla Bureau" (e.g., MI[R] or SOE). It includes such operational matters as intelligence, target selection, planning, weapons, tactics, and communications and provides ample consideration of geography and human populations, be they hostile, friendly, or neutral. Finally, it avoids the pitfall of assuming a passive enemy, instead providing instruction on enemy counteraction. The highlights are summarized in the "nine points of the guerilla's creed," ready for memorization by would-be insurgents.[101] The *PLH* covers similar topics at shorter length, augmented by eight appendices covering the practical details of ambushing, sabotage, hiding arms, and conducting intelligence activities.

Many of the principles contained within these works reflect themes that run through the conflicts in which Gubbins fought: the potential strength of guerrillas, particularly when possessed with quality intelligence; the danger guerrillas can pose to extended lines of communication; the psychological or moral effect of guerrillas simply remaining in the field; the need for guerrillas to maintain mobility; and the threat posed to guerrillas by extended engagements. In addition to learning from his own experiences (see chapter 2), Gubbins also examined various other conflicts for sources of inspiration. The balance of this chapter considers the lessons he learned from historical conflicts; his debt to contemporary wars will be discussed in chapter 4.

Learning from the Past

Although Gubbins and Holland both experienced irregular warfare themselves, particularly in Ireland, they also looked to historical examples. Indeed, as Foot observes, their "subject's importance should have been obvious to the British, for in 1899–1902 it had taken a quarter of a million men to put down an informal Boer army less than a tenth as large."[102] There is no doubt about GS(R)'s interest in history; its Report No. 2 considered "the Employment of Historians by the War Office in a consultative capacity."[103] An examination of the various conflicts known to have been studied by Holland and Gubbins reveals several things. At the most general level, such an examination shows that these men were very much products of their time. This is not to say that all military men in 1939 were interested in irregular warfare or believed in the usefulness of partisans. Nevertheless, the decades preceding the authorship of the *AGW* and the *PLH* were filled with irregular conflicts about which a great deal of information was available—in public books and articles and also in government memoranda—to those who were willing to look. And that was the crux of the matter. For although virtually every element of Gubbins's writings had precedent somewhere else, his claim that "there was not a single book to be found in any library in any language which dealt with this subject" should not be dismissed as mere hyperbole.[104] Works on guerrilla warfare certainly existed, but they were few. Moreover, most were historical, even anecdotal; a few were theoretical. Systematic tactical considerations were unusual. In addition, most works that seriously considered guerrilla warfare as a military phenomenon did so from the *counter*guerrilla's perspective not from the guerrilla's own. Thus, Gubbins's genius lay in synthesizing existing ideas into a concise and usable form.

At a more specific level, a careful consideration of the conflicts examined by GS(R) reveals parallels between specific tactics seen on the battlefield and also in Gubbins's thought. The extant documentation is rarely sufficient to definitively prove that on a particular point Gubbins was inspired by a single particular example. Nevertheless, by constructing a picture of irregular conflict in the decades before GS(R) came into existence—a picture informed by contemporary accounts, the subsequent writings of participants, and the known interests of GS(R)—one can better understand the context of Gubbins's work and draw probable, if not always certain, conclusions.

The Second Anglo-Boer War

Holland and Gubbins were certainly inspired by the example of the Boers in the Anglo-Boer War of 1899–1903. In a report to the DCIGS on 1 June 1939, GS(R) argued that "guerilla warfare, when carefully planned and conducted with skill, can have a marked influence on a campaign, out of all proportion to the numbers of guerillas actually engaged. Examples from our own history give adequate proof. In the Boer War, the number of Boers in the field probably never exceeded 25,000, while our own army was fully ten times as large before success was ultimately achieved."[105] The precise details of their study of the Boers are unknown; however, a delineation of the Boers' conflict with the British, alongside Gubbins's later writings, reveals likely areas of inspiration.

The Second Anglo-Boer War was Britain's largest conflict between the defeat of Napoleon and the Great War. Gubbins's interest in the Boers may have been further piqued at an early age by his Aunt Susie's service as a nurse in the conflict.[106] He continued to concern himself with the Boers after World War II, as well. In a lecture in 1973, for example, he observed that the Boer War and similar irregular campaigns exercised a "marked influence on the operations of regular armies."[107] Likewise, an article Gubbins wrote for *Chamber's Encyclopedia* explained the advantages of mobility that the Boer commandos had over the British forces.[108] The original draft added that British regulars were "cumbersome and . . . unsuited" to unconventional war, having to change their methods to achieve victory.[109] It is unsurprising, then, that Gubbins took note of the Boers and their irregular tactics when drafting his guides.[110]

Dutch refugees from British Cape Colony established the Orange Free State and the South African Republic (colloquially known as the Transvaal) in the 1850s. Gold was discovered in the Transvaal in 1886, eventually leading to war with Britain in 1899. Although the Boers scored early victories in British territory, Field Marshall Lord Roberts captured the Boer capital cities in May and June 1900. The war appeared to be over and Roberts returned to Britain, replaced by Lord Kitchener. But Boer commandos fought on for another two years in a costly guerrilla campaign.

The parallels between Gubbins's writings and the Boer experience are many. Gubbins did not leave detailed notes of which aspects of the conflict he and Holland studied. However, recalling the history of the Second Anglo-Boer War reveals the extent to which Gubbins's handbooks are congruent with the mindset of imperial campaigning. His ideas regarding the challenges posed by counterguerrilla forces; the importance to guerrillas of survival, mobility, initiative, and intelligence; stretching the enemy thin; raiding for supplies; and including civilians in a guerrilla war effort all find echoes in South Africa four decades earlier. If, however, we can detect broad similarities between Gubbins and the Boer style of warfare, and infer some degree of influence, we should not assume slavish emulation. Gubbins parted ways with the Boers on several matters, including discipline, the use of uniforms, and the need for a reasonable probability of success.

The counterguerrilla environment experienced by the Boers was similar to that anticipated by Gubbins. He expected guerrilla forces to be outclassed in weapons and equipment by an enemy employing all the technological advances of recent decades.[111] His guides warn about tactical concerns such as traps and raids but also the informational danger posed by mail censorship and prisoner debriefings, as well as threats from bureaucratic measures such as identity cards.[112] These techniques figured in Gubbins's experience of Ireland, but they could also describe the challenges faced by the Boers. Historian Byron Farwell observes that, when martial law was imposed on Cape Colony, "passes were required, . . . a curfew was imposed, . . . bicycles were registered; . . . farmers were ordered to give information; . . . the licences of travelling pedlars were suspended; hotels had to file daily reports on their guests; and there were harsh restrictions on a long list of 'prohibited goods.'"[113] Such were the countermeasures that Gubbins knew guerrillas would face.

The Boer commandos recognized that their ongoing presence in the field prevented Britain from claiming victory and therefore survival was more important than risky actions. Roberts complained that the Boers "slip away in the most extraordinary manner," something they did quite intentionally.[114] "It was impossible to think of fighting—the enemy's numbers were far too great," commented Christiaan de Wet, one of the Boer commanders. "Our only safety lay in flight."[115] Ambushes were sometimes utilized against pursuing forces to further ensure a safe retreat.[116] For the same reason, Gubbins's writings endorsed similar tactics, urging guerrillas to "never get involved in a pitched battle."[117] A "secure line of retreat" and a "quick get-away" are valued, while direct action should be avoided unless "in such overwhelming strength that success can be assured."[118]

In a third parallel, both Gubbins and the Boers emphasized weakening enemy forces by stretching them thin over a large area. Louis Botha, another Boer commander, explained, "We will split up into four or five commands, [and] continue operations independently."[119] By striking in one place, escaping, and then striking elsewhere, the Boers forced the British to dilute their forces across huge amounts of territory. Of the 164,000 men under Kitchener's command in June 1901, two-thirds of them were tied to defensive positions guarding rail lines.[120] Nearly forty years later, Gubbins likewise advocated harassing the enemy and thereby forcing him to disperse his forces to the point that he could not effectively wage war.[121]

Gubbins, like his Boer predecessors, understood the importance of mobility and initiative. With a culture of horsemanship and a history of raiding, the Boers deployed their men in small groups, often without wagons, for high mobility.[122] De la Rey eventually ordered his men to fire from the saddle, not even pausing long enough to dismount and fire.[123] Like the Boers, Gubbins saw mobility as one of a guerrilla's inherent strengths. Moreover, he advocated the use of light equipment permitting rapid strikes on ever-shifting locations.[124] And, like the Boers, Gubbins advocated small units, "self-contained, acting under their own leader's initiative . . . and maintaining the loosest organization compatible with effective action."[125]

The Boers retained the initiative in other ways as well. Deception was routinely used.[126] When the president of the Orange Free State crossed a heavily guarded railway, de Wet made a show of force elsewhere, distracting British pursuers from the presidential party.[127] At the Battle of Blood River Poort (17 September 1901), Col. Hubert Gough attacked "200 men of the enemy off-saddled," believing he had caught them in an unguarded moment. In fact, "he fell into a carefully-prepared trap in very difficult ground. . . . The whole force of the enemy [was] carefully concealed."[128] On another occasion de Wet found himself surrounded by British soldiers, who waited for him to attempt a breakout under darkness. All through the night they heard de Wet's artillery and equipment moving about, but at dawn his camp was empty. He had escaped through terrain deemed impassible by the British, while "two wagons had been loaded with sheet-iron and scraps to make a noise in imitation of artillery, and had for the benefit of the English watchers been industriously driven around the camp all night by two faithful . . . servants."[129] Similarly, Gubbins argued that among the principles of guerrilla warfare "surprise [is] first and foremost."[130] The later SOE syllabus—on which Gubbins had considerable influence (see chapter 6)—included the same lesson: "SURPRISE IS ESSENTIAL."[131] In order to achieve such surprise, Gubbins advised "finding out the enemy's plans and concealing your own intentions and movements."[132]

The Boers made heavy use of intelligence, a fifth parallel with Gubbins's writings; information about the enemy allowed the Boers to most effectively find and strike weak points, thereby retaining the initiative. The Boers' rural culture and many small wars had produced a people adept at scouting.[133] Their intimate knowledge of the geography was utilized by their commanders, who also tapped the British telegraph lines.[134] This emphasis on good intelligence was subsequently reflected by SOE. Its training syllabus observed that "the secret of every successful operation is detailed and accurate information."[135] "Superior information is the guerillas' greatest asset," wrote Gubbins; "it must be used. . . . to counteract the enemy's superior armament and equipment."[136] As seen in the Irish experience, such information could be "offensive"—useful for one's own operations—or "defensive"—preventing the enemy from achieving surprise on his raids.[137]

Information collection and utilization is only half of the intelligence battle; information must also be denied to the enemy. Those who collaborate with the enemy are a frequent source of information, either in the form of particular operational plans or more general insights into culture and tactics. In southern Africa, the British employed their own force of Boer scouts, many of them deserters from the enemy. De Wet lamented that these men were his "undoing."[138] Consequently, the families of Boers who surrendered were driven from their homes, while de la Rey cleared the eastern Transvaal of native African families, as a preventative measure against potential spies.[139] When Jan Smuts was promoted to the position of assistant commandant-general, he expelled all those suspected of disloyalty and executed those found guilty of treason.[140] Other Boer commanders did likewise.[141] One British soldier recalled that "the Boers killed any [scouts or spies] they caught and we found their bodies left as warning on the veldt."[142]

As already seen in the context of Gubbins's service in Ireland, he recommended similarly stern measures for collaborators: "In every community will be found certain individuals so debased that for greed of gain they will sell even their own countrymen. Against this contingency close watch must be set, and wherever proof is obtained of such perfidy, the traitor must be killed without hesitation or delay. By such justifiably ruthless action others who might be tempted to follow suit will be finally deterred."[143] To further heighten such deterrence, Gubbins advised that the local population should be convinced that the enemy would soon be expelled, at which time support to the resistance would be rewarded, but collaboration with the occupiers "ruthlessly punished."[144]

The practice of raiding for supplies is yet another parallel between the Boer experience and Gubbins's writings. With domestic production interrupted by the British occupation, the destruction of their farms, and only very modest material coming from abroad the Boers relied on captured equipment and materiel. Rifles, clothes, wagons, and other items taken from the British were utilized by the Boer commandos.[145] Captured enemy uniforms not only provided the Boers with protection from the elements but also sometimes confused the British, decisively so at the Battle of Elands River in September 1901.[146]

Similarly, Gubbins emphasized the importance of logistics and the need for guerrillas to rely upon the enemy: "When operating behind the enemy's lines, the maintenance of supplies from outside will be a matter of the very greatest difficulty. . . . It is most important therefore that every opportunity to *seize arms and ammunition from the enemy* should be grasped. . . . It will sometimes be necessary to organize raids whose primary object is the seizure of arms."[147] This emphasis on looting supplies was also reflected in the SOE syllabus, which discusses the matter in detail.[148] Nevertheless, SOE was far less dependent on raiding than the Boers had been, since arms and equipment could—with difficulty—be supplied to occupied areas from Britain; as Gubbins explained after the Second World War, the resistance movements had "a secure and accessible base from which [they could] be nourished."[149] Moreover, Gubbins never advocated using enemy uniforms or posing as enemy soldiers.[150]

A final parallel between the Boers and Gubbins concerns the role of civilians. The Boers frequently employed civilians, who provided supplies, intelligence, and concealment.[151] Women played a frequent role. A British officer recounted one occasion: "When we started to search the house the old woman stood in front of a door and said we couldn't enter, as her daughter was in bed going to have a baby, so we sent in Hardy, our doctor. The girl was in bed all right, and a Mauser [rifle] under the mattress, and her Boer lover under the bed."[152] Though often effective, this inclusion of Boer civilians in the war came with great cost. The British placed women and children in concentration camps where they died in numbers that shocked Victorian Britain. The same British officer described a region where "we have removed all the [native Africans], destroyed all the Boer farms, and the occupants have been taken to Concentration Camps; [we] knocked down all buildings, and bagged all the sheep and cattle and nearly every living animal."[153] British soldiers justified such actions as necessary, contending that the Boers used "their women and children as cover and their farms as arsenals."[154]

The Boer commanders were familiar with military history and could not claim ignorance of the sufferings often endured by civilians in guerrilla wars. William T. Sherman's campaign through Georgia and the Prussian capture of French franc-tireurs were recent examples. Historian Thomas Pakenham comments: "In short, here was a daunting moral problem. Was it fair to the folk (women and children, as well as the menfolk) to involve them in such a savage kind of war? . . . Women and children [were] pressed into service, . . . their homes looted and burnt, then forced to choose between going as refugees to the cities, or [going] into battle."[155] Although Smuts consoled himself with the unyielding morale of the Boer civilians who endured such trials, the question of its legitimacy remains.[156]

Gubbins, like the Boers who inspired him, believed the inclusion of civilians for communications, smuggling, and especially intelligence was worth the costs. He advises using women and children, "who are less suspect," for couriering messages.[157] When hiding weapons, Gubbins recommends—though only as a last resort—giving them to women. But Gubbins saw civilians' primary role in guerrilla warfare being that of intelligence collectors. He argues that the local population, frequently rubbing elbows with occupying troops, is the best source of information and should be trained to collect it well.[158]

Although there are many broad similarities between the doctrine Gubbins formulated and the Second Anglo-Boer War, which he studied, his thinking differed from that of the Boers in several notable ways. As we have seen, Gubbins did not encourage or even condone the use of enemy uniforms. A second departure concerns organization. The downsides to the Boers' grassroots organization and flexibility were chronic problems with ill discipline and incoherent strategy. Farwell describes the problem: "They had no overall strategy, no master plan for winning the war. The activities of the various commandos were not coordinated, and there was not even a statement of policy regarding purposes or objectives. From first to last the Boers were always long on tactics and short on strategy. Each independent commander was left to harass the British as he thought best."[159] This was a mistake Gubbins clearly sought to avoid. He advocated the formation of a Guerilla Bureau, "either an individual of the country concerned located with his small staff in the area of guerilla activities, or a section of the General Staff (Intelligence Branch) of the Army concerned, and located at its General Headquarters, or even a military mission from a third party," such as Britain.[160] This bureau would collect and disseminate intelligence, draft and coordinate plans, and provide arms to guerrillas. The bureau's chief would "frequently direct and lead . . . in person" large operations to ensure unity of effort.[161]

The most striking difference between Gubbins and the Boers is his refusal to engage in guerrilla resistance simply on principle, without hope of success. On this point, Farwell delivers a particularly scathing critique of the Boers:

> Their struggle was indeed without hope of success. . . . Their deliberate, hopeless prolongation of the war resulted in the deaths of additional thousands of brave men. It resulted in the destruction of their farms, which they and their fathers and grandfathers had worked so hard to build, and in the slaughters of their herds of cattle and sheep on which their future existence and way of life depended. Worst of all, it resulted in the decimation of their women and children. These proud, stubborn men had much to answer for.[162]

Gubbins's pragmatism would not admit such quixotic and costly resistance. "Sporadic risings are useless," the SOE syllabus warns.[163] Only actions with a reasonable probability of achieving tangible military success could justify the inevitable reprisals against civilians.[164]

T. E. Lawrence and the Arab Revolt

In October 1916, in the midst of World War I, a well-educated young British officer named T. E. Lawrence joined the Arabs then revolting against Turkish rule. The forces he led or advised attacked the Medina railway and captured Akaba and ultimately Damascus as well. Even after they linked up with the regular forces pushing east out of the Sinai, Lawrence's irregulars continued to operate as the right wing of the British Army.[165]

Lawrence not only helped lead the Arab Revolt but he also reflected on this group of irregular soldiers and their guerrilla campaign.[166] Whereas other campaigns, such as those fought by the Irish or Boers, are remembered through a variety of memoirs, government reports, and histories both official and scholarly, Lawrence's own writings were—and in many respects still are—the most important sources regarding the Arab Revolt. His memoir, *The Seven Pillars of Wisdom*, first published in 1926, was a best seller. Less well known is his pithy distillation of guerrilla theory, published in *Army Quarterly* in 1920/21 as "The Evolution of a Revolt," and republished with minor variation by *Encyclopædia Britannica* in 1929 as "The Science of Guerrilla Warfare." Until the advent of the Cold War, when he was eclipsed by Communist thinkers, Lawrence was probably the most oft-cited practitioner of guerrilla warfare. He was the writer who came to Wilkinson's mind when he attended MI(R)'s training school and was read and cited by MI(R).[167] Similarities exist between the thinking of Lawrence and Gubbins, suggesting the debt the latter may have owed to what he called "Lawrence's epic guerrilla campaign."[168] Nevertheless, the two thinkers offer different approaches to both the study and execution of guerrilla warfare, differences that, like Gubbins's departures from the Boers' practices, help us better understand Gubbins's doctrine.

T. E. Lawrence organized his thoughts on guerrilla warfare into three "elements, one algebraical, one biological, a third psychological."[169] In the case of the first, he notes that "perhaps a hundred and forty thousand" square miles of territory lay open to the Arabs in the southern Turkish empire. "How would the Turks defend all that?"[170] The numbers favored the Arabs: there was simply too much space for the Turks to protect.

Lawrence's second element, the "biological," concerned the components of war, "sensitive and illogical" human beings. Because of unknown human factors, commanders are forced to hold a body of men in reserve as a safeguard, thus stretching thin their other human resources. Lawrence worked to magnify his enemy's ignorance: "We were to contain the enemy by the silent threat of a vast unknown desert, not disclosing ourselves till the moment of attack."[171] Lawrence employed "a highly mobile, highly equipped type of army, of the smallest size . . . [used] successively at distributed points of the Turkish line, to make the Turks reinforce their occupying posts beyond the economic minimum."[172] Ignorance would cause the Turks to array their forces in a disadvantageous way, a weakness Lawrence happily exploited.

The third element, the "psychological," was of particular importance to Lawrence considering the Arabs' relative inferiority. "We were so weak physically that we could not let the metaphysical weapon rust unused."[173] He explains, "We had to arrange [our Arab soldiers'] minds in order of battle, just as carefully and as formally as other officers arranged their bodies."[174] For Lawrence, the use of psychology was primarily strategic, concerned with an individual's or group's commitment to the war at large. He describes this element as "the adjustment of spirit to the point where it becomes fit to exploit in action, the prearrangement of a changing opinion to a certain end. . . . We had won a province when we had taught the civilians in it to die for our ideal of freedom: the presence or absence of the enemy was a secondary matter."[175]

To a considerable degree, Gubbins follows two of Lawrence's three conceptual elements, though without the pseudoscientific language. With regard to Lawrence's second element, the "biological" quality of ignorance, Gubbins is in full agreement. He argues in the *AGW* that the enemy could be incapacitated by "compelling [him] to *disperse* his forces in order to guard his flank, his communications, his detachments, supply depots, etc."[176]

Gubbins also follows Lawrence regarding the importance of psychology or morale. Lawrence considers the psychological element primarily with regard to *his own* Arab forces and with an emphasis on the strategic. Gubbins recognizes this application, noting that, "Successful action by the guerillas ... will awaken in the people the spirit of revolt, of audacity and of endurance, and make them foresee and assist towards the victory that will be theirs."[177] However, Gubbins also gives extensive consideration to *enemy* morale, seeing it as a weak point that guerrillas might attack. "To inflict damage and death on the enemy and to escape scot-free has an irritant and depressing effect on the enemy's spirit."[178] Indeed, Gubbins even advocates very tactical and intimate ways to maximize the psychological impact of attacks on the enemy. When "sniping and killing sentries, stragglers, etc. ... use a knife or noose when you can. This has a great frightening effect. ... Night-time is best and has the best effect on enemy nerves."[179] Likewise, he advocates the "burning of soldiers' cinemas ... *during a performance*," an attack calculated to strike terror.[180]

There are other similarities as well. Both writers place considerable emphasis on the local population and the need for its sympathies. Lawrence insists that guerrillas "must have a friendly population, not actively friendly, but sympathetic to the point of not betraying rebel movements to the enemy. Rebellions can be made by 2 per cent. active in a striking force, and 98 per cent. passively sympathetic."[181] Gubbins likewise recommends that guerrillas should "endeavour not to offend the people ... but to encourage their patriotism and hatred of the enemy."[182] However, the population's role might be active—such as "providing information for the guerillas"—or passive—"withholding it from the enemy."[183]

Likewise, the two authors share mixed feelings about regular officers serving with guerrillas. Lawrence notes that there were "officers and men of Arab blood who had served in the Turkish Army," who could form "the beginning of an Arab regular army," but he downplays their importance, given the limited relevance of regular forces to an irregular war.[184] Gubbins notes that "any guerilla who has a background of military training is *ipso facto* a better partisan";[185] moreover, "it may ... frequently be advantageous to appoint certain serving army officers for duty with guerillas"[186] However, he also argues that leaders of partisan bands should ordinarily come from among the people they lead; if regular officers serve as "assistants to guerilla commanders," a division of labor should result, with the leader "ensuring the cohesion of his guerillas" while the officer "supplies ... the technical knowledge." Gubbins even goes so far as to say that regular officers must "clear their minds of all preconceived ideas regarding military procedure.... Training in the full military sense is not applicable to guerillas."[187]

In spite of the many similarities, Gubbins was no mere disciple of Lawrence, replicating his ideas. With regard to Lawrence's first element of guerrilla warfare, the "algebraical," we see significant difference in the thought of Gubbins. Lawrence argues that success was highly likely given the vast areas which the Turks could not possibly hold. Gubbins, in contrast, assumes an enemy presence, often a strong one. This led to divergence on three points: the likelihood of enemy countermeasures, the plausibility of an unassailable base, and the relation of guerrillas to conventional forces.

The greatest point of departure between Lawrence and Gubbins concerns enemy countermeasures. Although Lawrence mentions the sudden advance of Turkish forces at Rabegh, which threw the Arabs into disarray, his account generally implies a static enemy.[188] Arab forces could sweep out of the desert, strike the Turkish foe, and return to the desert without fear of being followed. Lawrence is little concerned with enemy spies or long-range patrols hounding his forces. In stark contrast, Gubbins insists that "the enemy will institute counter-measures as soon as guerilla activities against him commence," deploying flying columns, "detachments ... mobile by means of horses, lorries, etc.," to sweep the countryside, looking for guerrillas.[189] Gubbins expresses great concern about the way "modern developments, particularly in aircraft, mechanized forces and wireless, have profound influences on guerilla warfare, enabling the enemy rapidly to concentrate in opposition to any moves of guerillas that have been discovered."[190] Gubbins expects raids, traps, censorship of letters, interrogation of prisoners, and enemy infiltration of partisan bands.[191]

Lawrence does, however, give a nod to the problem of enemy countermeasures when he writes in the *Encyclopædia Britannica* version of his essay that "diversity threw the enemy intelligence off the track. By the regular organization in identical battalions and divisions information builds itself up, until the presence of a corps can be inferred on corpses from three companies."[192] Enemy intelligence could not discern Arab organization because there was so little. Likewise, Lawrence also references "security (in the form of denying targets to the enemy)" but does not mention most of the counterguerrilla tactics that later concern Gubbins.[193]

In a second point of divergence, Lawrence writes that "rebellion must have an unassailable base, something guarded not merely from attack, but from the fear of it."[194] For Lawrence, this base was the desert, adjacent to the more populated areas where the fighting occurred. Gubbins, however, is less sure about such a base. As we have already seen in relation to the Boers, he argued after the Second World War that in Britain the resistance forces had "a secure and accessible base from which [they could] be nourished."[195] Nevertheless, the very geographic separation from the continent, which made Britain secure, also militated against its accessibility. This was particularly the case with regard to eastern Europe, especially in the early days of the war when the RAF possessed limited resources. Thus, it is not a contradiction of his later thinking, but a practical complement to it when he writes in 1939 that "searches, raids, . . . curfew, passport and other regulations" will eventually force guerrillas to abandon their homes and "go on the run . . . in some suitable areas where the nature of the country enables them to be *relatively* secure."[196] Not everyone would have the liberty of fleeing to Britain's secure shores, nor could the underground war be carried on if everyone did. Unfortunately, "areas which offer good opportunities for concealment are usually just those areas where the maintenance and supply of large guerilla forces becomes difficult. They are usually wild, with little cultivation . . . and supplies have to be brought in specially."[197] This creates a supply tail, which ruins the guerrilla's advantage of mobility.[198] Thus, Gubbins recognizes the value of bases but also their limitations.

Finally, in a third area of divergence, Lawrence suggests that guerrillas might succeed alone: "By careful persistence, kept strictly within our strength and following the spirit of our theories, we were able eventually to reduce the Turks to helplessness, and complete victory seemed to be almost within our sight. . . . The experiment was a thrilling one. . . . We believed we would prove irregular war or rebellion to be an exact science, and an inevitable success, granted certain factors and if pursued along certain lines."[199] Such success required, however, that a guerrilla force face an "army of occupation too small to fulfill the doctrine of acreage: too few . . . to dominate the whole area effectively."[200]

Gubbins, on the other hand, is not interested in discerning the circumstances in which guerrillas could win by themselves; instead, he is concerned with drawing enemy forces away from the main front of a conventional conflict and pinning them down. Therefore, he argues that the goal of guerrilla warfare "is to harass the enemy . . . to such an extent that he is eventually incapable either of embarking on a war or of continuing one that may already have commenced. . . . The culminating state of guerilla warfare should always be to produce in the field large formations of guerillas, well-armed and well-trained, which are able to take a direct part in the fighting . . . in *direct conjunction with the operations of regular troops.*"[201]

With both convergence and divergence present between the works of these two thinkers, assessing what Gubbins learned from this important intellectual forebear and why he borrowed some ideas but not others can be difficult. Differences in the geographical settings of their thought do explain some of the variation, though ultimately the difference may be one of intellectual temperament.

During a pause in the fighting in Arabia, Lawrence sought "the equation between my book-reading and my movements," a reconciliation of theory and practice.[202] Gubbins's work can be seen as something similar, a refinement of Lawrence's theory to fit a new practice. Even when not writing explicitly about Arabia, Lawrence's works make the most sense in a context of open and desolate geography; for all his universal insights—and they are not inconsiderable—his vision sometimes remains bound to the particular location of his experience. Gubbins had a different set of experiences against which to measure Lawrence's thinking, notably the Irish Revolution. Moreover, although the Second World War had not yet occurred, Gubbins could foresee some of its basic contours, including European geography and society; he had to find a form of guerrilla warfare that could interact closely with the civilian population and nearby conventional forces and that could endure the repeated pressures of enemy countermeasures made possible by airpower and other technological changes.

Thus, Gubbins transforms Lawrence's "algebraical" element—inapplicable to Ireland or anticipated operations in Poland and Czechoslovakia—and changes its emphasis on space into an emphasis on people. If the land itself was not of overwhelming size, the occupied population was nevertheless too large and complex to be controlled by a foreign army. In one of his more colorful passages, Gubbins insists that "given the leadership, the courage, the arms and the preparation, . . . there is one thing . . . that [aggressor nations] cannot break, and that is the spirit of the people whose territory has been over-run, a spirit expressing itself in uncompromising and steadfast resistance."[203] Yet even this transformation of Lawrence's "algebraical" element must be qualified: the population's size alone was not sufficient; leadership, courage, arms, and preparation were also required.

In his original article, Lawrence calls irregular warfare "an exact science."[204] The *Encyclopædia Britannica* article utilizes the term as well. However, Lawrence writes elsewhere that "handling Hejaz Arabs is an art, not a science, with exceptions and no obvious rules."[205] In the midst of this apparent contradiction, Lawrence perhaps best explains himself when he writes that "irregular war is far more intellectual than a bayonet charge," a comment with which Gubbins would likely agree.[206] But whereas Lawrence looks for "pure theory and ... the metaphysical side, the philosophy of war," Gubbins's approach is more pragmatic.[207] This may best explain the differences between the two thinkers. Gubbins kept those elements of Lawrence's work that he deemed relevant, while transforming or qualifying those he did not. This approach might seem commonsensical, even obvious, but it was an approach that a genius of Lawrence's stripe might not choose.

Paul von Lettow-Vorbeck and the *Schutztruppe*

When the Great War broke out in the summer of 1914, young Colin Gubbins made his way out of Germany and back to Britain. T. E. Lawrence, then an archaeologist in the Middle East, offered his services to the British Army. Meanwhile, Col. Paul Emil von Lettow-Vorbeck found himself commander of Germany's *Schutztruppe* (colonial force) in German East Africa. He defended the colony by conventional means until the spring of 1915, when events compelled him to adopt guerrilla tactics.[208] Even after he was driven from German East Africa in November 1917, Lettow-Vorbeck waged his guerrilla war in Allied colonies, tying down vast numbers of enemy soldiers who might otherwise have participated in the fighting on the Western Front.[209] Undefeated, he surrendered on 25 November 1918, two weeks after the armistice in Europe.[210]

Mackenzie's official history of SOE explains that Gubbins drew inspiration from the activities of Lettow-Vorbeck, and Simon Anglim likewise observes that Holland read Lettow-Vorbeck's memoirs.[211]

However, it is particularly difficult to assess the influence of the German guerrilla experience on GS(R). Apart from the usual paucity of specific evidence, there is also the question of linguistic and cultural barriers. These would not have been insurmountable but would likely have inclined British soldiers more toward sources in English, particularly those written by their countrymen. Moreover, many of the insights that Holland or Gubbins found in *My Reminiscences of East Africa* would have confirmed lessons already learned elsewhere. This comes as little surprise. Lettow-Vorbeck studied German and foreign colonies for the German General Staff (1899–1900), saw action in the Boxer Rebellion in China (1900–1901), and served for several years in German South-West Africa against the Herero rebels (1904–1906). Most notably, he discussed guerrilla warfare with Louis Botha.[212] Though Lettow-Vorbeck wrote little in his memoirs about the Second Anglo-Boer War, he notes that he "gained abundant personal experience" from the Boers and that their "excellent qualities . . . commanded my respect."[213]

Even before the outbreak of hostilities in 1914, Lettow-Vobeck recognized the importance of attacking the enemy, since the *Schutztruppe*'s purpose was to tie down Allied forces that might otherwise deploy against the Fatherland. "Hostile troops would allow themselves to be held only if we attacked, or at least threatened, the enemy at some really sensitive point."[214] A prime example was the Uganda Railroad: the British could only protect it with extreme difficulty, stationing troops along its entire length of 440 miles.[215] Like the Boers, Lettow-Vorbeck forced his opponents to disperse huge numbers of men over a large area in the pursuit of his guerrillas. It was a strategy Gubbins also endorsed.[216]

In spite of his emphasis on the attack—or at least the threat thereof—Lettow-Vorbeck was not indiscriminate with his forces; instead, he carefully maximized every advantage. As with the Boers, surprise and deception were among the most useful tools. Even before the onset of guerrilla operations, Lettow-Vorbeck utilized night marches and rapid concentration to catch his opponents unawares, as at the Battle of Jassini (18–19 January 1915).[217] On other occasions he used the vegetation for concealment to achieve surprise.[218] German and British uniforms looked fairly similar, even more so after each had been weathered in the field; Lettow-Vorbeck's men magnified this similarity by wearing only their shirts—and not their coats—when in areas where the locals reported troop movements to the British.[219] As we have already seen, Gubbins's approach to concealment and surprise was similar.[220]

Like the Boers, Lettow-Vorbeck's troops were aided by their mobility and minimal logistics. As the war progressed, his European troops learned to get along with less, discarding many items they had previously considered necessities.[221] Fat was obtained from elephant hunting and sugar replaced with wild honey; quinine was produced from one kind of local bark, while another was used for bandages. Lettow-Vorbeck personally learned rudimentary bootmaking using antelope hide.[222] Jan Smuts, who had fought against the British more than a decade before and now commanded South African forces on their behalf, admitted that Lettow-Vorbeck's troops were "very mobile and able to live on the country, largely untroubled by transport difficulties."[223] Unencumbered by elaborate supplies, German forces moved faster than the Allies and across terrain considered impassable. "Increased independence and mobility," Lettow-Vorbeck explains, "used with determination against the less mobile enemy, would give us a local superiority in spite of the great numerical superiority of the enemy."[224] The *AGW* echoes similar sentiments, noting that "in total strength the enemy will normally have the superiority . . . but the distribution of his forces will necessitate the use of detachments against which superior guerilla forces can be brought."[225]

Finally, like the Boers, Lettow-Vorbeck relied on captured weapons, both out of necessity and to reduce dependence on supply lines.[226] Before the war began he planned on capturing weapons, since his native soldiers, known as "askaris," were armed with 1871 pattern rifles, which used smoky powder and were obsolete in modern warfare.[227] Most of the explosives used against the Uganda Railroad were captured from the British, while captured horses and mules were also utilized.[228] Whether in imitation of the Boers or the *Schutztruppe*, Gubbins similarly advocated using captured resources.[229]

Guerrilla leaders in nearly every instance have understood the importance of the local population; Lettow-Vorbeck was no exception. With only three thousand German soldiers at his disposal, nearly 80 percent of his force consisted of askaris.[230] Even most of the Germans in his army were not regular soldiers but local settlers enlisted in a Volunteer Rifle Corps. From among these came some of Lettow-Vorbeck's finest officers.[231] Native Africans were an excellent source of intelligence, as the German commander very quickly discovered, noting that "in their interchange of information the inhabitants tell each other everything that happens in their vicinity. Calls, fire signals, and the signal drums serve to exchange and quickly spread all news."[232] Likewise, natives aided Lettow-Vorbeck with their knowledge of local geography.[233]

Although the war in East Africa has been called a gentlemen's war, and in some ways was, Lettow-Vorbeck faced stiff countermeasures.[234] In March 1915, for example, "the Belgians made arrests on a large scale in Ubwari, the inhabitants of which had shown themselves friendly to us, and hanged a number of people."[235] Later on spies, drawn from native populations, were sent among the German forces.[236] Allied armies pursued Lettow-Vorbeck continually across German East Africa, Portuguese Mozambique, and into Northern Rhodesia. Unlike Lawrence, Lettow-Vorbeck could never assume the enemy's inaction. The *Schutztruppe*'s experience may have helped strengthened Gubbins's conviction that strong countermeasures are inevitable.[237]

While much of Lettow-Vorbeck's experience parallels that of the Boers specifically, and other guerrillas—such as those in Ireland—generally, two particular aspects of the German campaign deserve attention for their affinity with Gubbins's thinking: planning and leadership. Even before war broke out, Lettow-Vorbeck planned for battle, since its basic contours could be discerned in advance. While he traveled extensively, his friend and subordinate officer Tom von Prince organized the Volunteer Rifle Corps. Likewise, Lettow-Vorbeck tried to arm all the Europeans of the colony with uniform military rifles.[238] His strong emphasis on early planning may have influenced Gubbins, who argues that "a careful study must be made *as early as possible* of the territories concerned, so as to determine for what methods of warfare each territory is suited, and to make the necessary preparations *in advance*."[239] Likewise, Gubbins contends that the problem of supplying arms "is immensely simplified . . . if adequate supplies can be obtained *before hostilities commence*."[240] Finally, "the selection and training of regular army officers in the art of guerilla warfare" should begin in peacetime; preferably their "training should include a period of residence in the territory concerned."[241]

Reading Lettow-Vorbeck's memoirs, one quickly notices the strong leadership of the *Schutztruppe*. The German commander embodied his own conviction that "there is almost always a way out, even of an apparently hopeless position, if the leader makes up his mind to face the risks."[242] Throughout the war he demonstrated unbounded energy, creativity, and selfless determination. Moreover, Lettow-Vorbeck, with a strong group of subordinate officers, records that "the long war had produced a large number of capable leaders, and their example . . . roused unbounded enterprise and daring."[243] Such men were the kind Gubbins hoped would lead his new guerrillas. "In guerilla warfare, it is the personality of the leader that counts," he writes in the *AGW*. "He it is who has to make decisions on his own responsibility and lead his men in each enterprise. He must therefore be decisive and resourceful, bold in action and cool in council, of great mental and physical endurance, and of strong personality."[244] Lettow-Vorbeck clearly matched that description.

Conclusion

In the late 1930s the British government established several organizations to study and plan subversive warfare. Two of these—Section D and MI(R)—not only undertook this mission, but did so while cooperating in varying degrees with one another. Among the most important developments of this era was the formulation of a doctrine, most cogently expounded in Gubbins's the *AGW* and the *PLH*. Gubbins drew upon his own personal experiences of unconventional warfare but also extended his vision to encompass historical lessons learned from the Boers, from T. E. Lawrence and from the German commander, Paul von Lettow-Vorbeck. As we shall see in chapter 4, however, Gubbins did not limit his vision to case studies of yesteryear's guerrilla warfare but also drew inspiration from conflicts raging around him at the time of writing in 1939.

CHAPTER 4

FORMULATING A DOCTRINE

CONTEMPORARY EXAMPLES

When J. C. F. Holland was appointed to GS(R), he chose to study irregular warfare because he was impressed by contemporary fighting in Spain and China.[1] Conflicts of the past, examined in chapters 2 and 3, certainly provided valuable lessons to Britain's embryonic forces of subversive warfare. However, changed conditions often limited the utility of lessons from these earlier conflicts. Warfare in 1938 or 1939 did not look the same as it had in 1902 or 1918 due to technological changes—most notably the widespread introduction of airpower. Moreover, with the exception of Lawrence's Arabian activities, all the conflicts heretofore examined saw Britain playing the role of counterinsurgent. Several conflicts in the 1930s provided more up-to-date lessons in guerrilla warfare, with the added advantage that Britain's future opponents—Nazi Germany, Fascist Italy, and Imperial Japan—often fought on the counterinsurgent side, making the lessons more directly applicable.

The Spanish Civil War highlighted the general value of guerrillas but also gave examples of strong counterguerrilla action and the failure of guerrilla tactics. The Arab Revolt in Palestine revealed some of the far-reaching social complexity of irregular warfare, as well as the failures resulting from weak leadership. The Special Night Squads, deployed in Palestine, included many of the features Gubbins advocated: intelligence, initiative, deception, and strong leadership. They also demonstrated the kind of vigorous counterguerrilla capability he feared. The Second Sino-Japanese War highlighted the vulnerability of conventional forces trying to hold vast swaths of territory and provided a useful case study of the role of neutral territory in irregular warfare. Although it is unlikely that Gubbins was inspired by the guerrilla theories of Mao Tse-tung, MI(R) made early plans to conduct operations in China, plans that reflected Gubbins's new doctrine.

The analysis that follows not only draws on contemporary accounts and later scholarship but also on British Military Intelligence reports, to which MI(R)—as a component of the Military Intelligence Directorate—had access and to which it sometimes contributed. Making full use of such varied sources, a picture of irregular warfare in the years before the Second World War emerges. If, in some cases, the information from Gubbins, Holland, and MI(R) is too thin for more than generalizations, in other instances we can directly observe how Gubbins drew upon and synthesized existing models into one which fit Britain and its future needs.

The Spanish Civil War

In 1936, years of political unrest in Spain came to a head when tit-for-tat violence created an opening for an attempted coup by members of the military, who argued that they had to save Spain from a left-wing government and impending anarchy. The coup failed to seize control of the government or many of the major cities apart from Seville. Nevertheless, the rebels—known as the Nationalists—quickly captured large swaths of León and Old Castile, the more conservative regions of the country.[2] With Spain divided roughly in half between the Nationalists and the Republican government, or Loyalists, civil war followed.

The conflict quickly attracted international involvement. Germany and Italy airlifted Nationalist troops from Morocco to mainland Spain, the first major airlift in history. Both nations subsequently provided combat forces. Although the Soviets withheld major combat forces, they supplied planes, tanks, and artillery pieces to the Republicans, along with large numbers of advisors, including a contingent from the Soviet People's Commissariat for Internal Affairs (NKVD).[3] Lesser material support was also provided by Portugal and Mexico to the Nationalists and Republicans, respectively. In spite of the official policy of noninternvention by most foreign countries, large numbers of international volunteers fought on both sides.[4]

Military historians have viewed the Spanish Civil War primarily as a testing ground for the weapons and tactics of the Second World War, particularly in regard to the mobile warfare of German armored columns backed by close air support.[5] However, the Spanish Civil

War also provided a venue for irregular operations, with guerrillas organizing in Andalucia and the NKVD sending *aktivki*, small sabotage units, behind Nationalist lines.[6] Indeed, the conflict gave us the term "fifth column," used to describe subversive forces. Nationalist general Emilio Mola famously commented that he had four columns converging on Republican-held Madrid, but the assault would be led by a "fifth column" of Nationalist supporters already inside the city.[7] However, Mola's boast led to a brutal effort to root out right-wing sympathizers in Madrid, demonstrating the phenomenon Gubbins had witnessed firsthand: the destruction of partisan forces acting prematurely against overwhelming force.[8] It is uncertain whether Gubbins specifically studied the "fifth columnists" of Madrid, though it seems likely given the wide circulation of Mola's new phrase in the press and Gubbins's own use of the term; if Gubbins indeed examined this episode, it doubtless confirmed his careful approach to utilizing irregular forces.[9]

More generally, Gubbins commented that Spain was an "obvious" example of "the crippling effect of subversive and paramilitary warfare on regular forces."[10] The war likewise inspired Holland with its use of "gym-shoes, light equipment, evasive tactics, . . . mobility, etc."[11] Outside MI(R), others noticed the lessons of resistance as well. The reports of MI3a—the section of Military Intelligence responsible for Spain and France—suggested early on the possibility of guerrilla warfare, since the Nationalist army, "on occupying any large town . . . send out columns to dispose of any opponents in the neighbourhood."[12] If partisans could succeed in avoiding these sweeps by mobile columns, they might be able to resist for some time.[13] One report described the region of Asturias in northern Spain as "an amazing country. More difficult for an offensive than anything I have seen on the North West Frontier [of India] or in Abyssinia. From a guerilla point of view it looks as if it could be held for ever."[14] Another report noted that even after the loss of Asturias by the Republicans, "scattered bands of fanatics" took to the mountains.[15] Dennis Wheatley, a British writer, explained in 1940: "In the Spanish Civil War villagers often held up well-trained troops, and even tackled tanks, although in most cases they had only the most rudimentary arms. . . . Skillful planning, quick action and resolution can often offset superior arms."[16]

There were, however, voices of caution as well. Neither the Republican General Staff nor their Soviet tutors ever fully embraced guerrilla warfare, even when the conventional conflict was lost; thus, unconventional warfare was the exception, not the rule, in Spain.[17] Britain's assistant military attaché in Paris, who visited Spain during the conflict, described the conflict as "a war in which the majority of the participants are almost entirely untrained, a war in which comparatively small forces are strung out on a vast length of front, a war in which modern weapons are used but not on the modern scale, and, finally, a war in which there have been more assassinations than deaths in battle."[18] He argued that, due to its various abnormalities, "the greatest caution must be used in deducing general lessons from this war: a little adroitness and it will be possible to use it to 'prove' any preconceived theory."[19] Likewise, Gen. J. F. C. Fuller, another of the British officers who observed the war in Spain, describes it as "quite unlike any war I have so far taken part in." The front "is in no way continuous, but . . . hard to discover." Battles "appear to be quite small affairs."[20] The partisan warfare he described was much more urban than rural. He explains, "It is in no sense a great war, a trench war or even a guerilla war. Instead, if I may give it a name, it is a city war. . . . [Nationalist general Francisco Franco] can fight only where the Reds [Republicans] are, and as they dare not enter his area, . . . and as they are supported by the rabble in the towns . . . they are compelled to hold on to the cities, consequently it is there that Franco has to attack them."[21] Though Fuller resisted use of the term "guerilla," his description clearly left open the possibility of partisan warfare within the cities.

Spain certainly provided examples of subversion as well as guerrilla warfare. Every Nationalist battalion had "a loud speaker squad . . . which accompanies the unit into the line for the purpose of disseminating propaganda to the enemy."[22] Likewise, radio stations routinely broadcast propaganda, to friendly populations and also to the enemy.[23] The combatants, as observed by the British, were certainly aware of the effects of eroding morale on their troops. After one of his later visits, Fuller commented that Republican will to resist only held because "there is generally a firing squad at hand ready to restimulate it. In Barcelona, unless you do as you are told, you become a Trotskyite, and are liable to be shot on sight. This is not a normal war."[24] Likewise, he noted elsewhere that "so far as literature goes, the Red retiring forces were amply provided. Everywhere one moves a truly amazing number of pamphlets, leaflets and newspapers is to be found. . . . From what I picked up, one hundred per cent. was political."²⁵ Though commanders in all ages have to concern themselves with the morale of their troops, Spain provided Holland and Gubbins with new proof that the loyalty of soldiers—for or against their leaders—could not be assumed but was open to manipulation. One very common method of controlling men had been seen by Gubbins in Ireland a decade and a half before: killing suspected traitors and leaving their bodies about with an attached explanatory note. Republican placards accused the dead of being fascists; Nationalists pinned their victims' union membership cards to their chests as a sign of their perceived treachery.²⁶

The Nationalist cause in Spain inherited the bulk of the country's prewar military and with it its leadership, support services, and organization.²⁷ Republican forces, on the other hand, consisted of civilian volunteers and paramilitary formations, the kind of men and women Holland and Gubbins expected to mold into partisans. While both men were impressed by the possibilities of partisan warfare, the problems the Republicans faced in Spain were similar to those faced by the Boers and the IRA: poor discipline, disorganization, and factions. In August 1938, British Military Intelligence reported that Republican forces were in a state of "confusion and indiscipline," with "a complete absence of co-ordinated supply and medical organisation, each unit being fed by its own political organism regardless of others."²⁸ It was reported that the Republican war effort "is being carried on in separated districts by small parties, who are fighting each other for their political ideals independently of their respective acknowledged Governments."²⁹ If the South African and Irish examples had not already demonstrated the need for coordination—such as that provided by the *AGW*'s Guerrilla Bureau—study of the Spanish Civil War drove home the point once again.

The war provided other notes of caution as well. Fuller, for example, reported that he observed tanks that had been destroyed; "it was claimed that these machines . . . were put out of action by throwing bottles of petrol on them followed by a hand grenade. This I do not believe. They obviously were put out of action by A. P. [armor-piercing] bullets. . . . I am of [the] opinion that this petrol tactic has been purposely exaggerated to give confidence to the troops."³⁰ To would-be partisans, this is a sobering reminder that not all accounts of bold action by paramilitary irregulars are true; to act as though they were and to encourage others to do so would be dangerous. In 1939 Gubbins would encourage partisans by reminding them that "guerilla warfare is what a regular army has always most to dread. When this warfare is conducted by leaders of determination and courage, an effective campaign by your enemies becomes almost impossible."[31] In spite of this optimism, caution of the sort that Fuller provided led Gubbins to temper his comments. The same passage in the *PLH* warns that "the enemy will become more and more ruthless in his attempts to stop you," while the subsequent SOE syllabus explains that "sporadic risings are useless."[32] Fuller noted in 1938 that "battles are not won by clichés (slogans) or Liddell-Hartisms. That has been the Red mistake."[33] He and the men of MI(R) would have likely disagreed about the potential value of irregular operations or the indirect approach; however, the negative lessons of Spain may have caused them to hold back when others, such as future Minister of Economic Warfare Hugh Dalton, were more enthusiastic.

The Arab Revolt in Palestine, 1936–1939

Following the British conquest of Palestine during the Great War, the territory was given to Britain as a League of Nations mandate. Even before the creation of the mandate, many Zionists eyed the ancient home of the Israelites as a future Jewish state; an influx of Jewish immigration in the interwar years created difficulties between the resident Arab population and the growing Jewish population.[34] These communal tensions erupted when, on 15 April 1936, three Jews were shot by a group of Arab assailants.[35] Riots broke out at one of the funerals and two Arabs were killed in a Jewish revenge attack; on 18 April the Arabs called a national strike and the following day an Arab mob—driven on by rumors of wholesale murder by Jews—rampaged, engaging in "violent and indiscriminate attacks on every Jew or European, regardless of age or sex."[36] The British had a full-fledged revolt on their hands. The author of one staff college text concludes from the Arab Revolt that "modern rebellion has assumed a form which makes its prompt suppression essential."[37] Gubbins himself argues that "it has been shown countless times in history that where firm enemy action has been taken in time against small beginnings, such action has always met with success."[38] Palestine was not, however, such a case. One GS(R) report observed that "in Palestine, the active insurgents are believed never to have exceeded a total of 1,500," but they exerted influence far beyond their numbers.³⁹ By 1938 two infantry divisions, composed of some twenty-five thousand men, were deployed to put down the rebellion, which lasted until 1939.⁴⁰

Counterinsurgency was not new to the British military; it had faced such conflicts throughout the empire and recently in Ireland. Indeed, as historian Rory Miller explains, "many of those serving in the civil and military wings of the Palestinian administration in the late 1930s had served in Ireland or worked on Irish issues. . . . Many of the security tactics first applied in Ireland were used to respond to the revolt in Palestine."⁴¹ However, Tom Bowden argues that "those who transferred to Palestine appeared not to have retained any of the politico-military lessons taught by the course of the Irish War of Independence."⁴² Moreover, Philip Anthony Towle contends that "the Palestinian revolt resembled the post-1945 guerrilla uprisings much more closely than any other insurgency with which the British had to deal between the World Wars."⁴³ The rebels captured some of their weapons—notably Lewis machine guns—from their British opponents, while other weapons were smuggled in though French Syria or British Trans-Jordan.⁴⁴ The revolt was both rural and urban, motivated by nationalism and ethnic hatred as well as other issues; Arab operations were directed by a religious leader, the Mufti of Jerusalem, who fled to Lebanon in 1937, and received propaganda support via radio from both Italy and Germany.⁴⁵ Gubbins recognizes the importance of many of these aspects when he comments that a foreign mission to guerrillas "must study the languages, dialects, topography, etc. [of the country]; they must know the ethnological, political and religious groupings of the people, the history and aspirations of the country, its heroes of the present and martyrs of the past."⁴⁶ The Arab Revolt in Palestine demonstrated—and SOE would utilize—the extended social complexity of guerrilla warfare.

Tactically, British forces in Palestine faced an escalating series of challenges, from civil disturbances and rioting to "arson, sniping, bombing and attacks on motor cars," as well as assassination of police and security personnel.⁴⁷ Attacks against bridges, rails, and the trains that traveled on them were frequent.⁴⁸ The rebels certainly demonstrated Gubbins's claim that a rail ambush could "wreck the train, either by derailing it, by blowing a mine under the engine, or other means."⁴⁹ In addition to outright explosion, the Arabs "could spread or lift a rail" to derail a train.⁵⁰ Telephone communications, oil pipelines, and the Jerusalem water supply were also attacked, as were mail vans.⁵¹ To the men of MI(R), studying the revolt, these tactics looked familiar. "It is believed," Holland wrote, "that the Mufti's instructions to the Palestine rebels are, to some extent, based on Irish practice."⁵²

Taking a page from South Africa, Sir Charles Tegart, the special advisor to the Palestine Police, ordered the construction of blockhouses in the most rebel-infested areas.⁵³ British sources do not directly address the motive behind Arab attacks on railroads; the suggestion is often that they were attacked simply because they were there. But a history of the Palestine Police Force observes that "railways had to be placed under constant guard, and *this drained men from other important tasks*. In the end, to keep the railways running, an intolerable strain was placed upon the security forces."⁵⁴ A keen military observer would have perceived the potential value of guerrilla attacks against a larger conventional effort; Gubbins himself came to such a conclusion.⁵⁵

The Arab rebels did not limit their attacks to cities or infrastructure; vehicles on rural roads were ambushed as well. The *Military Lessons of the Arab Rebellion*, compiled by the General Staff of Palestine and Trans-Jordan, explains that "the great majority [of attacks] bore the same characteristics: most of them started with an attack on a convoy and ended with the arrival of aircraft and reinforcements rushed to the scene in response to a call from the wireless lorry of the escort. Where the enemy managed to escape heavy casualties it was usually due to darkness overtaking the action before the reinforcing aircraft and troops could strike."⁵⁶ On many occasions the road was "heavily blocked by huge boulders rolled down from the hillside."⁵⁷ A second line of stones was often deployed before a vehicle could get turned around, and mines were also used to destroy vehicles.⁵⁸ In the city of Jaffa, "nail-strewing in the main streets" was employed to support a strike of the city's buses and taxis by keeping other traffic off the roads. The same tactic was later employed on rural roads to stop British patrols.⁵⁹

Most guerrillas were not foolish enough to remain engaged against superior forces but escaped to the safety of nearby caves or slipped among the civilian population.⁶⁰ The *Military Lessons* explains that

> ambush parties would consist of anything from seven to twenty men fairly widely scattered, who often wore black cloaks and when

stationary were almost invisible.... They always chose their positions well as being easy to evacuate, while any approach from the road, either frontally or from a flank, would involve a difficult climb. They were seldom prepared to stand and fight, and took care not to stage an ambush at the same place more than once on any one day. Generally they retired in haste as soon as the troops had debussed and started to attack, so that by the time the attackers gained their [the rebels'] position the late occupants were several hills away.[61]

The British typically pursued ambushers, first with "light fast motor transport" on the roads and then with "motor-borne pack donkeys" once the pursuit moved "off the roads."[62] The objective for the British—and the situation to be feared by the rebels—was "to get to grips with the hostile elements and bring them into subjection."[63] Sustained contact was always a one-sided affair and repeatedly succeeded in destroying rebel formations.[64]

Attacks were not limited to lines of communication. On 16 May 1936 unidentified gunmen (presumably Arabs) entered a cinema in Jerusalem's Jewish quarter and opened fire.[65] In September 1937 the Nazareth district commissioner was assassinated by guerrillas.[66] As had happened in Dublin, murder was committed in broad daylight on the streets of Jerusalem.[67] The security forces and Jewish civilians were attacked by the rebels, but so too were Arabs who worked for the government, refused to participate in the strike, or were otherwise deemed unacceptable to the rebel cause.[68]

The rebels began the conflict with fairly large bands of partisans, but "these became split up owing to our [British] activities and owing to the fact that a large armed band is difficult to conceal and is liable to suffer heavy casualties."[69] This may have alerted Gubbins to the fact that "the speed of modern communications, i.e., motor, wireless, etc., and the presence of aeroplanes make it very difficult for a large party to remain concealed for any length of time."[70] In later stages of the Arab Revolt, partisan bands sometimes came together and operated as a single unit, but in so doing they decreased their mobility and increased their chances of being identified by the British; in due course severe defeats followed.[71] Gubbins's guerrillas would not commit the same error, as he warns them time and again that "the organization of guerillas must not be of a higher degree than circumstances will, with reasonable safety, and a view to efficiency, permit."[72]

Among the problems faced by British forces in Palestine was the heavily Arab composition of the police. While many Arab policemen served with impartiality and devotion to duty, others betrayed details of future operations to the rebels, as had been the case with the Royal Irish Constabulary in Ireland. This was not only the result of divided loyalties but also because of the assassination of Arab policemen and threats to their families.[73] So serious was the problem that the British worried about the "risk of [Arab police] going over to the rebels with their arms."[74] Intelligence collection among the general Arab population was even more difficult, confirming Gubbins's later observation that a hostile population "will actively co-operate in providing information for the guerillas" or at the least "withholding it from the [occupying] enemy."[75]

Apart from outright treasonous passage of information, the rebels also benefitted from "unguarded telephone conversations, discussion of operations in public places, and carelessness in handling secret documents in offices. . . . Information regarding the movement of troops was transmitted by inhabitants, who watched camps and roads and sent their messages by means of lights in houses, bonfires and smoke signals."[76] One contemporary account explains that rebel villages were "undisturbed unless a temporary military invasion burst suddenly upon them. As a rule, they had ample warning and could move out of the way till the activity died down and the troops went back to their camps."[77] Gubbins, recognizing the source of the guerrillas' strength and information, points out to his partisan leaders that "military action is greatly facilitated by the support of the local population. By this means, warning can be obtained of all hostile moves, and it will not be possible for the enemy to carry out surprise action."[78]

> In light of the rebels' "all-seeing" intelligence, British forces in Palestine attempted to deceive it. Many expedients were tried, but nearly all failed—however well executed—because of a leakage of plans almost at the source. Ruses tried included the spreading of false news, dropping troops quietly from moving vehicles at night, the use of "Q" buses containing troops disguised as Jewish passengers or workmen, and the adoption of circuitous routes by M.T. [mechanical transport] columns.[79]

"Road traffic was used . . . often as a bait with which to draw out armed bands and bring them to action."[80] In July 1936 the British attempted a major sweep of the Nablus area, hoping to encircle and capture some rebel bands. "Like most drives under such conditions," writes historian Charles Townshend, this effort was "a failure."[81] The 8th Division's summary of the conflict concurred that drives always failed.[82] As a result, later efforts involved occupying villages in an attempt to force rebels away from their usual sources of food and shelter and into the open, where they could more easily be engaged.[83]

Searches became a routine part of the British effort. Ambushes or firefights with the rebels were plotted on maps, allowing authorities to make an educated guess at which villages harbored rebel fighters. Such locations were usually cordoned off at night and searched at dawn, in accordance with the principles laid out in a 1934 military handbook, *Notes on Imperial Policing*.[84] A contemporary account explains that

> arms were usually well hidden at some distance from the houses. On one occasion, a group of women were seen seated on a rug near a village.... Someone had the bright idea of looking under the rug. The ladies at first failed to understand, and then combined protest with loud lamentation when they saw that bluff was useless. Under the rug the earth had been newly dug. The earth was dug up again, and in a narrow trench was found a little arsenal of arms and ammunition.[85]

Although viewed by British commanders as punitive measures aimed at "regaining the initiative," these searches generally strove to be civil and disciplined and were therefore broadly cautious in their approach.[86] The same could not be said of the Special Night Squads organized by Orde Wingate in 1938.

Wingate, who graduated from Woolwich in 1923, came to Palestine in late 1937; he was soon posted to general headquarters as an intelligence officer.[87] Wingate was a distant cousin of T. E. Lawrence, whom he studied in some detail. Although Wingate became known as a practitioner of unconventional warfare and is often placed alongside Lawrence in this regard, Wingate was highly critical of his relation, both as a soldier and as a man. Biographer Christopher Sykes explains, "He believed that Lawrence's military ideas were fallacious and he deplored the cult of which he was the centre."[88] Most specifically, Wingate quibbled with Lawrence's total reliance on native forces. In one episode that took place in Abyssinia a few years after the Arab Revolt, Wingate initially rebuffed the advances of a local chieftain who wanted to fight alongside him. Wingate only accepted his offer after the chieftain agreed to provide his own arms and Wingate had forced the chieftain into a subordinate position.[89] Wingate would utilize local forces only if he was certain he could retain control of their activities and would not be fleeced in the process. Otherwise he would rely on his own men.

Organized in 1938, the Special Night Squads (SNS) consisted of British soldiers and members of the Jewish Supernumerary Police, most of whom were also members of the unofficial Jewish defense militia, the Haganah.[90] These small mobile units engaged in aggressive patrolling and counterambushes against the rebels.[91] Simon Anglim has argued that the SNS are "often portrayed in 'popular' accounts . . . as a departure from established British Army methods," though "when placed in their context [of imperial paramilitary specialist units], the Night Squads can be seen as a culmination of existing practice."[92] While it is useful to note that the SNS were not sui generis, their distinct character, when compared to regular units and formal British practice, is worth highlighting.

The SNS certainly satisfied one British report's contention that "the secret of success in operations is always to retain the initiative and to do something new. The rebels soon get to know about a particular method and take steps to defeat it. They should be kept continually guessing."[93] In order to achieve the element of surprise, the SNS first made use of excellent intelligence, possibly from within rebel bands, which was always carefully checked to weed out double agents.[94] Wingate's forces then moved by circuitous routes, operating under the assumption that "in Palestine someone is always watching you."[95] In the approach to the Battle of Dabburiya (11 July 1938) the SNS "left their stations in the short twilight, some travelling east, and Wingate's party travelling north . . . with a party of girls in the car as further cover for his intentions. Then after dark all the lorries travelled along the Nazareth-Tiberias road, some going east, some west, dropping men off at prearranged intervals, the lorries never slowing down."[96] Just as Holland had been impressed by the use of rubber-soled shoes in Spain, so too in Palestine the SNS used the same, to make themselves both lighter and quieter.[97] Through innovative tactics and equipment, Wingate achieved his surprise.

The stations operated by the SNS were unlike ordinary British military instillations. On parade or operations Wingate was an autocrat, but the stations were democratic with elected committees of grievances.[98] This may seem like an odd approach to leadership, but the SNS's unusual composition—including both civilians and soldiers—and unconventional operations required a special arrangement. Wingate's leadership style is not so distant from Gubbins's description of a guerrilla leader, who must be able "to control his followers and win their unquestioning obedience without the close constraints of military organization and discipline which are the antithesis of guerrila action and a drag on its efficiency."[99]

Wingate also held unique ideas about training. Like many of Gubbins's writings, Wingate's surviving lecture notes "are precise, brief, to the point, and mainly technical."[100] But Wingate also commented on more general matters, arguing, for example, that "great soldiers were serious and diligent in their youth . . . and many of them were people of outstanding moral character." He was also critical of the professional soldier, admonishing his men to "learn his discipline and calmness . . . but don't imitate his brutality, stupidity and drunkenness."[101] Gubbins too questioned the usefulness of professional soldiers, though never in such strong language; likewise he could write with a flourish now and again, reaching beyond the details of guerrilla warfare to the heights of the human spirit.[102]

As Sykes explains, "Training and operation were not sharply divided [in the SNS], indeed to a large extent the squadsmen were trained through taking part in operations."[103] This contrasts both with Gubbins's 1939 publications and his subsequent work with SOE. In the *AGW*, Gubbins writes that "the narrow limits of the training [a guerrilla] requires . . . and the careful, detailed rehearsal of projected coups should enable him . . . to match even the best trained troops."[104] Thus, while Gubbins suggests that guerrillas need little training, he also calls for "detailed rehearsal," something Wingate's fast tempo may have left out. Likewise, Gubbins insists that "a few rounds spent on perfecting shooting, and testing of rifles, will be amply repaid."[105] While Wingate appears not to have objected to using "a few rounds" in training, such an allotment would be much scarcer for a guerrilla force than for the SNS; one can question what Wingate's priorities might have been under other constraints. In another departure between the SNS and the *AGW*, Gubbins insists that guerrillas be trained in the "use of the various destructive devices such as bombs, road and rail mines, etc., which are such a special and useful feature of guerila warfare."[106] While the roles of Gubbins's forces as guerrillas and Wingate's as counterguerrillas easily explain the absence of this element in the latter's training regime, this all-important matter highlights the imperfections of the parallel between the two thinkers. Finally, any notion of training through operations was undermined by the very existence of SOE's system of schools, which thoroughly trained agents before inserting them into occupied territory (see chapter 6).

Wingate's SNS were not all quirks and idiosyncrasy; he insisted on inspecting weapons cleaning after returning in the dawn hours from a long night of patrolling.[107] If perhaps a touch obsessive, this is simply good soldiering, though it too is paralleled in Gubbins's observation that weapons "must be protected against damp, rust, etc.; remember that your life and that of your friends may depend on a weapon in good order."[108] Such fundamentals, though not unique to unconventional warfare, can take on special importance, particularly when the supporting services enjoyed by many regular troops are absent.

The SNS were an aggressive antiguerrilla force but also functioned as a semi-guerrilla force of their own. Wingate eventually worked for MI(R)'s Middle East branch in 1940; it was their idea, not Wingate's, to operate native forces behind enemy lines in Abyssinia. By this time Gubbins was busy liaising with the Poles and Czechoslovaks and then commanding the Independent Companies in Norway (see chapter 5). However, MI(R)'s doctrine, crafted by Gubbins, had already been set in place and served as Wingate's guidelines in Abyssinia. Anglim explains: "Wingate inherited an existing operation applying Gubbins' recommended operational procedures faithfully, and produced afterwards a set of operational procedures of his own derived partially from Gubbins' as shaped by his [Wingate's] own experiences in Palestine and Ethiopia."[109] Thus, we know Wingate followed Gubbins's ideas; it is less clear if influence went the other way. Anglim continues:

> Perhaps the biggest difference [between the two] was that Wingate insisted, increasingly, on concentration of force and resources, rather than the dispersal and economy of effort that was the hallmark of other MI(R) operations, and his moving away from subversion and partisan warfare—about which he seems never to have been enthusiastic—towards use of purpose-designed regular forces to menace enemy lines of communication, with occasional support from local irregulars provided they didn't get in the way.[110]

In short, Wingate was a commando; he was not a true guerrilla in Abyssinia and probably had not been in Palestine either.[111]

Wingate's aggressive patrols did, however, confirm Gubbins's experience in Ireland that guerrillas will be hounded by antiguerrilla forces. These examples led him to conclude that only for a time could partisans live "in their own homes" before "this will soon be rendered impossible by the searches, raids, etc." Indeed, Gubbins expected "detachments . . . [to] be sent out to search the country, moving by circuitous and haphazard routes, employing scouts and advance guards, and probably assisted by aircraft."[112] While aircraft played only a supporting role in Ireland, they were a key part of the counterinsurgency effort in Palestine; Gubbins's description points to the new lessons learned from this conflict.[113]

Other aggressive actions by the British authorities likewise confirmed the dangers that irregular warriors are likely to face. The *Military Lessons of the Arab Rebellion* observes that "the best deterrent [against bombing of British vehicles] would probably have been the carrying of hostages." This is qualified, however, with a caveat of lamentation: "had it been permitted."[114] Other measures were, however, permitted. On 18 June 1936 the Royal Engineers entered the Old City of Jaffa, which had been evacuated of its inhabitants.

> Demolition work was started at once. By nightfall a road ten metres wide had been driven right through from one side of Jaffa to the other. . . . Later . . . a north and south circular road was blown through the Old City. . . . A notorious quarter of tin shanties, known as "Tin Town," was demolished amid a deafening clatter by the simple process of driving tanks across it after its occupants . . . had been deported to their native Syria.[115]

If this was how Britain dealt with rebellion, could anti-Nazi partisans expect gentler measures at the hands of the Third Reich? Gubbins's many cautions were not idle.

Any consideration of the lessons learned by MI(R) from the Arab Revolt must be qualified by the generally low opinion the British held of their Palestinian opponents. The *Military Lessons of the Arab Rebellion* describes "the Palestinian Arab" as "not a fighting man: even when led and reinforced by trained and experienced individuals from Iraq, Syria, and Trans-Jordan, the rank and file still retained their characteristics of carelessness, lack of enterprise, and a wholesome regard for their own skins. They had none of the military qualities of, for instance, the tribesmen of the North-West frontier of India."[116] The 8th Division's summary of the conflict notes that, "on the whole the enemy have been most unenterprising in their methods. They have not evolved any new tactics of note. They open fire from ambush and usually withdraw as soon as attacked."[117]

Throughout the fighting, both leadership and training were in short supply among the rebels.[118] Indeed, Fawzi al-Qawuqji, the Lebanese Druze who was arguably the single most important military leader among the rebels, explained to the radical Syrian newspaper *Al Kabas*: "I started to constitute an Iraqi band of young men who were trained in the Army, in order that the 'expedition' should be organised in military methods, in order not to repeat the anarchy that had prevailed in the Syrian revolt" of 1925–27.[119] The *Military Lessons of the Arab Rebellion* admits that "after Fauzi's arrival the [rebel] bands soon demonstrated more effective leadership and organization, while the extension of their sphere beyond the areas of habitual activity showed that their numbers had increased."[120] Nevertheless, Fawzi never enjoyed leadership of *all* the rebels, who were divided by tribal loyalties and by goals; some fought for political liberty, while others were mere thieves or unemployed opportunists. Under such conditions, it is unsurprising that the rebels fought piecemeal and ineffectively.[121] Someone studying the conflict, as MI(R) did, might draw the conclusion that in order to be effective, guerrillas must be organized by a single leader or a coordinating agency, the precise conclusion to which Colin Gubbins came.

In July 1939 the military commander in Palestine—by then Maj. Gen. Bernard Montgomery—declared that the rebellion was "now definitely and finally smashed." It was certainly winding to a close, though Townshend comments that "few observers would have shared Montgomery's conviction it was the outcome of his actions. Rather it seemed that . . . the insurgency had died away—in the nick of time for Britain, as international tension screwed up to the pitch of imminent European war."[122]

Irregular Warfare in China

The Second Sino-Japanese War

Several decades of poor relations between the ambitious empire of Japan and its Chinese neighbor began in the nineteenth century.

Japan defeated China in the First Sino-Japanese War (1894–95), annexing Taiwan and gaining hegemony over Korea.[123] During the Great War Japan seized the German concession of Shandong; though it was returned to China in 1922, Japanese and Chinese troops there came to blows in 1928.[124] China's transformation from a monarchy to a republic in 1912 did little to strengthen the country's ability to resist aggression and Japan continued to exploit ongoing instability in China, including the outbreak of civil war between Nationalists and Communists in 1927.[125] In September 1931, elements of the Japanese Army perpetrated an explosion against a Japanese rail line in Manchuria and blamed the event—known as the Mukden Incident—on Chinese troops. Under the pretext of defending its interests, Japan invaded Manchuria, quickly overrunning the area and establishing the puppet state of Manchukuo. Clashes continued for several years.[126]

On 7 July 1937, Japanese troops stationed at the Marco Polo Bridge, which provides access to Beijing, staged nighttime maneuvers. One of the Japanese soldiers went missing, possibly spending the night in a brothel. The Japanese commander insisted on searching the nearby town; the local Chinese commander refused, shots were exchanged, and by the following morning there was open fighting. Over the course of the next month, Japanese forces pushed deeper into China, capturing Beijing in early August. A few days later the fighting spread to Shanghai. This was not simply another "incident" but a full-scale conflict, the Second Sino-Japanese War.[127]

In spite of the Japanese onslaught, the Chinese learned to resist in various ways. One MI(R) officer argued that "the value and function of the guerillas was not recognised by the Chinese until after the fall of Nanking in December 1937. Since then, considerable attention has been paid, not without success, to increasing their sticking-power and effectiveness."[128] Chinese guerrillas harassed lines of communication and supplies.[129] They made use of speed and surprise, employing ambushes and other tactics, which allowed them to bring superior numbers to bear against small isolated units. When large attacks could not be conducted, so-called sparrow war, characterized by small pricks with sniping, landmines, or even firecrackers, was utilized. Such operations were frequently carried out by the Eighth Route Army, the Communist formation of the tentative anti-Japanese army of national unity.[130] Guerrilla operations were, however, also in accordance with the plan annunciated by Chiang

Kai-shek, the Nationalist leader, who exhorted his commanders "to use special operations units and plainclothes agents, scattering them everywhere, to deal with the enemy rear areas."[131]

British Military Intelligence believed the Chinese turned to irregular warfare not on ideological grounds or out of a Lawrence-esque belief in the efficiency of guerrillas but out of necessity. One British report explains that the Chinese, lacking adequate munitions, could not return fire against Japanese artillery.[132] Edgar Snow, an American who interviewed Mao Tse-tung in 1936, confirmed this view, observing that "both the air force and such mechanization as has taken place . . . are looked upon by many as costly toys . . . quite incapable of retaining a rôle of initiative after the first few weeks, since China is almost utterly lacking in the basic war industries necessary to maintain and replenish either an air force or any other highly technical branch of modern warfare."[133] This use of irregular forces in China did not go unnoticed by MI(R). Studying China was a significant part of Holland's task when he took his post.[134] Among the *Notes on the Sino-Japanese War* assembled by Military Intelligence one can find the cover page shorn from a report by GS(R) titled "Considerations from the Wars in Spain and China with Regard to Certain Aspects of Army Policy."[135] Although the contents of the report appear to be lost, the report's existence not only confirms that GS(R) produced analysis of the war in China but also demonstrates that this analysis was circulated beyond the doors of Holland's office to a wider audience in Military Intelligence and perhaps throughout the War Office. Some of the other documents within the *Notes on the Sino-Japanese War* are clearly not from GS(R)/MI(R), but other portions have ambiguous authorship and may come, in part or in whole, from Holland and his men.

The elements of guerrilla warfare noted by European observers in China mirrored earlier conflicts, underscoring once again the difficulty faced by conventional forces attempting to defend a vast territory and far-flung lines of communication. The war in China also confirmed the vigorous countermeasures that could be employed to protect such lines and defeat guerrillas. More uniquely, the fighting in China provided the British with important lessons regarding the role of neutral territory in a guerrilla conflict. It also provided a useful reminder that guerrillas are not always savory characters.

The Japanese suffered from the vastness of both the Chinese geography and the depths of popular opposition. The *North China*

Daily News reported in 1939 that Chinese youths recruited to fight for the Japanese were mutinying and going over to the guerrillas.[136] A British report concluded that "so long as the Chinese continue their guerilla tactics ultimately they may be able to defeat the Japanese because, in order to cope with the guerilla tactics the Japanese will require a much larger force than they have at present."[137] In addition to the casualties suffered by the Japanese, the guerrilla war tied down Japanese troops that might otherwise have been employed at the front and imposed huge—and, in the long term, arguably unbearable—financial costs.[138] Such a situation accords with Gubbins's observation that an invader "will be working usually amidst a hostile populace; without their co-operation his task will be more difficult and will require a larger number of his own men to carry it out."[139]

Japanese lines of communication were particularly hard hit by Chinese guerrillas. One Japanese telegraph official, who spoke to the British, admitted that "the lines were still frequently cut" by the Chinese. Foreign missionaries and Chinese chauffeurs reported that in some areas only "strongly protected convoys of 50 cars or more" were capable of traversing key roads, while railroad "track is frequently damaged," with the result that "the Japanese can no longer depend on [these] line[s] of communications."[140] A British officer with a sense of humor reported that "the new [Japanese] Garrison Commander . . . was installed and on 10th April the guerillas celebrated his arrival by dismantling 6,000 feet of telephone wire."[141] Henri de Fremery, a Dutch observer, notes that guerrillas posed such a threat that the Japanese tried to time their maneuvers with extreme precision so as to avoid far-flung lines of communication whenever possible.[142] All of this accords with Gubbins's argument that guerrilla warfare succeeds by "compelling the enemy to disperse his forces" to guard his communications and supplies.[143]

The Japanese resorted to holding village headmen responsible, on pain of death, for the integrity of telegraph and rail lines in their areas, in an effort to end the attacks.[144] Moreover, along railways a blockhouse was constructed every three miles and security forces were raised to protect the lines. Such a strategy of blanketing lines of communication had barely worked in South Africa, where the Boers were so few in number; in China, de Fremery observes that "despite [the Japanese defenses], a great many attacks are made against the lines."[145] All these reports find an echo in Gubbins's observation that "modern large-sized armies, entirely dependent as they are on the regular delivery of supplies, munitions, petrol, etc., for their operations, present a particularly favourable opportunity for guerilla warfare, directed against their communications by road, rail or water, and against their system of internal postal and telegraph communications."[146]

As with other conflicts, however, there were notes of caution regarding China. Some irregulars were drawn from Shanghai's notorious Green Gang; others were reported to be "quarrelsome," requiring that a "small body of [regular] troops" be dispatched to "improve organisation."[147] A British missionary, writing to the British ambassador, explained that the nearby guerrillas, though "a pretty harmless set of chaps [and] very pleasant" in their relations with him, were "not popular with the people as they help themselves to what they want" and "the farmers have to supply them with food."[148]

Although such actions made the guerrillas unpopular with the local population, the Japanese also worked to defame Chinese irregular forces through the use of *agents provocateurs*. On 13 August 1938, the first anniversary of hostilities in Shanghai, there were widespread fears of attacks by Chinese partisans; however, a British Military Intelligence report indicates that the only trouble came when members of the Japanese Special Service Section, operating in civilian clothes, attempted to intimidate and humiliate Chinese residents of the American and British sectors of the city, hoping to start incidents that might justify Japanese repression.[149]

Some members of British Military Intelligence did not subscribe to the implicitly pro-Chinese views expressed by their colleagues. Maj. Gen. F. S. G. Piggott, the military attaché in Tokyo, undertook a visit to Tientsin in April 1939. His report describes as "absolutely convincing" the Japanese "diagrams of [Chinese] terrorist organizations, statistics of outrages, [and] types of infernal machines."[150] Whether or not Gubbins shared Piggott's assessment of the Chinese resistance as "terrorists"—and it is likely he did not, given the tone of his writings in 1939 and his subsequent support for resistance movements elsewhere—there was still useful information to be gleaned from the attaché's reports. According to the Japanese briefings Piggott received, Chinese fighters were organized with a headquarters in the British Concession within Tientsin, a neutral territory where they could usually find safe haven. Three kinds of units operated in Japanese-occupied territory: "Army property destruction group[s]" that destroyed "stores, rations, ammunition, transport, etc."; "Terrorist Group[s], composed entirely of girls between the ages of 20 and 24," who utilized "inflammable and explosive substances . . . concealed in scent-bottles, cigarette cartons," and similar containers; and "Civil factory destruction group[s]," which targeted buses, rails, and shops.[151]

In Ireland the rebels made use of resources from Germany and the United States but, lacking geographic proximity to a third party, did not make considerable use of neutral territory. Likewise, neutral neighbors did not play a major role in the Russian Civil War or in most of the conflicts Gubbins studied (the role of ostensibly neutral France in the Spanish Civil War excepted). But in China partisan forces made use of neutral territory in a way Britain certainly noticed, since it was her own. In the same year as Piggott's report, Gubbins writes that the "field of action for guerilla warfare" includes "neutral countries," from which weapons and explosives may be run.[152]

Piggott does not explain why the Chinese utilized young women for their operations; these women may have operated where men would raise greater suspicions. This phenomenon would not have been foreign to Gubbins's experience in Ireland, where elderly women carried guns for the IRA, since women were usually exempt from searches.[153] Moreover, Gubbins himself later argues that "women and children . . . are less suspect and probably could enjoy greater immunity from search."[154] The female teams on which Piggott reported may have also used their feminine charms, another concept found in Gubbins's writings.[155]

Both praise and blame imply that Chinese operations were significant enough to merit notice. However, the majority of Chinese Nationalist Army officers lacked faith in guerrilla warfare and spent little time concerning themselves with its tactics. Even Dai Li, head of Nationalist intelligence and security, who organized one of the earliest Nationalist programs in guerrilla warfare, did so primarily to keep an eye on the Communists, who depended heavily on guerrilla warfare.[156] This ambivalence on the part of certain Chinese leaders seems to have trickled down the ranks; de Fremery observes that "guerrilla troops themselves are easily satisfied with a minimum performance, and it is only owing to their great strength of numbers that anything at all is achieved."[157] There were lessons to be learned in China, but it was hardly a perfect model for the future SOE.

Gubbins and Mao

Although Chiang Kai-shek spoke and wrote on guerrilla warfare, Mao Tse-tung eclipsed him in this field, not only during the decades of the Cold War but even during the Second Sino-Japanese War, in which the Communists held substantial control of the guerrilla movement.[158] De Fremery, the Dutch observer, argues that "red troops . . . have applied the tactical concepts suggested by Mao Tse Tung with success."[159] In 1937, Mao authored *On Guerrilla Warfare* (*Yu Chi Chan*), of which the first known English translation was made by Samuel Griffith of the U.S. Marine Corps in 1940, the year after Gubbins authored his handbooks.[160] There is no evidence that Holland, Gubbins, or anyone else at MI(R) read Mao's work in the late 1930s; however, the points of convergence and divergence between Gubbins's and Mao's doctrine are worth considering for several reasons. Firstly, Mao's work was certainly widespread; even in Nationalist zones of China it was "widely distributed . . . at 10 cents a copy."[161] Portions, the entirety, or a summary of *On Guerrilla Warfare* may have been available to MI(R). This could have come about through an unpublished (and presumably now lost) English translation, perhaps by one of the Chinese linguists in the War Office or SIS. MI(R) may have also come across a description or translation in a language other than English; after all, Gubbins was a qualified interpreter in both Russian and French, had passed the preliminary Urdu exam, and had a passing knowledge of German and Italian.[162] Secondly, apart from any knowledge of *On Guerrilla Warfare* itself, the men of MI(R)—though possibly ignorant of the text's existence—may have discerned some of its principles at work in the operations about which Military Intelligence reported.

Mao and Gubbins agree on a great many points. Like Gubbins, Mao stresses the importance of initiative, surprise, and mobility.[163] Both writers understand the importance of equipment captured from the enemy, the value of partisan leaders, the significance of local circumstances and populations, and the propaganda value of guerrilla successes.[164] Both Mao and Gubbins recognize the place of guerrilla warfare within a larger conventional conflict, though both show reservations about the direct use of regular troops with partisans.[165]

At a higher conceptual level, Gubbins and Mao agree that, because partisans' first task is survival, they should avoid decisive battles and instead attack enemy supplies and communications. However, Mao also includes the establishment of bases among the tasks appropriate to guerrillas, something not of interest to Gubbins.[166] That Mao wanted to occupy and control liberated areas of China, whereas Gubbins had no interest in seizing continental territory for Britain, may explain this different approach. Likewise, although both Gubbins and Mao recognize the dangers of large-scale counterguerrilla sweeps, Mao advocates counterattacks to break such efforts, while Gubbins acknowledges that flight might often be required.[167]

But three major divergences mark the differences between these two thinkers: the role of ideology, the level of organization, and the nature of operations. Whereas Gubbins's works are tactical, Mao's are mostly theoretical. Moreover, Gubbins—who acquired a fierce hatred of Bolshevism in Russia—writes virtually nothing about ideology; the closest he comes are a few passages about the ability of the human spirit to resist oppression. But Mao's work is suffused with ideology, arguing that anyone who divides the political and military aspects of guerrilla warfare "must fail."[168] Moreover, Mao places an extremely strong emphasis on the role of the people, contending, for example, that "the moment this war of resistance dissociates itself from the masses of the people is the precise moment that it dissociates itself from hope of ultimate victory."[169] Gubbins places a strong emphasis on the local population as well but does not ascribe to it Mao's pseudomystical significance.[170]

A more subtle point of departure involves the matter of organization. Mao argues that "guerrilla bands that spring from the masses of the people suffer from lack of organization" and calls for the organizing of guerrilla units up to the level of brigades.[171] As we have seen in the Irish context, Gubbins warns about overorganization and the opportunities it creates for counterguerrilla forces. The difference in views here may be explained by a difference in geography—large portions of China were never occupied by the Japanese, making organization less dangerous—or by Mao's ideological interest in organization stemming from the Marxist tradition.

Similarly, Mao's recommended organization is distinctly conventional, consisting of brigades with their own administration, engineers, and finance units; battalions include machine-gun and medical sections.[172] Very little in his model organization suggests the need for clandestine or mobile operations, nor an emphasis on ambushes or other tactics favorable to guerrillas. Likewise, Mao calls for the establishment of armories to produce—among other things—bayonets, a weapon Gubbins warns is "quite unsuitable for guerillas," being difficult to conceal and "only for use in shock action which should be eschewed."[173] That Mao's guerrillas would attempt such assaults, which provide little chance of escape in the event of failure, and would not be concerned with concealment suggests a considerable degree of regular operations.[174] Mao hoped to transition from guerrilla to conventional warfare; his forces therefore stand halfway between true guerrillas—conceptually distinct from regular forces—and militia units that, though distinct from regular forces, strive to emulate them.[175]

While the irregular warfare doctrines of Mao and Gubbins have much in common, these are mostly tactical matters of a nature to which guerrillas in most times and places could attest. Their considerable divergences on larger theoretical matters coupled with the absence of documentary evidence on a connection strongly suggest that Mao's influence on Gubbins was minimal, if it existed at all. But this, in turn, suggests an important finding: Gubbins was not influenced in the same way by all the conflicts he studied. If he was aware—directly or indirectly—of Mao's ideas, Gubbins appears to have rejected many of them. The more likely conclusion, that Gubbins was not familiar with Mao's writings in any meaningful way, also serves the useful purpose of reminding us that Gubbins's program of study was limited and pragmatic. For various reasons, even a thinker as eminent in the modern age as Mao could be overlooked or ignored.

Early Plans for China

MI(R)'s interests in China were not simply academic. On 1 August 1939, Peter Fleming, who had traveled through much of Asia in the interwar years, was recruited by MI(R) "as the leader of a small party of officers whose mission would be to stir Chinese guerrillas into more effective action against the Japanese."[176] At the request of MI(R), he also produced a paper titled "Notes on the Possibilities of British Military Action in China," in which he proposed a multipronged British mission to China, consisting of a liaison headquarters, a propaganda component, technical training for the Chinese, advisory details in the field, and "sub-missions." Following Gubbins's observation three months earlier that "it may . . . frequently be advantageous to appoint certain serving army officers for duty with guerillas," Fleming proposed that the sub-missions include junior officers who would "organise and, where possible ... *lead personally* local offensive action against the enemy."[177] He argued that the Chinese "would be pleasurably surprised to find foreign officers coming with them under fire. ... The average Chinese general will not take kindly to foreign direction or control, ... but he will view with gratitude, respect and astonishment a foreign officer who undertakes in person, and with success, the distasteful task of fighting."[178] Fleming also proposed the creation of a British, Indian, or Australian cavalry force in Inner Mongolia, arguing that the terrain was ideal for a small, high-impact force waging irregular warfare.[179]

Fleming's proposals were accepted within a week and plans were made to depart for China in November 1939. Fleming was permitted to recruit his own force, including men such as Martin Lindsay, an Arctic explorer who served for ten years in the regular army and had learned Chinese in Shanghai. These plans came to naught in mid-September when the Foreign Office vetoed even clandestine support to the Chinese, not wanting to exacerbate tensions with Japan, or find Britain in a second war, having recently acquired one in Europe. Fleming, however, stayed with MI(R), producing plans for anti-Japanese propaganda which effectively anticipated Japanese moves in 1941.[180]

German Subversive Forces

A final source of inspiration to Gubbins and the men at MI(R) was the enemy himself. In an address at Cambridge many years after the war, Gubbins explained how the British government was impressed by

> the tremendous harvest that Germany had reaped through the use of these [unconventional] means, for example the subversion of Austria in 1939, the rape of Czechoslovakia in 1939 all without a shot being fired—and then in 1940 the elimination of France as a combatant, fundamentally attributable to the rot in Government circles achieved by German "5th Column" activities before the War even began and the complete lack of confidence that ensued: subversion had won in the final round with a knock-out.[181]

In 1940, Minister of Economic Warfare Hugh Dalton echoed this sentiment in a letter to Lord Halifax, the foreign secretary: "We have got to organize movements in enemy-occupied territory comparable to . . .—one might as well admit it—to the organizations which the nazis themselves have developed so remarkably in almost every country in the world."[182] Not all the successes attributed to Nazi agents actually happened, but when understanding the thinking of Gubbins and his colleagues, what matters was perception in Britain, not reality on the continent. And the perception that the Allies had suffered at the hands of German fifth columnists is widely attested. It became dogma within SOE that "Britain and her Allies" had experienced "the strength and success of the enemy fifth column" before realizing that the Allies too could engage in subversive warfare.[183]

Nazi Germany's rise to power was a complex process involving various political and military factors. For those with an interest in irregular warfare, a clear line of subversion ran through events in various countries from the advent of the Third Reich in 1933 to the fall of France in 1940. Shortly after taking power in Germany, the Nazis began deploying clandestine forces, sending spies to France and assassins to Czechoslovakia and Switzerland, where they targeted anti-Nazi broadcasters and refugees.[184] In Austria, Germany supplied arms to the Austrian Nazi Party, which assassinated Chancellor Engelbert Dollfuss in 1934 and planned an armed insurrection.[185] In March 1938, following political bludgeoning of the Austrian government by Germany, Interior Minister Arthur Seyss-Inquart, a Nazi sympathizer, appointed himself chancellor and, on the orders of his German masters, invited German troops into the country, ostensibly to restore law and order.[186] Austria's independence was over. In Czechoslovakia, Konrad Henlein, leader of the *Sudetendeutsch Partei*, spouted Nazi propaganda and agitated for "rights" the Czechoslovak government could never grant its German-speaking minority. Meanwhile, Henlein's henchmen, receiving support from the *Abwehr* (German military intelligence), threatened armed insurrection, going so far as to revolt in Asch-Eger.[187] Although the revolt was quickly crushed, Henlein played an important role in fostering the political crisis that ended with German annexation of Sudetenland in October 1938, the first step in dismembering Czechoslovakia. Prior to the invasion of Poland in September 1939, Abwehr teams in Polish uniforms were tasked with seizing bridges, mountain passes, and economic targets such as iron and coal mines, as well as the Polish military intelligence archives.[188] Members of the Nazi paramilitary *Schutzstaffel* (SS) organization dressed as Polish soldiers and attacked a German radio station at Gleiwitz, providing the ostensible justification for Germany's invasion.[189]

Such clandestine and subversive operations continued even after the formal outbreak of war, often conducted by the Abwehr II Department's 800th Special Purpose Instruction Regiment Brandenburg, the brainchild of Hauptmann (Captain) Dr. Theodor von Hippel, a veteran of Lettow-Vorbeck's guerrilla campaign in Africa. Von Hippel envisioned a unit "to seize vital objects such as bridges, tunnels, crossroads and armaments plants and hold them until the arrival of the leading units of the German Armed Forces."[190] Drawing heavily on men fluent in the languages of Germany's neighbors, the Brandenburgers dressed in enemy uniforms and seized key infrastructure such as bridges during the invasions of Denmark, Norway, the Low Countries, and France.[191] In one instance German commandos posed as Dutch policemen escorting German Army deserters in order to clear a Dutch checkpoint. The Brandenburgers were further aided by local Dutch agents and volunteers from the Dutch National Socialists. In Reims, France, a truckload of secret files from the French Western Army was seized by a German agent posing as a French lieutenant. In Paris, Brandenburgers, posing as Belgian, Dutch, and French refugees, seized the files of French military intelligence headquarters before they could be evacuated.[192]

In Ireland, fears of German agents and fifth columnists persisted throughout the war. In May 1940, Sir Charles Tegart, who had previously advised the Palestine Police, stoked the fears of the new British prime minister, Winston Churchill, reporting that hundreds or even thousands of German agents were infiltrating Ireland to topple the Irish government in preparation for an invasion of Britain.[193] Tegart was but one member of a chorus of voices raising concerns about Ireland. It was not only the British who worried; following the fall of the Netherlands, Irish *Taoiseach* (prime minister) Éamon de Valera too became anxious about German agents. So concerned was he that he appealed to Britain for arms against this potential threat.[194] Worries that German U-boats were being resupplied in the rocky bays of western Ireland never seemed to go away, though they were never substantiated.[195]

Though not privy to all the details, the European public frequently heard about German subversive plots, both real and imagined. As early as 1934, Nazi paramilitary forces were rumored to work with ethnic Germans in Lithuania, in preparation for an imminent invasion.[196] In 1938, eighteen Abwehr agents were arrested in the United States. When Abwehr activities in the Soviet Union came to light, the German consulates in seven cities were closed.[197] Likewise, in the spring of 1939 nine Nazis were deported from Britain for similar activities.[198] An exposé by German refugees claimed there were forty-eight thousand Nazi agents across Europe; a document seized in Spain and translated into various languages, including English, further outlined German subversive activities. As Dutch historian Louis de Jong explains, "The general public, perhaps, was not much roused, but in police and judicial circles and in the secret services of many countries the publications were seriously studied."[199] Gubbins was among those who took notice.[200]

In the United States, Col. William Donovan, of subsequent OSS fame, and Edgar Mowrer, a journalist, authored a short work titled *Fifth Column Lessons for America*, in which they conclude that "no amount of genius would have accomplished what the Germans accomplished in so short a time without two [nonmilitary] elements. These were the Germans abroad and sympathizers in the victim countries."[201] Incredible actions were attributed to the tens of thousands of German operatives said to be in the field: "Germans disguised as Polish soldiers spread panic through the villages . . . [and] issued false instruction[s]. . . . Others . . . signaled objectives and instructions to German air men." In Norway and the Netherlands, German soldiers reportedly hid in the holds of civilian vessels in order to seize their objectives. In Denmark, German agents "by their constant threats and interference with the Danish Government, had produced a state of mind bordering on terror that contributed to drive any thought of real resistance from the Danish mind." In the Netherlands, "the 120,000 [German residents] occupied their leisure in propaganda and espionage for the Nazis. . . . When Hitler finally struck, the 120,000 turned on their placid hosts with the fury of dervishes and, where they could, shot them down in cold blood."[202] The effect of such clandestine efforts seemed nearly super-human.

Certainly not all of these allegations were true. As de Jong demonstrates, a great many of the reports of the German "fifth column" were bogus.[203] But perception matters a great deal; de Jong's comment on the Austrian Nazis' planned insurrection of 1938 may be applied more broadly: "People didn't worry about whether the Vienna rebels . . . had acted on direct orders from Berlin. . . . The complicity of the German *Reich* was evident."[204] This presumed knowledge was significant in two important ways. Firstly, it inspired fear. If Britain was threatened by German subversion—and by 1940 everyone agreed she was—some sort of response was needed. Irregular activities, ultimately centered in SOE, proved part of that response. Secondly, German subversion—real or imagined—provided an inspiration. "You will remember," Gubbins reminded the Danish-English Society after the war,

> in the years 1938 and 1939 and even earlier the success of the Nazi party and leaders in using unorthodox methods to subvert governments, to penetrate disputed territory, to created "fifth columns," to attack their potential adversaries from within so as to weaken resistance to eventual aggression. We were late in Britain in appreciating the immense effect of these activities but just before the War a very small nucleus of people were taken aside and told to study what actions of this nature could be planned and undertaken to harass Germany in the event of War.[205]

Gubbins and the men of MI(R) indeed studied. Before long war would be upon them and their ideas tested in practice.

Conclusion

In the late summer of 1939, Gubbins's days with MI(R) were drawing to a close, having authored the *AGW* and the *PLH*, leaving his intellectual stamp upon Holland's young organization. Although formally remaining with MI(R) for a time, Gubbins spent nearly the first year of World War II serving elsewhere: with the military mission to Poland, leading an Independent Company in Norway, and then planning for the defense of Britain itself with guerrilla forces. By the time he returned to MI(R) in 1940, it had evolved into the new SOE.

Gubbins was most certainly a man of his times who drew upon lessons available from a variety of sources. That most of the ideas he propagated while at MI(R) were not originally his own hardly detracts from the achievement of recognizing examples that proved useful and distilling them to a brief set of principles and guidelines.

In spite of this achievement, it should be mentioned that two notable subjects are omitted from the *AGW* and the *PLH*. Firstly, nowhere does Gubbins mention the aerial resupply of guerrillas, an essential aid to the resistance in both Europe and Asia during the Second World War; airpower is only ever mentioned as a *threat* to guerrillas.[206] Gubbins's gaze may simply have been too historical, looking only to existing examples. However, he or another member of MI(R) proposed in 1940 that "the ideal would be for the [guerrilla] force to . . . be supplied by air enroute, and . . . receive by parachute the explosives, special weapons, etc, which it requires."[207] Thus, any deficiency in Gubbins's conception of supply was swiftly corrected. Secondly, Gubbins does not directly address the question of reprisals that partisans and civilians were likely to face. Mackenzie comments that "General Gubbins's recollection is that this was deliberately omitted, as a point best passed by in silence."[208] A careful reading of the *PLH*, however, reveals a clear, if understated, grasp of this problem; Gubbins reminds those resisting, for example, that "as your activities develop, the enemy will become more and more ruthless in his attempts to stop you."[209] It was a reality with which SOE had to grapple.

CHAPTER 5

GESTATION OF GUBBINS'S THINKING AND THE CREATION OF SOE

Between August 1939 and November 1940, Colin Gubbins served in three different capacities that provided valuable experience, though none of the three could, in a strict sense, be described as leading a guerrilla force. At the outbreak of the war, Gubbins served with a British liaison mission in Poland, where he witnessed Nazi Germany's offensive power and also began fostering relationships with what soon became the Polish General Staff in exile, Britain's essential link to the Polish resistance. Gubbins then helped organize and lead the Independent Companies, small units intended to conduct guerrilla raids, in Norway. Although the vision was not fully realized and the new units were largely occupied with conventional operations, Gubbins gained firsthand experience training irregular forces and attempting to employ them in an asymmetric fashion against the German Army. If the Independent Companies' irregular aspirations were overtaken by events, Gubbins's third assignment, the Auxiliary Units, were truly a guerrilla force, though they never saw action. These highly secret units were intended to conduct sabotage against a German invasion of Britain, should it occur. Taken collectively, these three roles gave Gubbins considerable experience to complement the research and writing he had done at MI(R).

Britain's failure to predict and halt Germany's advance into western Europe left leaders shaken and willing to consider alternatives. In July 1940, after several configurations were proposed, a new organization, SOE, was created within the Ministry of Economic Warfare, incorporating Section D and, in time, MI(R). The new organization inherited many of the qualities and concepts that had characterized its two predecessors. Although Gubbins was not present at the creation of SOE, he joined shortly thereafter. Moreover, the first few months of SOE's existence were quite rocky, with the consequence that the organization remained in flux and open to his influence when Gubbins arrived. In addition to bringing his ideas and firmness of purpose, Gubbins also brought personnel. Many of these individuals were people Gubbins knew from Poland, the Independent Companies, or the Auxiliary Units; most of them had attended MI(R)'s early training program, which Gubbins himself had designed.

No. 4 Military Mission

Throughout the summer of 1939, Gubbins traveled to several countries in central and eastern Europe, which Germany appeared to be threatening. On 19 August he returned to London from his second visit to Warsaw, only to find that plans were being made for another trip. With intelligence suggesting that a German invasion of Poland would come by the beginning of September, military missions were planned to Poland and Romania.[1] Holland wanted to make sure these had an MI(R) element and he received permission from the CIGS to call up certain MI(R) personnel without waiting for a general mobilization.[2] Gubbins later explained, "My appointment to Warsaw in the event of War had been arranged in July with the D.M.I., so that I had two roles, the official one as Chief Staff Officer and the unofficial 'to stimulate and assist the Poles and Czechs in Guerilla warfare.'"[3] Gubbins was chosen for this unique role because he was one of the few who could fill it: he had the conventional credentials—including experience as an ADC and training at Staff College—to be a chief of staff but was also an acknowledged guerrilla warfare expert who had been with Holland since GS(R) days.[4]

The military mission—designated No. 4—was led by Gen. Adrian Carton de Wiart, whom Gubbins had met in France many years before. Never a man for peacetime service, Carton de Wiart had retired from the British Army and settled in eastern Poland, where he was a long-term guest on the estate of a Polish prince. Thus, when war seemed imminent, he was already in Poland, meeting with the Polish military in Warsaw before the other mission personnel ever left Britain.[5]

Gubbins and the rest of the party traveled the long way round Europe, across France and the Mediterranean, then to Egypt and Greece, and finally through Romania to Poland. They crossed the border on the night of 2/3 September, the Germans having invaded on the first.⁶ Earlier in the year Holland had written that "foreign General Staffs might be encouraged to leave behind selected and trained parties of troops to act as centres for local guerilla activities."⁷ But Gubbins had highlighted "the importance to Poland of *preparations* for guerilla warfare," in light of "the veritable withdrawals her armies will be compelled to carry out in the early stages of a war."⁸ Now that Polish forces were collapsing around them, however, there was little the MI(R) contingent could do to organize guerrilla bands. Nor was there much the rest of the military mission could offer the Poles. The result was depressing. Gubbins describes the scene the day after arriving in Poland:

> Lunch had been arranged for us at a hotel in Lyublin and we sat inside, still wearing our civilian clothes as our country was not at war. While having our meal we heard on the radio that Britain had declared war on Germany. I immediately ordered my officers and men to put on their uniforms and we went out into the town square to rejoin our buses. The square was completely filled by a huge crowd, cheering and shouting "England is beside us. Long live England." We were each of us lifted bodily into the air and carried into our buses already loaded with flowers. My heart was filled with sadness and foreboding.⁹

Shortly thereafter Gubbins made contact with Carton de Wiart.¹⁰ The Poles were in desperate straits and with the fighting quite fluid there was little concrete information. Gubbins dispatched one of his men, Tommy Davies, via the Baltic States to London to personally explain to the CIGS just how bad the situation was.¹¹ Gubbins and the men of MI(R) were unable to do much in the way of organizing guerrillas. To have brought up the matter of stay-behind parties before the fall of Poland might have appeared defeatist; besides, the German campaign unfolded far too quickly for joint planning.¹² The speed of the German advance was helped by the drought conditions that summer, which meant that rivers ran quite low and did not provide the obstacles that Polish plans expected.¹³ On the morning of 5 September the Polish General Staff—the British military mission's counterpart for liaison activities—left Warsaw for Lukow, fifty miles to the southeast. This was only the first of several moves. The military mission purchased two cars and a truck, struggling at each relocation to find out where the rapidly moving General Staff was going next and to follow it.¹⁴

At one point Gubbins was able to give a spare wireless set to Gen. Wacław Stachiewicz, the Polish chief of staff, who was out of touch with some elements of the army. But by and large there was little Carton de Wiart or the mission could do to stem the German tide.[15] Swift action by the RAF, the support Britain was best positioned to take at the moment, was beyond the military mission's authority. Meanwhile, General Stachiewicz freely confessed he lacked knowledge of the battle. A Polish artillery major encountered by Gubbins admitted that his unit had no guns, only their sidearms.[16] With the Red Army's crossing of Poland's eastern frontier on 17 September, any hope of staving off defeat evaporated.[17] Peter Wilkinson, a member of the mission, recalled that when Gubbins received official word from the Polish General Staff of the Soviet invasion, "he . . . made a moving little speech in French in which he expressed his sympathy for the Polish predicament and his admiration for the courage with which the army had fought against overwhelming odds. He promised that Britain would fight on until Poland was once more free and its territory restored. After this we shook hands and took our leave."[18] The No. 4 Military Mission stayed in Poland for a short while longer before making its way across the Romanian border with countless Polish refugees. Most of the mission's members quickly returned to Britain by sea, though Carton de Wiart and Gubbins stayed in Bucharest for an extra week to write up the official report.[19] The report's descriptions of blitzkrieg went unheeded, and those individuals mentioned in dispatches were ungazetted until the British Expeditionary Force was encircled by the Germans at Dunkirk in the following year.[20] It was a thoroughly sobering experience.

The Coming of War in Britain

Meanwhile, with the coming of war, Section D moved its headquarters to the countryside, sharing the widespread fear that London would soon be leveled by aerial bombardment. The Frythe, a Victorian neogothic private residential hotel in Hertfordshire, was requisitioned on 1 September, the very day the Germans invaded Poland. In spite of the war's advent, a spirit of amateurism, even levity, still prevailed at Section D. The entire section lived at the Frythe, with wealthy members supplying their own cars for transport. Darts and table tennis were common forms of diversion.

The only security incident in the autumn of 1939 was a bizarre series of episodes involving "ghostly whistling, banshee wailing and stealthy prowling round the house." At one point an army sentry was assaulted by an assailant who "escape[d] down 'spook alley' with a gleeful cackle of eery laughter."[21] The culprit? The hotel's manager, who had fiercely opposed the requisitioning of the property and was trying to scare away his new guests.[22]

With the coming of war, Holland decided to move himself and MI(R) back to the War Office. As Gubbins explained, Holland "had no faith in 'D' [Grand], with his wild cat and fantastical schemes, never getting down to brass tacks and specific achievements."[23] Nevertheless, cooperation continued between the two organizations. Wilkinson explains that, although he was employed by MI(R) in early 1940, he spent as much time at Section D, where he "was given a desk in their Balkan section and allotted the secret symbol DH/M."[24]

In addition to the MI(R) component of the No. 4 Military Mission, Holland and his staff were busy elsewhere. As Gubbins put it, Holland believed his "function was to produce ideas, work them up to a practical stage and then cast them off to grow under their own steam."[25] A prime example of this concept came in the autumn of 1939. Even before there were any British prisoners, Holland recognized that there would be soon, and so he began to consider how they might escape from the enemy and evade pursuers, making their way home. Norman Crockatt was brought on board as general assistant; the project rapidly grew, until Holland cast it off all together to become an independent agency, MI9, the War Office's escape and evasion service.[26] Similar schemes involving deception and raids into Italian-occupied Ethiopia were also spun off once they became too big for MI(R) (see chapter 7).[27] In December 1939 plans were begun to send an MI(R) mission to Finland and some secret preliminary scouting was conducted in Norway and Sweden in February and March 1940; these efforts, however, ended when the Finns capitulated to the Russians in March and Germany invaded Norway in April.[28]

While Holland was thinking up clever projects and the men of Section D were chasing ghosts, Gubbins was soon back on the continent. Although he and Carton de Wiart arrived in London on 4 October, there was no work for them there, the leadership of the British Expeditionary Force going to France already having been chosen. But Holland had other ideas: he sent Gubbins to Paris, as head of a reconstituted No. 4 Military Mission. The Polish and Czechoslovak General Staffs were both there in exile, so it was the obvious place from which to establish contact with underground forces in the two occupied countries. Gubbins left for Paris on 20 November.[29]

In theory the reconstituted mission was in Paris to liaise with the General Staffs; in practice, it was there to coordinate partisan warfare, something about which their French hosts were rather more skeptical.[30] Gubbins did not even try to visit the Polish or Czechoslovak training units under French command, nor did he visit the Polish divisions held in reserve behind the Maginot Line; the French would not have been pleased.[31] Further complicating the mission's work was the fact that Section D was also in Paris. A nominal division of labor was worked out between the two British agencies: MI(R) liaised with the French military, while Section D was responsible for work with the Deuxième Bureau, France's external intelligence agency.[32] This was quite natural, each working with the opposite of its own parent agency (though the Deuxième Bureau was under the auspices of the French military, unlike the civilian Foreign Office, which oversaw SIS). It was also, however, a gross oversimplification: Gubbins's primary contact was not a Frenchman at all, but his friend Stanislav Gano, who was now the deputy chief of Polish military intelligence.[33]

The Polish Home Army, the new underground force forming under Nazi occupation, had agents in Budapest and Bucharest. If MI(R) could get material aid to these agents, they could then get it into Poland. Alas, MI(R) had no means of getting material even to the Balkans. Section D, however, had numerous courier lines flung across the region and MI(R) utilized these. At first, cooperation was difficult: Gubbins could not provide Grand with the precise details of what was to be shipped; Grand refused to go forward without such information and jealously guarded the details of Section D's capabilities. To break the impasse, Gubbins sent Peter Wilkinson to work directly with the Balkan unit of Section D. Although MI(R) was eventually able to use Section D's channels, they could not handle the volume of material the Poles needed.[34]

Relations with the Czechoslovaks were also fraught, though for different reasons. The Czechoslovak government in exile resided in Britain but was not yet recognized by the British government in late 1939. That made any contact problematic. But further complicating MI(R)'s efforts to work with the Czechoslovaks was the fact that the commander of their intelligence service, Col. František Moravec, was working with SIS, which—for understandable security reasons—was not keen on sharing him. So in December 1939 Gubbins and Wilkinson simply got in direct touch with the commander-in-chief of the Czechoslovak Army, then resident in Paris. The Czechoslovak General Staff was in communication with the Czechoslovak Home Army via channels independent of Moravec, and so Gubbins was able to get in touch with the Home Army without infringing on SIS's authority.[35]

Gubbins's time with the No. 4 Military Mission came to an end once and for all on 23 March 1940, when he left Paris for London, to plead for a dramatic increase in the supplies given to the Poles; in his stead he left Wilkinson in charge.[36] Under Wilkinson the mission grew, with representatives in Budapest, Belgrade, and Bucharest who reported directly to him and met with Polish and Czechoslovak agents in the various Balkan capitals.[37] If Gubbins's time in Paris was marked by political frustrations and limited resources, it was a fitting summation of the mission's work, which served to remind him and others that supporting irregular warfare waged by resistance forces would be a formidable task.

The Independent Companies

On 9 April 1940, Germany invaded Denmark and Norway; in response, MI(R) was asked to plan amphibious raids against Norway's western coast.[38] Gubbins concluded that a typical infantry battalion was too large for such purposes, while a regular infantry company was too small; furthermore, neither was properly trained or equipped for autonomous operations.[39] Thus he settled upon the concept of an "independent company," small enough to engage in mobile harassment action but designed to operate on its own for up to a month, away from the ship that served as its floating base.[40] Four days after the German invasion, Holland submitted a proposal to the CIGS, recommending that elements of the Territorial Army (TA) should be trained for raiding operations.[41] The demands of wartime led to the rapid realization of MI(R)'s vision.

Gubbins's experience with the Independent Companies was not exactly practice in guerrilla warfare. In their conception the companies were designed "to act as guerillas and by successful action gradually to raise the morale of the local population and to organize from it local guerilla bands."[42] However, in practice they had few connections to the Norwegian resistance, and once the Independent Companies were placed within a conventional formation midway through the campaign, even the mobility envisioned for them was lost. Nevertheless, Gubbins's Norwegian experience was significant in that it gave him additional battlefield experience, this time against the German Army. Moreover, his brief service broadened his base of knowledge regarding small-scale irregular operations.

Holland's initial proposal of 11 April was quickly accepted and expanded. On 20 April the Independent Companies were formally approved: as many as ten companies would be raised from volunteers in Britain who had completed their training and were awaiting deployment to France.[43] Each company, composed of 20 officers and 270 other ranks, included its own engineers and signals, light machine guns, two-inch mortars, and an antitank gun.[44] As historian Eric Morris observes, "Gubbins was the obvious choice to command this scratch force," having served in a wide variety of relevant positions.[45] By 25 April the No. 1 Independent Company was filled with volunteers from the 52nd (Lowland) Infantry Division and made its way to Scotland, where it met up with Gubbins and its new staff.[46] Training was grueling, bringing TA soldiers up to regular infantry standards and then teaching them such necessary skills for irregular operations as night marches by compass, slitting throats, and sabotage.[47]

The Independent Companies were not MI(R)'s only project in Norway. Four MI(R) officers had just arrived as "assistant consuls" when the Germans invaded; one was captured and the other three only escaped with difficulty. On 13 April an MI(R) party under Capt. Peter Fleming—whose plans in China had been curtailed—landed in Namsos to conduct reconnaissance. A military mission to Norway—designated No. 10—was organized and dispatched via Stockholm on 16 April. MI(R) officers were included in the mission, which had the task of liaising with Norwegian forces and encouraging guerrilla warfare. The mission harried the German invaders as best it could, but its remnants were forced to cross into neutral Sweden on 12 May. Three days after the military mission was dispatched, Major Jefferis, Gubbins's coauthor of *How to Use High Explosives*, landed in Norway with a sergeant and one thousand pounds of explosives for demolition purposes. He was training Norwegians at Lillehammer in demolitions when the city was overrun; he fought as an infantryman with the retreating British force until evacuation on 28 April.[48]

On 2 May Gubbins received orders from Gen. Hugh Massy, commander of the British Expeditionary Force going to Norway, to command SCISSORSFORCE, a formation composed of Nos. 1, 3, 4, and 5 Independent Companies, assisted by eight Indian Army officers with experience in mountain warfare on the North-West Frontier.[49] The Germans had captured the northern port of Narvik early in the campaign, but, cut off by Britain's Royal Navy, this garrison was isolated from other German forces in Norway. Gubbins was given the task of keeping the Germans out of Bodø, Mo, and Mosjøen, three key towns straddling the Arctic Circle just south of Narvik, preventing the Germans from unifying their positions.[50] His orders stated he was to "ensure that all possible steps by demolition and harrying tactics to impede any German advance [be taken]. . . . Your companies . . . should not attempt to offer prolonged frontal resistance but should endeavour to maintain themselves on the flanks of the German forces and continue harrying tactics against their lines of communication."[51] It was a task with which he was quite familiar, having written about it only months before.[52] The commander of No. 1 Independent Company was specifically told to "get to know the country intimately. Make use of locals but do not trust too far. Use wits and low cunning."[53] Two days after receiving orders, Gubbins and his men sailed for Norway.[54]

SCISSORSFORCE faced stiff resistance as soon as it arrived. No. 1 Independent Company unsuccessfully engaged in fierce street-by-street fighting against an unexpected German amphibious landing near Mo. Mosjøen, the southernmost of Gubbins's three charges, was cut off and Gubbins chose to withdraw Nos. 4 and 5 Independent Companies to Bodø, rather than try to push the Germans back into the sea, a move consistent with his earlier admonition that irregular forces ought not engage in sustained contact with the enemy, except "in overwhelming strength and thus sure of success."[55] In spite of these setbacks, the Independent Companies had some opportunities to carry out their assigned role, when, for example, Capt. J. H. Prendergast, Indian Army, led members of No. 5 Independent Company and Norwegian forces in a successful ambush of German forces on the morning of 9 May. Nevertheless, the Independent Companies' intended role as harassing light infantry was compromised by the heavy ammunition and extensive food supplies they were expected to carry.⁵⁶ It was a problem Gubbins had anticipated when he advocated light equipment and cautioned that a conventional infantry battalion was too unwieldy.⁵⁷ Moreover, the collapse of organized Norwegian resistance cut short the opportunities for the companies to play their assigned role.⁵⁸ Unable to carry out their irregular mission, the companies were instead mostly "squandered in main force operations" against a German foe that advanced over 150 miles of difficult terrain in a single week.⁵⁹

Regrouping further north, SCISSORSFORCE was placed by General Massy under the command of 24th (Guards) Infantry Brigade and given an essentially conventional role. This organizational shift had major implications for Gubbins when 24th Brigade's commander was forced to withdraw the following day, due to an attack on his ship. This left acting Colonel Gubbins the most senior member of the unit and he assumed command.⁶⁰ The ensuing operations were not glorious. Gubbins was forced to relieve Lt. Col. T. B. Trappes-Lomax of his command of the 1st Battalion Scots Guards for refusing orders and retreating before the enemy.⁶¹ The guards and Independent Companies defended Bodø for a time, though they were hammered by German forces and evacuated before the city fell.⁶²

On the night of 31 May/1 June, Gubbins and the last of the men under his command were withdrawn from Norway. In spite of the setbacks, Gubbins acquitted himself well, leaving him one of the few officers to come out of the campaign with his reputation intact.⁶³ For his service he was awarded the Distinguished Service Order. Gen. Claude Auchinleck, who had overall command of the ground forces in Norway, commented in his final report that "the swiftness and efficiency with which the evacuation was carried out reflects great credit on Brigadier Gubbins and his staff." In a private letter to the CIGS, Auchinleck gushed, "Gubbins has, I think, been first-class. Should be a divisional commander or whatever the equivalent may be in the New Army!"⁶⁴ Such praise not only speaks to Gubbins's abilities but also to the opportunities that likely awaited him in the wartime army.

The Auxiliary Units

As Gubbins was evacuating his forces from Norway, a new problem arose: What if Britain itself was invaded? This question was answered, in part, by the Inter-Services Projects Board. Proposed in April 1940, the board had members from the Admiralty, Air Ministry, War Office, Chiefs of Staff, and SIS. It was created with a fourfold purpose:

1. To co-ordinate projects for attacking the enemy by irregular operations.
2. To prevent the lapsing of any project of value.
3. To provide Service planning staffs with advice and intelligence derived from the exchange of ideas between members of the Board.
4. To ensure that the operations of each service were complementary to the others.[65]

On 27 May the board agreed to raise a force that would operate in close cooperation with the military in order to resist an invasion of Britain.[66] Since Section D and MI(R) were the experts on sabotage and subversion, they were given the task of raising the nucleus of a resistance force, under the aegis of General Headquarters Home Forces.[67] A division of labor between MI(R) and Section D was agreed for the project: MI(R) would be responsible for those waging guerrilla warfare, while Section D officers would be attached to the dozen regional civil commissioners or (once an area came under martial law) the local military commander. These Section D officers arranged headquarters storehouses and carried out a whispering campaign to encourage resistance among the general population.[68]

Separate plans for MI(R) and Section D elements of these home defense units were curtailed in July 1940. An internal SOE history, which appears to have its roots in Section D, argues that the merger of these elements resulted from a decision that civilians should not carry out sabotage, for fear of enemy reprisals.[69] However, historian David Lampe contends, in agreement with Wilkinson and Astley, that Section D's overenthusiastic efforts raised the suspicions of local military commanders, who complained to General Headquarters Home Forces.[70] In either case, the Commander-in-Chief Home Forces, Gen. Edmund Ironside—with whom Gubbins had served in Russia—decided that all guerrilla resistance in Britain should be under military control. Thus he created the General Headquarters Auxiliary Units and placed Colin Gubbins—recently returned from Norway—in command.[71] As Gubbins explained, the new unit's mission was "to act offensively on the flanks and in the rear of any German troops who may obtain a temporary foothold in this country." Secondarily, "the other role is Intelligence."[72] A handful of men from Section D's operations were incorporated into the new "Aux Units," as they came to be called, though most were "told simply that their organization no longer existed."[73]

The Aux Units were anticipated somewhat by Gen. Andrew "Bulgy" Thorne, commander of the XII Corps in southeastern England. Concluding that the German Navy would be able to carry out no more than large-scale raids, and not a full invasion, Thorne believed stout defense of England's coasts could prevent the enemy from gaining a beachhead.[74] In the summer of 1940 he requested from the War Office someone who could organize and train a group of men to stay behind enemy lines and cause havoc in the rear, should the Nazis invade.[75] Accordingly, Peter Fleming, who had already done work for MI(R) and was recently returned from Norway, was sent. Beginning with a handful of TA soldiers, two aviators with a wireless set, and sapper subaltern Mike Calvert, Fleming set out recruiting locals and organizing the XII Corps's Observation Unit, a stay-behind resistance force. He and his men mined bridges, laid booby traps, and constructed underground hideouts for future resisters.[76] The unit was eventually rolled into the Auxiliary Units, becoming their local branch in Kent.[77]

In organizing his small staff, Gubbins drew upon men he knew from Poland and Norway.[78] These dozen men—known as intelligence officers to disguise the real nature of their work—were each responsible for a sector of the British coast, where they would organize cells of about half a dozen local men.[79] Ironside gave Gubbins authority to draw personnel from regimental depots to assist in training the Auxiliary Units.[80] Many members of the cells themselves came from the Home Guard, particularly veterans of the Great War. All were men who had extensive experience out of doors and knew their area well, as Gubbins had insisted since his time at MI(R).[81] Organization was intentionally kept loose; although coordination would at times be useful, tight organization could have been exploited by the Nazis to roll up the entire organization.[82]

Training was carried out at a manor located in the Berkshire Hills, west of London. Here new recruits were given intensive basic instruction, while some received specialized training in particular tactics or weapons.[83] Instruction was carried out under the sharp eye of an Indian Army officer, though Gubbins himself, a former trainer, also took a direct part in instructing new recruits.[84] The Aux Units were given a variety of new weapons and sabotage devices, often before units in the regular army.[85] In addition, they were issued with rubber-soled agricultural boots, allowing for quieter operations, as Holland and Wingate had advocated.[86]

Although the Auxiliaries would have operated when the Allies were on the strategic defensive, whereas resistance forces in Europe ultimately participated in the strategic offensive, the tactics of both were quite similar. The Aux Units emphasized, for example, nighttime movements, studying the habits of enemy posts, and the maintenance of silence, three topics later covered by the SOE syllabus.[87]

Peter Fleming's assessment of the Auxiliary Units was not particularly upbeat. Although they would likely have justified their existence, "reprisals against the civilian population would have put us out of business before long," he later reflected. "In any case, we would have been hunted down as soon as the leaf was off the trees. . . . I doubt if we should have been more than a minor and probably short-lived nuisance to the invaders."[88] Gubbins concedes that "their usefulness would have been short-lived," but he observes that "they were designed, trained and prepared for a particular and imminent crisis."[89] Besides, they cost practically nothing, a virtue SOE would also exhibit, relative to the total cost of the British war effort.[90]

As the war continued and the likelihood of a German invasion receded, increasing numbers of the Auxiliary Units' sharpest members left the organization to apply their expertise to more active work at the new SOE. Not least to make this move was Colin Gubbins. Lampe claims that Gubbins received "his first opportunity to test M.I.(R) theories about modern guerrilla warfare" at the Aux Units.[91] While it is true that the units' function was properly guerrilla, unlike the Independent Companies, their lack of actual combat makes it difficult to call this a proper test of MI(R) theory. Nevertheless, Gubbins here organized and trained a guerrilla force, valuable experience he would finally put to full-fledged use at SOE.

Creation of SOE

Proposals for a New Organization

In spite of intelligence received through the Poles, the German strike into the Low Countries and France in the spring of 1940 caught MI(R) and Section D almost as much by surprise as it did the War Office and SIS.⁹² As a result, Britain's clandestine response was not impressive. Officers from Section D managed to smuggle £500,000 of industrial diamonds out of Amsterdam and £84 million of gold out of Bordeaux; they failed, however, to evacuate Madame de Gaulle from France. MI(R) sabotaged the oil stocks at Gonfreville in Normandy but did little more.⁹³ Courier operations through the Low Countries, carrying propaganda or intelligence, became much less frequent; Italy likewise presented increasing difficulties. The Balkans alone remained open to courier lines, via Cairo, through the summer of 1940.⁹⁴ Although Section D and MI(R) had not halted the Nazi drive west, the prospect of the entire European continent in Nazi hands—with Britain itself on the brink of invasion—was the impetus needed to bring about reform of the clandestine services in order to better conduct sabotage and subversion.⁹⁵

On 25 May 1940, the Chiefs of Staff submitted to the War Cabinet an assessment that if France fell "Germany might still be defeated by economic pressure, by a combination of air attack on economic objectives in Germany and on German morale and the creation of widespread revolt in her conquered territories." Stimulating revolt was "of the very highest importance. A special organization will be required, and plans . . . should be prepared, and all the necessary preparations and training should be proceeded with as a matter of urgency" since otherwise "we should have no chance of contributing to Europe's reconstruction."⁹⁶

The Ministry of Economic Warfare (MEW) had been created in 1939 and was initially seen as a revival of the First World War's Ministry of Blockade, concerned with the economic isolation of Nazi-occupied Europe.⁹⁷ When Churchill came to the premiership, he asked Hugh Dalton to become minister of Economic Warfare in his new coalition cabinet.⁹⁸ Dalton had a high opinion of the ministry, believing it could win the war. However, he wanted to unite its economic work with a political role, creating a single entity conducting both political and economic warfare that could bring down the Nazis. After all, Dalton, a Labourite steeped in international socialism, considered the purpose of economic pressure to be political change in the enemy state; thus, political and economic warfare should be coordinated by a single ministry.⁹⁹

It is unclear how Dalton found out about the existence of Section D and MI(R). Dalton biographer Ben Pimlott suggests that Gladwyn Jebb, then private secretary to Sir Alexander Cadogan, the permanent undersecretary of the Foreign Office, informed him. In any case, almost as soon as he became minister, Dalton began planning how he might bring them into his orbit.[100] On 1 June 1940 he noted cryptically in his diary, "The D plan is being concocted."[101]

Meanwhile, as the British Expeditionary Force was evacuated from Dunkirk, DMI Beaumont-Nesbitt put forward two papers from J. C. F. Holland, which proposed a directorate of Irregular Activities within the War Office that would have "a measure of control" over EH and the more secretive services (i.e., MI5 and SIS), and would also liaise with the Air Ministry, Admiralty, and Foreign Office.[102] Both MI(R) and Section D would be rolled into the new creation.[103] Simultaneously, the Chiefs of Staff were working on other plans, and on 15 June they established Lt. Gen. A. G. B. Bourne, Royal Marines, as commander of Raiding Operations and advisor to the Chiefs of Staff on Combined Operations.[104] Under pressure from Churchill, and against the wishes of the chiefs, this post was superseded by the director of Combined Operations, first filled by Vice-Admiral Roger Keyes.[105] Out of the Independent Companies, Combined Operations built its signature force, the Commandos.[106] Although Combined Operations took up some of the raiding duties that had been previously discussed, as a purely military organization its role in subversion was limited. Thus did the need remain for something else.

On 28 June Cadogan circulated a paper summarizing this state of affairs, echoing the proposals given by Holland and affirmed by Beaumont-Nesbitt earlier in the month. Most broadly, Cadogan insisted that sabotage and subversion "should be concentrated under one control." More specifically, he argued that "they should probably be divorced from SIS, which is more concerned with intelligence, and has enough to do in that sphere." Instead, these functions should be "placed under military authority as an operation of war . . . , the whole thus coming under control of the DMI. If possible, the staff should be housed in the War Office." Under Cadogan's plan, Section D would be "amalgamate[d]" into MI(R); this would not be a merger of equals.[107] There was little support for Section D; as Foot explains, "Even more than MI R it had managed to antagonise a considerable number of established authorities, British and allied, whose help might have been of value had they been more tactfully approached."[108] Under Cadogan's plan "the DMI would . . . be responsible for (1) sabotage, (2) subversive propaganda, and (3) to some extent, propaganda in all countries." The funding, however, remaining secret, "would have to . . . be paid through the Director of the SIS."[109] Cadogan recommended that the DMI should be *jointly* responsible not only to the War Office, but also to the Foreign Office and the Ministry of Information.[110] Nevertheless, it is worth underscoring that he—the permanent undersecretary of the Foreign Office—was willing to invest considerable authority in the War Office and to fund it from the SIS, ultimately part of his own organization. Cadogan's commitment to sabotage reform ran deep enough that he was willing to lose this interministerial turf battle.

Dalton, on the other hand, was fiercely opposed to the plan. "It proposes to give too much to [the] D.M.I.," he wrote in his diary.[111] A few days before Cadogan's proposal, he recorded his desire to have an organization with civilian and military branches, led by a soldier jointly responsible to the MEW and the War Office.[112] Now he wanted it "under [Clement Attlee], with me doing a good deal of it."[113] The consistent theme, in spite of this vacillation, was Dalton's own role. Cadogan complained, "Dalton [is] ringing up hourly to try to get a large finger in the Sabotage pie."[114] In spite of broad agreement in favor of Cadogan's proposal, Dalton was adamant in discussions with his colleagues that while "war from without" could be waged by soldiers, subversive "war from within" would be "better conducted by civilians."[115] He was desperate to get the new organization within his ministry.

Dalton's relentless lobbying, which exasperated so many of his colleagues, ultimately paid dividends. Halifax met with the prime minister on 7 July; both agreed to the creation of a new sabotage and subversion organization, merging Section D and MI(R), under Dalton.[116] Cadogan came around a few days later.[117] On 16 July Churchill asked Dalton to take charge of sabotage and subversion.[118] Neville Chamberlain, lord president of the council, acting on the prime minister's authority, signed the paperwork creating "a new organization . . . to co-ordinate all action, by way of subversion and sabotage, against the enemy overseas. . . . This organization will be known as the Special Operations Executive," or, as Churchill affectionately called it, the "Ministry of Ungentlemanly Warfare."[119] Dalton was specified as chairman, "with such additional staff as . . . necessary," allowing him to pull officers from the services. However, Dalton was required to keep the Chiefs of Staff "informed in general terms of his plans, and, in turn, receiv[e] from them the broad strategic picture."[120] On 22 July the War Cabinet gave its blessing, finalizing the new creation. The meeting minutes noted that "it would be very undesirable that any Questions in regard to the Special Operations Executive should appear on the Order Paper" of the Commons.[121] The organization would remain entirely secret throughout the duration of the war.[122]

Throughout the discussions, Britain's political leaders looked to past and contemporary examples, as had Holland and Gubbins. Dalton, for example, argued in a letter to Halifax that "we have got to organize movements in enemy-occupied territory comparable to the Sinn Fein movement in Ireland, to the Chinese Guerillas now operating against Japan, to the Spanish Irregulars who played a notable part in Wellington's campaign or—one might as well admit it—to the organizations which the Nazis themselves have developed so remarkably in almost every country in the world."[123] The prime minister had long been intrigued by irregular warfare. As a young man Churchill had observed the Cuban War of Independence and particularly admired the way the guerrillas used intelligence to enhance the effectiveness of their limited forces.[124] He likewise observed the Second Anglo-Boer War at very close range—including capture by and escape from the Boers, giving him personal experience operating behind enemy lines.[125]

In the mythology that has grown up around SOE, Churchill's role in its creation and his uttering—according to Dalton—of the famous phrase "set Europe ablaze" have taken on legendary proportions. In parliament he had long been a supporter of intelligence, and his role in the creation of SOE was certainly important, but the original leadership came from Grand and Holland; Gubbins, Beaumont-Nesbitt, and others provided assistance in the development of what would become SOE.[126] Even so, serious historians continue to fall prey to the romance of Churchill as founder of the organization. John Keegan, for example, describes SOE as "Churchill's scheme" and "his conception."[127] Credit where credit is due: SOE was not Churchill's brainchild.[128]

SOE's Early Development

In late July and into August, the workaday details of SOE began to fall into place. Dalton was given control of Section D and the secret propaganda wing of EH.[129] Meanwhile, the open propaganda wing of EH was left at the Ministry of Information, for the time being.[130]

The chief of SIS was apparently not even informed of the creation of SOE—and the removal of Section D from his sphere—until three weeks after the fact.[131] For a time, MI(R) continued to live an independent existence, though its eventual incorporation into the new SOE was all but inevitable.[132] Gladwyn Jebb, who held the post of assistant undersecretary at MEW, became Dalton's de facto lieutenant for sabotage and subversion.[133]

By the end of July, SOE was organized into three branches. The secret propaganda operations of EH were established as SO1, under Rex Leeper. SO2, created from Section D, was responsible for operations. Finally, SO3 was responsible for research and planning. It was organized along regional and country lines, following the pattern of a similar research unit at MI(R). SO3 was quickly swamped with paperwork, however, and never functioned properly; it was soon absorbed into SO2.[134] SO1 was never an integrated part of SOE; Leeper was twelve years senior to Jebb, making oversight difficult. In November 1940, SO1 moved its headquarters from London to Bedfordshire, creating a physical division in addition to the bureaucratic one. Thus, SOE was an organization with two separate functions: sabotage and propaganda. The unified concept of "subversion," encompassing both, had been vigorously promoted by Dalton but was stillborn.[135] In December 1940 Dalton demanded that the Ministry of Information transfer the rump of EH—its open propaganda wing— to SOE. He lost the ensuing battle and in August 1941 EH's two branches were reunited as the Political Warfare Executive (PWE), under a committee composed of representatives of the Ministry of Information, the MEW, and the Foreign Office.[136] SOE's active role in propaganda was over.

On 28 August 1940 Sir Frank Nelson was named first executive head of SOE by Dalton. A former Bombay merchant who had served with the Bombay Light Horse and as a military intelligence officer during World War I, Nelson then served in the House of Commons as a Conservative before also conducting intelligence work for SIS out of the Basel consulate at the beginning of the Second World War.[137] When Nelson arrived, Grand remained within SOE as his deputy.[138] Nelson said he was impressed by Grand; however, he complained to Jebb that the organization he inherited had "no project anywhere near completion" and needed a "radical overhaul" and "drastic reorganizing on economic grounds alone." Not surprisingly, Nelson recommended that Grand be placed "outside the organisation."[139] Dalton, who referred to Grand in his diary as "King Bomba," believed him disloyal to the new organization and decided to remove him on 18 September 1940.[140] That same day Dalton sent the following message to Grand:

> I have given further thought to the arrangements concerning the D organisation and have reached the conclusion, with regret, that, under the re-organisation on which I have now decided, there will be no further opportunity for the use of your services. I must, therefore, ask you to take such leave as is due to you as from September 20th, and to consider yourself, as from that date, no longer a member of the D organisation. I am sending copies of this letter to Sir Alexander Cadogan, General Beaumont-Nesbitt, CD and C.[141]

Jebb contended this was done with good reason since, under Grand's leadership, Section D had "spent much of its time conducting subversive operations less against the enemy than against ... MI(R)."[142] Many of Grand's men appear to have resigned or been forced out; although some veterans of Section D were incorporated into the new SOE, their numbers were few.[143]

On 2 October 1940, MI(R) was officially dismantled, its assets migrating to SOE.[144] Holland's departure did not cause the fireworks that Grand's did, as he went on to serve as a major general in the Mediterranean Theater and was made a Knight of the Bath for his efforts.[145]

Gubbins at SOE

In November 1940, Gubbins was seconded to SOE at the personal request of Dalton. His arrival was certainly significant; Jebb comments that "the real motive force in the machine [SOE] always seemed to me to be Colin Gubbins."[146] Wilkinson and Astley argue that "Jebb's incisive mind and exceptionally wide inter-departmental experience, coupled with Gubbins's tenacity and military experience, made them ... a formidable combination" when it came to advancing SOE's mission.[147] Gubbins was offered a promotion to brigadier and higher pay at SOE than in the army, but the new organization hardly offered him the prestige of commanding the brigade or even a division that would have likely come to him by virtue of his performance in Norway. Wilkinson and Astley conclude that "his decision to join SOE can only be attributed to a conviction that, if properly coordinated with regular operations, guerrilla warfare on the mainland of Europe might prove decisive in what might otherwise be a single-handed struggle against Hitler. . . . Gubbins may well have believed that with his unique MI(R) background this is where his duty lay, at any rate for the time being."[148]

On 18 November Gubbins arrived at SO2, bringing his secretary, Margaret Jackson, and a staff officer, Peter Wilkinson, with him from the Auxiliary Units.[149] In December Gubbins was made director of Training and Operations. Admittedly, there were rather few operations to direct at that time, since George Taylor, an Australian from Section D, had specific responsibility outside of Gubbins's jurisdiction for most of the few projects that were actually up and running.[150] Indeed, this was, in many ways, a rather depressing time to join the organization. Although the War Cabinet concluded at the end of September that "the stimulation of the subversive tendencies already latent in most countries" was "likely to prove a valuable contributory factor towards the defeat of Germany," successes were few.[151] A month before Gubbins arrived, SOE made its first attempt at smuggling an agent into France, in this case via torpedo boat. The attempt failed.[152] The first attempt to drop an agent by parachute into the same country also failed in November.[153] Indeed, SOE did not successfully insert an agent into France until 5 May 1941, more than nine months after its creation.[154]

Gubbins explained that, at this time, "SOE was . . . under great pressure to commence operating as soon as possible in order to help maintain the morale of the occupied countries, to try and prevent the Germans making free use for war purpose of the rich countries they had over-run, and to hamper and delay their activities generally wherever possible."[155] "Speed was our guiding principle owing to the perilous position of our country. Improvisation had to be the order of the day."[156] The resources at his disposal were quite limited, however. With regard to his training duties, "there was . . . practically nothing existing, just one explosives school and a dozen officers and civilians." Operations were no better: "There was no contact with anyone in the occupied countries, no wireless, no personnel, no special equipment, no aircraft—in fact—blank. All this had to be built up from scratch."[157] SOE's small size did have its advantages, however. "In the early months of our existence," he explained, "no one was much interested in our activities . . . except the Prime Minister—to spur us on."[158]

In July 1941 SOE produced a paper that outlined the model for future operations, involving two distinct kinds of resistance groups. The first, sabotage groups, were to be quite small for security and were to be recruited and trained by SOE. These were a kind of elite force and would operate in advance of imminent liberation. The second group, secret armies, would be much larger and supported through conduits by SOE; held in reserve until such time as Allied liberation forces were on the offensive, these forces would then attack communications, seize airfields, and produce general disorder in the enemy's rear, forcing him to spread his forces across a wide area.[159] This was a refinement and a natural development of Gubbins's earlier writings. Gubbins had recognized the importance of sabotage in maintaining morale in occupied nations and undermining the enemy occupation; on the other hand, he understood the danger of reprisals and of premature activity.[160] This distinction allowed SOE to carry on a small amount of targeted sabotage without endangering all resistance assets by willy-nilly operations. The distinction does, however, introduce a degree of confusion into historical analysis: the natural inclination is to focus on the activities of the sabotage teams when measuring SOE's success, though support to resistance secret armies was every bit as much an SOE mission.

In his new work Gubbins drew upon his past experiences, not only for concepts, but also for personnel. "I was fortunate," he recalled, "in being able to call in as my key men certain officers who had been with me in Poland at the war's beginning, others who had been with me in the brief Norwegian operations of my Independent Companies, and again others whom I had used to raise and train the Auxiliary Units."[161] Although the new SOE was far more institutionalized than the little GS(R) operation Gubbins had run with Holland, the same spirit of irregularity prevailed. Of the men Gubbins brought in as his cadre, "only two were regulars, and 3 or 4 territorials." The rest had passed through MI(R)'s training program at Caxton Hall. "They were business men with foreign languages and experience, explorers and mountaineers, lawyers with international experience, yachtsmen and even one novelist—but he knew his Europe backwards and was all out for blood."[162]

As SOE grew and Gubbins began to organize larger operations, new challenges arose:

> As and when our operations began to impinge on those of the other services—e.g. ships seized by us in Norway—raids by us on the French coast—it obviously became necessary to co-ordinate our operations with all others. This was done through liaison officers at the three Ministries, and also finally by the Chiefs of Staff Committee where I frequently had to appear in some awe, and even the War Cabinet—when matters reached that level, which, of course, I always hoped they would not.[163]

Gubbins did not see much of Dalton, working more closely with the director of SOE, first Nelson and then his successor, Sir Charles Hambro. Nevertheless, from the interactions they had, Gubbins described Dalton as a man with "immense enthusiasm, & determination to get things moving."[164] Gubbins recalled one occasion when he and Dalton inspected a school in Scotland and Dalton suggested that, rather than taking cars, they walk from one facility to another, across the hills. Rain poured down as they ran the last mile and a half of their journey. In spite of temporarily losing a shoe in the mud, Dalton "talked without stopping as we splashed our way home; he had really enjoyed himself."[165] Although Gubbins admired this zeal, Dalton's left-wing tendencies could be grating, as when he assumed that any skepticism from within SOE was the result of conservative bias against him. Nevertheless, while Dalton loathed businessmen and civil servants, he gave a pass to Gubbins and other soldiers, since he had himself served on the Italian front during the Great War.[166]

Conclusion

Although it is tempting to read a tidy teleological progression onto the development of Gubbins's ideas and the creation of SOE, the path was neither direct nor inevitable. Nevertheless, by the summer of 1941, the ideas that Gubbins had formulated at GS(R), ideas that matured as Gubbins experienced the new battlefields of Europe, found a home in SOE, an organization that was gradually beginning to conduct the operations for which it was created. Gubbins and SOE imparted these resurrected ideas of irregular warfare not only to British agents but also to the Americans and to members of the various national resistance forces through a growing network of training schools, the subject of chapter 6.

CHAPTER 6

SOE TRAINING

SOE's extensive training system, developed under Gubbins, typifies the organization's varied inspirations as well as its widespread impact. Beginning with assets from both MI(R) and Section D, SOE also drew on War Department facilities first established for the Independent Companies. Training personnel came from varied walks of life, many from the distant corners of the empire. They often mirrored, in their personal experience, the experiences and studies of Gubbins, bringing together lessons in irregular warfare from around the globe. This system of schools trained not only agents from SOE and the various occupied nations but also individuals from SIS, the British military, and various Allied nations, including Canada and the United States.

Among the other organizations that SOE trained, none was more important than America's Office of Strategic Services (OSS), whose director, William Donovan, frequently visited Britain and conferred with British leaders. Like Gubbins, Donovan was a decorated soldier who had visited Russia in 1919 and Sudetenland in 1938. Unlike Gubbins, however, Donovan was a career lawyer with strong political connections; where Gubbins's experience was largely with guerrilla warfare, Donovan's leaned more toward espionage, a difference also reflected in the organizations they led. Although the United States had a tradition of irregular warfare on which it might have drawn, OSS was consciously modeled on the British clandestine services and received extensive doctrinal and training support from SOE, particularly at Camp X in Canada.

While Gubbins's first post at SOE was as director of training, in late 1941 he was also given responsibility for operations in western Europe. A few months later he became SOE's deputy director, and in 1943 he became director of SOE. This series of promotions marked the culmination of, not a departure from, his early work. From his earliest days at GS(R), Gubbins had articulated the ideas that later drove SOE. His work in training confirmed this vision and ensured that it was disseminated throughout the organization. By the time he became director, SOE already bore his distinctive stamp.

The SOE Training System

The Schools

Both MI(R) and Section D had training schools before the establishment of SOE. MI(R)'s classes at Caxton Hall have already been mentioned. Section D's school was established in June 1940 in Hertfordshire to train men of various nationalities who could then recruit and train others. Among the four instructors were Guy Burgess and Kim Philby, Soviet spies. The program of training, lasting six weeks, covered both theoretical and practical matters, including explosives, cover, counterespionage, and the use of firearms. The first class, consisting of Norwegians, Belgians, Frenchmen, and a Scot, completed their training on 12 October 1940. Discipline among the French was poor and the site's security was found to be lacking.[1]

Initially, the new SOE obtained permission from the War Office to train its agents at Lochailort, in the wilds of Scotland's western highlands. The training school there had been established by MI(R) for the Independent Companies and now served the Commandos.[2] The problem with this arrangement was that it was usually desirable for SOE to keep groups of different nationalities separated from one another, for security purposes; thus, what SOE needed was not a single school but a network of them. Under Gubbins's orders, the use of several houses in the nearby Arisaig area was acquired.[3] As seen in Section D's requisition of the Frythe in September 1939, government use of private residences during the war was common. With domestic help in short supply, traditional country house living became virtually impossible; the owners of many great houses found that having their home requisitioned for clandestine purposes was a blessing, since the government paid for upkeep.[4]

The system of schools that emerged was organized into several stages. Recruits first attended a preliminary school, usually destination specific, where they received two or three weeks of general military training, emphasizing physical fitness, map reading, and basic use of firearms.[5] A well-stocked bar was always maintained, to test how much students did—or did not—reveal when beguiled by alcohol.[6] Those who passed this initial course then attended one of the paramilitary schools in the Arisaig area for three or four weeks. Here students were trained in mountaineering, small boat work, armed and unarmed combat, and raiding techniques. Weapons instruction included major British, German, Italian, and American weapons. Railway sabotage was practiced against actual tracks and trains.[7] As many as a third of the recruits would fail this course.[8] Those who passed then attended parachute training school at RAF Ringway, outside Manchester. As Gubbins explained, "90% of our personnel went to their destinations in the field by air and parachute, hence the universal parachute training."[9] Although he recognized its necessity, SOE's director of training was not enthusiastic about this component: "Parachuting was then in its infancy—not much fun about it. I never enjoyed it myself nor did the bulk of our personnel." Nevertheless, parachuting was so important to SOE that Gubbins had all his staff jump.[10]

Only after these first three rounds of training were recruits asked if they would be willing to serve in an occupied country; prior to this point, the precise nature of SOE's work was kept secret.[11] Although, in theory, the recruit knew nothing of an essentially sensitive nature, those who failed their training or chose not to continue were often sent to an "Inter-Services Research Bureau Workshop" at Inverlair, Scotland, until any secret knowledge gained had become irrelevant. "The Cooler," as this holding pen was known, implied no treason or moral failing, and students were held only as long as necessary, before being released back to their military units or the civilian world.[12]

Having completed their preliminary, paramilitary, and parachute training, and having been told of their true mission, recruits were finally sent to finishing schools, located in Hampshire, near the village of Beaulieu. These were specific to the intended destination and mission.[13] These month-long courses covered such topics as cover stories, codes, forgery of documents, safe-breaking, enemy uniforms, and other knowledge needed to survive under cover in Axis-controlled territory.[14] Scotland Yard and MI5 assisted with some aspects of this training, explaining police and counterintelligence tactics.[15] Students were never physically harmed, but they were awoken in the dead of night by men in Gestapo uniforms and cross-examined at length; an agent whose cover story could not hold up under questioning from instructors playing dress up could hardly be expected to survive an encounter with the real enemy.[16]

Graduation from the finishing school usually involved a multiday test. Students were organized into small teams and given some sort of mission in the local area, typically the theft of military equipment or the placing of explosives. Often they had to rendezvous with a previously unknown accomplice, who would be known by certain signals. The local police were given rough descriptions of the students and told to be on the lookout. Before the exercise began, students were given a telephone number to memorize; if arrested, it would get them out of jail.[17]

Occasionally agents required additional specialized training, beyond the finishing school. This was provided by specialist schools that taught technical matters such as wireless telegraphy, industrial sabotage, clandestine printing, and advanced boat work.[18] To aid these schools, SOE drew on the knowledge of various experts. "Contact was made with the larger insurance companies," Gubbins explained, "whence we gained invaluable insight and knowledge as to the really vital parts of all types of installations and plants, the parts whose destruction involved their highest loss of profit claims."[19]

SOE's network of schools began in Britain but came to straddle the globe, with facilities in Palestine, Egypt, India, Ceylon, Australia, and Canada. As territory was liberated, new schools were also established in Algeria and Italy.[20] Gubbins frequently visited these schools, and when doing so often wore the Scottish kilt with his uniform, in defiance of army regulations.[21] In total, the SOE schools trained at least 6,810 students, of whom only 480 were British SOE agents; the rest came from sixteen foreign nations, as well as 872 students from Britain's SIS and 172 students from the Special Air Service.[22]

The People

The instructional staff of the training section mirrored the early pioneers of GS(R) and Section D. Many of these men, though not all, had military experience. They came from all walks of life, often from the distant corners of the empire. In many cases they brought with them lessons learned from foreign countries or irregular conflicts. As the war effort progressed, returned agents served as instructors, providing eyewitness descriptions of life in occupied territories.[23]

When Gubbins arrived at SOE's training section, his deputy, Jack Wilson, was already there. His knowledge and support would prove invaluable to Gubbins. Wilson had been deputy head of police in Calcutta, where he had considerable experience in countersubversion activities against Nationalists and Communists, and served under Sir Charles Tegart, who later advised the British administration in Palestine during the Arab Revolt.[24] In addition, Wilson was a friend of Robert Baden-Powell's and extremely active in the international scouting movement. He utilized the lessons of *Scouting for Boys* when training the Armed Police of India, and he later served as the chief instructor of the Boy Scout Training Centre at Gilwell Park, outside London.[25] With such an obvious background he had been recruited into MI(R) in 1940, trained the Independent Companies, and then moved to SOE.[26]

William E. Fairbairn was by far the most famous instructor at SOE's schools. If perhaps more colorful and intense than most, he typified the kind of instructors and recruits that SOE favored. Variously known as Fearless Dan, The Shanghai Buster, or Deacon, he was described by William Cassidy as "a quiet man, with the manners of a priest."[27] Swearing and drinking were unknown to him; in his spare time he never read and appeared to have no intellectual concerns. One of his students described him thus: "Off duty, his conversation was limited to two words: yes and no. . . . All his interest, all his knowledge, all his intelligence—and he was intelligent—concentrated on one subject and one subject only—fighting."[28]

Born in 1885, in Surrey, Fairbairn was one of fourteen children; he was named for the four-time prime minister William Ewart Gladstone. With an elder brother in South Africa and two in the navy, young Fairbairn left an apprenticeship as a leatherworker to join the Royal Marines at the age of fifteen years and ten months.[29] While serving with the legation guard in Seoul, Fairbairn got his first taste of Asian warfare. Since Britain and Japan were allied at the time of the Russo-Japanese War, celebrations were held for each Japanese success. These festivities were an excuse for various competitions, including in bayonet fighting. The Royal Marines prided themselves on their team, of which Fairbairn was a keen member, until they met their Japanese opposite. The British were trounced. "For the first time," he wrote, "we had been hit with the butt of the rifle, tripped and thrown and what was worse SHOUTED at by our opponents. This was not 'cricket.'"[30] Fairbairn did not, however, take the loss sitting down. After a month of practice—using the Japanese methods—the British called for a rematch and won.[31]

In 1907 Fairbairn, having left the Royal Marines, joined the Shanghai Municipal Police (SMP), which was responsible for law enforcement in the city's International Settlement.[32] After being beaten by criminals one day and left for dead, Fairbairn began the study of Asian martial arts; in the years ahead he studied under the leading instructors of the region, eventually becoming the first Caucasian to earn a black belt in jujitsu.[33] Moreover, Fairbairn created his own unarmed fighting system—"Defendu"—which drew upon jujitsu and boxing and was intended for use by members of the SMP. Fairbairn described his new method as offering a "number of admittedly drastic and unpleasant forms of defense but all are justifiable and necessary if one is to protect himself against the foul methods of a certain class."[34] In addition to growing in his personal knowledge of Asian martial arts, Fairbairn's position in the SMP also grew; in 1910 he assumed responsibility for training all SMP recruits: European, Japanese, Sikh, and Chinese. In response to three months of intense rioting, Fairbairn created the Reserve Unit, sometimes known as the Shanghai Riot Squad, a specially trained and equipped mobile unit. It was the first of its kind in the world, pioneering advanced methods of riot and crowd control, as well as handling armed robberies, criminal standoffs, and sniper situations.[35] If serving in the police force of one of the world's roughest cities was not experience enough, Sino-Japanese conflict created new difficulties for Fairbairn and the SMP. In 1932 the Shanghai Municipal Council was forced to declare a state of emergency and in 1937 the city experienced full-scale urban warfare between the Japanese and Chinese. By this time Fairbairn was assistant commissioner of the SMP and had a major role in trying to ensure safety in the middle of this warzone. In one instance he was single-handedly responsible for securing the release of 153 Chinese prisoners—men, women, and children—slated for execution by the Japanese.[36]

In 1940 Fairbairn reached fifty-five, the mandatory retirement age in the SMP. He left with full honors but was not idle for long; within weeks of his arrival back in Britain he was recruited to train his fellow countrymen and commissioned as a captain in the secret service, training MI(R), MI9, the British Commandos, and (when it came into existence) SOE.[37] Fairbairn taught unarmed combat, knife fighting, and pistol shooting. In the streets of Shanghai, he and his colleague Alan Sykes, who also came to work for SOE, had developed a new shooting technique that forewent the old-fashioned and time-consuming methods of duelists in favor of a quick draw and a pair of shots fired from the waist.[38] Likewise, they developed the Sykes-Fairbairn fighting knife, adopted by SOE, the Commandos, the Special Air Service, and America's OSS.[39] In addition to combat techniques, Fairbairn also taught a variety of clandestine skills, such as boarding and leaving moving trains, breaking into houses, and scaling cliffs.[40] As William Cassidy explains, his methods were highly effective: "Stripped of all the unnecessary trappings, his system of unarmed combat made it possible for a person of average strength and skills to meet and win against an opponent trained in the martial arts. His unparalleled experience with knife attacks and attacks with blunt instruments—unlikely to be duplicated in this day and age—provided a sound basis for instruction in the use of or defense against edge weapons, batons and clubs."[41] Fairbairn—and others who served at the fringes of the empire—brought to SOE a recognition of extreme circumstances and the extreme measures for which they call. In due time these lessons would be shared not only with SOE and other British clandestine organizations but with the Americans as well.

The Syllabus

The SOE training syllabus, a collection of outlines and summaries of lectures, was derived from the *AGW*, the *PLH*, and *How to Use High Explosives*, the work Gubbins had coauthored with Jefferis.[42] The syllabus was, however, constantly in flux; as agents returned from the field, they were debriefed and the lessons learned incorporated into the training program.[43] Nevertheless, its essential elements remained the same across the years of the Second World War, and its content, though differing somewhat from one school to the next, was centrally controlled by SOE's training section.[44] The syllabus may be broken into five unequal sections: (1) techniques of clandestine life, (2) enemy countermeasures, (3) propaganda, (4) communications, and (5) paramilitary fieldcraft.[45] Each of these sections echoes Gubbins's own writings, though only the first need be considered, since the general overview it offers prefigures the other four sections.

The first section of the syllabus begins with a description of the "objects and methods of irregular warfare." It notes that the Axis powers exploit "their own, . . . satellite and . . . occupied territories" politically, economically, and strategically. Thus the goal of irregular warfare is to coordinate "spontaneous resistance," since "sporadic risings are useless."[46] Those who participate in irregular warfare should see themselves as "a cog in a very large machine whose smooth functioning depends on each separate cog carrying out its part efficiently."[47] Thus, just as Gubbins's 1939 writings made clear that guerrillas must cooperate with regular forces as part of a larger effort, so too that same message was repeated to SOE agents from the very beginning of their training. The syllabus goes on to explain that the enemy must be fought politically, economically, and strategically, through espionage, propaganda, passive resistance, sabotage, and guerrilla warfare. Targets included "the enemy's morale and that of his collaborators . . . the enemy's man-power and communications . . . [and] material profitable to the enemy."[48] Such widespread attacks would accomplish Gubbins's stated goal of "compelling the enemy to disperse his forces in order to guard his flank, his communications, his detachments, supply depots, etc."[49]

This first section of the syllabus then goes on to discuss seven subtopics: (1) self-protection, including such various issues as security for wireless telegraphy, makeup and disguise, informants, and cover; (2) police methods and countermeasures, a matter more fully covered in the second section, but here discussing police techniques such as surveillance, searches, and interrogation; (3) agent management, including motives, recruiting, and handling; (4) organization of agents into cells; (5) communications, both within and outside a single resistance unit; (6) operations, from passive resistance and subversion of troops to selection of targets for attack; and (7) the emergency period, that is, when an agent first lands in occupied territory and must make contact with a reception committee.[50] Some of these topics correspond to Gubbins's writings more closely than others. He wrote nothing in 1939, for example, about makeup or disguises. One could speculate why Gubbins omitted this topic. Perhaps he considered himself unqualified to write about it; perhaps he thought it would have little relevance for a military organization such as MI(R), which was bound, by the terms of the Hague Convention, to utilize uniforms. Whatever the reason, disguises do not appear in his two guides, nor do management of individual agents or their organization into cells. One could see in these gaps a departure by the SOE syllabus from Gubbins's earlier writings. While the syllabus certainly represents the ideas of the *AGW* and the *PLH*, the case for continuity is easily seen when examining major topics from both periods: countermeasures, communications, and planning attacks.

As discussed earlier, Gubbins had a profound concern for enemy countermeasures, a worry shared by the SOE syllabus. Issues of particular emphasis are similar, including systems of control such as curfews and passports, raids, and penetration by enemy agents.[51] Gubbins observes in the *AGW*, however, that the enemy "will be working usually amidst a hostile populace; without their cooperation his task will be more difficult and will require a larger number of his own men to carry it out."[52] The tension that he anticipated between the occupier and the occupied is more explicitly discussed in the syllabus: "There will always be a conflict . . . between the desire to achieve maximum security through efficient [counterespionage] activity, and the need for the economic and politic life of the country to continue in as efficient and satisfactory a manner as possible. Recognition of this conflict is essential."[53] In other words, an occupier cannot lay down a perfect security net without angering the local population and making utilization of the region's resources cumbersome; spies and saboteurs can exploit the resulting security gaps.

On the matter of communications, Gubbins warns in 1939 that "all means of communication that are open to interception by the enemy must be used with the greatest discretion—i.e. civil postal service, telephone and telegraphs, etc."[54] In contrast, "the passing of information verbally and direct is clearly the safest and in many ways the most reliable means."[55] The syllabus likewise cautions that the mail was "fairly easily investigated by police" and gives a range of measures that should be taken when using it, from codes and secret inks to varied addresses and nondescript paper. In the end, however, "if suspected, do not use [the] post for subversive correspondence."[56] Likewise, the telegraph was "to be used sparingly." Like Gubbins's earlier writings, the syllabus concludes that couriers were "slow but surer than other methods."[57]

One final parallel from this section may suffice to demonstrate the development from the *AGW* and the *PLH* to the wartime training of SOE agents, with regard to both continuity and changes. Appendix 3 to the *PLH*—"Destruction of an Enemy Post, Detachment or Guard"—describes preparations for attacking a target and admonishes guerrillas that "you must get detailed information of the posts in your area."⁵⁸ Twenty-three specific points to observe are listed. The syllabus, covering the same topic, likewise insists that good information must be acquired before an attack and lists nineteen similar points to consider. A majority of the items covered in the syllabus were anticipated in the *AGW* and the *PLH*. The points unique to the syllabus fall into a handful of clearly defined topics. Point (o) asks whether "normal types of errors and accidents in [the target] factory . . . can . . . be reproduced artificially." Point (p) similarly asks about the presence of bottlenecks: "At what point will damage do most harm?" These two clearly represent the kind of technical knowledge gained from insurance companies and manufacturers, knowledge that was conveyed at the specialist schools. Another departure is found in point (r): "Can [landmarks for guiding aircraft] be created or found?"⁵⁹ This interest in the use of airpower by forces friendly to partisans represents less a change in ideas and more a change in battlefield realities. When Gubbins was writing in 1939, the most probable resisters were Poles and Czechoslovaks. British air support to either nation was likely to be extremely limited, due to both the finite range of aircraft and the intense antiaircraft defenses they would encounter while flying over long stretches of German territory. But by September 1943, when this particular form of the lecture was written, British and American forces had captured Sicily (Operation Husky) and were landing on the Italian mainland (Operations Avalanche, Baytown, and Slapstick); thus northern Italy, as well as occupied France and the Low Countries, were now within operational range of Allied aircraft, making it plausible for partisans to direct air strikes. As the war progressed, SOE made small adjustments to Gubbins's ideas, bringing them in line with the latest developments; however, the essential concepts of his 1939 writings remained at the heart of the SOE syllabus.

Teaching the Americans

"Wild Bill" Donovan

On 11 July 1941 the euphemistically titled Office of the Coordinator of Information (COI) was created. Unlike SOE, the COI's existence was not secret, though the new organization's stated purpose was simply to collect and organize information, masking its true mission of espionage, propaganda, and subversion.⁶⁰ In time this new organization, under the leadership of Bill Donovan, would become the OSS. At the beginning of its history, "Donovan was the OSS and the OSS was Donovan."[61]

William Joseph Donovan was born in 1883 into an Irish American family in Buffalo, New York, and studied law at Columbia College, where he also played football.[62] He practiced law in Buffalo and there organized an Army National Guard cavalry troop that saw limited action with Gen. John Pershing's expedition into Mexico in 1916. Donovan subsequently joined New York's famed Irish American 69th Regiment and served with it in France during the First World War, for which he was heavily decorated. He was wounded three times and it was in battle that he was given the nickname "Wild Bill."[63]

Donovan worked as a lawyer after World War I, but his eyes were always on political conflicts across the seas. In the summer of 1919, while Colin Gubbins was serving in Archangel as aide-de-camp to General Ironside, Donovan participated in another element of the Allied intervention. Traveling via Japan, he undertook a trip to Siberia, to collect information and try to make sense of the confusing situation there. Whatever the motive for his travels—about which historians disagree—Donovan concluded that Japan had designs on the region and that White Russian forces were of poor quality. Whether Pres. Woodrow Wilson took Donovan's assessment seriously is debated by Donovan biographers, but on 31 December Wilson ordered American forces out of Siberia and pressured Japan into doing likewise.[64] In the autumn of 1931 Donovan again returned to the region, unofficially investigating the Mukden Incident and informally communicating his thoughts on Japanese aggression to the U.S. government.[65]

In November 1935 Donovan traveled to Italy, where he met Benito Mussolini; convincing the dictator he was sympathetic to the Fascist cause, Donovan received permission to visit the Italian lines in Abyssinia, which Italy had invaded the previous month. Donovan spent two weeks touring facilities and interviewing Italian officers. Upon his return to the United States, Donovan—who had traveled at his law firm's expense—briefed an excited War Department, which had been unable to place spies among the Italian invaders.[66] Continuing to travel as a private citizen and making use of his network of contacts, he visited Germany in 1937 and observed German Army maneuvers; in 1938 he toured the Czechoslovak defenses in the Sudetenland, witnessed the fighting in Spain, and again observed maneuvers in Germany.[67]

Observing the British

In July 1940, having been tasked by President Roosevelt and Secretary of the Navy Frank Knox with assessing the strength of the British and studying German fifth column forces, respectively, Donovan left for Britain.[68] Lord Lothian, the British ambassador to Washington, D.C., cabled ahead to the Foreign Office, explaining that Donovan was a key advisor to Knox and therefore was likely to have strong influence over arms sales to Britain. This was an exaggeration, but it accomplished Lord Lothian's purpose, opening doors throughout Whitehall.[69] On arrival Donovan toured the island nation's defenses and formed strong relationships with the British leadership. Naval intelligence, MI5, and SIS all provided Donovan with briefings.[70] Hugh Dalton provided information on SOE, while Sir Frank Nelson granted access to SOE facilities throughout Britain and Colin Gubbins introduced Donovan to the SOE schools.[71] Conyers Read, an American historian of Britain who worked for OSS, argues that this visit by Donovan "marks the beginning of close cooperation with the British which was to characterize the whole history of . . . OSS. When Donovan later undertook to organize his secret intelligence . . . and his subversive operations . . . he turned frankly to British models."[72] On Donovan's return to the United States he concluded "that the British would hold out; that America must help, at least in the matter of supplies; and that fifth column activity had become a fact of major importance in modern warfare."[73] As was seen in chapter 4, the *Fifth Column Lessons for America*, which he coauthored with journalist Edgar Mowrer after his return, strongly pushed this same line.

In November 1940, the president again had need of Donovan's services, this time sending him to the Mediterranean to assess the situation there. He left the following month, first stopping in Britain, where he returned to SOE's network of training schools.[74] Donovan was once again impressed by the British, though this did not leave them above criticism. As the *War Report of the OSS* explains, "The Germans were exploiting the psychological and political elements. . . . Neither America nor Britain was fighting this new and important type of war. . . . Their defenses against political and psychological warfare were feeble."[75] Donovan urged President Roosevelt to take action in this sphere. After stopping in Britain, Donovan then traveled to Gibraltar, Malta, Egypt, Greece, Bulgaria, Yugoslavia, Turkey, Cyprus, Palestine, Iraq, Spain, and Portugal, before returning to the United States via Britain.[76] Of these dozen territories, half were British; Donovan's—and America's—priorities were clear.

The Coordinator of Information and the Office of Strategic Services

In the summer of 1941, vast amounts of information were flowing into Washington, D.C. Faced with this challenge, President Roosevelt asked Secretary of War Henry Stimson, Secretary of the Navy Frank Knox, and Attorney General Robert Jackson to consider this problem and that of intelligence in the broadest sense. When consulted by the committee, Donovan advised the creation of an organization with responsibility for intelligence, propaganda, and subversion, a vision as expansive as anything Dalton sought. Bold though this proposal was, the committee endorsed it in its report to the president.[77]

On 25 June 1941 the president created the Office of the Coordinator of Information, with Donovan at its helm. Over the next half year, leading up to America's entry into the Second World War, Donovan worked to establish his new intelligence and sabotage organization. Inspiration and assistance from the British was essential, and the British, desperate for U.S. resources, were happy to mentor the Americans. Indeed, historian Jay Jakub goes so far as to argue that the British played an instrumental role in selling the Americans on the idea of a central clandestine organization and seeing to it that the pro-British Donovan was at its head.[78] During these six months leading up to the United States' entry into the war, Donovan met with or telephoned Sir William Stephenson, the chief of British Security Coordination (BSC) in New York, at least thirty-six times, about once every five days.[79] One subsequent member of OSS, Carleton Coon, argues that Donovan modeled his new organization not on Britain's SIS, but on SOE.[80] Such actions on the American side were not surprising, considering that SOE, at the time keen to expand its operations in Latin America, was more eager for a relationship with the Americans than was SIS.[81]

On 10 October, a new section of COI was established, known simply as "Special Activities—K and L Funds." This office handled not only secret intelligence but also subversion and guerrilla warfare activities.[82] As part of the new venture, Donovan sent Lt. Col. Robert Solborg, an army intelligence officer seconded to COI, to Britain for three months to receive "extensive training in British [i.e., SOE] schools."[83] In the following months, Donovan lobbied hard for expansion in the area of special operations. In December he sent President Roosevelt an account of the British Commandos' development and a few days later argued "that there be organized now, in the United States, a guerrilla corps, independent and separate from the Army and Navy.... This force should, of course, be created along disciplined military lines, analogous to the British Commando principles, a statement of which I sent you recently."[84] SOE encouraged this development, since COI needed a significant special operations capability if SOE was to form a strong partnership.[85]

From the beginning, Donovan argued that intelligence and special operations, although closely collaborating, should be divided into different branches. Any doubt about this arrangement was removed by America's formal entry into the war after the Japanese attack of 7 December 1941. Although COI had worked with its British counterparts prior to that time, such cooperation grew exponentially afterward. In light of the fact that the British SIS and SOE had a strong rivalry and separate cabinet ministers, liaison was made much easier for the Americans if they came from two distinct branches of COI. In December 1941 Donovan divided "Special Activities—K and L Funds" into the Secret Intelligence Branch and the Special Operations Branch.[86]

As COI grew, its detractors in the military, the State Department, and the Federal Bureau of Investigation (FBI) increased. In March 1942 there was a major push to have it abolished; Archibald MacLeish, director of the War Department's Office of Facts and Figures, and Harold Smith, budget director, proposed creating a new propaganda organization and dividing COI's other assets among existing organizations. For a time Roosevelt delayed a decision, but on 13 June he divided COI into the Office of War Information (OWI) and the OSS, the latter under the broad authority of the Joint Chiefs of Staff.[87] It was a decision that mirrored the departure of Britain's PWE from SOE, though unlike its British counterparts, OSS united sabotage and intelligence within a single organization.[88]

A few days before the official creation of OSS on 13 June 1942, Donovan and Preston Goodfellow, his director of special operations, traveled to London to negotiate an arrangement with Sir Charles Hambro for cooperation with SOE in Britain and in the field. These negotiations between SOE and OSS regarding the precise terms of their collaboration were ongoing when Roosevelt signed the order dividing COI and creating OSS.[89] Although OSS worked out similar arrangements with SIS, the agreement with SOE was arguably the more important, for two reasons. Conceptually, a distinction can be made between intelligence and special operations. In the case of intelligence, information sharing and collaboration between agents in the field often posed a grave danger to the safety of agents, a danger which frequently outweighed the benefits of SIS-OSS cooperation. On the other hand, while Gubbins warned of the dangers posed to special operations by overorganization, duplication of effort could result in wasted lives and operational confusion; in this case, the benefits of close SOE-OSS cooperation often outweighed the costs. Moreover, well into 1942, OSS Special Operations felt it was "catching up" with its Secret Intelligence counterpart and thus needed to collaborate with SOE "without reservation."[90] Thus it proved to be a major boon when, among the final agreements of the Donovan-Hambro accords, was a provision that "all supply, operational and training facilities of SOE are at the disposal of OSS."[91]

Camp X

OSS eventually grew to have thirteen thousand personnel and a total budget of $135 million.[92] But in the months prior to the American entry into the war, Donovan faced very basic tasks in his effort to build a viable clandestine organization, tasks such as training American agents. A conversation in the summer of 1941 was emblematic of the situation. Meeting with Kenneth Baker, head of the Psychology Division of Donovan's Research and Analysis Branch, and Dr. J. R. Hayden, former vice-governor of the Philippines, Donovan told them,

> "I want you to start the schools."
> "What schools?"
> "The SI [secret intelligence] training schools."
> "But we don't know anything about espionage schools. . . ."
> "Who does?"[93]

The answer to the question was clear enough: the British. Since the United States was not officially at war, British training of American personnel would constitute a violation of neutrality. Such concerns were not enough to derail plans for joint training, but they had to be considered. Thus, it was decided to build a new school in Ontario, Canada, outside the United States but close enough for easy access.[94] As it turned out, Special Training School 103 did not begin operations until 9 December 1941, two days after the Japanese attack on Pearl Harbor, obviating the need for neutrality.[95]

Camp X, as it came to be known, was intended not only to *teach* the Americans, using the SOE training syllabus developed under Gubbins, but also to impress them and draw them into the British way of thinking about matters of irregular warfare. As David Stafford notes, "Gubbins envisaged far more than the training of agents. He wanted to help shape the mental universe of those in the United States who were preparing for American entry into the shadow war."[96] "A really efficient training school would impress the Americans," one British officer wrote after his visit to the United States in October 1941. "It would also provide us with valuable propaganda in obtaining their co-operation in the realm of subversive activities."[97] Another assessment from within SOE explained:

> American resentment at England's still playing the leading part in this war is going to cause difficulties in all spheres. SOE's best insurance against trouble of this sort is the development of close collaboration with OSS. It will be easy now, when we can be of great help to them while they are still floundering in their initial difficulties, to get them more or less on the right track. It might be very difficult indeed, later on, when they have got the bit between their teeth, particularly if they are given the impression in these early months, that we have gone ahead without bothering about them.[98]

Clearly, the American adoption of the British training syllabus was a good thing for the British, but it was also a good thing for the Americans, creating a "unity of doctrine and effort between OSS and SOE," something advantageous to both sides.[99] Even in its details, Camp X instilled a certain British style; Maj. Richard M. Brooker, the camp's first chief instructor and later commander, demanded strict attention to spit and polish. Part of this may well have been aimed at overawing the Americans with rarefied British custom, but it also instilled a sense of seriousness in the students;

Brooker believed attention to detail to be an integral part of intelligence. "If there's anything loose in the intelligence business, you're dead," he explained.[100]

At the camp American students received three to four weeks of intensive training. Where possible, the course would be tailored to match the future location or mission of the students; however, all students received the same basic elements and even variations did not usually represent something heretofore unseen somewhere in the SOE training system.[101] Students at Camp X were introduced to surveillance, disguises, codes, ciphers, invisible inks, propaganda, close-quarters combat, silent killing, recruiting and running agents, and adopting a cover, among other topics.[102] Instruction came through a mixture of lectures and hands-on field work.

By the summer of 1942, Gubbins began to think that Camp X, in its brief life, had served its purpose. In March of that year OSS had established its first training facility, Area B, in the Catoctin Mountains of Maryland, near the presidential retreat of Shangri-La.[103] As the OSS system of schools came on line, Camp X became increasingly redundant. Moreover, British security needs in Latin America—at one time a consideration—were diminishing. However, the view that Camp X had become "an expensive and unnecessary luxury" was not quickly accepted.[104] But in light of the scheduled Allied invasion of Sicily in July 1943 and the subsequent landings on the Italian peninsula, guerrilla efforts were stepped up in the Balkans and Gubbins argued that, with this new push, the staff at Camp X were needed in Britain more than in Canada. Few SOE recruits were coming out of North America now that the Americans had their own schools and Canada had largely been combed for agents. In May 1943, it was decided to close Camp X. The decision was postponed, due to a late wave of Canadian recruits for the Balkans, but in February 1944 the decision was again made to shut down the camp and in April its doors were permanently closed.[105]

The school had trained more than five hundred students from SOE, SIS, COI/OSS, the FBI, and the Royal Canadian Mounted Police, many of whom went on to train others in the ungentlemanly arts.[106] Among Camp X's graduates were men like Lt. Col. Garland Williams, who had directed the New York Bureau of Narcotics, served in the army, and joined COI in the autumn of 1941. Having been trained at Camp X, he returned to the United States to oversee the entire training program for OSS's Special Operations.[107]

Historian Mark Wheeler has described the Anglo-American partnership as "troublesome intimacy."[108] In spite of the many squabbles, the cooperation between these two nations and their clandestine services was astounding, with planning and operations often conducted in concert, and several formations—among them, the JEDBURGHS (see chapter 7)—composed of members from both sides. Camp X, as one of the earliest avenues of Anglo-American clandestine cooperation, was the first step toward many future successes.

Influence beyond Camp X

Even after the closure of Camp X, the British continued to influence OSS. This influence was continued most concretely through the work of British instructors who served at OSS schools. Fairbairn was among those who moved to the United States, where, one historian explains, he "made a lasting impression on just about everyone he met, including OSS, who got him on more or less permanent loan from the British.[109]

Brooker, who served as Camp X's first chief instructor and commanding officer from August 1942 until March 1943, was widely credited with being the single largest contributor to the school's overall success.[110] Though he was "very aggressive and sometimes not too diplomatic," gaining "many detractors within OSS," Brooker also gained many supporters. He was frequently described as a natural salesman and "a brilliant and convincing lecturer."[111] After leaving Camp X, Brooker was seconded to OSS as advisory director of training. One official history explains: "His contribution to the subsequent reorganizations and the consolidation of training programs was very important—if not the determining factor.... He visualized a flexible, yet standardized, type of training to accommodate all needs. ... The plan was solidly founded on the British experience. OSS had no tradition or practical experience in the field at this time."[112] As another OSS history explains, "During 1943, S&T [Schools and Training Branch] continued to lean heavily on the British for assistance by sending potential instructors to British schools and by borrowing instructors from the British for varying periods of time."[113] The OSS Maritime School, located in Area D, a wooded section of the Potomac across from Quantico, began its work in February 1942 under a British officer on loan from the Royal Navy.[114]

In addition to the British instructors who served at OSS schools, the OSS's official *History of the Schools and Training Branch* explains that almost all of OSS's own instructors first "trained in the Canadian SOE school near Toronto [Camp X] in a month-long course.... The Canadian school furnished lecture syllabi which S&T adapted for use at all the training areas."[115] The course of instruction for OSS Basic School, training common to both intelligence and special operations personnel, strongly parallels the corresponding SOE syllabus.[116] The handwritten notes of students in the OSS course clearly follow, sometimes verbatim, the SOE lecture outlines.[117]

Finally, the British supplied OSS's earliest classroom demonstration devices, including "incendiary pencils, fog-signals, lead delays, limpets, escape files, concealed compasses and models of ships and aircraft."[118] In addition, when Camp X was closed in the autumn of 1944, its entire stock of teaching aids and equipment was passed to OSS for use in the growing OSS school system.

The Question of Relative Influence

OSS and its agents were certainly influenced by a variety of experiences and ideas pertaining to irregular warfare. *The War Report of the OSS* explains:

> The problem of training personnel for... OSS was a complex one.... There was no precedent in America for such an undertaking and it was necessary at first to piece together various fragments of seemingly relevant knowledge from other agencies of the Government, to borrow instruction techniques from the British, and to adapt certain technical aspects of orthodox military training to the probable conditions under which guerrilla units and resistance organizers might operate.[119]

The unprecedented nature of OSS's work has been overstated, just as SOE's has. American soldiers had engaged in espionage, guerrilla warfare, and various forms of skullduggery in the Philippines, Hawaii, Central America, and the Caribbean for half a century by the time OSS came into being; law enforcement officers had faced not dissimilar problems.[120] The *War Report*'s own admission that orthodox military training had some bearing on guerrilla problems acknowledges, to some extent, that past models could be utilized.

The above passage from the *War Report* also highlights the fact that the influence upon OSS was not monocausal; it included the British example as well as American sources, both civilian and military. Thus, the question is not which of these played a role in shaping American thinking on irregular warfare—they all did—but which played the *preeminent* role. While individual Americans were influenced by their experiences of places like the U.S.-Mexican border, it is difficult to make the case that, with regard to doctrine and tactics, America's clandestine warriors were more influenced by their own background than by British tutelage.

Historian Rhodri Jeffreys-Jones observes: "It could be argued that, while the Americans did have a tradition, they kept on forgetting about it and having to start from scratch, while the British remembered intelligence lessons from the past."[121] However, Jeffreys-Jones contends that this line of thinking exaggerates the extent of an ongoing British clandestine tradition; instead, he argues, British secret services only managed to get themselves organized in the late 1930s, just in time for war.[122] Jeffreys-Jones's argument pertains more to intelligence than sabotage or guerrilla warfare, but it is an accurate description of GS(R) and Section D as well. Nevertheless, it is worth making an additional distinction: the United States had a tradition of irregular warfare but failed, by and large, to draw upon it when the time came. Although Britain stood in danger of also ignoring its own irregular tradition, it was recovered and codified through the efforts of J. C. F. Holland and Colin Gubbins, who in turn shared it with the Americans.

The results of SOE's deep influence on OSS can be seen both in the doctrine it espoused and the structure of its training regime. In one of Donovan's earliest statements of guerrilla policy, he argued to Roosevelt in December 1941 that guerrilla warfare should have two facets, first, "setting up of small groups working as bands under definite leaders." These partisans would be drawn from "those people and those territories where the issue is to be fought," echoing the focus Gubbins had also placed on local resistance forces.[123] Moreover, Donovan called for "the establishment of guerrilla forces military in nature, in order to secure cohesion and successfully carry out a plan of campaign."[124] As the *War Report of the OSS* explains, "The organization and administration of the [Special Operations] Branch was along military lines and its first personnel were drawn from the armed services, principally the Army." From its inception,

Special Operations "was to operate in support of local area [military] commands," again mirroring Gubbins's own advocacy of paramilitary forces operating in conjunction with—if not necessarily a part of—the military.[125]

This emphasis on both local populations and the need for militarily valuable partisans may also be found in the training curriculum for OSS's Operational Groups (OGs), units of foreign language–speaking soldiers created on 23 December 1942.[126] Their stated mission was "to create Guerilla Units capable of operating in various occupied countries; these units are recruited from the various nationals and first generation Americans. . . . *They will be militarily organized, disciplined and trained* to go into the country of their origin *to organize, and instruct, local resistance groups into effective Guerrilla units.*"[127] Although the methods of the OGs differed from those of conventional military forces, that their work was directly complementary was made clear in the training curriculum: these units existed "to harass the occupying forces; by so doing they would render effective assistance to the main effort."[128]

In addition, the basic shape of OSS training followed the British model. American agents attended a preliminary school for about two weeks, where they learned fieldcraft and weapons, and at which their taste for alcohol was carefully observed. Next they moved to two weeks at a basic school, the American version of SOE's paramilitary schools, where students practiced sabotage and raids. Then it was off to an advanced school (equivalent to SOE's finishing schools), where they learned to operate under cover, and finally to parachute school. Additional OSS schools, which focused on maritime operations, industrial sabotage, and particular overseas locations, filled the role of SOE's specialist schools.[129]

Like their British counterparts, American students of sabotage also studied the basics of intelligence. As one OSS history explains, "In COI, the tendency for [intelligence and operations] to find considerable value in each others' training courses had already appeared." But rather than ascribing this duality in OSS's double mission, this account instead attributes it elsewhere:

> This tendency probably can be ascribed to the influence of the British SOE training. It will be remembered that the British SOE combined in one organization both para-military and intelligence functions. . . . OSS men trained in British schools, either in Canada

or England, received a rounded picture of operations in modern war and returned to OSS imbued with the idea that OSS students should receive training in the many facets of subversive operations.[130]

While Britain had a dedicated intelligence organization—the SIS—SOE's clandestine character meant that it straddled the line between intelligence and military operations, occupying a bureaucratic gray zone that remains difficult to demarcate even in the present day. This ambiguity was in turn inherited by OSS and manifested in its training, which frequently united intelligence and special operations.

Promotion

Reshuffles

In November 1941, Sir Charles Hambro, a former Eton cricket captain, Coldstream Guard, prominent banker, and chairman of the Great Western Railway, became Sir Frank Nelson's deputy at SOE.[131] Hambro was a brilliant amateur, a man who Jebb said "lives by bluff and charm."[132] At the same time, Gubbins had become responsible for SOE's operations in western Europe.[133] A few months later, in February 1942, following the fall of Singapore, the British government was reshuffled. Hugh Dalton, minister of Economic Warfare, was moved to the Board of Trade. He was replaced at the MEW by Roundell Cecil Palmer, at the time Viscount Wolmer, though a few days later he succeeded his father as the 3rd Earl of Selborne.[134] At the time Cadogan believed Selborne "would work" in the post, "but he's not very inspiring."[135] Nevertheless, Gubbins and many others were relieved to see the departure of Dalton, always a micromanager of SOE and source of friction with Whitehall. Moreover, Selborne listened to Gubbins and was willing to champion his cogent and professional views on irregular warfare. Whereas Dalton had sometimes viewed SOE's work as a rather melodramatic socialist crusade, Selborne was more practical and focused.[136]

A few months after Dalton's departure and Selborne's arrival, Sir Frank Nelson stepped down as the head of SOE. Nelson had performed the valuable but exhausting task of trying to check Dalton's more extravagant plans, and in the process he had burned himself out.[137] Decades after the war, Gubbins remained polite in his treatment of Dalton, though his assessment of the situation was clear:

[Dalton] drove himself hard & his leading figures in SOE equally hard, perhaps too hard in one or two cases as in that of Sir Frank Nelson our first Chief. Politically they were poles apart & I would say that neither of the two tried to hide the fact: further Sir Frank felt that Dalton was conducting affairs as if he, Dalton, were the Chief Executive ... & interfering in the running of the show. There was considerable truth in Sir Frank's complaints on this score.[138]

Before their departures, Nelson and Dalton discussed the matter of SOE's next director. Gubbins's name was proposed; although Nelson suggested that Gubbins was "on his merits the best choice," he cautioned, according to Dalton's diary, that "he is difficult personally and likes only to work with people whom he himself has picked."[139] Instead, Nelson was replaced by Hambro. Gubbins was initially unsure of him, but under Hambro's leadership SOE became a regular and respected element of the war effort. One of Hambro's first acts upon arrival was to appoint Gubbins his deputy for operations; in recognition of this new position, Selborne managed to wrestle out of the War Office a brevet promotion to major general.[140]

Director of SOE

In September 1943 a fierce disagreement broke out between the commander-in-chief of the Middle East, Gen. Sir Henry Maitland Wilson, and SOE regarding Balkan policy. The Chiefs of Staff and Foreign Office were pulled into the squabble as well. The resulting compromise placed SOE's operational activities under the relevant theater commander, an outcome unacceptable to Hambro and his deputy for administration, Sir John Hanbury-Williams. Both resigned. This left Gubbins, a man who had argued since his GS(R) days that irregular forces need to be closely coordinated with regular operations, the most senior SOE officer. Selborne had no difficulty obtaining Churchill's approval for Gubbins's appointment as director of SOE.[141] Gubbins would remain at the helm of SOE until its dissolution on 1 January 1946.

Gubbins's new position merely confirmed the central role he already played, as "the real motive force in the machine," to borrow Jebb's phrase.[142] This final promotion allowed Gubbins to complete the work of creating SOE in his own image, according to the ideas he had first formulated four years before. Whereas Hugh Dalton had envisioned a "Fourth Arm" that would employ propaganda and subversion to foment a general rising of the working class, Gubbins was more realistic about what his agents might achieve, instead envisioning a paramilitary effort that would work alongside local resistance forces and in cooperation with the theater commander. Having seen the potential effectiveness of indigenous resistance movements and believing that resistance would have to be on a large scale to be effective and justify the inevitable reprisals against civilians, Gubbins concluded that success would necessarily come in cooperation with the governments-in-exile in London, many of which were in contact with—if not always in control of—resistance forces in their home countries. Perceiving the need for larger efforts and disciplined coordination, Gubbins shifted SOE away from its civilian past, creating a paramilitary organization capable of integrating with regular troops.[143]

Dennis Wheatley, who worked at the London Controlling Section devising deception operations, provides an unusual picture of Gubbins during his time as director of SOE. Like earlier accounts, Wheatley describes Gubbins as having little interest in official dress: "[He was] a dapper little man. Instead of the slacks or battle-dress worn by the majority of Army officers employed in War Departments, he always wore beautifully cut Bedford cord breeches, highly polished field boots and spurs." His parties were attended by military officers of the various governments-in-exile: the Poles and Czechoslovaks he so admired, as well as Frenchmen, Norwegians, Belgians, and Dutch, all the adventurous kind of men SOE dropped behind enemy lines. The most unexpected part of Wheatley's description involves Gubbins's relationship with women. He was a "man who excelled in surrounding himself with lovelies. . . . The hostesses [at his parties] were a score or more of beauties, mostly ex-débutantes, hand-picked by Gubby from the hundred or more girls that he employed in his office."[144] Wheatley provides few other details, but the suggestion is risqué.

Gubbins had been distant from his first wife, Norah ("Nonie"), for a long time—they eventually divorced in 1944—and he certainly enjoyed the cosmopolitan life of intelligence.[145] However, Wheatley's picture should be taken with more than a grain of salt, not only because Wheatley was an author of pulp fiction in peacetime. SOE certainly employed a large number of women, something in the neighborhood of 3,200 of them, many of them from the First Aid Nursing Yeomanry (FANY). These women served as wireless operators, drivers, secretaries, and domestic help at the country house schools.[146] Wheatley's suggestion of impropriety involving such women appears misplaced, however. After the war Donald Hamilton-Hill asked Gubbins to look over the manuscript of a novel about SOE. Gubbins replied:

> I do not mind your "conversational details" [but] . . . I do think that you should be very careful in laying any stress on female relationships and luscious F.A.N.Y's and things of that nature. . . . I think you do want to avoid anything which would make your book a "succès de scandale" and would hope that you would not denigrate our own F.A.N.Y's in any way, who were of course as signal personnel at the core of our success: I would not like people to think that male/female relations entered into our daily tough work in any degree.[147]

Perhaps Gubbins was simply interested in preserving his good name or that of SOE, though this was only one of a raft of books that appeared about secret operations after the war, and a book with which he had no official connection. Indeed, Gubbins acknowledges in the letter that spies and sex was a theme that had "already been abused by cheap authors."[148] His intercession with Hamilton-Hill appears to have arisen from genuine motives.

Joan Bright Astley, who herself worked for Gubbins, provides a considerably different take on a scene not so different from Wheatley's:

> Whatever their rank or status, [the FANYs] looked to Gubbins as their patron. He, for his part, always took a personal interest in their welfare. To celebrate the New Year [in 1942] he organized at one of the training schools an all-ranks dance for members of his staff to which he invited the FANY drivers. Presided over by Mrs. [Phyllis] Bingham [Commander of the FANYs], it was as decorous as an end of term party at a girls' school; however, Gubbins wore the kilt and led the Scottish dancing until the small hours of the morning. At a time when senior officers were not expected to enjoy all-ranks dances, Gubbins proved an exception. . . . In staff relations, as in much else, he was ahead of his time.[149]

Conclusion

The four years from the outbreak of war in September 1939 to Gubbins's appointment as director of SOE in September 1943 were a significant and dynamic period, for the war generally, for SOE, and for the growth of its American counterpart, the OSS. Likewise, Gubbins's time at SOE's helm, lasting two additional years, saw the zenith of the organization's operations. Nevertheless, as SOE grows the story of its doctrine tapers off. Although the experiences of war led to innovations in irregular operations, SOE's basic doctrine became increasingly fixed. Gubbins's ideas were continually reinforced, as one layer was added to another: his significant contribution to the thinking of MI(R), itself a major component of the new SOE; his impact as SOE's first director of training, beginning in 1940, upon thousands of new agents; his increased influence when Selborne, a man willing to listen, became minister in 1942; and, finally, his leadership as director after 1943. Thus, the history of ideas settled down even as the pace of SOE's operations quickened. To those activities we now turn our attention.

CHAPTER 7

OPERATIONS AND ASSESSMENT

A comprehensive account of SOE's operations is beyond the scope of this book. Nevertheless, a brief consideration of some of SOE's operations is merited for several reasons. Firstly, SOE's doctrine bore fruit in its operations; the former cannot be discussed without at least mentioning the latter. Secondly, the diversity of operations and theaters in which SOE conducted them speaks to the flexibility of the organization and the doctrine behind it. SOE's wartime record was by no means unblemished; it ranged from confusion in the Balkans to tragedy in Poland to model operations in Abyssinia, Norway, and Burma. That it succeeded as often as it did, and in such a wide variety of difficult situations, indicates the robustness and universality of Gubbins's ideas. Thirdly, SOE had and continues to have its critics. A brief survey of its operations goes some distance toward answering those critics or at least informing the debate.

In addition to a rough sketch of some of SOE's global operations, two case studies follow. SOE was active in many dissimilar theaters, making it difficult for one or two cases to represent the whole. However, Normandy and Burma, between them, provide a decent approximation of the various conditions in which SOE operated. The two areas differ from one another in several substantial ways. Firstly, the geography could hardly be less similar. Northern France is broadly level, populated by frequent towns and villages, and knit together by a developed system of roads and other communications. In stark contrast, Burma, particularly in the northern and eastern regions where resistance forces resided, is extremely mountainous, covered with dense jungles, and almost completely devoid of roads or other forms of European-style development. So different and demanding was Burma's tropical climate that even elite personnel arriving in the theater required new training in jungle warfare and were sometimes rejected as physically unsuitable for the region.[1] Secondly, these theaters represent diverse political and cultural situations. France was an independent nation whose government-in-exile SOE supported; in contrast, Burma was a British colony that

SOE sought to return to British rule. Moreover, whereas France and Britain had a long history involving many shared cultural, political, and religious values, Burma's various ethnic groups had virtually nothing in common with their British counterparts, except for certain members of the colonial administration who had come to know the local languages. Thus, although these two case studies do not exhaustively cover SOE, they do provide two very different windows into its operations.

Survey of SOE Operations

SOE's mission of stimulating indigenous resistance with the eventual goal of armed risings, coordinated with the Allies' larger strategic and conventional efforts, played out differently in the various countries in which it operated. Factors such as the terrain, the level of industrialization, the extent of existing underground organization, as well as the attitudes of the local population and long-term political goals resulted in a multiplicity of arrangements.[2] In Denmark, France, and the Low Countries, resistance activities consisted largely of underground organizations, often nonmilitary in character, organized into small independent cells for security. Such groups primarily provided intelligence and engaged in sabotage. SOE also prepared many of these groups to assist with the preservation of law and order following the liberation of their territories. In contrast, resistance forces in Burma, Italy, Yugoslavia, Albania, and Greece consisted of much larger paramilitary formations.[3]

Although particular arrangements varied, SOE generally worked through the many governments-in-exile in London. The Czechoslovaks, for example, selected their own agents; these men were then sent to SOE schools, before being briefed by Czechoslovak handlers. In the field, these agents acted on behalf of the Czechoslovakian government, not SOE. Likewise, the Poles had a significant presence within SOE's Force 139, located in Brindisi, from which they operated a training school, signal station, and a wing of RAF aircraft, all manned by Poles under general British supervision.[4] In virtually every theater, SOE spent many long months building networks, establishing wireless communications, and inserting weapons and individuals into occupied territory. The operations described below resulted from such painstaking, and often frustrating, work. As Mackenzie points out, some of these episodes "had little future, but bulked large at the time."⁵ But given that resistance is as much psychological as material, such symbolic deeds were often quite important. Although SOE's largest areas of focus, as measured in numbers of agents, were France and Yugoslavia, followed by Greece and Italy, less active theaters also provided political and military successes as well as valuable lessons learned.⁶

Abyssinia

The MI(R) section in the Middle East, known as G(R), was heavily integrated with Gen. Archibald Wavell's Headquarters Middle East, though MI(R) provided expert advice and a lobby in the War Office.⁷ One of G(R)'s subordinate formations was Mission 101 in Khartoum, commanded by D. A. Sandford, a former farmer in Abyssinia and consul in Addis Ababa. The British attack on Italian-occupied Abyssinia offered one of the earliest models of how conventional and clandestine forces could work together.

After preparatory work by Sandford in Italian-occupied territory, conventional forces invaded Abyssinia from the north and southeast in November 1940, while two G(R) columns, supported by thousands of camels, moved into the west of the country. Several small groups, called Operational Centres, preceded the main G(R) columns, organizing local forces and attacking enemy communications. These centers consisted of a single British officer, five noncommissioned officers (NCOs), and two hundred British-trained locals. The southerly column, known as Gideon Force, was commanded by Orde Wingate, organizer of the Special Night Squads in Palestine. Through a mixture of rapid maneuvering, superior marksmanship, and deception, the small British force and its local allies routed larger Italian forces.⁸

Although, in the scheme of the global war, the liberation of Abyssinia was a minor operation, "experience gained there was to prove of value in the next four years."⁹ SOE learned tradecraft such as packing supplies and utilizing wireless communications. More importantly, two lessons, taught in Gubbins's writings, were proven in the field: that guerrilla warfare could be effective, especially when conducted in conjunction with regular forces, and "that patriot forces . . . could be given a sharper cutting edge by the presence of small groups of officers and NCOs trained in tactics, especially the tactics of sabotage and attack."¹⁰

Poland

Because Poland was the only country in occupied Europe with a meaningful resistance in 1940, it was an early area of SOE operations, aided by Gubbins's contacts with the exiled Polish military intelligence.[11] Gubbins deeply loved the country and it "formed a burden that weighed extra heavily on [his] heart."[12] From the very beginning, SOE's greatest struggle in Poland was overcoming the tremendous distance that RAF planes had to fly—through German-occupied airspace—to parachute agents and supply the Polish Home Army. SOE's first ever liaison flight to occupied territory was to Poland, in February 1941; although Gubbins's report was upbeat, the route was too demanding for routine traffic.[13] Indeed, so long were flights that they could not be done under cover of darkness during the summer because the night was too short.[14] By mid-1941, most interested parties in the British government concluded that major support to Polish or Czechoslovak uprisings was unrealistic and no longer needed, with the German invasion of the Soviet Union in June 1941 pulling vast numbers of enemy troops eastward. Although successful flights resumed in the winter of 1941/42, they were always limited by weather, German defenses, and the demands for aircraft elsewhere.[15] In total, the British made 485 air drops in Poland during the war, delivering 600 tons of materiel, 40 percent of it to the ill-fated Warsaw Uprising, though at great cost to the RAF. In all, 318 agents were dropped into Poland, virtually all of them Poles trained by SOE but acting on orders from the Polish government-in-exile.[16] Although Poland was an early recipient of SOE's support, its story was almost inevitably tragic; being situated closer to the Soviets, with whom the vast majority of Poles understandably refused to cooperate, than to the Western Allies posed enormous, if not insurmountable, challenges.

On 1 August 1944, with the Red Army at Warsaw's door, the Polish Home Army revolted against the Nazis. For two months the rebels fought in the ruined streets. The Red Army, keen to see this reborn Poland strangled at birth, did not come to their aid. Though the RAF, U.S. Army Air Forces, and South African Air Force flew hundreds of sorties, few of the supplies actually reached the beleaguered resistance fighters.[17] On 2 October the rebels were forced to capitulate. As many as ten thousand members of the Polish Home Army and perhaps twenty times as many civilians perished.[18]

As historian E. D. R. Harrison points out, the failure to adequately support the uprising occurred at several points. The leadership of

Poland's Home Army was naïve, perhaps to the point of negligence, with regard to the tremendous technical difficulties involved in flying supplies to Poland and dropping them to small rebel units in a dense urban area. Polish leadership in London understood these difficulties and the improbability of receiving significant aid but failed to adequately communicate these harsh realities to their colleagues in Poland. British leaders, not least among them Gubbins, genuinely desiring to support the Polish resistance, did not outright prohibit a rebellion or refuse all support to it, though they knew that very little support could be provided.[19] Poland's Home Army leadership pressed ahead in tragic ignorance. It is, however, doubtful that better information would have changed its plans; this was the hour when Poland had to wager everything, irrespective of the odds. Gubbins's description of his experience in Poland in 1939 was again apropos: "My heart was filled with sadness."[20]

Czechoslovakia

When the Germans partitioned Czechoslovakia, Edvard Beneš, the former president, and František Moravec, head of the Czechoslovak intelligence service, managed to flee the country, along with their files and key elements of their staff.[21] The Czechoslovak General Staff was established, for a time, in Paris, where it was in contact with Gubbins and MI(R), in spite of its position under French command. In early 1941, Gubbins was among the senior SOE leaders who negotiated an agreement with the Czechoslovak government-in-exile whereby SOE began to train Czechoslovak agents.[22] Britain eventually parachuted a score of agents into occupied territory, the first in April 1941.[23] In spite of these efforts, Czechoslovak leaders were aware that their country offered only modest terrain for waging guerrilla warfare, that it was far from the Allied centers of power, and that, as a small nation, its future was uncertain. Early resistance in September 1939 was ruthlessly crushed. Thus, they trod cautiously in the realm of resistance activities.[24]

In September 1941, Reinhard Heydrich was named *Reichsprotektor* in Prague. His draconian policies earned the ire of Beneš and Moravec, who—in spite of their general caution—determined to kill him, both in retribution and to demonstrate that the Czechoslovak underground was capable of active resistance. Gubbins characteristically warned that an attempt on Heydrich's life would likely result in widespread reprisals and initially cautioned against it, until he learned that Heydrich took a particular interest in rooting out resistance in northwest Europe, which Gubbins saw as a direct threat to SOE.[25] On 27 May 1942, two of Moravec's SOE-trained agents attacked Heydrich's car in Prague, fatally wounding him. As a propaganda coup, it was a tremendous blow. Heydrich, who took a wealth of information to his grave, was replaced by a man of far less capability. However, the German reprisals that followed the assassination left five thousand people dead, including many children. Subsequent SOE missions to the country were few and limited to intelligence, not sabotage.[26]

Nevertheless, the exiled Czechoslovak General Staff worked to rebuild its army; an Anglo-Czech Planning Committee was formed to aid these efforts and Gubbins chaired its first meeting in September 1942. Wilkinson, who had worked with the Czechoslovaks in Paris after Gubbins's departure, was a regular participant in the committee's efforts.[27] In May 1945, Prague rose up as the Germans departed. Although this was essentially a popular revolt, SOE had a liaison team on the ground throughout the rising and dropped several tons of stores to the Czechoslovaks in the preceding months, providing modest support.[28]

Italy

In their first directive to SOE, the Chiefs of Staff called for both "co-ordinated and organised revolts in the occupied countries" and "a popular rising against the Nazi party inside Germany." From this broad range of possible targets, the chiefs specified that "the elimination of Italy comes first among our strategic aims."[29] Nevertheless, SOE's efforts in Italy were stymied by political sensitivities about working with individuals within an enemy regime, particularly after the formal demand for unconditional surrender made at the Casablanca Conference in January 1943. Moreover, following the chiefs' first directive to SOE, the Axis powers added to their conquests Yugoslavia, Greece, and—after June 1941—large sections of the Soviet Union. These and the occupied territories in western Europe proved more promising opportunities for sabotage and subversion than either Germany or Italy.[30] In April 1941, Peter Fleming—who had earlier proposed forming a guerrilla force in China—led a small mission tasked with recruiting saboteurs from among Italian prisoners captured in Africa, only to discover that reports of anti-Fascist sentiments among the prisoners were much exaggerated.[31] Although discontent existed within the Axis nations, occupied countries were always more amenable to SOE's work, as Gubbins himself foresaw when he noted that the "justice of his cause will inflame [the] embitterment" of a man fighting occupiers.[32]

Five SOE parties went ashore with Allied troops during Operation HUSKY, the invasion of Sicily, in July 1943; SOE members likewise took part in the Anzio landing in January 1944. Among them was Gubbins's own son, Michael, who was killed in action.[33] One of SOE's most notable successes in Italy was the role it played in the Italian armistice that followed HUSKY. SOE provided the wireless set, codes, and operator used to communicate between Gen. Dwight Eisenhower and Marshal Pietro Badoglio, a key member of the anti-Fascist coup who became prime minister after Benito Mussolini was ousted.[34] While this about-face by the Italian state was not an act of guerrilla warfare per se, it fit a pattern of action Gubbins had advocated five years earlier, when he argued that "the [enemy] people's will to war must be sapped and undermined . . . so as to induce a craving for peace and for a change in the regime. . . . What is required is to divide the population of the enemy against itself."[35] SOE's efforts in this matter were relatively modest but proved extremely valuable at a very critical time.

As soon as the government switched sides, the Germans lost no time occupying northern Italy. While a loss for the Allies, this move was a boon for SOE, since most Italians now saw the Germans as occupiers and Mussolini's reconstituted Italian Socialist Republic as a puppet state. SOE worked with elements of Italy's Military Intelligence Service, once an enemy, now turned friend, as well as various semiautonomous partisan bands. SOE provided supplies and wireless communications; in turn, these groups provided intelligence and helped escaping Allied prisoners. SOE dispatched dozens of missions to work with partisans, improving their training, armaments, leadership, and effectiveness in attack; primarily British, these missions also included Italian members. By 1 April 1945, SOE fielded 125 British agents and 92 Italians recruited and trained by SOE.[36] As Allied fears of a Communist takeover grew, SOE's vision for Italian partisans shifted from major offensive operations to prevention of sabotage by departing German forces and maintenance of order in newly liberated territories, similar to the role played in the Low Countries (see below).[37]

Yugoslavia

Prior to the Italian invasion of Greece in October 1940, SOE faced pressure to limit its activities in the Balkans, lest they provoke German action in the region. Following the invasion, however, German involvement seemed increasingly likely. SOE attempted to prepare sabotage and guerrilla forces in Romania, Bulgaria, and Yugoslavia, though to limited effect.[38] Drawing upon assets it inherited from Section D, SOE also played a small role in the March 1941 overthrow of the Axis-leaning Prince Paul, the Regent of Yugoslavia, in favor of seventeen-year-old King Peter, whose minority was declared over.[39]

The benefits of Prince Paul's removal were short-lived; in April the Axis powers invaded Yugoslavia. For SOE, the country became a political quagmire and it has remained such for many historians. A comment from SOE's war diary could almost cover the entire experience: "Measured in tangible results, the achievements of the [Balkans] Section have not been particularly striking. At the same time it must be remembered that emphasis has been transferred from sabotage undertakings to political work and that to some extent these two lines of action are mutually exclusive."[40] In September 1941, SOE attached Capt. D. T. Hudson to a party of three Yugoslavs sent by the government-in-exile into the country via British submarine. Hudson, tasked with assessing resistance forces, met Josip Tito, commander of the Communist-led Partisans. Though friendly, Tito was uninterested in close cooperation with the British. Hudson also met with Draža Mihailović, a royalist resistance commander, who gave a cold reception and refused to work with anyone who had contacts with Tito.[41] In spite of these first impressions, by October 1941 both the Yugoslav government and SOE concluded that Mihailović was their man. Meanwhile, the Russians, hard pressed by the German invasion of their country, called for all possible support to Yugoslav resistance forces as a means of diverting German forces. The British Chiefs of Staff feared that a revolt in Yugoslavia was premature and could not be adequately supported by the Allies, but Gubbins argued that "at this moment . . . supplies dropped in Yugoslavia are worth any number of bombs dropped in Germany."[42] The resulting compromise was a schizophrenic policy of supporting a revolt under Mihailović's leadership, while providing so little material assistance that his position was never secure and the revolt's success was in doubt.[43]

Repeated attempts in late 1941 and 1942 to insert mixed parties of Yugoslav and British agents into the country proved fruitless. Yugoslav agents trained by SOE but responsible to the Yugoslav government were also dropped in, but they did not accurately report on local politics and often received instructions from their own government, which were at odds with Britain's.[44] The system of working through the governments-in-exile, which often proved successful elsewhere, was a failure in Yugoslavia. Throughout 1942, the situation in Yugoslavia deteriorated, as conflict between Mihailović and Tito became acute. Britain attempted to broker a deal between them, while Russia staunchly backed Tito, whose forces were ideologically aligned with Moscow and engaged in heavy fighting against the Axis, while Mihailović's hung back.[45] As Allied forces took to the offensive in North Africa and then Sicily, the need to divert Axis forces away from the main front became more significant, but British missions dropped into Mihailović's territory found his troops unreliable and they accomplished virtually nothing. In February 1944, the British finally switched their support to Tito.[46]

Although SOE had numerous missions in Yugoslavia by the summer of 1943, they observed, rather than organized or led, guerrilla operations, which received minimal material support from Britain. By the time the shift to Tito came about, Britain's aid became more overt, making SOE's role as coordinator of clandestine warfare less necessary.[47] As military forces, such as No. 2 Commando, played a growing role, SOE shifted its efforts toward overseeing the supplies—for the first time at meaningful levels—that were provided by the RAF to Partisan forces and needy civilians.[48] At the time of Operation OVERLORD in June 1944, the Partisans launched their own Operation BEARSKIN, which successfully attacked major infrastructure and tied down German troops; similar operations in September 1944 coincided with an Allied attempt to break the Gothic Line in northern Italy.[49] At various times, guerrilla warfare in Yugoslavia engaged as many as thirty-two Axis divisions, of which half were German units that could have otherwise deployed elsewhere. These were primarily Tito's own operations; SOE could claim little credit for them. Nevertheless, SOE only sent 215 men to Yugoslavia over the course of the war, of whom 25 were killed. Even if SOE's share of the credit was small, its costs, in the context of the global war, were negligible.[50]

Greece and Albania

In the days before SOE's creation, preparations for the possible Axis occupation of Greece were divided between MI(R), responsible for Crete, and Section D, responsible for the mainland. The arrangement changed slightly when British troops landed in 1941 and organized defenses along the Olympus Line. Demolitions north of the line were the responsibility of the Greeks, supported by Section D; south of the line, demolitions were the responsibility of the British military, acting through MI(R) personnel, among them Peter Fleming. Understandably, the Greeks were not particularly cooperative in such destruction, though the harbor and defenses at Salonika were very thoroughly destroyed when the Axis powers invaded in the autumn of 1940.[51]

Like Yugoslavia, Greece was a political nightmare. Mackenzie comments that "Greek politics are almost inexplicable except in terms of personalities" and he begins his discussion with Thucydides's account from the fifth century BC.[52] The hyperbole is merited. SOE was tasked with stimulating resistance in Greece; however, there was a natural tension between this mission and the Foreign Office's firm policy of supporting the king, since many would-be resisters were not monarchists, notably the Communist-led National Liberation Front (EAM). The situation was clarified somewhat when Lord Selborne assumed the helm of SOE and insisted that "SOE policy in Greece . . . must be in conformity with that of His Majesty's Government. . . . We cannot all be Foreign Secretaries."[53] Nevertheless, SOE continued to receive guidance prone to misconstrual, as when it was told in 1943 that

> there can be no question of SOE refusing to have dealings with a given group merely on the grounds that the political sentiments of the group are opposed to the King and Government, but subject to special operational necessity SOE should always veer in the direction of groups willing to support the King. . . . Nothing should be neglected which might help to promote unity among the resistance groups in Greece.[54]

Such advice, however sage, was open to a variety of interpretations in the field.

The British military mission to Greece, which became the center of gravity for all SOE's efforts there, parachuted into the country in September 1942, made contact with Greek guerrillas, and destroyed the Gorgopotamas bridge, an essential link between the Greek port of Piraeus and central Europe, two months later. The two leaders of the attack remained in Greece, with one commanding all British forces in the country and the other establishing the first of many subordinate liaison missions.[55] In June 1943, Greek partisans, acting on British coordination, conducted a series of attacks on lines of communication, preventing the withdrawal of German troops from Greece and giving the false impression of an impending Allied attack in Greece, rather than in Sicily.[56] When the Italian government capitulated in July 1943, SOE opened negotiations with Italian garrisons in northern Greece, with the result that the first Italian units to join the Allied cause anywhere were those that surrendered to SOE. Likewise, Italian forces on several of the Greek islands came over to the Allies, though in some cases the Germans managed to retake these weak garrisons.[57]

Although the campaign of June 1943 was a rousing success, EAM's prominent role in the action marked an advance in its efforts to gain control of the country. In October 1943, EAM moved against its rival resistance organizations and in so doing sparked an all-out civil war, an outcome the retreating Germans happily encouraged. Only in February 1944 were the feuding resistance fighters again yoked together under a simulacrum of united guerrilla policy.[58]

In September 1944, as Russian forces pushed into Romania and German troops prepared their final withdrawal from Greece, the Allies launched Operation NOAH'S ARK, a sustained effort over three weeks to harry the German retreat while British forces landed in the Peloponnese. In addition to destroying hundreds of locomotives and motor vehicles and killing thousands of German soldiers, the attacks by Greek guerrillas also held in place enemy forces, making them easy targets for Allied air attacks. The liberation of Greece was aided in the Piraeus area by the Apollo network, which conducted sabotage against Axis ships beginning in 1943 and successfully smuggled at least a hundred people out of the country. In the final phase of the German occupation, the network prevented sabotage of the valuable Piraeus port.[59]

Albania was occupied by Italy in April 1939, the same month Gubbins arrived at GS(R), and held an early interest for SOE's predecessors. However, Albania played only a small role in the larger strategy and had few industrial targets for sabotage. SOE first attempted to land an agent in April 1941; when he was captured, another effort was not undertaken until April 1943, though four additional missions rapidly followed. As in Yugoslavia and Greece, SOE worked in Albania to build a coalition of anti-Axis guerrilla organizations, in spite of their disagreements—often violent—about domestic politics. In the end the Communists proved most effective and received the bulk of SOE's support.[60] In 1944, aid to the Albanian resistance increased, with money and weapons provided by air and sea, in addition to close air support. In September 1944, as NOAH'S ARK was going on in Greece, forty veterans of the Long Range Desert Group parachuted into Albania, providing valuable assistance to the guerrillas and inflicting heavy losses on retreating German troops.[61]

Scandinavia

Although Norway was not viewed by the British Chiefs of Staff as a likely area of operations, and therefore received very limited air support to resistance activities, Churchill was periodically intrigued by the Norwegian resistance, which SOE supported via the "Shetland Bus," a group of vessels crewed by Norwegian seamen.[62] Norway was, in many respects, an ideal country for resistance: rough terrain, a largely rural or maritime population, a tradition of local government, a strong sense of national unity, the absence of divisive domestic politics, and a long border with neutral Sweden.[63]

In early 1942 the Anglo-Norwegian Coordinating Committee was established to ensure smooth operations between SOE and its Norwegian counterparts; the committee was eventually expanded to include America's OSS as well. Early plans to maintain separate organizations—one centered on the local home front resistance forces, the other supported by SOE and external Norwegian forces—were scrapped when it became apparent that the country was too sparsely populated for two organizations. Nevertheless, the home front succeeded in running a parallel government within Norway, which avoided political infighting and allowed SOE to focus almost exclusively on military objectives.[64]

The Norwegian resistance, which was aided by training, supplies, and communications from SOE, collected intelligence, conducted attacks on rail lines, and guided RAF bombers. In addition, SOE assisted with the planning and execution of Combined Operations' raids on Norway. All of these operations had to be conducted with great caution: Norway's small population meant that the German occupiers could deal terrible blows against the nation, so only the most valuable operations could be justified.[65] SOE's greatest success in Norway was Operation GUNNERSIDE, an attack on the Norsk Hydro plant, which produced heavy water for the German atomic program. Einar Skinnarland, a member of the Norwegian resistance who was familiar with the plant, arrived in Britain in March 1942. He was trained by SOE and parachuted back into Norway, where he remained for nearly a year. Following the failure of Combined Operations' glider attack on the plant in November 1942, the target was entrusted to SOE and in February 1943 the plant was successfully attacked by Norwegian resistance forces that approached across ground deemed impassible by the Germans.[66] Similar, though less spectacular, attacks occurred on various mines and railroads. As a result of the rail campaign, the German capacity to move troops out of Scandinavia fell from four divisions per month to a mere one per month by the spring of 1945, a significant contribution to Allied forces pushing through the Rhineland.[67] SOE's official history describes one group of SOE-trained fighters in Norway, the Norwegian Independent Company (Oslo) as having "some reason to think itself the best team of saboteurs in Europe."[68] This group waged a campaign against German shipping in Norwegian waters and effectively prevented the implementation of a Nazi labor mobilization scheme by conducting thefts and attacks aimed at its bureaucratic infrastructure.[69]

Resistance in Denmark faced some unique challenges, since the country capitulated to Germany mere hours after being invaded, not out of ideological sympathy but pragmatism. The king, government, and military remained in the country, nominally collaborating with the Germans. Although the beginnings of resistance were slow, they had ties to the Danish General Staff and enjoyed broad, if quiet, support from the population.[70] As it turned out, first contact with the Danish resistance's intelligence network came through SOE, and SIS agreed that SOE, though not formally an intelligence agency, should act as SIS's sole agent in Denmark, as well as acting on behalf of MI9, the escape and evasion service, which had been formed out of MI(R).[71] A sabotage campaign in 1943 caused the Germans to put unacceptable pressure on the elected Danish government, which resigned in protest. The General Staff was driven into exile and the occupiers, now forced to do their own dirty work, drove the population into the arms of the resisters. The Danish resistance primarily engaged in industrial sabotage and strikes. Although its contribution to the war effort was modest, through SOE's careful intervention the nation shifted from formal collaboration to open resistance, and from political division to unity of effort, valuable assets in the postwar reconstruction.[72]

The Low Countries

SOE's activities in the Low Countries were often frustrating. This resulted from terrain unfavorable to guerrilla warfare, German diligence, and incompetence and personality clashes among the Allies.[73] SOE had difficult relations with the Belgians. The basic conundrum was understandable from both sides: the Belgians wanted to keep their resistance forces intact until the time of liberation; SOE, while broadly amenable to this plan, also understood the need to justify itself and the resistance movements it supported with action in the short term. So acrimonious did relations become that they were broken off entirely between August and November 1942.[74]

By the time of Belgium's liberation in September 1944, resistance forces reportedly numbered fifty thousand men. Prior to the Normandy landings, the Belgian resistance focused largely on denying the country's industrial capacity to the Germans, through such actions as coordinated rail cuts to disrupt supply chains.[75] Following the Normandy landings, Belgian partisans cut hundreds of rail lines, destroyed bridges, sabotaged trains, and generally made transportation of German troops to the beachhead difficult. One German division in Flanders had to travel through Holland and Germany in order to reach Normandy because the direct route had been made impassable. In Antwerp, a Belgian officer, trained in Britain for the specific task, organized resistance forces, which seized the city's valuable port facilities shortly before the arrival of Allied troops, attacking German demolition parties, removing charges, and saving the port for Allied use. Belgian resistance forces guarded the flanks of Allied forces operating in the area, as well as guarding captured airfields, bridges, and other key points, and took prisoner some ten thousand Germans.[76]

The most outstanding event in the history of SOE's operations in the Netherlands was a colossal disaster generally known by its German names, Operation NORDPOL ("North Pole") or *Das*

Englandspiel ("the England game"). German military intelligence, working with the SS, penetrated SOE's network and arrested every SOE agent who landed in the country for eighteen months, nearly fifty individuals in all. The failure had several causes. The Dutch government-in-exile mishandled its resistance operations and sent only mediocre candidates to SOE. The Germans engaged in rigorous police work to break the network and keep up the false impression that nothing was amiss. SOE was negligent in its running of agents, refusing to believe the clear warning signs that things had gone wrong.[77] As in Poland, there was blame aplenty to go around.

Case Study: Normandy

SOE in France

Although the French arguably loom largest in popular imagination of any of the European resistance movements, early on SOE faced two major hurdles in France. First, the existence of Marshal Philippe Pétain's Vichy regime, however tainted, caused many Frenchmen to forego resistance activities, such that there was very little organized resistance through 1941.[78] Second, SOE had trouble finding Frenchmen to serve in its ranks, since Charles de Gaulle's Free French forces, to whose banner most Frenchmen in Britain rallied, often believed SOE was trying to subvert them.[79]

In March 1941, SOE conducted its first major effort in France, parachuting a team of Gaullist volunteers "blind" into German-occupied France, with the purpose of attacking Luftwaffe aircrews in Brittany. Although the attack itself was a failure, the operation demonstrated the ability to insert agents into France, have them travel a considerable distance to their targets, and then exfiltrate via submarine. A second operation in June, following the same pattern, successfully destroyed a power station.[80] But the real beginning of operations in France, though less exciting, came in May 1941, when the first agent was dropped into Vichy France, not with the purpose of staging a particular attack but instead building networks to support an Allied invasion. This was the real purpose for which SOE worked. Another major advance came in September when Jean Moulin, a Gaullist resistance leader, reached London. There he accepted SOE's offer of support, while simultaneously convincing de Gaulle to establish a National Council of Resistance. Although de Gaulle often displayed extreme reluctance to work with SOE or the British government, Moulin's involvement with SOE's Free French section was a key factor in the development of the SOE–Free French relationship.[81]

Industrial sabotage possesses several virtues. It can strike an enemy's rear areas when direct military confrontation is impossible or undesirable. Because sabotage is generally conducted by a handful of individuals at very close range, it can be done with great precision and economy of effort. Finally, sabotage is much more politically sensitive than wanton destruction, particularly when the country in question is not the enemy's own but a friendly nation that has been occupied and has an eye toward preserving its industry. Sabotage operations in France demonstrated all of these advantages.

Due to the intense Allied air campaign, Luftwaffe aircraft in France required frequent maintenance and repairs. In January 1944, an SOE agent, using only nine pounds of explosives, disabled one of France's largest and most sophisticated propeller plants for the duration of the war. Across southwestern France, SOE launched attacks against the transformers of several manufacturers of aircraft parts, disrupting their operations without destroying the plants themselves. High-altitude Luftwaffe fighters depended upon oxygen produced at plants in northern France. A series of five attacks between November 1943 and July 1944 against these plants effectively limited the operational ceiling of Luftwaffe fighters in the region to fifteen thousand feet.[82]

Allied planners identified German ball bearing production as an industrial bottleneck and sought to exploit this fact. Factories producing ball bearings in Germany were bombed from the air, but those in occupied France were located in densely populated areas, making bombing politically problematic. Therefore, SOE orchestrated a series of six precision attacks against these French factories between November 1943 and August 1944.[83] Political issues were again mitigated by SOE when concerns arose regarding French railroad locomotives. Allied aircraft frequently engaged these locomotives in the lead-up to the Normandy landings; such attacks often produced only temporary damage to transportation infrastructure but considerable loss of life among French railroad engineers, who supported the resistance and engaged in sabotage on behalf of the Allies. Understandably, these air attacks resulted in significant anger on the French side. As a result, in some areas responsibility for attacking locomotives was shifted to the resistance, with no small effect: between August 1943 and June 1944, over 1,700 French locomotives were attacked by resistance forces, with more than 1,400 immobilized, most requiring total rebuilds.[84]

In early 1943, Britain and the United States established the Allied Inter-Service Planning Staff, under the auspices of the Supreme Headquarters Allied Expeditionary Force (SHAEF), to prepare for a cross-channel invasion in 1944; likewise, SOE stood up a new directorate to assist in planning operations in northwestern Europe.[85] To better integrate SOE and OSS efforts into the conventional campaign, and ensure adequate input from the French side, coordination centers were established: one, known as Special Force Headquarters, under SHAEF, and a second, known as SO(M), responsible to the Supreme Allied Commander Mediterranean. British and American units deploying to France received Special Force Detachments with direct wireless communications to Special Force Headquarters, to ensure coordination. These detachments also provided conventional commanders with the means by which they could task resistance forces.[86]

The JEDBURGHs

The idea of the JEDBURGH teams apparently came from Gubbins himself, who referred to them as "my pet project." He proposed in July 1942 "the dropping behind ... the enemy lines, in cooperation with an Allied invasion of the Continent, of small parties of officers and men to raise and arm the civilian population to carry out guerrilla activities."[87] The concept was validated at the SPARTAN war games of March 1943, which convinced the British Army that SOE could, with limited expenditure, stimulate resistance and provide reliable support to an advancing conventional force.[88] In their final form, the JEDBURGHs consisted of three members: a French officer, an SOE or OSS officer, and an American, British, or French radio operator. They would be parachuted into France immediately following the Operation OVERLORD landings at Normandy, to support the French resistance and the Allied agents already in place. Members required excellent intelligence, skill with small arms, and fluency in French.[89] These teams epitomized not only Gubbins's commitment to working with foreign resistance forces but also SOE's close relationship with OSS.

Although these men wore uniforms, unlike many SOE and OSS agents, they functioned in accordance with the well-established doctrine of organizing and aiding local forces. As Gubbins had written in 1939, "The culminating state of guerilla warfare should always be to produce in the field large formations of guerillas, well-armed and well-trained, which are able to take a direct part in the fighting by attacks on suitable hostile formations . . . in direct conjunction with the operations of regular troops."[90] The JEDBURGH teams were designed for that mission. As the *Secret War Report of the OSS* explains, they were "to help in the coordination of resistance activities with the needs of the invading armies, to train men at new resistance centers following the landings and to direct the delivery of additional supplies by air."[91] Moreover, Gubbins had observed in 1939 that

> it may . . . frequently be advantageous to appoint certain serving army officers for duty with guerillas . . . to serve as specially qualified staff officers or assistants to guerilla commanders. In such cases, it will often happen that the serving officer works hand and glove with the titular leader, the latter, owing to his local connections, etc., ensuring the cohesion of his guerillas, while the former supplies to the partnership the technical knowledge necessary for the most effective direction and co-ordination of the guerillas' operations.[92]

This the JEDBURGHS did, organizing and arming recruits, participating in operations, liaising with British and American forces, and advising resistance leaders, but leaving command of resistance operations in French hands.[93] Indeed, the JEDBURGH teams themselves were placed under the operational control of the General Staff of the French Forces of the Interior.[94]

The JEDBURGHS received a pared-down version of typical SOE or OSS training, which included parachuting and making contact with friendly elements, as well as radio operation, close combat, weapons training (including foreign weapons), and demolitions. In addition, JEDBURGH training placed special emphasis on "preventing demolition of main bridges, etc." by retreating German forces, a task of particular concern in the period immediately following the Allied invasion.[95] Omitted were those topics pertaining to operating under cover, since the JEDBURGHS would land in uniform a relatively short distance in advance of the Allied forces.[96]

Invasion

Both SOE and OSS had agents in France prior to the Allied landings at Normandy on 6 June 1944. These men and women, augmented by JEDBURGH teams and OSS OGs immediately after the landings, helped arm, organize, and lead members of the resistance. In total, ninety-three JEDBURGH teams were parachuted into Europe.[97] SOE, with the help of the RAF, armed as many as half a million French partisans, while OSS provided twenty thousand tons of weapons, ammunition, and supplies.[98] On the night of 5/6 June, the British Broadcasting Corporation broadcast the code phrase, "The wine is red." It was the signal for the resistance to strike, conducting sabotage with the primary purpose of preventing German reinforcements from reaching the beachhead.[99] As a result, Allied forces were able to break out of their initial positions and push into France.

Nearly a thousand rail lines in France were cut by partisans the night of 5/6 June 1944.[100] Several thousand more were cut over the course of the next three weeks.[101] SOE estimated that, on average, German forces south of the River Loire were delayed two days in their move north to Normandy. In some cases the delay was much longer. The 2nd SS Panzer Division was held up for two weeks as it fought partisans on its journey from Toulouse to Saint Lô. In the central French region of Corrèze, five thousand German troops had to be deployed against partisans in June 1944—five thousand soldiers who otherwise would have been sent to Normandy. The following month the Germans had to redeploy elements of two divisions against the fighters on the Vercors plateau in eastern France, and another division against partisans along the Dordogne River in the southwest.[102] These German redeployments give lie to the criticism that resistance at Vercors and elsewhere was put down "at trifling cost to the German forces."[103] Even when guerrillas were unable to inflict significant casualties, they forced the shuffling of German troops and thereby changed the balance of forces at the crucial decision point in Normandy. After the initial Allied breakout from Normandy, the resistance continued to show its worth. One column of twenty thousand German troops fleeing from southwest France found that it could not travel directly east, as it wanted, since partisans controlled the roads. Instead, it was forced to turn north into the Loire valley, where eighteen thousand of its number surrendered to JEDBURGH-led resistance forces.[104]

One might justly ask to what extent SOE or OSS were responsible for these successes. Indeed, though the activities of the JEDBURGHS have been well recorded, the way they were used and the value of their operations remain open to debate.[105] "How much Resistance was mobilized by the 'Jedburghs,' which would otherwise have been ineffective?" Mackenzie asks. "There is no means of measuring this: but practically every 'Jedburgh' which was in the field for any length of time found much to do on the lines intended for it—reconciling factions, suggesting targets, bringing supplies, instilling good guerilla doctrine. They were certainly a reinforcement to Resistance out of proportion to their numbers."[106] In addition to delaying German movements, SHAEF noted that organized resistance also aided regular forces "by disrupting enemy telecommunications . . . , by enabling allied formations to advance with greater speed through being able to dispense with many normal military precautions, e.g. flank protection and mopping up, by furnishing military intelligence, [and] by providing organised groups of men in liberated areas able to undertake static guard duties at short notice and without further training."[107] Moreover, SHAEF recognized the larger role played by the resistance when "setting the oppressed peoples at loggerheads with the occupying power." This opposition not only made it difficult for the Germans to exploit fully their conquered territories, but it also fostered the will to resist. "This morale factor was, of course, greatly enhanced by the feeling of support from and contact with the Allies. . . . As resistance met with success, national self-respect and confidence were restored, and the desire and ability to resume responsibilities after liberation revived."[108] This is no small accomplishment considering that SOE was never as large as a single infantry division.[109]

Gubbins's vision of subversive forces working in close conjunction with regular forces was certainly achieved in France. In the days following Germany's defeat, Gen. Dwight Eisenhower, overall commander of Allied forces in northwestern Europe, wrote him a letter of thanks. In it, Eisenhower observed that "in no previous war, and in no other theatre during this war, have resistance forces been so closely harnessed to the main military effort."[110]

Case Study: Burma

SOE in the Far East

SOE's activities in the Far East were dwarfed by those in Europe. One of the chief reasons was time: the war in Europe began more than two years before the war with Japan but, due to the atomic bombs, fighting in the Far East ended only three months after that in Europe. Thus, many of SOE's Far Eastern efforts never reached the maturity of their European counterparts. Moreover, the Japanese capitulation meant that many territories, in which resistance forces had diligently waited to time their revolt with an Allied invasion, never saw open guerrilla warfare.

SOE's efforts in the Far East were initially organized into two missions, one headed by Valentine Killery, initially out of Singapore, and a second led by Colin Mackenzie out of Meerut, India. Mackenzie's mission, initially called GSI(k) and formally located within the General Headquarters, India, was expected to focus on Persia, Afghanistan, Russia, Tibet, and China—in sum, the old Great Game stomping grounds.[111] Indeed, fears of Axis subversion in these territories impelled the creation of this mission and provided its earliest assignments.[112] However, the Japanese invasion of Burma in 1942 brought India to the front lines and shifted Mackenzie's focus.[113]

In July 1941, SOE established Special Training School 101 in Singapore, one of its many schools around the globe. Although the fall of Singapore in 1942 forced the school's closure, it trained civilians from half a dozen nations as well as British officers and NCOs, many of whom went on to teach at subsequent SOE schools.[114] Early plans for stay-behind parties in Malaya were mired in poor coordination between relevant British officials and got off to a late start. But by the end of January 1942, approximately two hundred men were trained, armed, and deployed. Of these, more than two-thirds were ethnic Chinese, most affiliated with the Communist Party. Although these stay-behind parties inflicted considerable damage on the invading Japanese and the infrastructure upon which they relied, they had insufficient time to organize local guerrillas and could not sustain operations.[115]

In 1942, SOE established a school in China to train Nationalist partisans; the trainers were to be closely integrated into Chiang Kai-shek's army and enthusiasm initially ran high on all sides. But the British soon found themselves micromanaged by their Chinese superiors and the arrangement collapsed, never to be replaced. SOE later contributed funds to Chinese intelligence and propaganda efforts and received intelligence in return, but Chiang remained skeptical of sabotage.[116] Under SOE's agreement with OSS, the Americans were given preeminence in Nationalist China, further limiting SOE activities. SOE's attempts to circumvent the agreement by assisting Mao's Eighth Route Army instead came too late in the war to bear fruit.[117]

Special Operations (Australia) (SOA) was established in April 1942, on the orders of the commander-in-chief of the Australian Military Forces, Gen. Sir Thomas Blamey. Gubbins saw in SOA a way in which Australia could, with modest expenditure, make considerable impact on behalf of the empire in what was essentially an American theater of the war. Although not directly subordinate to SOE, SOA did not undertake operations with approval from SOE. Lt. Col. John Chapman-Walker, SOA's commander, was held in high esteem by Gubbins and successfully defended the autonomy of his organization against predators in the Australian and American militaries, while still enjoying excellent relations with both Blamey and Gen. Charles Willoughby, director of intelligence for Gen. Douglas MacArthur.[118] Together SOE and SOA conducted two notable operations, JAYWICK and RIMAU. In September 1943, a joint team sailed from Australia in a fishing vessel. Under the cover of darkness, small assault parties paddled into Singapore harbor, where they destroyed fifty thousand tons of enemy shipping.[119] An attempt to repeat this success in the autumn of 1944, however, ended in failure, with the entire team lost.[120]

Burma

Japan invaded British Burma in January 1942, overrunning the entire country in a few months. However, members of the native Burma Rifles who either did not retreat to India with the main British force or who returned to Burma after having done so formed the core of organized resistance. Among such resistance forces, the hill peoples —particularly the Karens and Kachins—predominated.[121] These men formed themselves into guerrilla units that not only harassed Japanese patrols and supply columns but also rescued downed Allied airmen.[122]

SOE's Burma section, which worked closely with the Karen forces in southeastern Burma, was led by John Gardiner, who had worked in forestry and served on the Municipal Council of Rangoon before the war. As historian Louis Allen explains, the Burma section's goal was "to contact nuclei of local resistance against the occupying enemy force, assess their potential, arm them if it was considered that an armed rising would assist the returning British, and lead and control the rising when it occurred."[123] The Karens represented just such local resistance.

Several months before the Japanese invasion, Noel Stevenson, an assistant superintendent of the Burma Frontier Service, began organizing and training guerrillas. Maj. Hugh Seagrim was recruited by Stevenson and organized a guerrilla force of Karens, built around a core of fifty-five policemen. By April 1942 Seagrim, now living and dressing like a Karen, and his guerrilla force in the hills were totally cut off from the British Army, a problem only rectified when SOE succeeded in dropping a radio and agent to him in October of the following year. So much did the Japanese fear Seagrim's force—and their proximity to the communication lines connecting Rangoon to Mandalay—that a punitive expedition (*tōbatsu*) was launched into the Karen Hills. To end the egregious violence against innocent civilians, Seagrim voluntarily gave himself up and was executed by a Japanese court. However, his Karen guerrillas remained in contact with SOE and also with elements of the collaborationist Burma National Army, including its Karen battalion, which had become resentful of the Japanese and their false promises of independence.[124]

In August 1943, Lord Louis Mountbatten, former chief of Combined Operations, was named Supreme Allied Commander, South East Asia. Gubbins understood that Mountbatten's coming heralded a shift from defensive to offensive operations in the theater and therefore worked to expand SOE's operations and ensure they supported military plans. Given the relatively short timelines anticipated, rather than training and inserting significant numbers of secret agents, indigenous guerrilla forces would be utilized.[125] The various forces that had been organized out of loyal tribes nicely fit the bill.

In 1945 the British Fourteenth Army returned to Burma and, after the capture of Mandalay, began pursuing Japanese forces southward. Historian Charles Cruickshank describes the problem the geography imposed, and the solution SOE and the Karen fighters offered:

> The Irrawaddy and Sittang Rivers run parallel in the centre of the country, north to south. . . . The Irrawaddy is flanked to the west by the Arakan Yomas Range, and the Sittang to the east by the Karen Hills. It was down these valleys that the XIV Army proposed to drive the Japanese forces; but since the mountains precluded outflanking movements on any great scale, the enemy would have every opportunity of making an orderly withdrawal, and re-forming troops. . . . [SOE] was to make that orderly withdrawal impossible.[126]

"I gave the word, 'Up the Karens!'" Gen. William Slim, commander of the Fourteenth Army, recalls in his memoirs.[127] And up the Karens rose. Under Operation CHARACTER, SOE deployed teams of British officers and nearly twelve thousand irregulars, all in radio communication, with weapons provided by air drop.[128] Following the long-standing British practice of empowering traditional Karen leadership, these forces were raised through local Karen chiefs.[129] General Slim recalls: "Japanese, driving hard through the night down jungle roads . . . ran into ambush after ambush; bridges were blown ahead of them, their foraging parties massacred, their sentries stalked, their staff cars shot up."[130] The Karens were so effective that in June 1945 they inflicted more casualties than the vastly larger regular forces of the Fourteenth Army. CHARACTER cost the Japanese 10,964 dead, while SOE's total losses in Burma for the entire war were a mere 303 officers, NCOs, and native levies.[131] In addition to its own operations, CHARACTER supplied valuable intelligence to the RAF. By the time Allied forces closed in on Rangoon, CHARACTER supplied virtually all of the targeting data used by the RAF's 224th Group, indeed, more high-value targets than it had assets to attack.[132]

The Karens were not the only people in Burma to resist the Japanese occupation; the Kachins in the north of the country did the same. Like the Karens, most Kachins returned to their villages after the initial British defeat, to conduct guerrilla warfare and await the British return.[133] Richard Dunlop observes that the Japanese made the mistake of believing that they "could terrorize the Kachin mountain warriors into making peace by carrying out ferocious attacks on the . . . villages. Fire, rape, and the mutilation of young boys would intimidate the Kachins into surrender," or so the Japanese thought.[134] Instead, the Japanese earned for themselves the wrath of a fearsome people who inhabited one of the most inhospitable corners of the world and had a long history of violence.

Though the British Army did not return in large numbers until 1945, in January 1943, British officers infiltrated into Burma to organize the Kachin Levies.[135] Crucially, these forces defended Fort Hertz, an obscure outpost in the extreme northern corner of Burma, of almost no consequence except that it had an airfield. It was from Fort Hertz that the Allies were able to infiltrate men and equipment further into Japanese-occupied Burma.[136] Beginning in earnest in the spring of 1944, the British organized a number of Kachin units, with a total strength of three thousand men. However, in the autumn of 1944 SOE withdrew from the area, at the insistence of Gen. Joseph Stilwell, the regional American commander, who resented the British presence.[137]

OSS sent its first paramilitary unit, Detachment 101, to northern Burma, where it operated under Stilwell. The detachment worked with the Kachins, organizing guerrilla forces and rescuing downed airmen.[138] The American Kachin Rangers, recruited by Detachment 101, eventually numbered 10,200 men.[139] They provided intelligence to Stilwell's American and Chinese forces as they worked to capture the Japanese garrison at Myitkyina, an operation in which the British Kachin Levies also participated.[140]

Like the Karens, the Kachins were praised by their Western colleagues for their skill in irregular warfare. "As guerrilla soldiers they were ideal," Col. William Peers, who eventually commanded Detachment 101, recalls. "The difficulties of following invisible tracks through jungle or crossing towering peaks they looked upon as a natural contest. Weapons they understood as a fact of life; demolitions were not beyond their powers."[141] Kachin resistance forces not only supplied intelligence and launched sabotage missions against Japanese targets but also played a vital role by controlling the jungle and securing its trails, allowing Stilwell to move his forces unmolested. The Kachin Rangers alone were responsible for 5,428 known enemy dead and possibly as many as 10,000 more. In the course of the war they destroyed 51 bridges and 277 enemy vehicles and rescued 574 Allied personnel from the jungles.[142]

As with the war in Europe, the contribution made by resistance forces in Burma, supported by SOE and OSS weapons and coordination, was substantial, even when considering the massive scale of modern industrial warfare. General Slim, commander of the Fourteenth Army, could be a fierce critic of special forces, arguing that they were "expensive, wasteful, and unnecessary."[143] But he believed the resistance played a significant role in Burma.

Our own levies led by their British officers were a most valuable asset and had a real influence on operations. . . . They could not and were not expected to stand up to the Japanese in pitched battles but they could and did in places harry them unmercifully. . . . They had an excellent jitter effect on the Japanese, who were compelled to lock up troops to guard against attacks on the lines of communication.[144]

This was precisely the role Colin Gubbins had envisioned in 1939: threatening communications and forcing the enemy to spread himself thin, thereby diluting the power of his conventional capabilities.

Assessing SOE

The value of sabotage and subversion has been hotly debated. As noted in the introduction, some historians, such as John Keegan, conclude that SOE was expensive and ineffective.[145] Assessments of Anglo-American clandestine relations have likewise sometimes been scathing. Anthony Cave Brown argues that at the end of the war "nobody . . . stepped forward from the grimy London headquarters of SIS to speak well of Donovan."[146]

As the preceding case studies indicate, there is ample evidence that the forces of resistance and the clandestine services that supported them made a meaningful contribution to the ultimate Allied victory. The British Chiefs of Staff concluded that "S.O.E. activity forced the Germans to retain considerable forces in areas of no immediate military value to us. These forces could have been used elsewhere and were contained by economical expenditure of effort."[147] SHAEF concluded that "without the organisation, communications, material, training and leadership which SOE supplied (with the assistance of OSS . . .), 'resistance' would have been of no military value. In DENMARK and HOLLAND, indeed, there might have been no resistance at all but for the work of SOE."[148] Moreover, though it is difficult to measure, SOE and the resistance activities it supported contributed to the Allied effort in indirect ways. By attacking communications lines, for example, the French resistance forced German forces to make greater use of wireless transmissions, which were vulnerable to Allied intelligence collection.[149]

But these benefits must be weighed against the costs. The Second World War was a massive conflict, with millions of men under arms and nearly unimaginable quantities of war materiel expended. Casualties give some sense of scale: Britain lost 264,000 servicemen, the British Empire 125,000, and the United States 300,000. The numbers of German, Japanese, and Soviet servicemen and -women killed—not to mention civilians—runs into the millions for each country.[150] In a war of such staggering scale, the clandestine services were never very large. As of 29 May 1944, the number of SOE personnel in occupied territories stood at only 1,599 in Europe and 352 in the Far East.[151] SOE's total personnel around the globe peaked in September 1944, just shy of 10,000.[152]

The materiel consumed by SOE was quite small; the sum total of its industrial sabotage attacks in France utilized about three thousand pounds of explosives, roughly equivalent to the bomb load of a single Lancaster bomber. Nearly one hundred factories, mines, and other industrial installations were damaged or destroyed by these sabotage efforts.[153] In support of resistance forces, SOE made frequent demand upon the other services, particularly the RAF, but such demands were limited. In 1941 a mere 0.13 percent of RAF Bomber Command's sorties were for SOE purposes. That proportion grew as the war progressed, and by 1945, when Bomber Command flew more sorties for SOE than in the previous four years combined, that proportion rose to 11.47 percent. Still, for the five-year period from 1941 through 1945, only 4.13 percent of Bomber Command's sorties were for SOE.[154] Any argument based on what *might have been* should be treated with caution, but it is difficult to make the case that these resources could have made a substantially better contribution to the war effort in other hands.[155]

But what of the human costs incurred by those who put their trust in SOE? John Keegan argues that three failed rebellions against the Nazis—the Vercors massacre, in which hundreds of French fighters were killed in July 1944; the Slovak revolt of 1944, which was brutally suppressed; and the Warsaw Uprising—demonstrate that SOE raised false hopes, encouraged resistance, and then proved unable or unwilling to support it when revolt finally came.[156]

It is hard to overstate the tragedy of these events, but Keegan's criticisms must be qualified. They are most trenchant when weighed against the hopes of Hugh Dalton and those who fancied that sabotage and subversion could, on their own, win the war. But Gubbins never made such claims; indeed, SOE saw itself as "a cog in a very large machine."[157] As early as his GS(R) days, Gubbins argued that irregular forces must be closely integrated with regular efforts and he rose to the head of SOE precisely because he was willing to work in such close collaboration while his predecessors were not.[158] Indeed, it was because of their commitment to resistance within the context of the larger war effort that the British repeatedly admonished the Polish Home Army *not* to rise up, since the Allied ability to aid the resisters was minimal.[159] The failures here were in the careful balance between encouraging resistance and marrying it to larger strategy, a marriage sometimes requiring restraint. Resistance, with support from SOE and OSS, *was* capable of great achievement. SOE's successes reveal that there was no intrinsic reason why resistance could not make a substantial contribution to the war effort, as it often did.

Conclusion

From humble beginnings in J. C. F. Holland's GS(R) office, Colin Gubbins's vision of irregular warfare grew into a worldwide element of the Allied war effort, both British and American. SOE's brief organizational history concealed decades of wisdom that Gubbins and his colleagues distilled from their own experiences and half a dozen other conflicts into a concise and usable framework. Even before the outbreak of the Second World War, Gubbins identified the principles which produced SOE's greatest successes, among them the paramount importance of indigenous resistance and the need to coordinate irregular warfare with conventional efforts.

Although SOE was not solely responsible for the Allied victory, it played an important role and its story deserves to be told. Likewise, neither Gubbins nor his ideas were solely responsible for SOE's successes. However, there are occasions in history where individuals exercise a strong influence, and Gubbins's place in SOE is one of them. Moreover, if ideas are not the only force in history, they are an important one, and so long as that is the case, intellectual history will matter. Tracing the pedigree of Gubbins's irregular warfare doctrine—sometimes with certainty, sometimes only probabilities—provides a deeper understanding of the exchange of ideas in the world of the twentieth century and, in particular, within the British Empire.

Epilogue

In spite of the successes of SOE in France, Burma, and elsewhere, the organization was disbanded in early 1946, with any leftover assets transferred to SIS.[1] Gubbins, an acting major general at the time, was unwanted by the British Army, which had more generals than it needed, many of them with far more experience commanding in the field than Gubbins, whose work was entirely secret. Lord Selborne fought to have Gubbins's rank made substantial, so that he could retire with a major general's pay, but the War Office refused to grant any exceptions: he could keep the rank as an honorific but would retire with the pay of his substantial rank of colonel.[2] Britain was on the brink of bankruptcy. On 1 February 1946, Gubbins wrote to Selborne, thanking him for his efforts. The letter reveals Gubbins's mixed feelings.

> I know that the War Office decision is wrong, both ethically and on the practical basis of my past career, the appointments I have held, my age etc., without taking into account my service in SOE, but I bear no grudge whatever against them & am only sorry that they can be so stupid.
>
> I am retiring without any feelings of bitterness. I feel it a real privilege to have been in SOE for five years, & know that I was thereby enabled to do far more for our country than if I had been a substantive major-general in any other appointment whatever, and that there are not many people as lucky as that.[3]

Having previously been made a Companion in 1944, Gubbins was promoted to Knight Commander of the Order of Saint Michael and Saint George in the New Year's Honours of 1946.[4]

If Gubbins was virtually forgotten by the bureaucrats of the British government, the same could not be said of foreign governments. In addition to the Order of Saint Stanislaus (third class) he received from the White Russians, Poland awarded him the Croix de Vaillance in 1940, and a raft of honors came after the war's end:

the Légion d'Honneur and Croix de Guerre from France, the Order of Leopold and Croix de Guerre from Belgium, the Royal Order of Saint Olaf from Norway, the Order of Merit from the United States, the Order of the White Lion from Czechoslovakia, Order of the Dannebrog from Denmark, the Order of Orange Nassau from the Netherlands, as well as Greek and Italian awards. The British government agreed to waive the usual rule limiting British soldiers to four foreign awards.[5]

The transition to civilian life was not easy for Sir Colin, who had been in the army since 1914. With only a colonel's retirement, he sought employment. He tried business management, working at a rubber company and then a textile manufacturer. He appears to have been successful, but not outstandingly so, and his heart was not in it. His real interests lay elsewhere. His great passion of the postwar era was the Special Forces Club, an organization he founded for former members of SOE, which also cared for the widows and orphans of those who had served and not returned.[6] Before agreeing to write a preface or foreword to an author's book, Gubbins would always request that the author or publisher make a small donation to the club's benevolent fund.[7]

In 1950 Sir Colin remarried; his new bride, Anna Elise Tradin, was the widow of a Norwegian pilot who had died flying for the RAF. The matter of her citizenship highlights the disregard Gubbins was shown after the war; when she applied for British citizenship, she was told that her husband, who had been born in Japan while his father was on consular service, qualified as a British *subject*, but not a British *citizen*, a status that was only created under the British Nationality Act of 1948. (The Home Office unhelpfully suggested that, since Sir Colin's father had been born in British India, he might be able to claim Indian citizenship.) Sir Colin had to apply for British citizenship before his new bride could claim the same.[8]

In spite of such difficulties, he settled into and profoundly enjoyed his new married life. He took up gardening and, feeling the deprivation of never having attended university, took to intellectual and aesthetic pursuits, reading widely, visiting art galleries, and attending the ballet. He eventually returned to his Scottish roots and retired to the Isle of Harris; he served as colonel in command of the local Home Guard from 1952 to 1956. On 23 January, 1976, he was commissioned the deputy lieutenant of the Isles Area, Western Isles, an honor he deeply valued. Two weeks later, on 6 February, he suffered a heart attack, and died on 11 February.[9]

Far from disappearing, insurgency and guerrilla warfare became common in the decades following the Second World War. So long as they remain, the studies of SOE and OSS maintain their relevance. For historians and policymakers interested in understanding these organizations and the ideas they utilized, Colin Gubbins is indispensable. As Lord Selborne observed, "It is not too much to say that the Organisation over which he presided was mainly his creation."[10] In that creative capacity he built a clandestine service that embodied the lessons of his own life and of the British military experience around the globe.

Notes

Chapter 1

1. Gubbins address to the Danish/English Society (elsewhere given as "Anglo/Danish Club"), Copenhagen, 29 April 1966, 4, Gubbins papers 4/1/20, Imperial War Museum (IWM).
2. Brief History of SOE, 1, The National Archives: Public Record Office (TNA: PRO), HS 7/1. This anonymous document is marked "1st Draft Used on 1st Course." Its purpose remains obscure, since it appears to have been written in 1946, too late to be utilized in one of SOE's many wartime training schools.
3. Hargreaves, *Special Operations in World War II*, 10–11.
4. Regarding *SOE in France*, Gubbins wrote to Foot: "May I say at once that I was immensely impressed by the way you have marshaled the multiplicity of events and evidence into a continuous narrative which reads so convincingly and—if I may so presume—by the balanced judgment you have achieved and given from a welter of conflicting opinions." Gubbins to Foot, 1 January 1964, Gubbins papers 3/2/57, IWM.
5. Anglim, *Orde Wingate and the British Army*, 105.
6. The term Irish Revolution encompasses both the Irish War of Independence (1919–21) and the Irish Civil War (1922–23). Gubbins's time in Ireland included both.
7. Note that Gubbins spells "guerilla" with only one "r," whereas the accepted spelling today is "guerrilla." However, his original spelling will be preserved in this title and in quotations.
8. Gubbins, quoted in Wilkinson and Astley, *Gubbins and SOE*, 34.
9. Cassidy, introduction to Gubbins, *Art of Guerilla Warfare*, vi. The 1981 reprints of the *Art* and *Partisan Leader's Handbook* by Interservice Press should not be taken for books in the ordinary sense; they are pages stapled together between construction paper covers. The author observed them in the Rare Books, Manuscripts and Archives section of the Georgetown University Library.
10. Garliński, *Poland, SOE and the Allies*, 25.
11. Selborne to Churchill, 13 May 1942, Gubbins papers 3/1/8, IWM. Churchill eventually replied: "I am glad it has been possible to meet your wishes in this matter and that Brigadier Gubbins will be able to continue on the important work on which he is now engaged." Churchill to Selborne, May 1942, Gubbins papers 3/1/9.
12. William Strange (Foreign Office) to Gubbins, 10 December 1949, Gubbins papers 3/2/48, IWM.
13. Robin Brook to Foreign Secretary, September 1970, Gubbins papers 3/2/57, IWM.
14. Foot, *SOE in France*, 450.

15. Gubbins to Foot, 31 January 1964, 2, Gubbins papers 3/2/57, IWM.
16. C. B. Townshend's report of 17 December 1974 held by SOE Advisor; quoted in Stuart, "'Of Historical Interest Only,'" 222.
17. Stuart, "'Of Historical Interest Only,'" 222–23.
18. "CG's Comments on Foot's Book," n.d., 1, Gubbins papers 3/2/57, IWM.
19. On the existence of this war diary, see Astley, *Inner Circle*, 42. GS(R) was followed by MI(R), whose war diary *is* extant, though it begins only with the outbreak of war in September 1939. It may be found in TNA: PRO, HS 8/263.
20. Keegan, *Second World War*, 483–85. It should be noted, however, that Keegan's criticism of SOE is part of his larger argument—found across numerous works—that "victory is . . . bought with blood rather than brains." Thus, in addition to criticizing SOE, he also qualifies the utility of intelligence, calling it "the handmaiden, not the mistress, of the warrior" (Keegan, *Intelligence in War*, 6). Benjamin Grob-Fitzgibbon replies to Keegan that in an insurgency "force will indeed become necessary and inevitable, but force without intelligence will often do more harm than good" ("Intelligence and Counter-Insurgency," 72).
21. Foot, "Was SOE Any Good?" 167–81.
22. Wilkinson and Astley, *Gubbins and SOE*, 2–8, 12–14.
23. Howarth, *Undercover*, 3.
24. Astley, *Inner Circle*, 21.
25. Wilkinson and Astley, *Gubbins and SOE*, 242.
26. Seaman, "A New Instrument of War," 17.
27. Foot, *Memories of an SOE Historian*, 125.
28. Marks, *Between Silk and Cyanide*, 222–28, 362, 380–82, 406, 453, 562–63, 593.
29. Lord Selborne to the Rt. Hon. J. J. Lawson, PC, MP, 17 October 1945, 2, Papers of Roundell C. Palmer, 3rd Earl Selborne, MS Eng. Hist. c. 1002, fol. 10, Bodleian Library, Oxford University.
30. Sir Frank Nelson to Gubbins, 5 May 1942, Gubbins papers 3/2/5, IWM.
31. Weale, *Secret Warfare*, 4–6. Weale includes a fifth task, counterterrorism, though such operations are essentially variations on intelligence collection and offensive action.
32. Paddock, *U.S. Army Special Warfare*, 40, 152; Weale, *Secret Warfare*, 6–10.
33. The joint U.S. Army and U.S. Marine Corps *Counterinsurgency Field Manual*, released in 2006, has been central to many discussions. Arguably most eminent among the previous generation of studies is David Galula, *Counterinsurgency Warfare: Theory and Practice* (Westport, CT, 1964). For a history of the American experience, see Andrew J. Birtle's two volume *U.S. Army Counterinsurgency and Contingency Operations Doctrine*.
34. Indicative of the broad trend, see Patrick F. McDevitt, *May the Best Man Win: Sport, Masculinity, and Nationalism in Great Britain and the Empire* (Basingstroke, UK, 2004); William Beinart and Lotte Hughes, *Environment and Empire* (Oxford, 2007); Frank Trentmann, *Free Trade Nation: Commerce, Consumption, and Civil Society in Modern Britain*

(Oxford, 2008); Esther Breitenbach, *Empire and Scottish Society: The Impact of Foreign Missions at Home* (Edinburgh, 2009); John E. Crowley, *Imperial Landscapes: Britain's Global Visual Culture* (New Haven, 2011); Ryan Johnson and Amna Khalid, eds., *Public Health in the British Empire* (New York, 2012). So wide-ranging has this scholarship become that one of the leading journals in the field is simply titled *Britain and the World.*

Chapter 2

1. Gubbins, quoted in Wilkinson and Astley, *Gubbins and SOE*, 14.
2. Ibid., 15.
3. Army Form B 193A, Gubbins papers 3/1/6, IWM; Wilkinson and Astley, *Gubbins and SOE*, 16.
4. Supplement to the *London Gazette*, 22 September 1916, 9275. See also Letter from Deputy Assistant Adjutant and Quartermaster General, 4th Division to commander of the 4th Division Artillery, n.d., Gubbins papers 3/1/1, IWM.
5. Army Form B 193A, Gubbins papers 3/1/6, IWM; Wilkinson and Astley, *Gubbins and SOE*, 17. Wilkinson and Astley record that the promotion happened on 16 August, though this is likely a scribal error, arising from the fact that the above-mentioned form generally gives only months and the last two digits of the year, for example, "August 16."
6. Edward Beddington-Behrens, letter to his uncle, date unknown, quoted in Wilkinson and Astley, *Gubbins and SOE*, 18. See also (London) *Times* wounded list, 26 October 1916, and telegram of 9 October 1916, Gubbins papers 3/1/2, IWM.
7. Army Form B 193A, Gubbins papers 3/1/6, IWM; Wilkinson and Astley, *Gubbins and SOE*, 18.
8. Supplement to the *London Gazette*, 9 September 1916, 8869.
9. Carton de Wiart, *Happy Odyssey*, 89.
10. Gubbins, note for a book by Peter Fleming [never finished], n.d., 1, 3, Gubbins papers 5/11, IWM.
11. Supplement to the *London Gazette*, 5 April 1918, 4113; Wilkinson and Astley, *Gubbins and SOE*, 20.
12. Jack Gubbins [Colin's father], date unknown, quoted in Wilkinson and Astley, *Gubbins and SOE*, 20.
13. Supplement to the *London Gazette*, 17 May 1918, 5839; Army Form B 193A, Gubbins papers 3/1/6, IWM.
14. Wilkinson and Astley, *Gubbins and SOE*, 20–21.
15. Ibid., 21; Army Form B 193A, Gubbins papers 3/1/6, IWM.
16. Army Form B 193A, Gubbins papers 3/1/6, IWM; Wilkinson and Astley, *Gubbins and SOE*, 24. The Royal Artillery Cadet Officer School is referred to as a college in some documents.
17. Ironside, *Archangel*, 17; Kinvig, *Churchill's Crusade*, 23–24.
18. Kinvig, *Churchill's Crusade*, 41.
19. Ibid., 43. General Ironside, reflecting on this matter in his memoirs more than thirty years after the fact, comments, "It was thought that the coup should have been detected and prevented, and in Russian

quarters General Poole was accused of having favoured it. There was, of course, no truth in such a stupid accusation" (*Archangel*, 21).
20. Kinvig, *Churchill's Crusade*, 46.
21. Despatch No. 3, Ironside to Churchill, 1 November 1919, published in the Supplement to the *London Gazette*, 6 April 1920, 4117.
22. Ironside, *Archangel*, 66.
23. Albertson, *Fighting without a War*, 77. Cf. Rhodes, *Anglo-American*, 48.
24. Ironside, *Archangel*, 71.
25. Supplement to the *London Gazette*, 28 March 1919, 4139. Army Form B 193A, Gubbins papers 3/1/6, IWM, gives his date of appointment as March 1919. Prior to Gubbins's appointment, Ironside had no ADC; see Ironside, *Archangel*, 61.
26. Ironside to Secretary of State War Churchill, 1 November 1919, 1, TNA: PRO, WO 32/5705.
27. Kinvig, *Churchill's Crusade*, 44n.
28. Ironside, *Archangel*, 170.
29. Wilkinson and Astley, *Gubbins and SOE*, 25, 95; Supplement to the *London Gazette*, 28 October 1919, 13229; Army Form B 193A, Gubbins papers 3/1/6. His Russian language skills likely came about from dealing directly with Russian citizens. General Ironside had a Russian groom and a Russian driver. See Ironside, *Archangel*, 61, 67.
30. Letter to J. B. Astley from Maj. Gen. Douglas Wimberley, 8 July 1977; quoted in Wilkinson and Astley, *Gubbins and SOE*, 25.
31. Ironside, *Archangel*, 173.
32. Gubbins, "Regular and Irregular Warfare: Problems of Co-Ordination," lecture at University of Manchester, 29 November 1967, 4–5, Gubbins papers 4/1/27, IWM. This lecture was part of the Military Studies public lecture series, "Subversion, Intelligence, Resistance."
33. Ibid., 5–6.
34. Gubbins, "The Underground Forces in Britain 1940–1944," lecture given to the Cerne Abbas Discussion Club, Dorchester, April [?] 1973, Gubbins papers 4/1/42, IWM.
35. Rhodes, *Anglo-American*, 57.
36. Soutar, *With Ironside in North Russia*, xi.
37. Northern Russia Expeditionary Force to Director of Military Operations, 9 December 1918, quoted in Occleshaw, *Dances in Deep Shadows*, 281–82.
38. Rhodes, *Anglo-American*, 59.
39. Ironside, *Archangel*, 174.
40. Kinvig, *Churchill's Crusade*, 48.
41. Ironside, *Archangel*, 58.
42. Ironside to Churchill, 1 November 1919, 2, TNA: PRO, WO 32/5705.
43. Rhodes, *Anglo-American*, 61. See also Ironside to War Office, 6 and 8 November 1918, TNA: PRO, WO 158/714/HM06495. In Ironside's memoirs, however, he writes that, "Soldiers can only be affected by whispering campaigns conducted from inside, and the Allies had no

subversive elements in their ranks in Russia. I never found the British soldier touched by foreign-made propaganda. His kindly but marked contempt for all 'foreigners' provides him with an armour which is difficult to pierce. The Bolshevik propagandists certainly had no sort of idea how the ordinary Britisher lived and worked" (*Archangel*, 58).

44. Ironside, *Archangel*, 58. The conflict involved a variety of other quirks as well. Allied forces at Pinega, for example, "had been unpaid for some time owing to the lack of currency and they had very naturally protested. The wretched pay officer had been sent up with nothing lower than 1,000 rouble notes, in the hope that he might be able to exchange them in the villages. The supply of smaller notes had run out. . . . A wire to [Governor-General] Miller soon brought up a plane with the requisite small notes and all was peace once more" (ibid., 138).
45. Kinvig, *Churchill's Crusade*, 47.
46. Ironside, *Archangel*, 67.
47. Ironside to Gen. Lord Rawlinson, ADC General Commanding-in-Chief, North Russia, 1 November 1919, 1, TNA: PRO, WO 32/5705; Ironside, *Archangel*, 68, 84. Cf. Notes on Administration since Arrival of Relief Brigades in May 1919, 1-2, TNA: PRO, WO 32/5705.
48. Notes on Administration since Arrival of Relief Brigades in May 1919, 2, TNA: PRO, WO 32/5705; Lt. Col. Barrington C. Wells to Maj. Gen. Edmund Ironside, 8 July 1919, TNA: PRO, WO 32/9545; Ironside to Secretary of State for War Winston Churchill, 17 July 1919, TNA: PRO, WO 32/9545; Napper Tandy to Maj. Gen. Neil Malcolm, British Military Mission Berlin, 1 January 1921, TNA: PRO, WO 32/9545; Ironside, *Archangel*, 68-69, 112-14, 126-27, 161-62. The episode that most upset the British psyche was the mutiny of C Company, 1st Battalion (Dyer's Btn.), Slavo-British Legion. Around 2:30 A.M. on 6 July 1919, the mutineers "murdered three of their own British officers and four Russian officers in cold blood in their billets and then intimidated a certain number of the rank and file to desert and join the Bolsheviks" (T. Harrington to Maj. Gen. Neil Malcolm, 1 October 1920, TNA: PRO, WO 32/9545). An unknown writer described three of the ringleaders as "guilty of the blackest treachery conceivable" (unidentified letter, 10 August 1919, TNA: PRO, WO 32/9545).
49. Ironside to Churchill, 17 July 1919, TNA: PRO, WO 32/9545.
50. Royal Engineers, Allied Forces, Archangel, Report for Period: May 27th 1919 to Evacuation [Sept. 27th], 2, TNA: PRO, WO 32/5705.
51. Ironside, Notes on Operations . . . to Accompany Despatch, Appendix C: "Report on Operations Covering Period 1st October 1918 to 26th May 1919," 11, TNA: PRO, WO 106/1164. In his memoirs Ironside does not explicitly mention Callwell's book, though he notes that "the strategy and tactics employed [at Archangel] were those of 'small wars,' which have played such an important part in the history of the British Empire" (*Archangel*, 192). On the lack of interest in northern Russia, see also Ironside, *Archangel*, 23.
52. Douglas Porch, introduction to C. E. Callwell, *Small Wars*, v-vi.

53. Callwell, *Small Wars*, 44.
54. Ibid., 27.
55. Ibid., 40.
56. Ironside, *Archangel*, 165. The phrase "a blow in the air" is repeated again on 173. One ought not, of course, assume that the war was civil just because Ironside excludes its darker elements. He makes no mention, for example, of the fact that the British utilized poison gas against their Bolshevik enemies. See Kinvig, *Churchill's Crusade*, 244–47.
57. Silverlight, *Victor's Dilemma*, 256, 352.
58. Callwell, *Small Wars*, 42.
59. Hargreaves, *Special Operations*, 10.
60. Callwell, *Small Wars*, 32. Cf. ibid., 99.
61. Ibid., 53.
62. Ibid., 53–4, 242.
63. Colin Gubbins, *Art of Guerilla Warfare*, Gubbins papers 6/1, IWM (hereafter *AGW*), 12 § 43; Gubbins, *The Partisan Leader's Handbook*, Gubbins papers 6/2, IWM (hereafter *PLH*), 2 § 3. These pamphlets can also be found in TNA: PRO, HS 8/256. Cf. *AWG*, 4 § 12; 16 § 58.
64. Callwell, *Small Wars*, 47.
65. *AGW*, 2 § 5b.
66. Callwell, *Small Wars*, 76–77. Similar ideas were also found in the *Field Service Regulations (FSR)*, which Callwell influenced. See Anglim, "Callwell versus Graziani," 593.
67. Callwell, *Small Wars*, 72–73.
68. *AGW*, 5 § 15. Years later, Gubbins commented, "Countries may be technically defeated, their Governments compelled by lack of means to accept the enemy's presence, or to seek temporary exile in friendly territory: but *peoples* do not necessarily surrender, do not accept the technical situation, when they have the heart and will to continue the struggle for their homeland, though maybe momentarily stunned by the cataclysm that has struck them and left them in disarray" (Address to the Special Forces Club on the occasion of their Silver Jubilee dinner, 21 April 1965, 2, Gubbins papers 4/1/16, IWM).
69. This approach is echoed by the historian M. R. D. Foot, who himself served in the Special Air Service during World War II, in which capacity he rubbed shoulders with SOE; after the war he became SOE's first—and arguably still greatest—historian. Ralph White, writing of Foot, explains:

> A propos its contribution to the military and economic side of the Allied war effort, the scholar acknowledges the difficulties in making final or unequivocal judgments, and comes to his measured conclusions as to its real but limited role—with the important proviso that more could have been made of it. A propos the political, psychological and moral dimension, his conclusions are more confident and emphatic. At their core is the conviction that resistance "gave back to people in the occupied countries the self-respect that they lost in the moment of occupation." . . . The greatest value of resistance was, therefore, moral and exemplary. (White, "Teaching the Free Man," 113; internal quotation from Foot, *Resistance*, 319)

70. Callwell, *Small Wars*, 85.
71. *AGW*, 6 § 16d.
72. Callwell, *Small Wars*, 86.
73. *AGW*, 8 § 25.
74. Callwell, *Small Wars*, 115.
75. "Minor Tactics" (G.1), in Rigden, *SOE Syllabus*, 248.
76. *AGW*, 1 § 1; cf. *PLH*, 2 § 2, 12 § 14.
77. Callwell, *Small Wars*, 90.
78. Ibid., 91.
79. *AGW*, 5 § 15; *PLH*, 2 § 2f.
80. *AGW*, 6 § 16b.
81. Callwell, *Small Wars*, 135–43.
82. *AGW*, 15 § 55–56.
83. Anglim, *Orde Wingate*, 31. Cf. Moreman, "'Small Wars,'" 110.
84. Callwell, *Small Wars*, 23.
85. Ibid., 230–34, 248–55.
86. Porch, introduction to Callwell, *Small Wars*, xv.
87. Ibid., xvi. As it turned out, guerrillas in Lawrence's day and after had a weapon those facing Callwell often did not: unity. "In the pre-1914 era, native resistance usually failed because it lacked a common ideology or sense of self-interest. . . . [Post-1914,] nationalism, Marxism or Islam supplied ideologies that rationalized and focused discontent" (xvi).
88. Fitzpatrick, *Two Irelands*, 132–33.
89. Wilkinson and Astley, *Gubbins and SOE*, 26.
90. Ibid., 26–27.
91. Ibid., 27.
92. Sources disagree on the exact date of his arrival in Ireland. One letter states that he joined the 47th Battery on 2 December 1919. See Vera Long to Eric Mockler-Ferryman, 9 January 1978, Gubbins papers 12/2, IWM. However, his Army Form B 193A states that he joined the 47th Battery in November. See Gubbins papers 3/1/6, IWM.
93. War Diary, Headquarters, Royal Artillery, 5th Division (hereafter War Diary, RA5D), April 1922, TNA: PRO, WO 35/93A.
94. War Diary, Headquarters, Royal Artillery, Dublin District (hereafter War Diary, RADD), September 1922, TNA: PRO, WO 35/93A. On 1 October 1922 Gubbins relinquished his position as temporary brigade major. See *London Gazette*, 6 October 1922, 7044.
95. Gubbins to General Staff 5th Division, 9 April 1922; and Gubbins, order Z/298, 17 May 1922, TNA: PRO, WO 35/93A.
96. War Diaries, RA5D, January and April 1922; and Gubbins, order CA/301/21, TNA: PRO, WO 35/93A.
97. 5th Division Letter 13990-G, TNA: PRO, WO 35/93A.
98. Gubbins, orders of 16 April 1922, TNA: PRO, WO 35/93A. On 29 April Gubbins issued orders transferring all of the artillery from 5th Division to the Dublin District; in these orders, only about half of the artillery was converted to infantry. See Gubbins, orders CA/385/34, TNA: PRO, WO 35/93A.
99. Gubbins, orders Z/298/1, Table A, 24 June 1922, TNA: PRO, WO 35/93A.

100. Wilkinson and Astley, *Gubbins and SOE*, 26–27; Cassidy, introduction to Gubbins, *Art of Guerrilla Warfare*, v.
101. Hart, *British Intelligence*, 12–13. Kenneth Strong recalls that "my first Intelligence appointment was accidental. . . . Largely because I had recently attended a seemingly irrelevant education course, I found myself appointed Detachment Intelligence Officer" (*Intelligence at the Top*, 1).
102. Hart, *British Intelligence*, 10–11; Hart, *The IRA*, 74–75.
103. War Diary, RA5D, December 1921, TNA: PRO, WO 35/93A. This document is incorrectly marked "December 1922" on the top, but the entries below begin with "5.12.21" and make clear that headquarters is located at the Curragh, which was true in December 1921; by December 1922 British forces had left Ireland.
104. War Diaries, RA5D, January and February 1922, TNA: PRO, WO 35/93A.
105. War Diary, RA5D, February 1922, TNA: PRO, WO 35/93A.
106. Gubbins, orders 3542, 20 May 1922; War Diary, RADD, June 1922, TNA: PRO, WO 35/93A.
107. Divisional Artillery Operation Order No. 1, 3 June 1922, TNA: PRO, WO 35/93A. See especially appendix 6: "Co-operation with Royal Air Force."
108. War Diary, RA5D, August 1922, TNA: PRO, WO 35/93A.
109. *Record of the Rebellion in Ireland*, vol. 4: *Record of the 5th and 6th Divisions and Dublin District, Part I: 5th Division*, chapter 3: "Introduction of Martial Law in the South," June 1920–December 1920, 35, TNA: PRO, WO 141/93.
110. War Diary, RA5D, March 1922, TNA: PRO, WO 35/93A.
111. War Diary, RA5D, April 1922, TNA: PRO, WO 35/93A.
112. War Diary, RA5D, June 1922, TNA: PRO, WO 35/93A.
113. War Diary, RA5D, June 1922, TNA: PRO, WO 35/93A.
114. Wilkinson and Astley, *Gubbins and SOE*, 27.
115. War Diary, RA5D, June 1922, TNA: PRO, WO 35/93A.
116. War Diary, RADD, July 1922, TNA: PRO, WO 35/93A. Although the War Diaries are not explicit on this point, as early as December 1921 Gubbins mentioned "the possibility of Extremists causing a rupture by attacking British Troops." At least some of the antitreaty-ites may have hoped that drawing the British back into the conflict would unite the rival factions of the IRA. See Costello, *Irish Revolution*, 293, 298.
117. War Diaries, RADD, August and September 1922, TNA: PRO, WO 35/93A.
118. Quoted in Wilkinson and Astley, *Gubbins and SOE*, 27. They cite the Gubbins papers, though this author could not locate it among the papers at the Imperial War Museum.
119. Wilkinson, lecture titled "Gubbins: A Resistance Leader," given at Cambridge on 28 April 1990, Gubbins papers 4/1/50, 2, IWM.
120. "He was not one of those who yearned to follow in the footsteps of Colonel T. E. Lawrence" (Wilkinson, "Gubbins: A Resistance Leader," Gubbins papers 4/1/50, 1, IWM).

121. *Record of the Rebellion in Ireland*, vol. 4: *Record of the 5th and 6th Divisions and Dublin District, Part I: 5th Division*, chapter 6: "Training, Sport and Education," 68, TNA: PRO, WO 141/93.
122. Ibid., emphasis added.
123. Ibid., 69.
124. Hart, *British Intelligence*, 11, 13.
125. War Office, *Notes on Guerrilla Warfare in Ireland* (hereafter *Notes*), § 11.i.a-i.
126. *AGW*, 11 § 38.
127. *PLH*, 10 § 11; *AGW*, 3 § 6.
128. *AGW*, 12 § 38. Likewise, Gubbins insists that enemy documents found during ambushes should always be taken and examined. See *PLH*, 16 (appendix 1: "Road Ambush") § 4.
129. *AGW*, 13 § 45. Cf. *PLH*, p. 37 (appendix 7: "Guerilla Information Service"), § 4.
130. *PLH*, 11 § 12. Two months before Gubbins penned these words, a report by Section D (see chapter 3) included a passage on organization of Romanian guerrillas. "Where possible they would endeavour to execute members of the Gestapo with as much show as possible, in order to produce in the minds of the local inhabitants that the guerrillas were more to be feared than the occupying secret police. In this way, (a technique which was learnt from the Irish in 1920) the business of collection of intelligence would become more and more difficult for the enemy." See untitled document, 20 March 1939, TNA: PRO, HS 8/256.
131. *Notes*, § 2.
132. *AGW*, 11 § 37.
133. *AGW*, 11 § 37; *PLH*, 10 § 11, 37 (appendix 7: "Guerilla Information Service"), § 1. Gubbins never mentions prostitutes; either he considered them ineffective or his sense of decorum caused him to include them among "camp followers" rather than giving them their own category. However, Gubbins does note that "domestic servants and café attendants are particularly valuable agents; they must be encouraged to gain the confidence of the enemy soldiers, and be on easy and intimate terms with them. Suitable agents of this type should be introduced into houses where enemy officers are billeted, etc. It is a natural weakness of soldiers in a hostile country to react favourably to acts of courtesy and kindness from women; such men will frequently drop unsuspecting hints that they are shortly going on patrol, etc." (*PLH*, 37 [appendix 7], § 2.)
134. *PLH*, 10 § 11.
135. *Record of the Rebellion in Ireland*, vol. 4: *Record of the 5th and 6th Divisions and Dublin District, Part I:* "5th Division," chapter 4: "January 1921 to Date of The Suspension of Activities," 40, TNA: PRO, WO 141/93. The *Record of the Rebellion in Ireland* has a curious history; William Sheehan claims it was never published or even completed, while Peter Hart contends that it was printed, but with an unknown run. The memoranda and letters in TNA suggest that the

project was scaled back while in progress, but in April 1923 the chief of the Imperial General Staff made clear that "Vols. I & II have already been printed and a very limited issue has been made." Discussion was underway regarding the printing of a final volume, containing unit histories; the chief recommended that it be printed "as a secret document." See Chief of the Imperial General Staff, 18 April 1923, TNA: PRO, WO 141/93; Hart, *British Intelligence*, 16; Sheehan, *Hearts & Mines*, xvi. Sheehan and Hart agree that officers in Ireland collaborated on the project. It is unlikely, though not impossible, that Gubbins was also involved. More probable is that these and similar pieces of intelligence crossed his desk while in Ireland.

136. *Notes*, § 3.
137. *AGW*, 5 § 15, 6 § 16g, 6 § 16b.
138. *PLH*, 2 § 2f, 1 § 2b. Cf. *AGW*, 5 § 15, 6 § 16f; *PLH*, 1 § 2b; *PLH*, 14 (appendix 1: "Road Ambush") § 2d.
139. *Notes*, § 3.
140. See *PLH*, 13–20 (appendix 1: "Road Ambush"), and 20–27 (appendix 2: "Rail Ambush").
141. *AGW*, 5 § 16a.
142. *PLH*, 1 § 2a.
143. Ibid., 4 § 6.
144. *AGW*, 4 § 12. Cf. *PLH*, 4 § 6.
145. *Notes*, § 12.
146. *PLH*, 5 § 7; 15 (appendix 1: "Road Ambush") § 4b.
147. Ibid.
148. *Notes*, § 12; *AGW*, 6 § 16c; *PLH*, 13 (appendix 1: "Road Ambush") § 2a, emphasis added. The same point is stressed again in *AGW*, 5 § 15; *PLH*, 1 § 2c and *PLH*, 7 § 9.
149. *AGW*, 4 § 12. Cf. *Notes*, § 12. As the troubles in Ireland were winding to a close, the War Office had instructed its various unit commanders to compile detailed reports of their time in Ireland, reports that would then become the raw material for a brief work on partisan warfare. Thomas Mockaitis writes that "such a worthwhile manual seems never to have been written." It is possible, however, that GS(R) had access to these reports and that the manual was indeed written by Gubbins, though no evidence of this has yet been found. Mockaitis, *British Counterinsurgency*, 180.
150. Hart, *British Intelligence*, 12.
151. *AGW*, 15 § 54. Confusingly, the IRA used the term "flying column" to refer to bands out in the wilds trying to avoid capture, rather than for the mobile columns hunting them. Gubbins notes that the size of parties on the run will vary depending upon the terrain and that more rugged terrain is able to conceal larger parties. See *PLH*, 8 § 10.
152. *PLH*, 3 § 3; *AGW*, 10 § 33.
153. *Notes*, § 4–11. Cf. *AGW*, 14–16 § 53–60; *PLH*, 11–12 § 13.
154. *Notes*, § 1.
155. *PLH*, 1 § 2c. Cf. *AGW*, 6 § 16b.

156. J. C. F. Holland, Duties of the New Branch, 3 April 1939, 2, TNA: PRO, HS 8/256, emphasis added.
157. Gubbins, "The Underground Forces in Britain 1940–1944," lecture given to the Cerne Abbas Discussion Club, Dorchester, April [?] 1973, Gubbins papers 4/1/42, IWM.
158. O'Halpin, "The Irish Experience," 70.
159. Ibid., 71.
160. Ibid., 71.
161. Popplewell, *Intelligence and Imperial Defence*, 297.
162. Moreman, *The Army in India*, 103–20; Popplewell, *Intelligence and Imperial Defence*, 303.
163. Army Form B 193A, Gubbins papers 3/1/6, IWM; Wilkinson and Astley, *Gubbins and SOE*, 27–28. Wilkinson and Astley record that he sailed for India on 2 March and arrived at Lucknow on 1 April. Mhow is located south of Indore in modern-day Madhya Pradesh.
164. Wilkinson and Astley, *Gubbins and SOE*, 28. It was around this time that Gubbins was inducted into the Masons, a source of some concern when Foot was writing *SOE in France*. The initial draft was to include mention of the fact that Gubbins was a Mason, but Gubbins strongly objected to this inclusion. "I was initiated into the craft in about 1923," he wrote to Foot on 27 January 1964, "but have taken no active part of any kind since then, and am not even able to recognize fellow members of the Craft. If you mention it in your book nobody would believe that it did not affect my policies in some way or another. . . . Further I have no desire to be approached again by other Free Masons, which will surely happen if this point is mentioned." Foot replied two days later: "My dear Sir Colin, Thank you very much for your letter of the 27th. I quite see your point, and the passage shall be deleted. Yours sincerely, Michael Foot." See Gubbins papers 3/2/57, IWM. This author mentions this detail in the hope that modern readers will not jump to conclusions or weave silly conspiracy theories. Moreover, Sir Colin, now in the grave, is beyond the pesterings of his fellow Masons.
165. Army Form B 193A, Gubbins papers 3/1/6, IWM; Wilkinson and Astley, *Gubbins and SOE*, 28. Jubbulpore, now generally spelled Jabalpur, is located in Madhya Pradesh.
166. Army Form B 193A, Gubbins papers 3/1/6, IWM; Wilkinson and Astley, *Gubbins and SOE*, 28.
167. Gubbins, "The Underground Forces in Britain 1940–1944," lecture given to the Cerne Abbas Discussion Club, Dorchester, April [?] 1973, 4, Gubbins papers 4/1/4, IWM.
168. Bowyer, *RAF Operations*, 156.
169. Army Form B 193A, Gubbins papers 3/1/6, IWM.
170. Colonel Hillyard, 23 June 1925, Gubbins papers 3/1/4, IWM.
171. Army Form B 193A, Gubbins papers 3/1/6, IWM. Wilkinson and Astley contend that he took his Urdu exam in the summer of 1924. If that is correct, the date on the form is either a scribal error or the

date on which the results of his exam were officially processed. His SOE personnel file refers to this as an Army Proficiency Exam in Hindustani. See SOE Record of Service, TNA: PRO, HS 9/630/8.
172. Peter Wilkinson, "Gubbins: A Resistance Leader," lecture given at Cambridge on 28 April 1990, 2, Gubbins papers 4/1/50, IWM; Army Form B 193A, Gubbins papers 3/1/6, IWM; Wilkinson and Astley, *Gubbins and SOE*, 29.
173. Hopkirk, *Setting the East Ablaze*, 3-4, 15; Popplewell, *Intelligence and Imperial Defence*, 306.
174. Quoted in Hopkirk, *Setting the East Ablaze*, 1.
175. Ibid., 2. In January 1918, for example, the British consulate in Kashgar, in far western China, acquired a wireless set that it used not only to communicate with the British government but also to listen in on radio traffic from Moscow going out to Tashkent and other posts in Soviet Central Asia. Ibid., 96.
176. Popplewell, *Intelligence and Imperial Defence*, 312. Cf. Andrew, *Her Majesty's Secret Service*, 259, 269. Unfortunately, the leading works on the Comintern and India, by Sobhanlal Datta Gupta, are histories of the Comintern as an organization and its internal intellectual debates. *Comintern, India and the Colonial Question, 1920-37* (Calcutta, 1980) and *Comintern and the Destiny of Communism in India, 1919-1943: Dialectics of Real and a Possible History* (Calcutta, 2006) give virtually no details on actual subversive efforts in India.
177. *AGW*, 13 § 47.
178. Ibid., 18 § 67.
179. Adrian Weale argues that the practitioners of the Great Game, many of whom lived into the interwar period and continued to be celebrated in British popular culture, constitute "the real roots of modern Anglo-American-influenced special forces," since "the legacy of the Great Game, and the *Boys' Own* accounts that it inspired, undoubtedly helped to convince later generations that brave and intrepid individuals or small groups could make a difference" (*Secret Warfare*, 8, 10). While certainly plausible, this argument needs further development. While Gubbins learned important lessons in British India, he never named the Great Game among the models that inspired his work.
180. Army Form B 193A, Gubbins papers 3/1/6, IWM; Moreman, *The Army in India*, 125; Wilkinson and Astley, *Gubbins and SOE*, 29-30. In the preceding years, there had been intense debate about the provisional 1920 *FSR*, various textbooks on irregular warfare and the role frontier training in military education. The basic argument centered on whether military men needed specific training to meet the needs of the North-West Frontier—as the recent war against the Afghans and Waziri tribesmen suggested—or whether emphasis should be placed on more general skills of universal application. See Moreman, *The Army in India*, 123-24.
181. Wilkinson and Astley, *Gubbins and SOE*, 29-30.
182. Gubbins to Helen, 16 May 1929; quoted in Wilkinson and Astley, *Gubbins and SOE*, 30.

183. Wilkinson and Astley, *Gubbins and SOE*, 29.
184. Army Form B 193A, Gubbins papers 3/1/6, IWM.
185. Kinvig, *Churchill's Crusade*, 34. Cf. Baron, *The King of Karelia*, 185.
186. Bowyer, *RAF Operations*, 38; Rhodes, *Anglo-America*, 53.
187. Ironside to Gen. Lord Rawlinson, Commander-in-Chief, North Russia, 1 November 1919, TNA: PRO, WO 32/5705.
188. Sheehan, *Hard Local War*, 88, 113,145, 181.
189. *An t-Ólgach*, May 1921; quoted in Sheehan, *Hard Local War*, 145.
190. Government of India, *Army in India*, 177; Wilkinson and Astley, *Gubbins and SOE*, 29. In the 1920s RAF Squadron 5 was stationed at Quetta; see Bowyer, *RAF Operations*, 154.
191. SOE Record of Service, TNA: PRO, HS 9/630/8.
192. Bowyer, *RAF Operations*, 60.
193. Undersecretary of State's report on Somaliland, 17 February 1920, TNA: PRO, AIR/9/12; quoted in Towle, *Pilots and Rebels*, 12. Cf. Bowyer, *RAF Operations*, 62.
194. Bowyer, *RAF Operations*, 65–72, 75; Towle, *Pilots and Rebels*, 13–17.
195. Quoted in Bowyer, *RAF Operations*, 120.
196. Bowyer, *RAF Operations*, 135, 142; Towle, *Pilots and Rebels*, 49–51.
197. Moreman, *The Army in India*, 130; Bowyer, *RAF Operations*, 161, 167.
198. *Operations in Waziristan, 1919–20*, 2nd ed. (London, 1924), quoted in Bowyer, *RAF Operations*, 154.
199. Bowyer, *RAF Operations*, 170–72, 180.
200. *AGW*, 14 § 52.
201. Ibid., 16 § 59.
202. Ibid., 15 § 55.
203. *PLH*, 3 § 3.
204. Ibid., 35 (appendix 6: "How to Counter Enemy Action"), § 1.
205. Ibid., 14 (appendix 1: "Road Ambush"), § 2b.

Chapter 3

1. Army Form B 193A, Gubbins papers 3/1/6, IWM; Letter from Maj. Gen. D. Forster to General Officer Commanding, Aldershot Command, 19 November 1930, Gubbins papers 3/1/5, IWM.
2. Wilkinson and Astley, *Gubbins and SOE*, 31.
3. Army Form B 193A, Gubbins papers 3/1/6, IWM.
4. Wilkinson and Astley, *Gubbins and SOE*, 31–32.
5. Army Form B 193A, Gubbins papers 3/1/6, IWM; Wilkinson and Astley, *Gubbins and SOE*, 32.
6. Gubbins, quoted in Wilkinson and Astley, *Gubbins and SOE*, 33. There appears to be little other material available on this episode of Gubbins's life.
7. Wilkinson and Astley, *Gubbins and SOE*, 33.
8. Bond, *British Military Policy*, 7, 257–58; Bond, "Leslie Hore-Belisha at the War Office," 115; Gibbs, "British Strategic Doctrine," 209; Howard, *Continental Commitment*, 99, 114, 116.

9. Adams, *British Foreign Policy*, 17; Bond, "Leslie Hore-Belisha," 110–11.
10. Bond, *British Military Policy*, 215–16.
11. Bond, "Leslie Hore-Belisha," 111.
12. Bond, *British Military Policy*, 8.
13. Chiefs of Staff, Annual Review, 1933, quoted in Howard, *Continental Commitment*, 104. Cf. Annual Reviews, 1930 and 1935, quoted in Barnett, *Collapse of British Power*, 337, 413.
14. Sir Edmund Ironside, *Time Unguarded: The Ironside Diaries, 1937–1940*, ed. Roderick Macleod and Denis Kelly (London, 1962), 47, quoted in Bond, *British Military Policy*, 263. Cf. Adams, *British Foreign Policy*, 62–64; Barnett, *Collapse of British Power*, 494, 496–505; Gibbs, "British Strategic Doctrine," 209; Howard, *Continental Commitment*, 109–10.
15. Adams, *British Foreign Policy*, 131; Bond, *British Military Policy*, 290, 293–94; Bond, "Leslie Hore-Belisha," 117, 120.
16. Bond, *British Military Policy*, 11; Lloyd, *British Empire*, 291–92. Cf. Howard, *Continental Commitment*, 100.
17. Bond, *British Military Policy*, 214.
18. Sir John Burnett-Stuart, unpublished memoirs, 120–22, quoted in Bond, *British Military Policy*, 216. Burnett-Stuart served as General Officer Commanding-in-Chief of the Southern Command from 1934 to 1936 and was considered a strong candidate for chief of the Imperial General Staff.
19. Bond, *British Military Policy*, 217.
20. Ibid., 246. Basil Henry Liddell Hart, a strong supporter of T. E. Lawrence and indirect warfare, published a biography of Lawrence in 1934.
21. Anglim, "Callwell versus Graziani," 590.
22. Cadogan, *Diaries*, 182 [18 August 1939]; Pownall, *Chief of Staff*, 1:187; Aster, *1939*, 57–59; Hinsley et. al, *British Intelligence*, 47–48; Middlemas, *Diplomacy of Illusion*, 91–92.
23. Historians disagree about when EH was established; M. R. D. Foot argues for late March 1938 (*SOE in France*, 1–2). Charles Cruickshank contends that Stuart "was invited by the Prime Minister to set up a new propaganda department" in September 1938, though the Munich crisis delayed its operations until the following September (*Fourth Arm*, 10, 17). William Mackenzie's account is similar to Cruickshank's, though he assigns the initiative to Adm. Hugh Sinclair, chief of SIS, and places the beginning of operations in January 1939 (*Secret History of SOE*, 6; Mackenzie's *Secret History of SOE* is the official history of SOE, completed in 1948, but withheld from the general public until 1998.). The differences between these accounts may be the result not of fact but of definition. What qualifies as establishment or constitutes an agency changes the "official" date of creation for EH.
24. For a broader treatment of the PWE, see Cruickshank, *Fourth Arm*, and Garnett, *Secret History of PWE*.
25. "SOE Early History to September 1940," chapter 1, "Early History," 1, TNA: PRO, HS 7/3. (It appears that this history and all the items in HS 7/3 were written in July 1943, though this is not certain. See "Activities of the Section up to the Fall of France," TNA: PRO, HS 7/3.)

Cf. Foot, *SOE in France*, 2, quoting "a paper of recommendations on control of para-military activities, 5 June 1939, MIR file 3; Foot, "Was SOE Any Good?" 168; Mackenzie, *Secret History of SOE*, 4; Seaman, "A New Instrument of War," 8.
26. Wilkinson and Astley, *Gubbins and SOE*, 35. Cf. Sweet-Escott, *Baker Street Irregular*, 20.
27. Wilkinson and Astley, *Gubbins and SOE*, 35.
28. Gladwyn, *Memoirs*, 101; obituary for Maj. Gen. L. D. Grand, (London) *Times*, 28 November 1975, 19.
29. "SOE Early History to September 1940," chapter 1, "Early History," 7, TNA: PRO, HS 7/3; Seaman, "New Instrument of War," 9; Wilkinson and Astley, *Gubbins and SOE*, 35. At this time SIS had its headquarters on Broadway. The St. Ermin's Hotel was utilized by part of the Ministry of Munitions during World War I and remains an operating hotel today at the same location on Caxton Street.
30. "SOE Early History to September 1940," chapter 1, "Early History," 1, 3, TNA: PRO, HS 7/3; Foot, *SOE in France*, 2; Mackenzie, *Secret History of SOE*, 5.
31. "SOE Early History to September 1940," chapter 1, "Early History," 3, TNA: PRO, HS 7/3. These proposals were titled "Preliminary Survey of Possibilities of Sabotage."
32. Ibid., 4; Seaman, "New Instrument of War," 10.
33. Foot, *SOE in France*, 2; Mackenzie, *Secret History of SOE*, 33–34.
34. Seaman, "New Instrument of War," 10; West, *Truth Betrayed*, 114–19.
35. Mackenzie, *Secret History of SOE*, 23–30; Sweet-Escott, *Baker Street Irregular*, 22. Kim Philby, a Soviet spy, worked for Section D. Regarding plans to sabotage narrows on the Danube he writes, "I had seen the Iron Gates, and was duly impressed by the nerve of colleagues who spoke of 'blowing them up,' as if it were a question of destroying the pintle of a lockgate in the Regent's Canal. Such an attempt was hopelessly out of keeping with the slender resources of Section D in 1940" (*My Silent War*, 12).
36. Memo by Lord Hankey, 24 May 1940, TNA: PRO, CAB 127/375 (files retained in Cabinet Office), and George Rendel to Alexander Cadogan, 11 February 1940, PUSD papers, FCO, both cited in Jeffery, *Secret History of MI6*, 414. Cf. Stafford, *Britain and European Resistance*, 22.
37. "The Balkans," n.d., TNA: PRO, HS 7/3. This document also argues that Section D's limited successes of this period "were sufficient to convince even the most conservative of diplomats that there were certain activities that it was necessary to undertake but which could not be undertaken by official missions."
38. "SOE Early History to September 1940," chapter 1, "Early History," 6–12, TNA: PRO, HS 7/3; "Activities of the Section up to the Fall of France," TNA: PRO, HS 7/3; Mackenzie, *Secret History of SOE*, 30–33. While Section D provided intelligence, SIS provided Section D with most of its communications ("SOE Early History," chapter 1, "Early History," 20).

39. "SOE Early History to September 1940," chapter 1, "Early History," 14, TNA: PRO, HS 7/3. Much of Section D's propaganda centered on "self-generating material, such as chain letters," allowing the organization to sidestep the "volume of output" (ibid., chapter 3, "Propaganda," 1, TNA: PRO, HS 7/3).
40. Ibid., chapter 3, "Propaganda," 1, TNA: PRO, HS 7/3.
41. Mackenzie, *Secret History of SOE*, 35–36.
42. "SOE Early History to September 1940," chapter 1, "Early History," 12, TNA: PRO, HS 7/3; Mackenzie, *Secret History of SOE*, 34–35. The Oxford Group, a conservative evangelical organization, was led by Dr. Frank Buchman, who had ties to Nazi leader Heinrich Himmler and sometimes made statements praising the anti-Communism of the Nazis. See "SOE Early History to September 1940," chapter 2, "Censorship," TNA: PRO, HS 7/3.
43. GS(R) charter, quoted in Mackenzie, *Secret History of SOE*, 8.
44. "CG's Comments on Foot's Book," n.d., 1, Gubbins papers 3/2/57, IWM; Foot, *SOE in France*, 2; Wilkinson and Astley, *Gubbins and SOE*, 33.
45. DCIGS, quoted in Mackenzie, *Secret History of SOE*, 8. Mackenzie cites the "MI(R) War Diary 'Introduction,' (MI(R) File 3)." Alas, as Foot observes,

> an extra difficulty awaits those who try to take up Mackenzie's references to SOE papers. He complained himself of the troubles of trying to cope with "two superimposed systems of filing, both radically imperfect": a third system has been imposed even on them. In the early 1970s, the surviving operational and headquarters files were all gone through by Mr. Townsend of the PRO and reduced to what that office regarded as a sensible arrangement. Townsend's index to them did include cross-references to the original file numbers, where they survived, but it will be a nightmare task to try to fix which of the AD/S.1 files to which Mackenzie so often refers have survived. (Foot, forward to Mackenzie, *Secret History of SOE*, xiv–xv)

46. Foot, "The IRA and the Origins of SOE," 68; Foot and Langley, *MI9*, 31; Wilkinson and Astley, *Gubbins and SOE*, 33–34.
47. Foot, *SOE: An Outline History*, 14. Wilkinson and Astley, writing after Foot, note that Holland "served for some months in Ireland during the 'troubles' but, if he and Gubbins met, there is no record that they discussed irregular warfare" (34).
48. Gubbins, "The Underground Forces in Britain 1940–1944," lecture given to the Cerne Abbas Discussion Club, Dorchester, April [?] 1973, 4, Gubbins papers 4/1/42, IWM; Astley; *Inner Circle*, 21.
49. "CG's Comments on Foot's Book," n.d., 2, Gubbins papers 3/2/57, IWM.
50. Astley, *Inner Circle*, 19, 30.
51. Chamberlain to B. H. Liddell Hart, March 1937, quoted in Bond, *British Military Policy*, 252.

52. "CG's Comments on Foot's Book," n.d., 1, Gubbins papers 3/2/57, IWM; Wilkinson and Astley, *Gubbins and SOE*, 34; Astley, *Inner Circle*, 20.
53. Astley, *Inner Circle*, 22. Jefferis arrived in May 1939, after Gubbins, and after the transformation to D/M Section (see below). See "CG's Comments on Foot's Book," n.d., 1, Gubbins papers 3/2/57, IWM. Jefferis had already been attached to Section D's technical branch. Holland may have known Jefferis from earlier work, or he may have met him while working under Section D's umbrella. Whether Jefferis transferred from Section D to GS(R), or worked for both, is unclear. See Wilkinson and Astley, *Gubbins and SOE*, 35. On Jefferis's subsequent career with MD1—the Ministry of Defence's research and development agency, a spin-off from MI(R)—see Patrick Delaforce, *Churchill's Secret Weapons: The Story of Hobart's Funnies* (London, 1998), 16–47; and R. Stuart Macrae, *Winston Churchill's Toyshop* (New York, 1971).
54. Wilkinson and Astley, *Gubbins and SOE*, 34–35.
55. Foot, *SOE: An Outline History*, 11–12. Cf. Gubbins, "The Underground Forces in Britain," lecture to Cerne Abbas Discussion Club, Dorchester, April [?] 1973, 4, Gubbins papers 4/1/42, IWM. Mackenzie, author of the official history of SOE, claims that "it is plain ... that the doctrine" contained in the *AGW* not only came from the examples already mentioned but also "from the German experience of Wassmuss" (*Secret History of SOE*, 39). Wilhelm Wassmuss, a German diplomat in Persia during the Great War, attempted to bring Persia into the war on the Axis side, or at least lead a revolt against British occupation of a portion of the country. While he succeeded in fomenting revolt among several tribes, the hoped for Lawrence-esque conflagration, tying down British troops, never came. The limits of Wassmuss's success, combined with the fact that no other source mentions him as an inspiration to Gubbins, make it unlikely—though not impossible—that Mackenzie's claims are true. For more on Wassmuss, see Christopher Sykes, *Wassmuss: "The German Lawrence"* (New York, 1936), and Peter Hopkirk, *Like Hidden Fire: The Plot to Bring Down the British Empire* (New York, 1994).
56. David McKittrick, "Joan Bright Astley: Secretary to Winston Churchill's War Cabinet," *Independent*, 28 January 2009.
57. Astley, *Inner Circle*, 3, 8–12.
58. Gubbins to Foot, 28 April 1964, Gubbins papers 3/2/57, IWM. He explained that she was "a women of considerable culture and great verve, working really as a GSO2 not as a Secretary. . . . We shared some tough times." Eric Mockler-Ferryman worked in the War Office and later at SOE; having recently met her for the first time, he commented, "I can well imagine that you ruled visiting generals and admirals with an iron hand in a velvet glove." Eric Mockler-Ferryman to Joan Bright Astley, 7 December 1976, Gubbins papers 12/2, IWM.
59. Wheatley, *Deception Planners*, 18.
60. Grand, "Scheme D," 12 April 1939, 1, TNA: PRO, HS 8/256. Mackenzie claims the paper was submitted to Sir Stewart Menzies, the acting SIS chief. See *Secret History of SOE*, 8–9. Foot claims that the report

was first sent to Viscount Gort, CIGS. See *SOE in France*, 3. Seaman asserts that on 20 March Grand *alone* submitted the report to Sir Hugh Sinclair, head of SIS, a copy of which was also sent to Maj. Gen. F. G. Beaumont-Nesbitt, director of Military Intelligence. See Seaman, "New Instrument of War," 11.

61. Mackenzie, *Secret History of SOE*, 8.
62. Grand, "Scheme D," 20 March 1939, 1, TNA: PRO, HS 8/256.
63. Ibid., 1–6, quotation from 3.
64. Mackenzie, *Secret History of SOE*, 9.
65. Grand, "Scheme D," 12 April 1939, 1, TNA: PRO, HS 8/256; Foot, *SOE in France*, 3; Mackenzie, *Secret History of SOE*, 9; Seaman, "New Instrument of War," 11; Stafford, *Britain and European Resistance*, 21. This meeting does not appear in Cadogan's diary, which lacks an entry for that day. See Cadogan, *Diaries*, 265.
66. Foot, *SOE in France*, 3; Seaman, "New Instrument of War," 11.
67. Mackenzie, *Secret History of SOE*, 10.
68. "Duties of the New Branch," 3 April 1939, TNA: PRO, HS 8/256. This document, approved by the CIGS and DCIGS on 13 April, referrs to the desirability of "officers in the Reserve, or in the Territorial Army, possessed of means, who are not tied to civil jobs, who are keen for active work now, and who are sufficiently experienced already."
69. "CG's Comments on Foot's Book," n.d., 1, Gubbins papers 3/2/57, IWM; Astley, *Inner Circle*, 20; Wilkinson and Astley, *Gubbins and SOE*, 34–35.
70. Record of Meeting Held in the War Office on June 27th, 1939, To Settle the future of G.S.(R) and Certain Connected Questions, No. M/I.7, 1, TNA: PRO, HS 8/256. This change of name creates confusion in this period, as the terms GS(R) and MI(R) are used loosely and interchangeably by many participants and historians. The term D/M Section (or Branch) is rarely used, and will generally be avoided in this work.
71. Peter Fleming, quoted in Hart-Davis, *Peter Fleming*, 215.
72. Astley, *Inside Circle*, 19.
73. "SOE Early History to September 1940," chapter 1: "Early History," 12, TNA: PRO, HS 7/3. In a similar manner, another document titled "SOE in Europe, 1938–1945," claims that Section D was "divided into civil and military branches. . . . The Military Branch of 'D' Section was transferred to the War Office where, as M.I.R., it became responsible for para-military operations, while the Civil Branch continued in the Secret Service and organised subversive operations" (1, TNA: PRO, HS 7/1).
74. Seaman, "New Instrument of War," 13, 11.
75. Foot, *SOE in France*, 4. Cf. "CG's Comments on Foot's Book," n.d., 1, Gubbins papers 3/2/57, IWM. Joan Bright Astley clarifies, or perhaps confuses further, these claims when she comments, "Grand was a volatile dreamer, Holland an unsmiling visionary" (*Inner Circle*, 20).
76. "Suggested line of demarcation between War Office and 'D,'" 25 August 1940, TNA: PRO, HS 8/258. The same text is quoted in Mackenzie,

Secret History of SOE, 11; there it is attributed to Beaumont-Nesbitt, 11 February 1940. The date on the copy in TNA: PRO, HS 8/258 appears to be incorrect, since SOE had been created by August 1940. Mackenzie's date makes more sense.

77. MI(R) memorandum, 4 September 1939, quoted in Seaman, "New Instrument of War," 13.
78. "SOE Early History to September 1940," chapter 1: "Early History," 1–2, TNA: PRO, HS 7/3; Seaman, "New Instrument of War," 11.
79. Wilkinson and Astley, *Gubbins and SOE*, 35.
80. Mackenzie, *Secret History of SOE*, 38.
81. Holland, "General Instructions," 13 April 1939, 3, TNA: PRO, HS 8/256.
82. Holland, memorandum, No. M/I.6, June 1939, TNA: PRO, HS 8/256.
83. Record of Meeting Held in the War Office on June 27th, 1939, To Settle the future of G.S.(R) and Certain Connected Questions, No. M/I.7, 2, TNA: PRO, HS 8/256.
84. Foot, *SOE in France*, 4.
85. Wilkinson and Astley, *Gubbins and SOE*, 35. Cf. Gubbins to Foot, 24 January 1964, Gubbins papers 3/2/57, IWM.
86. "CG's Comments on Foot's Book," n.d., 1, Gubbins papers 3/2/57, IWM; Wilkinson and Astley, *Gubbins and SOE*, 36.
87. Astley, *Inner Circle*, 25; Wilkinson, *Foreign Fields*, 63. Wilkinson's personal assessment of the first MI(R) courses is mixed: "Colin Gubbins gave a good but somewhat superficial lecture on the principles of guerrilla warfare.... I enjoyed the two lectures given by the head signal officer of MI6.... I cannot say that I learned very much from the course and remember remarking ... that we might have been more profitably employed spending a weekend re-reading T. E. Lawrence's *Seven Pillars of Wisdom*."
88. Holland, quoted in Wilkinson and Astley, *Gubbins and SOE*, 36.
89. Gubbins, Report for D.C.I.G.S. No. 8—Investigation of the Possibilities of Guerilla Activities, appendix 1: "Preliminary Report on a Tour to Poland, Baltic States, and Roumania, 1 June 1939," 1, TNA: PRO, HS 8/260.
90. Ibid., 9.
91. Gubbins, address to the Danish/English Society, Copenhagen, 29 April 1966, 2, Gubbins papers 4/1/20, IWM; Garliński, *Poland, SOE and the Allies*, 24; Mackenzie, *Secret History of SOE*, 44–45; Seaman, "New Instrument of War," 11–12; Wilkinson and Astley, *Gubbins and SOE*, 36. These trips appear to have occurred in June and August, though it is unclear which countries were visited on which trips.
92. Wilkinson and Astley, *Gubbins and SOE*, 46–47. Gano had studied in Moscow and served as chief of the East Section of the Intelligence Department, military attaché in Helsinki, and head of the Independent Technical Section of II Bureau before World War II; in November 1939 he became head of the chief of the Intelligence Department as the Poles reorganized themselves in exile. See Pepłoński and Suchcitz,

"Organisation and Operations," 81, 102; Maresch, "SOE and Polish Aspirations," 212n5.
93. "CG's Comments on Foot's Book," n.d., 1, Gubbins papers 3/2/57, IWM.
94. Andrew, "British-Polish Intelligence Collaboration," 56; Gubbins, "The Underground Forces in Britain," lecture given to the Cerne Abbas Discussion Club, Dorchester, April [?] 1973, 12a, Gubbins papers 4/1/42, IWM.
95. Holland, "General Instructions," 13 April 1939, 2, TNA: PRO, HS 8/256. Holland explained: "I took a paper over recently to the War Office to secure the C.I.G.S.'s approval for the objects of this branch. In the prevailing excitement C.I.G.S. could not give the attention merited to this paper, but D.C.I.G.S. told me that it could be taken as approved."
96. Ibid., 2.
97. "G.S.R.," 18 April 1939, 1, TNA: PRO, HS 8/256; Mackenzie, *Secret History of SOE*, 39.
98. Astley, *Inner Circle*, 23.
99. GS(R), "Report for D.C.I.G.S. No. 8—Investigation of the Possibilities of Guerilla Activities," 1 June 1939, 5, HS 8/260.
100. *AGW*, 1 § 1. Cf. *PLH*, appendices 1 and 2.
101. *AGW*, 5 § 16.
102. Foot, *SOE in France*, 2.
103. Mackenzie, *Secret History of SOE*, 8n2.
104. Gubbins, quoted in Wilkinson and Astley, *Gubbins and SOE*, 35.
105. GS(R), Report for D.C.I.G.S. No. 8—Investigation of the Possibilities of Guerilla Activities, 1 June 1939, 1, TNA: PRO, HS 8/260.
106. Unfinished Gubbins memoirs, quoted in Wilkinson and Astley, *Gubbins and SOE*, 8. A draft of this chapter, "The Schools 1902–1913," including the quotation from Gubbins's unfinished memoirs, may be found in the Gubbins papers 12/2, IWM.
107. Gubbins, "The Underground Forces in Britain," lecture given to the Cerne Abbas Discussion Club, Dorchester, April [?] 1973, 14, Gubbins papers 4/1/42, IWM.
108. Gubbins, "Guerrilla," *Chamber's Encyclopedia* (London, 1968).
109. Gubbins, "GUERRILLA or, more commonly GUERILLA," n.d., Gubbins papers 5/8, IWM.
110. For an earlier treatment of the Second Anglo-Boer War and SOE, see Linderman, "Afrikaner Influence," 33–63.
111. *AGW*, 4 § 10, 8 § 24; *PHL*, 3 § 3.
112. *PLH*, 11 § 13, 32–33 (appendix 5: "The Enemy's Information System and How to Counter It"), § 1–6.
113. Farwell, *Great Anglo-Boer War*, 329.
114. Lord Roberts to Lord Lansdowne, 29 April 1900, Home & Overseas Correspondence of Lord Roberts, War Office Library, London, vol. 1, 107–108; quoted in Pakenham, *Boer War*, 445. Cf. Grew, *Field-Marshal Lord Kitchener*, 120; Arthur, *Life of Lord Kitchener*, 2:298–99.
115. De Wet, *Three Years' War*, 141.

116. Cakars, "Koos de la Rey," 133.
117. *PLH*, 2 § 2f. Cf. *AGW*, 5 § 15.
118. "Minor Tactics" (G.1), Rigden, *SOE Syllabus*, 248; *AGW*, 5 § 15. Cf. *AGW*, 6 § 16f; *PLH*, 1 § 2b; 14 (appendix 1: "Road Ambush") § 2d.
119. Louis Botha, quoted in Archibald, *Blue Shirt and Khaki*, 139.
120. Arthur, *Life of Lord Kitchener*, 2:2, 309. Cf. Hiley and Hassell, *Mobile Boer*, 251–52.
121. *AGW*, 1 § 1; *PLH*, 2 § 2, 12 § 14. Cf. "Minor Tactics" (G.1), Rigden, *SOE Syllabus*, 248.
122. De Wet, *Three Years' War*, 79–80, 85, 125; Hiley and Hassell, *Mobile Boer*, 269; Cakars, "Koos de la Rey," 128; Pakenham, *Boer War*, 348. The Boers' mobility initially contrasted with British efforts. "Our speed on this trek was . . . slow," writes one trooper, "limited by . . . our ox teams" (Perham, *Kimberley Flying Column*, 19). By the war's end, however, even Jan Smuts acknowledged that "the mounted columns of the enemy were about as mobile as the Boer commandos" (Smuts, *Smuts Papers*, 628).
123. Cakars, "Koos de la Rey," 139–40.
124. *AGW*, 3 § 6, 4 § 11, 6 § 16d; *PLH*, 1 § 2e, 2 § 2.
125. *AGW*, 3 § 5b. Cf. "Street Fighting" (G.6), Rigden, *SOE Syllabus*, 284.
126. Marling, *Rifleman and Hussar*, 284; Cakars, "Koos de la Rey," 134; Farwell, *Great Anglo-Boer War*, 346.
127. De Wet, *Three Years' War*, 144.
128. Lord Kitchener to William St. John Brodrick, 20 September 1901, quoted in Arthur, *Life of Lord Kitchener*, 2:48.
129. Hiley and Hassell, *Mobile Boer*, 243–44.
130. *AGW*, 5 § 16a.
131. "Minor Tactics" (G.1), Rigden, *SOE Syllabus*, 248. Emphasis in original.
132. *AGW*, 5 § 16a. Although Gubbins wrote little about actual deception as such—as opposed to mere concealment—Britain's efforts at strategic deception during the Second World War are well documented. Some leading texts on the topic include Sir Michael Howard, *Strategic Deception* (Cambridge, 1990); Jon Latimer, *Deception in War* (London, 2001); J. C. Masterman, *The Double-Cross System in the War of 1939 to 1945* (New Haven, 1972); and Ewan Montagu, *The Man Who Never Was* (Philadelphia, 1954). The Inter-Service Security Board, which coordinated many of Britain's deception activities, began as an MI(R) project, though Holland was happy to spin it off when it grew beyond MI(R)'s scope. See Holland, "Duties and Activities of M.I.R.," 22 July 1940, 2, TNA: PRO, HS 8/256; Mackenzie, *Secret History of SOE*, 48–49.
133. Smuts, *Smuts Papers*, 633; Archibald, *Blue Shirt and Khaki*, 129; Arthur, *Life of Lord Kitchener*, 2:11; Cakars, "Koos de la Rey," 128.
134. De Wet, *Three Years' War*, 125; Pakenham, *Boer War*, 498. However, the Boers took no interest in reading the enemy's mail. See De Wet, *Three Years' War*, 101.
135. "Street Fighting" (G.6), Rigden, *SOE Syllabus*, 284.

136. *AGW*, 12 § 43, 11 § 36.
137. *AGW*, 11 § 36. Cf. *PLH*, 4 § 6, 9 § 11, 11 § 13.
138. De Wet, *Three Years' War*, 18.
139. Pakenham, *Boer War*, 523, 590.
140. Ibid., 504, 517.
141. Farwell, *Great Anglo-Boer War*, 333, 346.
142. Bruce Hamilton, quoted in Parritt, *The Intelligencers*, 198.
143. *AGW*, 12 § 40. Cf. "Objects and Methods of Counter-Espionage" (A.6), Rigden, *SOE Syllabus*, 62; "Agent Management—Handling" (A.14), Rigden, *SOE Syllabus*, 95.
144. *PLH*, 5 § 6.
145. De Wet, *Three Years' War*, 102; Cakars, "Koos de la Rey," 139; Farwell, *Great Anglo-Boer War*, 341; Pakenham, *Boer War*, 504, 551.
146. Pakenham, *Boer War*, 555–56. Cf. Hiley and Hassell, *Mobile Boer*, 60; Kitchener, telegraph to unspecified recipient, quoted in Arthur, *Life of Lord Kitchener*, 2:44; Farwell, *Great Anglo-Boer War*, 342-43. Such wearing of the enemy's uniform was, however, a violation of accepted norms of warfare. International law, as it exists today, was just coming about in the late nineteenth century. The Hague Convention of 1899 on the Laws and Customs of War on Land banned the "improper use of . . . the enemy's uniform" (Scott, *Hague Conventions*, 116, article 23f). "While there was some justification . . . for wearing the [British uniforms]," observes Farwell, "there was no excuse for not removing the badges and insignia, and there was no excuse for not discarding the uniforms altogether when . . . [civilian] clothing became available" (Farwell, *Great Anglo-Boer War*, 343). Nevertheless, the Boers utilized international norms when it was to their advantage. One British soldier recalled, "I rode up to a house with a big red cross painted on the door, and an old woman sitting outside. I asked if it was the hospital. She could only speak Dutch, and handed me a piece of paper on which was written: 'This is to certify that Anna Sauerkraut is a qualified midwife, and as such is under the protection of the Geneva Convention [of 1864]'" (Marling, *Rifleman and Hussar*, 275).
147. *AGW*, 11 § 35, emphasis added. Cf. ibid., 10 § 33; *PLH*, 16 (appendix 1: "Road Ambush") § 4.
148. "Ambushes" (G.4), Rigden, *SOE Syllabus*, 271.
149. Gubbins, "The Underground Forces in Britain," lecture to Cerne Abbas Discussion Club, Dorchester, April [?] 1973, 15, Gubbins papers 4/1/42, IWM.
150. Gubbins makes no mention of posing as the enemy in either of his pamphlets. Moreover, the lecture in the SOE syllabus on "Cover, Make-up & Disguise" (A.4) only discusses disguising oneself as a member of various civilian occupations, not as a policeman or soldier (Rigden, *SOE Syllabus*, 46–58).
151. Jan Smuts to L. Botha, 23 January 1901; Smuts to J. H. de la Rey, 17 February 1901; Smuts to L. Botha, 27 February 1901, *Smuts Papers*, 363, 378, 383; Farwell, *Great Anglo-Boer War*, 326, 338; Pakenham, *Boer War*, 551.

152. Marling, *Rifleman and Hussar*, 275. Cf. ibid., 277, 285.
153. Ibid., 295. In the period from 15 April until the end of the war on 31 May 1902, Marling reported burning sixty-three farms on thirteen occasions, as well as an entire town.
154. "Experiences at the Front," *Cornish Guardian*, 30 August 1901, 3; quoted in Spiers, *Victorian Soldier*, 171.
155. Pakenham, *Boer War*, 500.
156. Jan Smuts to F. W. Reitz, 29 November 1900 (Smuts, *Smuts Papers*, 346).
157. *AGW*, 13 § 45. Cf. *PLH*, 37 (appendix 7: "Guerilla Information Service") § 4 and *PLH*, 5 § 7, 15 (appendix 1: "Road Ambush") § 4b.
158. *PLH*, 32 (appendix 4: "Concealment and Care of Arms and Explosives") § 4; *AGW*, 11 § 37. Cf. *AGW*, 4 § 12.
159. Farwell, *Great Anglo-Boer War*, 324. Cf. Pakenham, *Boer War*, 508.
160. *AGW*, 9 § 28.
161. Ibid., 9 § 31.
162. Farwell, *Great Anglo-Boer War*, 325.
163. "Opening Address: Objects and Methods of Irregular Warfare" (A.1), Rigden, *SOE Syllabus*, 35.
164. Rigden, introduction, *SOE Syllabus*, 1–2; Wilkinson and Astley, *Gubbins and SOE*, 105, 107.
165. Lawrence, *Seven Pillars of Wisdom*, 8–18. This conflict is generally known as the Arab Revolt; confusingly, the revolt in Palestine two decades later is also known by the same name. The dates (1916–18 and 1936–39) are sometimes used to distinguish the latter from its better-known predecessor.
166. "As a boy, T. E. always thought that he was going to do great things, both 'active and reflective'—'I hadn't learned you can't do both'" (note by B. H. Liddell Hart on a conversation with Lawrence, 1 August 1933; quoted in Wilson, *Lawrence of Arabia*, 19).
167. Wilkinson, *Foreign Fields*, 63; Anglim, *Orde Wingate and the British Army*, 17, 53, 109.
168. Gubbins, "GUERRILLA or, more commonly GUERILLA," n.d., Gubbins papers 5/8, IWM. The editors reduced this choice phrase to the more prosaic "Lawrence's guerrilla campaign." See Gubbins, "Guerrilla."
169. Lawrence, "Evolution of a Revolt," 59.
170. Ibid., 59.
171. Ibid., 59–61. Lawrence also extended this "biological" notion of ignorance and scarce resources to matériel as well. Although the Turks had relative abundance of manpower, they faced a relative shortage of equipment. "The death of a Turkish bridge or rail, machine or gun, or high explosive was more profitable to us than the death of a Turk." Thus attacks were directed "not against his men, but against his materials" (61).
172. Ibid., 63. Lawrence's forces were indeed highly equipped: "In his operative bodyguard, normally about thirty men, every other man was armed with a light automatic, so that his handful possessed more

firepower than battalions of a thousand men in 1914" (Liddell Hart, *T. E. Lawrence*, 471). Liddell Hart exaggerates somewhat: assuming 550 rounds per minute for a light automatic and 25 rounds per minute for a trained rifleman, the battalion could fire 25,000 rounds per minute while Lawrence's bodyguard only about 8,625. Still, that it is even worth making the comparison proves Liddell Hart's general point.
173. Lawrence, "Evolution of a Revolt," 62.
174. Ibid., 62.
175. Ibid., 61–62.
176. *AGW*, 1 § 1, emphasis added. Cf. *PLH*, 2 § 2; 12 § 14. Like Lawrence, Gubbins appreciated that destruction of enemy equipment could be at least as important as killing enemy soldiers; among Gubbins's suggested targets are supplies (*AGW*, 3 § 8; *PLH*, 3 § 4; 4 § 5e, 7 § 8c–e), roads (*AGW*, 3 § 8; *PLH*, 1 § 1; 3 § 4; 3 § 5a, 7 § 8b), rail lines (*AGW*, 3 § 8; *PLH*, 1 § 1, 3 § 4, 3 § 5a, 7 § 8a–b), canals (*AGW*, 3 § 8; *PLH*, 3 § 5a, 7 § 8b), postal systems (*AGW*, 3 § 8; *PLH*, 1 § 1, 4 § 5b, 7 § 8f), and telegraphs (*AGW*, 3 § 8; *PLH*, 1 § 1, 7 § 8b). The detachments forced to guard all these things, because of guerrilla attacks, become targets as well (*AGW*, 4 § 8; *PLH*, 4 § 5c).
177. *AGW*, 22 § 82.
178. Ibid., 5 § 15. Cf. *PLH*, 4 § 6.
179. *PLH*, 39 (appendix 8: "Sabotage") § 7.
180. Ibid., 40 § 12, emphasis in original.
181. Lawrence, "Evolution of a Revolt," 69.
182. *PLH*, 4 § 6.
183. *AGW*, 4 § 12. Cf. *PLH*, 4 § 6.
184. Lawrence, "Guerrilla."
185. *AGW*, 13 § 48.
186. Ibid., 7 § 18.
187. Ibid., 7 § 19, 13 § 48.
188. Lawrence, "Evolution of a Revolt," 56.
189. *AGW*, 2 § 5a, 15 § 55. Cf. *PLH*, 12 § 13.
190. *AGW*, 8 § 24. Cf. *PLH*, 3 § 3.
191. *PLH*, 11 § 12–3, 32–4 (appendix 5: "The Enemy's Information System and How to Counter It") § 1–7.
192. Lawrence, "Guerrilla." Gubbins concurs. "Over-organization is more dangerous and detrimental to guerilla operations than too loose an organization. . . . To err on the side of over-organization . . . is to court disaster" (*AGW*, 8 § 22, 12 § 38). "It is valueless and dangerous prematurely to organize partisan bands, acting independently as they normally should, into platoons, companies, squadrons, etc. and then into regiments or brigades, with nominated commanders, skeleton orders of battle, intelligence services, etc.; such organization necessitates documents, written orders, files, etc. all or any of which, falling into the enemy's hands, may enable him to destroy the guerrilla movement at a blow" (*AGW*, 2–3 § 5b).
193. Lawrence, "Evolution of a Revolt," 69.
194. Ibid., 69.

195. Gubbins, "The Underground Forces in Britain," lecture to the Cerne Abbas Discussion Club, Dorchester, April [?] 1973, 15, Gubbins papers 4/1/42, IWM.
196. *AGW*, 15 § 54, emphasis added.
197. *AGW*, 8 § 25.
198. Ibid., 8 § 25.
199. Lawrence, "Evolution of a Revolt," 68–69. Lawrence unhappily concludes, "We did not prove it, because the war stopped" (69).
200. Ibid., 69.
201. *AGW*, 1 § 1, 1 § 4, emphasis added.
202. Lawrence, *Seven Pillars of Wisdom*, 191.
203. *AGW*, 22 § 83.
204. Lawrence, "Evolution of a Revolt," 59, 61, 69.
205. T. E. Lawrence, "Twenty-Seven Articles," in Wilson, *Lawrence of Arabia*, appendix 4, 960. Lawrence penned the "Twenty-Seven Articles," in August 1917; this collection of suggestions explains how to deal with Bedouins. Although Lawrence insists that "they are meant to apply only to Bedu: townspeople or Syrians require totally different treatment," (960) many of the points are of broader consideration for officers operating with foreign guerrillas.
206. Lawrence, "Evolution of a Revolt," 68.
207. Ibid., 58.
208. Lettow-Vorbeck, *My Reminiscences*, 63–64. Lettow-Vorbeck's memoirs were originally published in 1920 in Leipzig under the title *Meine Erinnerungen aus Ostafrika*.
209. Lettow-Vorbeck, *My Reminiscences*, 229.
210. Ibid., 317–21.
211. Mackenzie, *Secret History of SOE*, 39; Anglim, *Orde Wingate and the British Army*, 106.
212. It is unclear from Lettow-Vorbeck's memoirs of East Africa precisely when this happened. His more general memoirs, *Mein Leben*, do not discuss the matter. But Edwin P. Hoyt argues that Lettow-Vorbeck met various Boers when he was in South Africa, on his way home to Germany after having been wounded in South-West Africa in 1906. See Hoyt, *Guerrilla*, 10.
213. Lettow-Vorbeck, *My Reminiscences*, 16.
214. Ibid., 4.
215. Ibid., 4. In addition to threatening infrastructure, German patrols attacked transport columns behind Allied lines, slowing their resupply, inflicting casualties, and distracting additional troops. Ibid., 142, 187. Cf. 170.
216. *AGW*, 1 § 1; *PLH*, 2 § 2, 12 § 14.
217. Lettow-Vorbeck, *My Reminiscences*, 58. At the same battle he attempted an ambush of British columns, though the Arab troops tasked with the operation failed to spring it properly (59).
218. Ibid., 167. "The dense bush and high forest in which our camps were hidden" made aerial reconnaissance by the enemy of little value (120; cf. 152).

219. Ibid., 137. Since the enemy's uniform was not worn or directly imitated, and since the British were not made to believe they had rights or privileges which the Germans did not intend to honor, this would not appear to be the war crime of perfidy, although that is open to debate.
220. *AGW*, 5 § 16a; *PLH*, 5§ 7.
221. Lettow-Vorbeck, *My Reminiscences*, 78.
222. Ibid., 192–95. In January 1917 Lettow-Vorbeck put strict controls on attendants who accompanied the *Schutztruppe* to reduce its need for food. Starvation was a real possibility. Hunting became a major source of food and experiments began involving ways to make unripe maize edible. However, Lettow-Vorbeck's decisions were not simply measures of desperation; keeping his numbers to a minimum and living off the land made him less vulnerable to attacks in food-producing regions. Ibid., 175–77.
223. J. C. Smuts, introduction to Crowe, *General Smuts' Campaign*, vi-vii. The tone of Smuts and Crowe stand in marked contrast to that of Lettow-Vorbeck. As is typical in war writing, both sides claim brilliance and victory at every turn. Since Lettow-Vorbeck, though vastly outnumbered and cut off from outside support, remained in the field—indeed, in British territory—at the end of the war, the balance of truth appears to rest with his account.
224. Lettow-Vorbeck, *My Reminiscences*, 222. Cf. 141, 145, 172.
225. *AGW*, 4 § 10.
226. Lettow-Vorbeck, *My Reminiscences*, 166, 186, 199, 211, 217–18.
227. Ibid., 8.
228. Ibid., 64–65, 67, 112. On at least one occasion German askaris charged the enemy crying "Wahindi, kameta frasi!" ("They are Indians, catch the horses!"). See Lettow-Vorbeck, *My Reminiscences*, 106.
229. *AGW*, 11 § 35.
230. Thomas P. Ofcansky, introduction to Lettow-Vorbeck, *My Reminiscences*, no pagination.
231. Lettow-Vorbeck, *My Reminiscences*, 4–5, 8.
232. Ibid., 13. Other sources of intelligence included radio intercepts and captured enemy papers. Ibid., 34–35, 61, 63. 104.
233. Ibid., 132, 201.
234. Thomas P. Ofcansky, introduction to Lettow-Vorbeck, *My Reminiscences*, no pagination. One example of gentlemanly behavior is found in the case of Major Buller and Lieutenant von Ruckteschell: the former, a British officer, put a bullet through the latter's hat, but the German returned fire, wounding Buller, who was then nursed in captivity by von Ruckteschell's wife. See Lettow-Vorbeck, *My Reminiscences*, 147.
235. Ibid., 95.
236. Ibid., 108.
237. *AGW*, 10 § 33, 14–16 § 53–60; *PLH*, 3 § 3, 11–12 § 13.
238. Lettow-Vorbeck, *My Reminiscences*, 4–6.
239. *AGW*, 2 § 5a, emphasis added. Cf. *AGW*, 21 § 77a.

240. Ibid., 10 § 33, emphasis added. Cf. *AGW*, 21 § 77b; *PLH* 31 (appendix 4: "Concealment and Care of Arms and Explosives").
241. *AGW*, 21 § 77c.
242. Lettow-Vorbeck, *My Reminiscences*, 188.
243. Ibid., 179.
244. *AGW*, 8 § 17.

Chapter 4

1. Foot, *SOE in France*, 2.
2. Beevor, *Battle for Spain*, 50–70; Preston, *Spanish Civil War*, 98–108; Thomas, *Spanish Civil War*, 196–220.
3. Beevor, *Battle for Spain*, 73, 163, 174, 198–200; Preston, *Spanish Civil War*, 154–58, 357; Thomas, *Spanish Civil War*, 427–34, 455–56, 937–41, 943n7.
4. Thousands of Portuguese and hundreds of Irish and Romanians fought for the Nationalists; the International Brigades, composed of men and women from across Europe and North America, fought for the Republicans. See Beevor, *Battle for Spain*, 139–40, 157–63, 198, 427; Preston, *Spanish Civil War*, 170–76; Thomas, *Spanish Civil War*, 378, 438–47, 939, 941–43.
5. Cf. Temperley, "Military Lessons," 34–43; Corum, *Luftwaffe*, 200; Edwards, *Panzer*, 25–26.
6. Beevor, *Battle for Spain*, 205.
7. Preston, *Spanish Civil War*, 181. Historian Louis de Jong comments, "I have not been able to trace the exact date nor the precise text of General Mola's words. An examination of all the works by him and about him remained without result. From Spain I have received information that no positive indications could be found in the nationalist press of those days either. Spanish experts, however, believe that there is little reason to doubt that Generla Mola—who died on June 3, 1937—uttered words of the above mentioned purport" (*German Fifth Column*, 3).
8. Beevor, *Battle for Spain*, 172–74; Preston, *Spanish Civil War*, 181–86; Thomas, *Spanish Civil War*, 473.
9. For an example of Gubbins's use of the term "fifth column," see his address to the Danish/English Society in Copenhagen, 29 April 1966, 2, Gubbins papers 4/1/20, IWM.
10. Gubbins, "SOE and the Co-Ordination of Regular and Irregular War," 86. This is a reprint of Gubbins's lecture, "Regular and Irregular Warfare: Problems of Co-Ordination," given at the University of Manchester, as part of the series, "Military Studies: Subversion, Intelligence, Resistance," 29 November 1967. The original text may be found in the Gubbins papers 4/1/27, IWM. Cf. Gubbins, "Guerrilla." The original text, with the title "GUERRILLA or, more commonly GUERILLA," can be found in the Gubbins papers 5/8, IWM.
11. Gubbins, "CG's Comments on Foot's Book," n.d., 1, Gubbins papers 3/2/57, IWM. Cf. Gubbins, "The Underground Forces in Britain

1940–1944," lecture given to the Cerne Abbas Discussion Club, Dorchester, April [?] 1973, 3, Gubbins papers 4/1/42, IWM.
12. "The Spanish Civil War: Summary of Information received 8th–10th August, 1936," § 4, TNA: PRO, WO 106/1576.
13. Cf. *PLH*, 11–12 § 13.
14. Maj. Gen. J. C. F. Fuller, Report on a Visit to Nationalist Spain, October 1937, 7, TNA: PRO, WO 106/1579.
15. Sir Henry Chilton, 29 October 1937, 1, TNA: PTO, WO 106/1580. Cf. Beevor, *Battle for Spain*, 302.
16. Dennis Wheatley, "Village Defence" (6/7 July 1940), reproduced in *Stranger than Fiction*, 78–79. Wheatley later served with the Joint Planning Staff and London Controlling Section.
17. Beevor, *Battle for Spain*, 314, 429.
18. Maj. C. A. de Linde, Report of the Assistant Military Attaché (Paris) on His Visit to Nationalist Spain, 26 April 1938, 2, TNA: PRO, WO 106/1588.
19. Ibid., 2.
20. Maj. Gen. J. F. C. Fuller, Report on Visit to General Franco's Army in Spain, March 1937, 1, 4–5, TNA: PRO, WO 106/1578.
21. Ibid., 1–3.
22. Interview between Wing-Commander A. James, MP, and MI3 (colonel), 8 October 1937, 2–3, TNA: PRO, WO 106/1581.
23. Ibid., 3; Beevor, *Battle for Spain*, 248; Diez, "La censura radiofónica," 103–24.
24. Maj. Gen. J. F. C. Fuller, Report on Visit to Spain, April 1938, 2, TNA: PRO, WO 106/1585.
25. Maj. Gen. J. F. C. Fuller, "Rag-Picking on the Spanish Battlefields," article manuscript, 20 April 1938, 1, TNA: PRO, WO 106/1585.
26. Beevor, *Battle for Spain*, 84, 88. Cf. *AGW*, 12 § 40; *PLH*, 11 § 12.
27. Maj. Gen. J. F. C. Fuller, Report on a Visit to Nationalist Spain, October 1937, 5, TNA: PRO, WO 106/1579.
28. "Spain," 23 September 1936, no. 12, § 3, TNA: PRO, WO 106/1576.
29. "Spain," 14 September 1936, no. 11, § 7, TNA: PRO, WO 106/1576.
30. Maj. Gen. J. F. C. Fuller, Report on Visit to General Franco's Army in Spain, March 1937, 7, TNA: PRO, WO 106/1578. To say that these tactics were exaggerated does not mean they were not used; other sources clearly attest to them. See, for example, Lt. Col. A. F. G. Renton, "Some Impressions of the Nationalist Army in Spain, May 1938," 5, TNA: PRO, WO 106/1583.
31. *PLH*, 13 § 14.
32. Ibid., 13 § 14; "Opening Address: Objects and Methods of Irregular Warfare" (A.1), Rigden, *SOE Syllabus*, 35.
33. Maj. Gen. J. F. C. Fuller, Report on Visit to Spain, April 1938, 4, TNA: PRO, WO 106/1585.
34. The year 1929 saw communal violence, though significant conflict was limited. For an account of these riots that was available to Gubbins, see Gwynn, *Imperial Policing*, 221–52. In October 1935 "an abortive attempt

was made to smuggle a large quantity of arms and ammunition through the Port of Jaffa, and every Arab firmly believed that these were intended for Jews for purposes of aggression" (General Staff, Headquarters, British Forces Palestine & Trans-Jordan, *Military Lessons of the Arab Rebellion in Palestine, 1936,* 7, TNA: PRO, WO 191/70). In 1936 tensions again rose when plans for a legislative council—which the Arabs would have dominated—were scrapped. See Mockaitis, *British Counterinsurgency,* 88. As of June 1936, the population of Palestine, excluding His Majesty's forces, consisted of nearly 1 million Arabs (of whom about 87,000 were Christians), approximately 370,000 Jews and 24,000 of other backgrounds. See General Staff, Palestine & Trans-Jordan, *Military Lessons of the Arab Rebellion,* 4, TNA: PRO, WO 191/70.

35. Such incidents were not uncommon; this one was only notable for its consequences. The motive of the attack appears to have been apolitical. See Horne, *Job Well Done,* 206. Accounts of the number killed vary. *Al-Jami'a al-Islamiyya* reported on 16 April that three Jews were killed; *el-Carmel* reported on 18 April only two. See Hughes, "Lawlessness Was the Law," 141.
36. General Staff, Palestine & Trans-Jordan, *Military Lessons of the Arab Rebellion,* 7, TNA: PRO, WO 191/70.
37. H. J. Simson, *British Rule and Rebellion* (London, 1938), 60, quoted in Mockaitis, *British Counterinsurgency,* 26.
38. *AGW,* 2 §5a. Cf. Foot, *SOE: An Outline History,* 11–12. See also Gubbins's comments about the Arab Revolt in "SOE and the Co-Ordination of Regular and Irregular War," 84; and "Guerrilla." The conflict was known at the as "The Arab Troubles," though it became a full revolt. Today the term "Arab Revolt" is usually used, though this is often followed by the dates 1936–39, to distinguish this conflict from the "Arab Revolt" in which T. E. Lawrence participated. See Horne, *Job Well Done,* 205.
39. GS(R), "Report for D.C.I.G.S. No. 8—Investigation of the Possibilities of Guerilla Activities," 1 June 1939, 1–2, HS 8/260.
40. Hughes, "Lawlessness Was the Law," 141.
41. Miller, "'An Oriental Ireland,'" 164.
42. Bowden, *Breakdown of Public Security,* 1.
43. Towle, *Pilots and Rebels,* 46.
44. General Staff, Palestine & Trans-Jordan, *Military Lessons of the Arab Rebellion,* 21, 23, TNA: PRO, WO 191/70; Bowden, *Breakdown of Public Security,* 203. Trans-Jordan was not in rebellion and therefore had fewer restrictions in place.
45. The Grand Mufti conferred with Adm. Wilhelm Canaris, chief of German military intelligence, on the topic of sabotage. See Kahn, *Hitler's Spies,* 233. One farmer in Palestine complained he was "constantly watched by a net of spies and Nazi officials" (*Palestine Post* [Jerusalem], 17 August 1939, quoted in de Jong, *German Fifth Column,* 21).
46. *AGW,* 7 § 21.
47. Ibid., 9. Cf. Townshend, *Britain's Civil Wars,* 104; Horne, *Job Well Done,* 211.

48. General Staff, Palestine & Trans-Jordan, *Military Lessons of the Arab Rebellion*, 9–11, 15–16, 19, 23, TNA: PRO, WO 191/70; Simson, *British Rule*, 196–97, 215–16.
49. *PLH*, 20 (appendix 2: "Rail Ambush").
50. Simson, *British Rule*, 242.
51. General Staff, Palestine & Trans-Jordan, *Military Lessons of the Arab Rebellion*, 11, 19, 23, TNA: PRO, WO 191/70; Sykes, *Orde Wingate*, 151. "Night sabotage was chiefly favoured [by those attacking the oil pipeline] as darkness not only made the saboteur's work safer but also contributed to the spectacular effect." General Staff, Palestine & Trans-Jordan, *Military Lessons of the Arab Rebellion*, 131, TNA: PRO, WO 191/70.
52. Holland, "Duties of the New Branch," 3 April 1939, 2, TNA: PRO, HS 8/256.
53. Townshend, *Britain's Civil Wars*, 111.
54. Horne, *Job Well Done*, 213, emphasis added.
55. *AGW*, 22 § 81.
56. General Staff, Palestine & Trans-Jordan, *Military Lessons of the Arab Rebellion*, 15, TNA: PRO, WO 191/70.
57. Ibid., 11. Cf. 134.
58. Ibid., 20, 23, 75, 135; Bierman and Smith, *Fire in the Night*, 109; Horne, *Job Well Done*, 214; Simson, *British Rule*, 261; Sykes, *Orde Wingate*, 168.
59. General Staff, Palestine & Trans-Jordan, *Military Lessons of the Arab Rebellion*, 8, 133, TNA: PRO, WO 191/70.
60. Simson, *British Rule*, 235.
61. General Staff, Palestine & Trans-Jordan, *Military Lessons of the Arab Rebellion*, 136, TNA: PRO, WO 191/70.
62. Ibid., 77.
63. *FSR* (1935), quoted in General Staff, Palestine & Trans-Jordan, *Military Lessons of the Arab Rebellion*, 128, TNA: PRO, WO 191/70.
64. Anglim, "Callwell versus Graziani," 596. Cf. *AGW*, 5 § 15, 6 § 16; *PLH*, 1–2 § 2, 14 (appendix 1: "Road Ambush") § 2d, 30 (appendix 3: "The Destruction of an Enemy Post") § 5.
65. General Staff, Palestine & Trans-Jordan, *Military Lessons of the Arab Rebellion*, 10, TNA: PRO, WO 191/70. Cf. *PLH*, 40 (appendix 8: "Sabotage") § 12.
66. Townshend, *Britain's Civil Wars*, 108.
67. General Staff, Palestine & Trans-Jordan, *Military Lessons of the Arab Rebellion*, 10, TNA: PRO, WO 191/70. Cf. Nankivell and Loch, *Ireland in Travail*, 60.
68. Horne, *Job Well Done*, 211. "The disciplining and terrorizing psychological effects upon the Arab community of the assassination of community leaders was traumatic. If not moved as a result actually to participate, Palestinian Arabs at least ceased to display openly any disaffection towards the Arab cause" (Bowden, *Breakdown of Public Security*, 180).

69. The 8th Division, *Notes on Lessons of Arab Rebellion, 1938–39*, 10, TNA: PRO, WO 201/326.
70. *PLH*, 3 § 3.
71. Bowden, *Breakdown of Public Security*, 204.
72. *AGW*, 2 § 5b.
73. General Staff, Palestine & Trans-Jordan, *Military Lessons of the Arab Rebellion*, 45–46, TNA: PRO, WO 191/70; Bowden, *Breakdown of Public Security*, 157, 171; Mockaitis, *British Counterinsurgency*, 93.
74. General Staff, Palestine & Trans-Jordan, *Military Lessons of the Arab Rebellion*, 13, TNA: PRO, WO 191/70. There were also concerns about Arabs employed on the telegraph lines and at the various pump stations of the pipeline that brought water to Jerusalem; in the event, however, they caused no trouble. See General Staff, Palestine & Trans-Jordan, *Military Lessons of the Arab Rebellion*, 131, 133, TNA: PRO, WO 191/70.
75. *AGW*, 4 §12. Cf. Mockaitis, *British Counterinsurgency*, 93–94.
76. General Staff, Palestine & Trans-Jordan, *Military Lessons of the Arab Rebellion*, 51, TNA: PRO, WO 191/70. Cf. 8th Division, *Notes on Lessons of Arab Rebellion*, 16, TNA: PRO, WO 201/326.
77. Simson, *British Rule*, 240–41.
78. *PLH*, 4 § 6.
79. General Staff, Palestine & Trans-Jordan, *Military Lessons of the Arab Rebellion*, 52, TNA: PRO, WO 191/70.
80. Ibid., 136.
81. Townshend, *Britain's Civil Wars*, 106.
82. The 8th Division, *Notes on Lessons of Arab Rebellion*, 9, TNA: PRO, WO 201/326.
83. Townshend, *Britain's Civil Wars*, 108.
84. Thomas Mockaitis, *British Counterinsurgency*, 33.
85. Simson, *British Rule*, 196–97, 227. This tactic was not new to observant British forces. In Ireland "it was nothing strange to be stopped by the military in the street and searched for arms, and the custom was growing to let women carry the guns until they were wanted and receive them again afterwards, for women were not allowed to be searched except in emergency by women searchers. The British Government was paternal in some things to the end, and earned the righteous scorn of Loyalist and Republican alike" (Nankivell and Loch, *Ireland in Travail*, 248).
86. Townshend, *Britain's Civil Wars*, 104. Cf. Mockaitis, *British Counterinsurgency*, 34.
87. Anglim, *Orde Wingate and the British Army*, 1; Sykes, *Orde Wingate*, 120.
88. Sykes, *Orde Wingate*, 133. Cf. Anglim, *Orde Wingate and the British Army*, 48–49.
89. Sykes, *Orde Wingate*, 291.
90. Bowden, *Breakdown of Public Security*, 245.
91. According to historians Thomas Mockaitis and Tom Segev, torture was not beneath the SNS. See Mockaitis, *British Counterinsurgency*, 34,

and Segev, *One Palestine*, 430–31. Biographer Christopher Sykes takes issue with this claim, writing:

> If it seems undeniable that some bad things to the contrary happened in the S.N.S., it is equally undeniable that Wingate, except on this occasion [of one engagement near Beisan in the summer of 1938, when civilian bystanders were killed], was throughout an influence of restraint on the more reckless spirits among his squadsmen, and insisted, even at peril, on humane conduct. Many allegations were made against him, sometimes by shocked Jewish followers who came from the decency of civilian surroundings. None of the allegations, except those regarding the indiscriminate shooting south of Beisan, can withstand scrutiny, and experience shows that unidentifiable events are usually imaginary ones. Wingate had many enemies in Palestine who (not without goading from him) tried to discredit him. But when they came to make definite accusations they made none of the kind indicated here. (Sykes, *Orde Wingate*, 170, cf. 107)

Simon Anglim is likewise cautious about claims of torture. See Anglim, *Orde Wingate and the British Army*, 59.
92. Anglim, "Callwell versus Graziani," 597.
93. The 8th Division, *Notes on Lessons of Arab Rebellion*, 9, TNA: PRO, WO 201/326.
94. Anglim, *Orde Wingate and the British Army*, 80; Bowden, *Breakdown of Public Security*, 245–46; Dekel, *Shai*, 328.
95. Wingate, quoted in Sykes, *Orde Wingate*, 151.
96. Sykes, *Orde Wingate*, 156–57.
97. Ibid., 150. Wingate was not entirely unique in this; elsewhere in Palestine British forces wore "P.T. shoes" for quiet at night, though the same report concluded that "it is necessary for boots to be worn for rough work and fighting." See 8th Division, *Notes on Lessons of Arab Rebellion*, 17, TNA: PRO, WO 201/326. On Holland's interest in light shoes, see Gubbins, "CG's Comments on Foot's Book," n.d., 1, Gubbins papers 3/2/57, IWM.
98. Sykes, *Orde Wingate*, 154. Simon Anglim suggests that the grievance committees were not to Wingate's liking and that his occasional authoritarianism was an attempt to enforce discipline that was lacking elsewhere. See *Orde Wingate and the British Army*, 82.
99. *AGW*, 6 § 17.
100. Sykes, *Orde Wingate*, 174. The surviving notes from eight lectures are held in the Israeli Ministry of Defence Records.
101. Wingate, quoted in Sykes, *Orde Wingate*, 174.
102. On the limited utility of regular soldiers, see *AGW*, 7 § 19. For examples of Gubbins's brief literary flourishes, see, for example, *AGW*, 2 § 4, 5 § 13, 12 § 40, 22 § 82.
103. Sykes, *Orde Wingate*, 151.
104. *AGW*, 5 § 13.
105. *AGW*, 14 § 51.
106. Ibid., 14 § 48. Cf. *PLH*, 22–27 (appendix 2: "Rail Ambushes").
107. Sykes, *Orde Wingate*, 155.

108. *PLH*, 31 (appendix 4: "Concealment and Care of Arms & Explosives") § 2. Arab weapons, in contrast, were almost always old and frequently unreliable. See Bowden, *Breakdown of Public Security*, 204.
109. Anglim, *Orde Wingate and the British Army*, 102.
110. Ibid., 102.
111. Wingate and Sir Edmund Ironside, Gubbins's superior in Russia, were friends, first meeting in Palestine when Ironside was governor of Gibraltar and commander-in-chief designate of the Middle Eastern Theatre. The occasion came at Tiberias in the aftermath of a firefight.

> Near the top of the hill leading out of Tiberias [Ironside] encountered a grim-looking man in an antique sun-helmet superintending the laying-out of robed corpses and the piling of captured weapons.
> "And who are you?" asked General Ironside.
> "I'm Wingate," was the reply. . . . The younger man had spoken as though his name must inevitably be known to the other as that of a famous person. . . . Wingate told him about the S.N.S. and explained how he had laid the ambush and collected six bodies, adding that he calculated that he must have accounted for forty. . . . When he was back in Gibraltar Sir Edmund . . . retained a lasting memory of the grim Captain on the heights over Tiberias. He noted that he had commanded the only force to meet, fight and punish the assassins on that night of slaughter. He decided that his name was not one to forget. (Sykes, *Orde Wingate*, 180)

112. *AGW*, 15 § 54–55.
113. Other elements in Palestine were not new: passes, identity cards, traffic regulations, curfews, and detentions under emergency regulations. The 8th Division, *Notes on Lessons of Arab Rebellion*, 1, 4–8, TNA: PRO, WO 201/326; Bowden, *Breakdown of Public Security*, 249–50.
114. General Staff, Palestine & Trans-Jordan, *Military Lessons of the Arab Rebellion*, 135, TNA: PRO, WO 191/70.
115. Ibid., 15. The actions described were apparently successful: "The Jaffa operations put an end forever to the use of the Old City as a citadel of lawlessness and refuge of fugitives of justice."
116. Ibid., 1. Cf. Bierman and Smith, *Fire in the Night*, 85. The *Military Lessons of the Arab Rebellion* explains that "so far as the bridges were concerned the most surprising thing is the small success achieved by rebels in this direction in spite of the many opportunities resulting from a widespread use of explosives for civil purposes all over the country. In no case was traffic ever stopped for more than 24 hours on account of damaged bridges" (134).
117. The 8th Division, *Notes on Lessons of Arab Rebellion*, 10, TNA: PRO, WO 201/326.
118. Bowden, *Breakdown of Public Security*, 192–93.
119. Fawzi al-Qawuqji, quoted in Bowden, *Breakdown of Public Security*, 198.
120. General Staff, Headquarters, British Forces Palestine & Trans-Jordan, *Military Lessons of the Arab Rebellion*, 21–22, TNA: PRO, WO 191/70.

121. Bowden, *Breakdown of Public Security*, 192–93.
122. Townshend, *Britain's Civil Wars*, 112.
123. E. Krueger, "Sino-Japanese Relations Reviewed," *China Quarterly* (Fall 1937): 578–86, reprinted in Johnsen, *Chinese-Japanese War*, 49; Peattie, "Dragon's Seed," 48.
124. Dreyer, *China at War*, 46–47; Peattie, "Dragon's Seed," 65; Wilson, *When Tigers Fight*, 5–6. There are several methods of Romanizing Chinese names; disagreement reigns in both primary sources and recent scholarship. Spellings here simply follow the most common usage in the sources.
125. Dreyer, *China at War*, 117–69; Peattie, "Dragon's Seed," 65; Samuel B. Griffith, introduction to Mao Tse-tung, *On Guerrilla Warfare*, 15. Mao later recalled, "From 1927 to 1936, the Chinese Red Army fought almost continually and employed guerrilla tactics constantly. . . . There are many valuable lessons we can learn from the experience of those years" (62–63).
126. Krueger, "Sino-Japanese Relations," in Johnsen, *Chinese-Japanese War*, 55–60; Dreyer, *China at War*, 170–81; Peattie, "Dragon's Seed," 66–67.
127. Krueger, "Sino-Japanese Relations," in Johnsen, *Chinese-Japanese War*, 61–62; Dreyer, *China at War*, 210–13; Wilson, *When Tigers Fight*, 14–26, 34–46.
128. Peter Fleming, Notes on the Possibilities of British Military Action in China, August 1939, 1–2, TNA: PRO, HS 8/260. One pro-Nationalist account explains somewhat differently: "With the outbreak of full-scale war in 1937, our country adopted the strategy of attrition which employed guerrilla operations to supplement regular operations. Accordingly, guerilla warfare manuals were published and guerilla cadres trained. Elements of regular force and local militia were dispatched to conduct guerilla operations. . . . Had the Chinese Communists not taken advantage of this opportunity to swallow local forces and attack guerilla forces, the effectiveness of our guerilla warfare would have been much greater" (Hu, *Brief History*, 128).
129. Hu, *Brief History*, 131. Cf. 129–30.
130. Yang, "Nationalist and Communist Guerrilla Warfare," 309–10.
131. Quoted in Yu, "Juntong," 136. Cf. de Fremery's Report No. 16, c. 1938, in *A Dutch Spy in China*, 245. The original reports by de Fremery, a former colonel of the Royal Netherlands Indies Army, have been lost, though copies are preserved in the Dutch Colonial Archives. This history may explain why his reports, in this published form, are undated. On attacking the enemy's rear areas, see also Mao, *On Guerrilla Warfare*, 67.
132. Notes on the Sino-Japanese War, 17 February 1938, 1, TNA: PRO, WO 106/5572. Edward Dreyer takes an even more cynical view: "'Fighting withdrawal' meant rout and 'guerrilla warfare' meant disintegration in the Chinese communiqués of this time [c. May 1938]." "A declared strategy of guerrilla warfare may often be merely a

rationalization for the desire to avoid battle. Preserving one's forces by not fighting and 'harassing' the enemy by following at a safe distance without actually making contact, were consistent with the warlord-derived vices of most Chinese military units, but were not really guerrilla warfare" (*China at War*, 228, 238–39).
133. Snow, *Red Star over China*, 90–91.
134. "CG's Comments on Foot's Book," n.d., 1, Gubbins papers 3/2/57, IWM; Astley, *Inner Circle*, 20; Wilkinson and Astley, *Gubbins and SOE*, 34.
135. GS(R)—Report for DCI, GS No. 7: "Considerations from the Wars in Spain and China with Regard to Certain Aspects of Army Policy," TNA: PRO, WO 106/5572.
136. *North China Daily News*, 22 July 1939, quoted in Booker, *News Is My Job*, 304. Cf. G. P. Young to Viscount Halifax, 23 March 1938, TNA: PRO, WO 106/5574; and de Fremery, Report No. 16, c. 1938, in *A Dutch Spy in China*, 249, 257–58.
137. Notes on the Sino-Japanese War, 17 February 1938, 2, TNA: PRO, WO 106/5572. Although Chinese accounts should be read with caution, one observes that the Japanese "were only able to occupy major cities and a 10-km narrow corridor along their lines of communication, while our guerilla forces possessed the vast areas surrounding and harassing them" (Hu, *Brief History*, 132).
138. De Fremery, Report No. 10, c. April 1938, in *A Dutch Spy in China*, 170; Zarrow, *China in War*, 311.
139. *AGW*, 12 § 39.
140. Lt. J. H. G. Cooper, RA, "Report on visit to Shihchiachuang, Changteh, and Taiyuanfu," c. May 1938, 7, 9, TNA: PRO, WO 106/5572. Cf. Report No. 24, Japanese Intentions and Prospects, 21 February 1938, 2, TNA: PRO, WO 106/5572.
141. Col. V. R. Burkhardt, Report on a Visit to North China, 9, TNA: PRO, WO 106/5576.
142. De Fremery, Report No. 12, c. August 1938, in *A Dutch Spy in China*, 209.
143. *AGW*, 1 § 1; emphasis added. Cf. *PLH*, 2 § 2, 12 § 14.
144. *New Statesman and Nation* (15 January 1938): 74, reprinted in Johnsen, *Chinese-Japanese War*, 140.
145. De Fremery, Report No. 17, c. 1938, in *A Dutch Spy in China*, 257.
146. *AGW*, 3 § 8. Cf. *PLH*, 1 § 1.
147. British Consulate, Chefoo, Chefoo Political Report for September Quarter, 1938, 30 September 1938, 1, TNA: PRO, WO 106/5574. Cf. Yu, "Juntong," 137–38.
148. Arthur R. Kennedy to His Majesty's Ambassador, 26 July 1938, 3, TNA: PRO, WO 106–5573. Cf. Yang, "Nationalist and Communist Guerrilla Warfare," 316. Subsequent scholarship has confirmed that, particularly in the first years of the war, the guerillas "were not much more than bandit gangs preying on the peasantry" (Dreyer, *China at War*, 228). Mao gave special attention to this problem, insisting that

his guerrillas should "not steal from the people" but instead "be courteous, be honest in your transactions, return what you borrow, replace what you break . . . [and] do not without authority search the pocketbooks of those you arrest" (*On Guerrilla Warfare*, 92.) His efforts apparently paid off. "The Eighth Route [Army] always pays for its food and never abuses folks," reported one old villager from Shanxi (Yang, "Nationalist and Communist Guerrilla Warfare," 317).

149. "Shanghai Local Situation: 15 July–15 August, 1938," 43–44, TNA: PRO, WO 106/5573. A report by a British liaison officer explains the form that some such repression took: "When terroristic outrages occur in the Settlement which are suspected of being anti-Japanese, the [Japanese] Military police are very much in evidence. They usually co-operate with the Shanghai Municipal Police but sometimes refuse them access to such places as they think fit. They also conduct searches, make arrests and generally proceed with their investigations regardless of the consent or otherwise of the civil and military authorities of the area concerned." (Lt. P. Pender-Cudlip, RA, Report on Attachment to British Military Headquarters, Shanghai as Liaison Officer to the Japanese Forces, November 1937 to July 1938, 11, TNA: PRO, WO 106/5573).

150. Maj. Gen. F. S. G. Piggott, Report on Visit to Tientsin, by Military Attaché, Tokyo, 3 to 9 April 1939, 7, TNA: PRO, WO 106/5584. The suspicions of Piggott and others who viewed the Chinese as terrorists were supported by a bomb attack carried out against the Japanese ship *Tazima Maru* while in the port of Bremen. Moreover, the Japanese consul told the British he had reports suggesting Chinese and foreign students at European universities would attempt subsequent acts of sabotage against Japanese ships in European ports. See "The following may be of interest," 2 April 1938, TNA: PRO, WO 106/5572. The initial claims of damage to the ship were reported by the Japanese consul. British authorities confirmed the damage when the ship came through Port Said. While attacking Japanese ships in Europe may seem novel, it accords with the strategy—observed in China and espoused by Gubbins a short time later—of attacking enemy communications and transportation. Cf. *AGW*, 3 § 8; *PLH*, 3 § 4.

151. Piggott, Report on Visit to Tientsin, 7, 12, TNA: PRO, WO 106/5584. The "Resist Japan Assassination Society" was reported to have "a very similar system of control and administration, but works independently" (8).

152. *AGW*, 17 § 64. Cf. *AGW*, 19 § 69. Most of Gubbins's comments about neutrals, however, pertain to neutral states from which an enemy receives supplies, making these states potential targets for partisans. See *AGW*, 19–20 § 71–73.

153. Nankivell and Loch, *Ireland in Travail*, 182, 248.

154. *AGW*, 13 § 45.

155. *PLH*, 37 (appendix 7) § 2.

156. Yu notes that "historians on the two sides of the Taiwan Strait give different accounts as to how and why the LPA [Loyal Patriotic Army,

Dai Li's guerrilla force] was formed. Nationalist historians in Taiwan insist on the anti-Japanese tradition of the LPA, while historians in mainland China have denounced it for its anti-Communist orientation. The Communists have largely denied any connection between the LPA and China's resistance struggle" ("Juntong," 137).

157. De Fremery, Report No. 22, c. October 1938, in *A Dutch Spy in China*, 262.
158. Dreyer, *China at War*, 233; Yang, "Nationalist and Communist Guerrilla Warfare," 308.
159. De Fremery, Report No. 16, c. 1938, in *A Dutch Spy in China*, 246.
160. Beckett, *Modern Insurgencies and Counterinsurgencies*, 76; Marlow, *David Galula*, 29. Evans Fordyce Carlson, U.S. Marine Corps, spent a considerable amount of time with Mao's guerrillas in 1937 and 1938. He resigned his commission in 1939 to take up public speaking and published his memoirs in 1940. See Carlson, *Twin Stars of China*. Carlson may have read *On Guerrilla Warfare* or heard about it while in China; he may have lectured on its contents. However, he did not produce a public translation before Griffith.
161. Griffith, translator's note to Mao, *On Guerrilla Warfare*, 37.
162. SOE Record of Service: Colin McVean Gubbins, TNA: PRO, WO 9/630/8. Marlow argues that Mao's *On Guerrilla Warfare* was only translated into French in 1950, though the possibility of unpublished translations remains. See Marlow, *David Galula*, 27. Likewise, Walter Laqueur notes that the first Russian translation of *On Guerrilla Warfare* was published in 1952 (*Guerrilla Warfare*, 177).
163. Mao, *On Guerrilla Warfare*, 96–97, 101–105. Cf. *AGW*, 5 § 14.
164. On captured equipment, see Griffith, introduction to Mao, *On Guerrilla Warfare*, 24; *AGW*, 11 § 35. Cf. Mao, *On Guerrilla Warfare*, 83: "The enemy is the principal source of [guerrillas'] supply." Mao told Snow that "the Red Army has equipped its present forces from the Kuomintang: for nine years they have been our 'ammunition-carriers'" (*Red Star over China*, 87). Likewise, Colonel Burkhardt observed the Chinese practice of capturing weapons for use. See Report on a Visit to North China, 4–5, TNA: PRO, WO 106/5576. On leaders, see Mao, *On Guerrilla Warfare*, 45, 52, 85–86; *PLH*, 2 § 3. On local conditions, see Mao, *On Guerrilla Warfare*, 49, 80, 93; *AGW*, 1 § 3, 11 § 37. On the propaganda value of success, see Mao, *On Guerrilla Warfare*, 64; *AGW*, 2 § 4, 5 § 15, 22 § 82.
165. Mao, *On Guerrilla Warfare*, 41–2, 54–55, 57, 74, 95; *AGW*, 1 § 4, 2 § 4, 7 § 19, 18 § 68. Chiang also advocated coordination of guerrilla activities with regular forces. See Booker, *News Is My Job*, 329–30 and Yu, "Juntong," 136. MI(R) was certainly aware of this strategy. One report noted that "Lawrence could not have won his war without [the regular forces of General] Allenby: Allenby could have won his war without Lawrence. Chinese high strategy recognises that guerillas can only represent a subsidiary military effort" (Fleming, Notes on the Possibilities of British Military Action in China, August 1939, 2, TNA: PRO, HS 8/260).

166. *AGW*, 3-4 § 8; Mao, *On Guerrilla Warfare*, 53, 112; Mao, quoted in Snow, *Red Star over China*, 91-92.
167. *AGW*, 15 § 55; *PLH*, 12 § 13; Mao, *On Guerrilla Warfare*, 111-12.
168. Mao, *On Guerrilla Warfare*, 43. Cf. Griffith, introduction to Mao, *On Guerrilla Warfare*, 27.
169. Mao, *On Guerrilla Warfare*, 44. Cf. Mao, quoted in Snow, *Red Star over China*, 87.
170. "The people will actively co-operate in providing information for the guerillas and withholding it from the enemy.... Fighting in his own country, among his own people, against a foreign foe who has invaded his land, the justice of [the guerrilla's] cause will inflame his embitterment" (*AGW* 4 § 12, 5 § 13). In spite of his emphasis on discipline, Mao also contends that "a primary feature of guerrilla operations is their dependence upon *the people themselves* to organize battalions and other units" (*On Guerrilla Warfare*, 51, emphasis added). Gubbins contradicts this in several places. After the Second World War, Gubbins wrote to Foot, "I sincerely do not think that there would have been any possibility of significant resistance in France, unless there had existed an S.O.E. to spark it off and not only co-ordinate it" (Gubbins to Foot, 29 January 1964, IWM, Gubbins papers 3/2/57, IWM). While his comments elsewhere demonstrate Gubbins's belief in the power of popular resistance, he certainly also understood its frequent dependence on outside organization and support.
171. Mao, *On Guerrilla Warfare*, 45, cf. 79-80.
172. Ibid., appendix, tables 2 and 4. This is in contrast to the organization General Piggott described in Tientsin, which was clearly configured for guerrilla or terrorist operations.
173. Ibid., 83; *AGW*, 10 § 34.
174. Admittedly, Mao's description of training does include demolitions, particularly of rail lines in enemy territory. See *On Guerrilla Warfare*, 83.
175. In one battle guerrillas literally filled such a middling role. Colonel Burkhardt describes the Chinese as arrayed "in three echelons[:] Red Spears [a local militia], Guerillas and Regular troops." See Report on a Visit to North China, 10, TNA: PRO, WO 106/5576.
176. Hart-Davis, *Peter Fleming*, 214.
177. *AGW*, 7 § 18; Fleming, Notes on the Possibilities of British Military Action in China, August 1939, 3-5, TNA: PRO, HS 8/260, emphasis in original. Fleming suggests that the advisory "details (not more than 4 men, including one driver, per officer) might consist of British-trained Chinese, or of Indian troops, or of (non-Burmese) troops from Upper Burma," that is, Kachins (see chapter 7).
178. Fleming, Notes on the Possibilities of British Military Action in China, August 1939, 4, TNA: PRO, HS 8/260. William Donovan, coordinator of information and then director of the Office of Strategic Services (OSS—see chapter 6), concocted a similar plan in December 1941. See Dunlop, *Donovan*, 339-40.

179. Fleming, Notes on the Possibilities of British Military Action in China, appendix B, August 1939, 1–2, TNA: PRO, HS 8/260.
180. War Diary, MI(R), September 1939, TNA: PRO, HS 8/263; Hart-Davis, *Peter Fleming*, 215–16.
181. Gubbins address to Cambridge University Officers Training Corps, 26 October 1962, 1–2, Gubbins papers 4/1/6, IWM. The reference here to Czechoslovakia pertains not to the Munich agreement of 1938, which gave Germany control of the Sudetenland, but the subsequent German occupation of the rump in 1939.
182. Dalton, *Fateful Years*, 368.
183. "Brief History of SOE," 1, TNA: PRO, HS 7/1.
184. Blandford, *SS Intelligence*, 82, 96–103; De Jong, *German Fifth Column*, 10; Kurowski, *Brandenburger Commandos*, 15.
185. Adams, *British Foreign Policy*, 82; Blandford, *SS Intelligence*, 81; Taylor, *The Origins of the Second World War*, 139–40. Taylor claims that "Hitler knew nothing of these plans, which had been prepared despite his orders" (140). However, Ian Westwell contends that the Abwehr's II Department (Sabotage) was involved in the Austrian Nazi intrigues. See *Brandenburgers*, 8. Whatever the actual case, an MI(R) officer, looking back from 1939, would have perceived a clear line of Nazi subversion.
186. Adams, *British Foreign Policy*, 82–83; Taylor, *Origins of the Second World War*, 147–48. Seyss-Inquart requested the troops in a telegram sent at 9:10 P.M.; the order to the German military to deploy troops to Austria had already been sent at 8:45 P.M.
187. Adams, *British Foreign Policy*, 91, 93–94, 106; Westwell, *Brandenburgers*, 8.
188. Kurowski, *Brandenburger Commandos*, 17, 41; Westwell, *Brandenburgers*, 13–14.
189. Westwell, *Brandenburgers*, 15.
190. Theodor von Hippel, quoted in Kurowski, *Brandenburger Commandos*, 6.
191. Kurowski, *Brandenburger Commandos*, 50, 52; Heilbrunn, *Warfare in the Enemy's Rear*, 58–61; Westwell, *Brandenburgers*, 15.
192. Kurowski, *Brandenburger Commandos*, 26–28, 53, 59, 62.
193. Fisk, *In Time of War*, 141–42; O'Halpin, *Spying on Ireland*, 93–94.
194. Fisk, *In Time of War*, 174. De Valera subsequently even asked Britain to come to Ireland's aid if she were attacked by Germany. See Fisk, *In Time of War*, 186–87.
195. Ibid., 142–50; O'Halpin, *Spying on Ireland*, 42, 52–53, 57, 66, 73, 252.
196. *Vier Dokumente zum Prozess Neumann, Von Sass und Genossen* (Kaunas, 1934), 16; quoted in de Jong, *German Fifth Column*, 10.
197. Kurowski, *Brandenburger Commandos*, 12.
198. De Jong, *German Fifth Column*, 20.
199. Ibid., 12–14.
200. Gubbins address to the Danish/English Society in Copenhagen, 29 April 1966, 2, Gubbins papers 4/1/20, IWM.

201. Donovan and Mowrer, *Fifth Column Lessons*, 1.
202. Ibid., 4.
203. De Jong, *German Fifth Column*, 147–248.
204. Ibid., 5.
205. Gubbins address to the Danish/English Society in Copenhagen, 29 April 1966, 2, Gubbins papers 4/1/20, IWM.
206. Cf. Mackenzie, *Secret History of SOE*, 40.
207. "An Appreciation of the capabilities and composition of a small force operating behind the enemy lines *in the offensive*," 7 June 1940, 2, TNA: PRO, HS 8/259. Cf. MI(R) No. 283/40, "Irregular Tactics and Strategy," August 1940, TNA: PRO, HS 8/259. This later document, likely authored by Holland, advocates the use of helicopters and autogyros to spearhead mobile forces, which would then be supported by parachute and glider-borne troops and supplies dropped by parachutes.
208. Mackenzie, *Secret History of SOE*, 41n1.
209. *PLH*, 13 § 14.

Chapter 5

1. At the time Romania bordered both Poland and the German puppet state of Slovakia. Today it borders neither.
2. Wilkinson and Astley, *Gubbins and SOE*, 36. Cf. Wilkinson, *Foreign Fields*, 67.
3. "CG's Comments on Foot's Book," n.d., 2, Gubbins papers 3/2/57, IWM.
4. Sir Peter Wilkinson, lecture titled "Gubbins: A Resistance Leader," given at Cambridge on 28 April 1990, 3, Gubbins papers 4/1/50, IWM; Wilkinson and Astley, *Gubbins and SOE*, 38.
5. Carton de Wiart, *Happy Odyssey*, 122–23, 153–56; Wilkinson, *Foreign Fields*, 78; Wilkinson and Astley, *Gubbins and SOE*, 38. Carton de Wiart may have collected intelligence for Britain even when he was not on the government payroll. See Pepłoński, Suchcitz, and Tebinka, "Intelligence Co-operation," 171.
6. Maj. Gen. Carton de Wiart, "British Military Mission to Poland," 2, TNA: PRO, WO 106/1757; Mackenzie, *Secret History of SOE*, 45; Wilkinson, *Foreign Fields*, 68–71; Wilkinson and Astley, *Gubbins and SOE*, 39–40.
7. Holland, "Duties of the New Branch," 3 April 1939, 4, TNA: PRO, HS 8/256.
8. Gubbins, "Report for D.C.I.G.S. No. 8—Investigation of the Possibilities of Guerilla Activities," appendix 1: "Preliminary Report on a Tour to Poland, Baltic States, and Roumania," 1 June 1939, 2, TNA: PRO, HS 8/260, emphasis added.
9. Gubbins, address to Anglo-Polish Society, 18 November 1972, 2, Gubbins papers 4/1/41, IWM.
10. Carton e Wiart, "British Military Mission to Poland," 2, TNA: PRO, WO 106/1757.
11. Bethell, *The War Hitler Won*, 166.

12. Wilkinson and Astley, *Gubbins and SOE*, 46.
13. Carton de Wiart, "British Military Mission to Poland," part 2: Lessons of the Campaign, 7, TNA: PRO, WO 106/1757.
14. Wilkinson and Astley, *Gubbins and SOE*, 41–43. The official report places this move on 6 September. The discrepancy may simply cover the time it took for the general staff and all its personnel to move. See Carton de Wiart, "British Military Mission to Poland," 2, TNA: PRO, WO 106/1757.
15. Wilkinson and Astley, *Gubbins and SOE*, 44.
16. Ibid., 43–44.
17. Carton de Wiart, "British Military Mission to Poland," 10, TNA: PRO, WO 106/1757.
18. Wilkinson, *Foreign Fields*, 82.
19. Ibid., 83–85; Wilkinson and Astley, *Gubbins and SOE*, 45.
20. Wilkinson, *Foreign Fields*, 86.
21. "SOE Early History to September 1939," 8, TNA: PRO, HS 7/3.
22. Ibid., 8.
23. "CG's Comments on Foot's Book," n.d., 1, Gubbins papers 3/2/57, IWM. Cf. Astley, *Inner Circle*, 27.
24. Wilkinson, *Foreign Fields*, 87. "I was also given a special identity card which seemed of questionable value since I was instructed by the security officer to keep it in a sealed envelope and never show it to anybody. I never did."
25. "CG's Comments on Foot's Book," n.d., 1, Gubbins papers 3/2/57, IWM.
26. Ibid., 2; Foot and Langley, *MI9*, 31–34; Mackenzie, *Secret History of SOE*, 42.
27. "CG's Comments on Foot's Book," n.d., 2, Gubbins papers 3/2/57, IWM; Mackenzie, *Secret History of SOE*, 46.
28. Astley, *Inner Circle*, 30; Mackenzie, *Secret History of SOE*, 48; Seaman, "A New Instrument of War," 14.
29. Wilkinson and Astley, *Gubbins and SOE*, 46.
30. Ibid., 47.
31. Bennett, "Polish-British Intelligence Co-operation," 159; Wilkinson, *Foreign Fields*, 91–92; Wilkinson and Astley, *Gubbins and SOE*, 49. See "Activities of the Section up to the Fall of France," TNA: PRO, HS 7/3, for an example of an anti-Nazi French agent arrested by his own government because he worked directly for the British and not through a French intermediary.
32. "Brief History of SOE," 2, TNA: PRO, HS 7/1. This document incorrectly identifies the Deuxième Bureau as the "Civilian Secret Organization"; in fact it was the Second Bureau of the general staff, a military organization, though an autonomous one. The Second Bureau also gave birth to a smaller Fifth Bureau, specifically responsible for sabotage; Section D also liaised with this organization. See "Activities of the Section up to the Fall of France," TNA: PRO, HS 7/3.
33. Maresch, "SOE and Polish Aspirations," 199; Wilkinson and Astley, *Gubbins and SOE*, 47.

34. Wilkinson and Astley, *Gubbins and SOE*, 47.
35. Ibid., 48.
36. Maresch, "SOE and Polish Aspirations," 199; Wilkinson, *Foreign Fields*, 90; Wilkinson and Astley, *Gubbins and SOE*, 49.
37. Wilkinson, *Foreign Fields*, 91. Among the useful information received from Polish agents were reports of the planned German offensive in the Low Countries in May 1940. MI(R) passed the information to SIS, though it is uncertain what was done with it. See Wilkinson, *Foreign Fields*, 92.
38. Foot, *SOE in France*, 6. "It had been known for weeks that the Germans were preparing an invasion." See Wilkinson and Astley, *Gubbins and SOE*, 50. This may have had to do with Gubbins's withdrawal from Paris not three weeks before. The involvement of the War Office, rather than the Royal Marines, in these amphibious plans, stemmed from the fact that the Royal Marines were seriously under strength at this time. See Macksey, *Commando*, 5.
39. Wilkinson and Astley, *Gubbins and SOE*, 50.
40. Harvey, *Scandinavian Misadventure*, 227; Macksey, *Commando*, 5; Wilkinson and Astley, *Gubbins and SOE*, 50.
41. Wilkinson and Astley, *Gubbins and SOE*, 50.
42. Major-General Richardson, Director of Training, 24 April 1940, TNA: PRO, WO 106/1889.
43. Morris, *Churchill's Private Armies*, 18; Wilkinson and Astley, *Gubbins and SOE*, 50.
44. Adams, *Doomed Expedition*, 72; Harvey, *Scandinavian Misadventure*, 227; Wilkinson and Astley, *Gubbins and SOE*, 51.
45. Morris, *Churchill's Private Armies*, 30; Wilkinson and Astley, *Gubbins and SOE*, 50.
46. Wilkinson and Astley, *Gubbins and SOE*, 50.
47. Morris, *Churchill's Private Armies*, 25–26, 28.
48. Mackenzie, *Secret History of SOE*, 49–51.
49. General Hugh Massy, Instructions to Lieutenant-Colonel C. McV. Gubbins, M.C., Commander, Independent Companies, 2 May 1940, TNA: PRO, WO 106/1889; Wilkinson and Astley, *Gubbins and SOE*, 51.
50. Morris, *Churchill's Private Armies*, 34; Wilkinson and Astley, *Gubbins and SOE*, 51.
51. General Hugh Massy, Instructions to Lieutenant-Colonel C. McV. Gubbins, M.C., Commander, Independent Companies, 2 May 1940, TNA: PRO, WO 106/1889.
52. *AGW*, 6 §16.
53. General Massy to Officer Commanding, No. 1 Independent Company, S. S. Orion, 30 April 1940, TNA: PRO, WO 106/1889.
54. General Massy, Instructions to Lieutenant-Colonel C. McV. Gubbins, M.C., Commander, Independent Companies, 2 May 1940, TNA: PRO, WO 106/1889; Wilkinson and Astley, *Gubbins and SOE*, 51. No. 1 Independent Company had sailed ahead of the main force. The staff of SCISSORSFORCE was mostly men with whom Gubbins was already familiar. Among their number were Capt. Roland W. Urquhart, who functioned as brigade major; Capt. Andrew Croft and Lt. Col. Quintin

Riley, RNVR, both holders of the Polar Medal and previously recruited and trained by MI(R), served as intelligence officers; and Maj. Kermit Roosevelt, Scots Guards, a son of U.S. president Theodore Roosevelt, who had seen action with the British Army in Mesopotamia in World War I before the American entry.

55. *AGW*, 6 §16f; Adams, *Doomed Expedition*, 73. Cf. Haarr, *Battle for Norway*, 282; Harvey, *Scandinavian Misadventure*, 230–31; Morris, *Churchill's Private Armies*, 36–37. Many historians criticize Gubbins for this withdrawal. "Gubbins should have kept his nerve," Morris writes. "Gubbins had surrendered 35 miles of most difficult mountain road. . . . It was perfect ambush country in a situation tailor-made for guerrilla warfare" (37). However, Independent Companies Nos. 4 and 5 were already battered from trying to hold a snow-covered road against the advance of German alpine troops. They lacked the equipment necessary for a conventional defense and the ski equipment needed for mobile operations. See Wilkinson and Astley, *Gubbins and SOE*, 53.
56. Adams, *Doomed Expedition*, 72–73; Harvey, *Scandinavian Misadventure*, 227–28; Morris, *Churchill's Private Armies*, 36; Wilkinson and Astley, *Gubbins and SOE*, 52–53.
57. *AGW*, 6 § 16d; Wilkinson and Astley, *Gubbins and SOE*, 50.
58. Wilkinson and Astley, *Gubbins and SOE*, 53.
59. Morris, *Churchill's Private Armies*, 34. Cf. Haarr, *Battle for Norway*, 277; Wilkinson and Astley, *Gubbins and SOE*, 53.
60. Haarr, *Battle of Norway*, 289; Morris, *Churchill's Private Armies*, 41; Wilkinson and Astley, *Gubbins and SOE*, 54–55.
61. Wilkinson and Astley, *Gubbins and SOE*, 55–64. Trappes-Lomax receives kinder treatment in other accounts, such as Adams, *Doomed Expedition*, 77–78, and Harvey, *Scandinavian Misadventure*, 236, 240–42. Wilkinson and Astley provide an exhaustive blow-by-blow account of these events; while their narrative one-sidedly supports Gubbins's decision, it also gives a clear explanation for why he made it. Gubbins's reputation with the Scots Guards was not improved by the rumor that he "borrowed" a car used by one Major Graham. "In the boot of this car was the battalion's stock of precious Scotch whisky, which was never seen again," or so the story goes. See Adams, *Doomed Expedition*, 77.
62. Adams, *Doomed Expedition*, 79–85, 89; Haarr, *Battle for Norway*, 297–98, 300.
63. Wilkinson and Astley, *Gubbins and SOE*, 67.
64. Ibid., 67. Internal quotations from Gubbins personal papers and Alanbrooke papers (Liddell-Hart Center, King's College, London). General Auchinleck's report was written after Gubbins's subsequent promotion to brevet brigadier.
65. "SOE Early History to September 1940," 9, TNA: PRO, HS 7/3.
66. Ibid., 16.
67. Wilkinson and Astley, *Gubbins and SOE*, 69.
68. "SOE Early History to September 1940," 16, TNA: PRO, HS 7/3; Lampe, *Last Ditch*, 86–87.

69. "SOE Early History to September 1940," 16, TNA: PRO, HS 7/3.
70. Lampe, *Last Ditch*, 87; Wilkinson and Astley, *Gubbins and SOE*, 69.
71. "SOE Early History to September 1940," 16, TNA: PRO, HS 7/3; Colin Gubbins to Rory Gubbins, 1970, Gubbins papers 3/2/69, IWM; Wilkinson and Astley, *Gubbins and SOE*, 69. Lampe contends that Gubbins was given charge of the MI(R) stay-behind operation and—seeing its limits—appealed to Ironside for assistance. In either case, the result was the same: Gubbins in charge, under Ironside's authority. See Lampe, *Last Ditch*, 88.
72. Colin Gubbins, "Auxiliary Units, Home Forces," 26 July 1940, 1, TNA: PRO, WO 199/738.
73. Lampe, *Last Ditch*, 91.
74. Ibid., 12.
75. Hart-Davis, *Peter Fleming*, 233. Cf. Lampe, *Last Ditch*, 13.
76. Calvert, *Fighting Mad*, 47–48; Hart-Davis, *Peter Fleming*, 234–35; Fleming, *Operation Sea Lion*, 269–70.
77. Lampe, *Last Ditch*, 107; Wilkinson and Astley, *Gubbins and SOE*, 70.
78. Lampe, *Last Ditch*, 89; Wilkinson and Astley, *Gubbins and SOE*, 70.
79. Gubbins, "Auxiliary Units, Home Forces," 26 July 1940, 2, TNA: PRO, WO 199/738; Lampe, *Last Ditch*, 89.
80. Lampe, *Last Ditch*, 90.
81. Calvert, *Fighting Mad*, 48; Lampe, *Last Ditch*, 91–92; AGW, 6 §16d.
82. Lampe, *Last Ditch*, 96. Cf. Gubbins, quoted in Wilkinson and Astley, *Gubbins and SOE*, 69. In spite of this, Gubbins insisted, per his earlier teaching, that the Aux Units should operate "in co-operation with the regular forces" (Gubbins, "Auxiliary Units, Home Forces," 26 July 1940, 1, TNA: PRO, WO 199/738).
83. Gubbins, 11 August 1940, TNA: PRO, WO 199/2151; Lampe, *Last Ditch*, 97–98.
84. Lampe, *Last Ditch*, 105; Wilkinson and Astley, *Gubbins and SOE*, 70–71. Col. G. H. B. "Billy" Beyts of the 6th Rajputana Rifles had fought against the Burma Rebellion of 1937, earning a Military Cross.
85. Lampe, *Last Ditch*, 98.
86. Ibid., 103. Cf. Gubbins, "CG's Comments on Foot's Book," n.d., 1, Gubbins papers 3/2/57, IWM; Sykes, *Orde Wingate*, 150.
87. Gubbins, "Auxiliary Units, Home Forces," 26 July 1940, 1, TNA: PRO, WO 199/738; Hart-Davis, *Peter Fleming*, 236. Night movement is discussed in "General Movement by Night" [Minor Tactics, appendix 3]; enemy posts in "Selection and Appreciation of Targets" [A.23], especially § 2–3; and silence in "General Movement by Day" [Minor Tactics, appendix 2].
88. Fleming, quoted in Hart-Davis, *Peter Fleming*, 237. Cf. Fleming, *Operation Sea Lion*, 272–73.
89. Gubbins, quoted in Wilkinson and Astley, *Gubbins and SOE*, 74.
90. Cf. Foot, "Was SOE Any Good?" 176–77.
91. Lampe, *Last Ditch*, 144.

92. Seaman, "A New Instrument of War," 14. Indeed, Cadogan records that as late as 14 May Churchill himself was "still doubtful" that a "big attack [was] coming in [the] West" (*Diaries* , 283).
93. "SOE Early History to September 1940," 12, TNA: PRO, HS 7/3; Foot, *SOE in France*, 5; Seaman, "A New Instrument of War," 14.
94. "SOE Early History to September 1940," 14–15, TNA: PRO, HS 7/3. Flying boats were now sometimes used to deliver materials.
95. Gubbins address to Cambridge University Officers Training Corps, 26 October 1962, 2, Gubbins papers 4/1/6, IWM. Even as the need for reform grew, so did the sabotage services. In July 1940 Section D's officer strength reached 140. By August 1940 its personnel outnumbered all the rest of SIS. See Seaman, "A New Instrument of War," 17.
96. Quoted in Foot, *SOE in France*, 6–7. Cf. Bell, *Certain Eventuality*, 50.
97. Cookridge, *Set Europe Ablaze*, 4.
98. Pimlott, *Hugh Dalton*, 277. The specific request came on 14 May 1940. Gubbins later commented that Dalton's "most unique qualification in my mind . . . was his knowledge & interest in foreign affairs, arising to some extent from having been Under-Secretary in the Foreign Office in 1929–1930: our work in SOE was clearly going to be concerned wholly with the Occupied Countries whose leading politicians & governments were in temporary exile in Britain. Dalton knew many of them personally so that high level contact could be quickly established" (Gubbins to John Peart-Binns, n.d., c. April 1974, 1, Gubbins papers 3/2/76, IWM).
99. Pimlott, *Hugh Dalton*, 282, 294.
100. Ibid., 295.
101. Dalton, *Second World War Diary*, 33 (1 June 1940).
102. Foot, *SOE in France*, 7. One paper was put forward on 3 June, the other on 5 June 1940.
103. Astley, *Inner Circle*, 39. In subsequent discussions with the prime minister and select members of the cabinet, the plan was broadened from a single-service outfit to a larger organization coordinating both raiding and subversion under a single minister. See Foot, *SOE in France*, 7; Seaman, "New Instrument of War," 15. Unfortunately the third volume of Stephen Roskill's biography *Hankey*, covering the period 1931–63, sheds no light on any of the events surrounding SOE's creation, though Hankey was involved in the discussions.
104. Smith, *Mountbatten*, 171–72; Ziegler, *Mountbatten*, 153.
105. Ziegler, *Mountbatten*, 154. In October 1941 Keyes was forced out of this position and replaced by Lord Louis Mountbatten.
106. Smith, *Mountbatten*, 172; Ministry of Information, *Combined Operations*, 5.
107. Cadogan, quoted in Seaman, "A New Instrument of War," 15. Seaman does not cite his source.
108. Foot, *SOE in France*, 5.
109. Cadogan, quoted in Seaman, "A New Instrument of War," 15.

110. Seaman, "New Instrument of War," 15.
111. Dalton, *Second World War Diary*, 50 (29 June 1940).
112. Ibid., 45 (21 June 1940).
113. Ibid., 51 (29 June 1940).
114. Cadogan, *Diaries*, 308 (Friday, 28 June 1940).
115. Dalton, quoted in Seaman, "A New Instrument of War," 16.
116. Foot, *SOE in France*, 8; Foot, "Was SOE Any Good?" 169; Seaman, "A New Instrument of War," 16. One Section D history argues that being directly answerable to a minister, rather than to the head of SIS, would ultimately be advantageous to SOE, giving it a greater voice in the War Cabinet. This is true, though by early July the argument seems to have been whether Dalton or the DMI would take control; SIS appears to have faded from the debate. See "Brief History of SOE," 4, TNA: PRO, HS 7/1.
117. Seaman, "A New Instrument of War," 16; Cadogan, *Diaries*, 312 (Thursday, 11 July 1940).
118. Dalton, *Fateful Years*, 336.
119. Quoted in Foot, *SOE in France*, 8–9; D'Este, *Warlord*, 456.
120. Quoted in Foot, *SOE in France*, 8–9.
121. Quoted in Foot, *SOE in France*, 9. Chamberlain entered the hospital a few hours later. In Foot's words, "He never lived to do anything of importance again" ("Was SOE Any Good?" 170).
122. Foot comments: "Not only was SOE to be outside parliamentary control, it was to remain secret and inadmissible, while other departments were expected to assist it. With such a start, it could hardly fail to be unpopular" ("Was SOE Any Good?" 170).
123. Foot, *SOE in France*, 8. Part of this passage is quoted, without a date, in Dalton, *The Fateful Years*, 368.
124. Gilbert, *Churchill*, 58–60; Stafford, "Churchill and SOE," 48.
125. Gilbert, *Churchill*, 107–31; Stafford, "Churchill and SOE," 48.
126. Stafford, "Churchill and SOE," 48.
127. Keegan, *Intelligence in War*, 308. Cf. Brown, introduction to *Secret War Report*, 2–3.
128. Stafford makes this point clearly when he argues that "Churchillian rhetoric and imagery is a misleading guide . . . to the strategy those actually involved in turning SOE into a functioning organisation envisaged for the resistance movements in Europe" (*Britain and European Resistance*, 27).
129. Seaman, "A New Instrument of War," 17.
130. Cruickshank, *Fourth Arm*, 17.
131. Foot, forward to Mackenzie, *Secret History of SOE*, xvii; Hinsley et al., *British Intelligence*, 278.
132. Astley, *Inner Circle*, 39; Seaman, "A New Instrument of War," 17.
133. Gladwyn, *Memoirs*, 100. Cf. Lockhart, *Diaries*, 68 (19 July 1940).
134. Foot, *SOE on France*, 18.
135. Gladwyn, *Memoirs*, 102.
136. Cruickshank, *Fourth Arm*, 18, 31.

137. Rigden, *SOE Syllabus*, 27; Stafford, *Camp X*, 5–6; Sweet-Escott, "Nelson, Sir Frank," 393. Nelson was technically just the head of SO2 at first, but as the organization changed, he soon found himself in charge of all that remained.
138. Seaman, "New Instrument of War," 17.
139. Nelson, quoted in ibid., 17.
140. Dalton, *Second World War Diary*, 83 (18 September 1940).
141. Dalton to Grand, 18 September 1940, quoted in Seaman, "New Instrument of War," 19. CD refers to the leader of SOE, at this time Nelson; C refers to the chief of SIS, at this time Sir Stewart Menzies.
142. Gladwyn, *Memoirs*, 101.
143. Ibid., 101; Lockhart, *Diaries*, 74 (17 August 1940); Philby, *My Silent War*, 22; Mackenzie, *Secret History of SOE*, 12.
144. Astley, *Inner Circle*, 40; Seaman, "New Instrument of War," 17, 19. Stafford places this event in the following month; see Stafford, *Britain and European Resistance*, 26.
145. "Holland, Major-General John Charles Francis," 533.
146. Gladwyn, *Memoirs*, 101.
147. Wilkinson and Astley, *Gubbins and SOE*, 101.
148. Ibid., 76–77.
149. Ibid., 77.
150. Maj. G. M. Forty, "History of the Training Section of SOE, 1940–1945," September, 1945, 3, 6, 10, TNA: PRO, HS 7/51; Wilkinson and Astley, *Gubbins and SOE*, 77–78. (Forty's history may also be found in TNA: PRO, HS 8/435.) The Polish and Czech Country Sections (known as MP and MX, respectively) did, however, fall under Gubbins's specific purview. By the end of 1941 additional country sections would be grouped under him. See Forty, "History of the Training Section," 6.
151. War Cabinet, quoted in Foot, *SOE in France*, 9–10. Foot does not cite the internal quotation.
152. "Brief History of SOE," 5, TNA: PRO, HS 7/1.
153. Ibid., 5.
154. Ibid., 5.
155. Gubbins lecture titled "Special Operations Executive," possibly for the Special Forces Club, June 1959, Gubbins papers 4/1/4, IWM.
156. Gubbins to the Bradford Junior Chamber of Commerce, 6 December 1961, 1–2, ibid., 4/1/5.
157. Gubbins address to the Danish/English Society in Copenhagen, 29 April 1966, 4, ibid., 4/1/20.
158. Gubbins address to Cambridge University Officers Training Corps, 26 October 1962, 24, ibid., 4/1/6.
159. "Brief History of SOE," 6–7, TNA: PRO, HS 7/1.
160. *AGW*, 2–3 § 5b–6, 5 § 15.
161. Gubbins to the Bradford Junior Chamber of Commerce, 6 December 1961, 2, Gubbins papers 4/1/5, IWM. In addition to Wilkinson, Gubbins also acquired Capt. H. B. Perkins, who had served on the No. 4 Military Mission to Poland. The deputy he inherited at Training,

Maj. J. S. Wilson, was an MI(R) veteran. See Wilkinson and Astley, *Gubbins and SOE*, 77.
162. Gubbins to the Bradford Junior Chamber of Commerce, 6 December 1961, 2, Gubbins papers 4/1/5, IWM.
163. Gubbins address to Cambridge University Officers Training Corps, 26 October 1962, 24, ibid., 4/1/6.
164. Gubbins to John Peart-Binns, n.d., c. April 1974, 1, ibid., 3/2/76.
165. Ibid., 1–2.
166. Wilkinson and Astley, *Gubbins and SOE*, 80.

Chapter 6

1. "SOE Early History to September 1940," 21, TNA: PRO, HS 7/3; Maj. G. M. Forty, "History of the Training Section of SOE, 1940–1945," 2, TNA: PRO, HS 7/51. Burgess departed from the scene as Section D became SOE. Lord Gladwyn, as he was then styled, records that it was on his recommendation that Burgess's appointment was terminated. "Not that I had any reason to suspect that Burgess was a Communist, still less a Soviet agent, but having met him once or twice I had formed the opinion that he was quite exceptionally dissolute and indiscreet and certainly unfitted for any kind of confidential work" (*Memoirs*, 101).
2. Wilkinson and Astley, *Gubbins and SOE*, 85.
3. Ibid., 85.
4. Foot, *SOE: An Outline History*, 63.
5. Forty, "History of the Training Section of SOE," 3, 14, 16–17, TNA: PRO, HS 7/51; Gubbins address to Cambridge University Officers Training Corps, 26 October 1962, 11, Gubbins papers 4/1/6, IWM; Foot, *SOE: An Outline History*, 63; Rigden, *SOE Syllabus*, 2.
6. Foot, *SOE: An Outline History*, 63.
7. Forty, "History of the Training Section of SOE," 3, 25–28, TNA: PRO, HS 7/51; Gubbins address to Cambridge University Officers Training Corps, 26 October 1962, 12, Gubbins papers 4/1/6, IWM; Foot, *SOE: An Outline History*, 64. The paramilitary schools, numbered Special Training School (STS) 21 to STS 25c, are sometimes referred to as the Group A Schools. See Foot, *SOE: An Outline History*, 66; Rigden, *SOE Syllabus*, 4.
8. Foot, *SOE: An Outline History*, 66.
9. Gubbins address to Cambridge University Officers Training Corps, 26 October 1962, 21, Gubbins papers 4/1/6, IWM; Forty, "History of the Training Section of SOE," 30–31, TNA: PRO, HS 7/51; Foot, *SOE: An Outline History*, 69. Although SOE students jumped alongside paratroopers and others at RAF Ringway, they lodged in special SOE houses, designated STS 51a and 51b. See Rigden, *SOE Syllabus*, 5.
10. Gubbins address to Cambridge University Officers Training Corps, 26 October 1962, 21, Gubbins papers 4/1/6, IWM.
11. Ibid., 12; Foot, *SOE: An Outline History*, 64.
12. Forty, "History of the Training Section of SOE," 15n, TNA: PRO, HS 7/51; Rigden, *SOE Syllabus*, 4.

13. Forty, "History of the Training Section of SOE," 3–4, 33, TNA: PRO, HS 7/51; Foot, *SOE: An Outline History*, 66; Rigden, *SOE Syllabus*, 5–6. In contrast to the Group A (paramilitary) Schools in Scotland, the finishing schools, numbered STS 31 to STS 37b, were known as Group B Schools or the Beaulieu Area.
14. Forty, "History of the Training Section of SOE," 35, TNA: PRO, HS 7/51; Gubbins address to Cambridge University Officers Training Corps, 26 October 1962, 13, Gubbins papers 4/1/6, IWM; Foot, *SOE: An Outline History*, 66, 68.
15. Foot, *SOE: An Outline History*, 67.
16. Ibid., 67.
17. Forty, "History of the Training Section of SOE," 37–38, TNA: PRO, HS 7/51; Foot, *SOE: An Outline History*, 69.
18. Gubbins address to Cambridge University Officers Training Corps, 26 October 1962, 14, Gubbins papers 4/1/6, IWM; Foot, *SOE: An Outline History*, 69. The propaganda school, STS 39, not only served SOE, but also the PWE. Cf. Forty, "History of the Training Section of SOE," 77, TNA: PRO, HS 7/51.
19. Gubbins to the Bradford Junior Chamber of Commerce, 6 December 1961, 5, Gubbins papers 4/1/5, IWM.
20. Foot, *SOE: An Outline History*, 70.
21. Wilkinson and Astley, *Gubbins and SOE*, 80.
22. Forty, "History of the Training Section of SOE," 206, TNA: PRO, HS 7/51. Weale places the total figure much higher, at 11,500 total graduates of SOE schools (*Secret Warfare*, 75).
23. Foot, *SOE: An Outline History*, 67.
24. Wilkinson and Astley, *Gubbins and SOE*, 85. In India Tegart was concerned with bombings, assassination, rebellion, and propaganda. See Tegart, *Terrorism in India*, 2–8, 14–21, 29–30, 33–37. This work is the printed form of an address Tegart gave to the Royal Empire Society in November 1932.
25. Wilson, *Scouting Round the World*, 18–19, 49; Howarth, *Undercover*, 5.
26. Forty, "History of the Training Section of SOE," 3, TNA: PRO, HS 7/51; Wilkinson and Astley, *Gubbins and SOE*, 85.
27. Cassidy, "Fairbairn in Shanghai," 71.
28. Langelaan, *Knights*, 65.
29. Cassidy, "Fairbairn in Shanghai," 66; Robins, *Legend of W. E. Fairbairn*, 9–12. Fairbairn's illegally young enlistment was only made possible with the help of a recruiter willing to look the other way with regards to his age. His agreed enlistment was for twelve years, though he was eventually discharged after only seven.
30. Fairbairn, quoted in Cassidy, "Fairbairn in Shanghai," 67.
31. Ibid., 67. These techniques, borrowed from the Japanese, were later adopted by all British forces.
32. Following their defeat in Russia, large numbers of White Russians, particularly Cossacks, came to Shanghai, where many were hired by the SMP. See Dong, *Shanghai*, 131. These men doubtless brought

their experience of irregular warfare with them. Thus, Fairbairn, like Gubbins, may have learned lessons derived from the Russian Civil War.
33. Cassidy, "Fairbairn in Shanghai," 68; Robins, *Legend of W. E. Fairbairn*, 88–95.
34. Fairbairn, *Scientific Self-Defence*, vii-viii; originally published as *Defendu: Scientific Self-Defence* (Shanghai, 1926), by the North China Daily News and Herald. Cf. Langelaan, *Knights*, 66–67.
35. Cassidy, "Fairbairn in Shanghai," 68; Robins, *Legend of W. E. Fairbairn*, 129–56.
36. Cassidy, "Fairbairn in Shanghai," 68–69.
37. Ibid., 70. As war escalated, the SMP was increasingly scattered to the four winds; however, Fairbairn was not its only member to find his way into the Allied secret service. He recruited one SMP veteran to help him train students, while others worked for SIS in China or SOE in India. One joined the Naval Volunteer Reserve in Hong Kong, only to be captured by the Japanese. Escaping, he made his way to the Nationalist Chinese forces and rejoined the war. See Bickers, *Empire Made Me*, 319–20.
38. Foot, *SOE: An Outline History*, 64; Langelaan, *Knights*, 68–69. These ideas were later complied into their book *Shooting to Live with the One-Hand Gun* (London, 1942) and adopted by police and military units around the world.
39. O'Donnell, *Operatives, Spies and Saboteurs*, 4–5. The famed Fairbairn knife was "first developed from Boer War bayonets in the armoury of the Shanghai Municipal Police" (Stafford, *Camp X*, 96).
40. Langelaan, *Knights*, 72–74; Stafford, *Camp X*, 94.
41. Cassidy, "Fairbairn in Shanghai," 71.
42. Wilkinson and Astley, *Gubbins and SOE*, 85.
43. Rigden, *SOE Syllabus*, 6.
44. Forty, "History of the Training Section of SOE, 1940–1945," 8, TNA: PRO, HS 7/51.
45. Denis Rigden describes a slightly different scheme, omitting paramilitary fieldcraft and describing instead "exercises related to the matters taught" in the first section (Rigden, *SOE Syllabus*, 6). Such exercises may have been frequent and organized separately, but they do not appear in the February 1944 syllabus that Rigden introduces, which can also be found in TNA: PRO, HS 7/55 and 7/56.
46. "Objects and Methods of Irregular Warfare" (A.1), Rigden, *SOE Syllabus*, 35.
47. Ibid., 37.
48. Ibid., 35–36. On the question of morale, which also occupied the entire third section of the SOE syllabus, see *AGW*, 18 § 66, 18 § 67; *PLH*, 39 (appendix 8: "Sabotage") § 7, 40 (appendix 8: "Sabotage") § 12.
49. *AGW*, 1 § 1.
50. Rigden, *SOE Syllabus*, 31.
51. *AGW*, 12 § 41, 14–15 § 53–55; *PLH*, 11 § 12–13; "Objects and Methods of Counter-Espionage" (A.6), Rigden, *SOE Syllabus*, 61–62.
52. *AGW*, 12 § 39.

53. "Objects and Methods of Counter-Espionage" (A.6), Rigden, *SOE Syllabus*, 61.
54. *AGW*, 13 § 44.
55. Ibid., 13 § 45.
56. "Communications—Internal" (A.19), Rigden, *SOE Syllabus*, 115.
57. Ibid., 117.
58. *PLH*, 28 (appendix 3: "Destruction of an Enemy Post, Detachment, or Guard") § 3.
59. "Selection and Appreciation of Targets" (A.23), Rigden, *SOE Syllabus*, 134.
60. Roosevelt, *War Report*, 5.
61. Brown, *Secret War Report*, 6. At the end of World War II, Kermit Roosevelt oversaw the writing of OSS's official history. It was published in two volumes in 1976. The first volume, titled *War Report of the OSS*, covered its headquarters operations, and was edited with a new introduction by Roosevelt. It was published by Walker and Co. of New York. The second volume, similarly titled *The Secret War Report of the OSS*, covered the organization's foreign operations, and was edited with an introduction by Anthony Cave Brown. This volume was published by Berkley Medallion, also of New York. The first section on Donovan's early activities on behalf of the president may be found in both documents.
62. Dunlop, *Donovan*, 13–26; Waller, *Wild Bill Donovan*, 10–13. Donovan's grandfather may have had some contact with the Fenian Brotherhood, the North American wing of the Irish Republican Brotherhood (IRB) terrorist organization. See Brown, *Last Hero*, 15–16.
63. Dunlop, *Donovan*, 28, 32–33, 44–113; Waller, *Wild Bill Donovan*, 15–16, 18–31. Cf. Harris, *Duffy's War*.
64. Dunlop, *Donovan*, 117–29; Waller, *Wild Bill Donovan*, 32–33. Dunlop contends that Donovan traveled at the personal request of President Wilson, but Waller points out that Donovan was hostile to Wilson. Moreover, Roland Morris, the U.S. ambassador to Japan, claimed that Donovan begged to join Morris on his tour of the White Russian forces in Siberia, an approach that would likely have been unnecessary if he were traveling on presidential business.
65. Dunlop, *Donovan*, 177.
66. Ibid., 185–90; Waller, *Wild Bill Donovan*, 51–54.
67. Dunlop, *Donovan*, 192–93.
68. Roosevelt, *War Report of the OSS*, 5; Dunlop, *Donovan*, 204–208; Jakub, *Spies and Saboteurs*, 3; Waller, *Wild Bill Donovan*, 59.
69. Waller, *Wild Bill Donovan*, 59.
70. Stephenson, *British Security Coordination*, 10–11; Dunlop, *Donovan*, 209–17; Jakub, *Spies and Saboteurs*, 5–7; Waller, *Wild Bill Donovan*, 60. Jakub provides one of the most well-researched accounts of Donovan's trips to Britain, as well as other aspects of Anglo-American clandestine cooperation in this period.
71. Dunlop, *Donovan*, 212; Jakub, *Spies and Saboteurs*, 9; Wilkinson and Astley, *Gubbins and SOE*, 95. It appears, however, that Donovan did not personally meet Sir Frank until February 1941. Moreover, according

to the official history, Donovan's tours of SOE facilities were "conducted" (i.e., limited). See Mackenzie, *Secret History of SOE*, 388.
72. Conyers Read, manuscript, in the possession of and quoted by Dunlop, *Donovan*, 212–13.
73. Roosevelt, *War Report of the OSS*, 5.
74. "CG's Comments on Foot's Book," n.d., 3, Gubbins papers 3/2/57, IWM; Stephenson, *British Security Coordination*, 24; Dunlop, *Donovan*, 270; Jakub, *Spies and Saboteurs*, 14; Hyde, *Quiet Canadian*, 151.
75. Roosevelt, *War Report of the OSS*, 6.
76. Stephenson, *British Security Coordination*, 13–14; Roosevelt, *War Report of the OSS*, 6; Dunlop, *Donovan*, 230–70; Jakub, *Spies and Saboteurs*, 11, 13–18; Waller, *Wild Bill Donovan*, 43–45. Cf. Makenzie, *Secret History of SOE*, 388.
77. Roosevelt, *War Report of the OSS*, 7; Dunlop, *Donovan*, 280–84. At this point Donovan was not exclusively interested in clandestine work; he had also taken the preliminary step of passing an army physical in May 1941, exploring the possibility of commanding a combat division. Secretary Stimson even went so far as to offer Donovan command of the 44th Division, if he wanted it. See Dunlop, *Donovan*, 289; Waller, *Wild Bill Donovan*, 69.
78. Jakub, *Spies and Saboteurs*, 22, 24–27, 29, 31, 33. Jakub notes that, in addition to Lend-Lease aid which was authorized in March 1941, U.S. assistance to Britain also came in the form of unvouchered funds transferred from COI to BSC, SIS, and SOE.
79. Dunlop, *Donovan*, 317. This figure comes from Donovan's appointment book; unrecorded meetings may push the figure even higher. Cf. Stephenson, *British Security Coordination*, 25–29.
80. Dunlop, *Donovan*, 317–18.
81. Mackenzie, *Secret History of SOE*, 329; Jakub, *Spies and Saboteurs*, 31. In addition to information and training, SOE also provided COI such services as operating its communications when the London station was first established. See Jakub, *Spies and Saboteurs*, 33.
82. Roosevelt, *War Report of the OSS*, 70. "The letters 'K' and 'L' were arbitrarily chosen; they have no significance" (85).
83. Donovan to Adjutant General, "Stephenson, William Samuel—Recommendation for Award of Distinguished Service Medal," 19 June 1944, J. Russell Forgan Papers, Box 1, Folder (unmarked envelope), Hoover Institution Archives on War, Revolution, and Peace, Stanford University; quoted in Jukab, *Spies and Saboteurs*, 39. Cf. Roosevelt, *War Report of the OSS*, 72; Stephenson, *British Security Coordination*, 28; Dunlop, *Donovan*, 327. Solborg's visit was among the more notable of a raft of American personnel sent to observe the British. Another significant trip came in September 1941 when William Whitney and Bob Sherwood visited SOE, SIS, and PWE with the "intent . . . to gain some idea of how the British were fighting the irregular war" (Donovan to FDR, 1 October 1940, Donovan Papers, Box 81B, vol. 34, U.S. Army Military Historical Archive, Carlisle, PA, quoted in Jakub, *Spies and Saboteurs*, 32).

84. Donovan to Franklin Roosevelt, 22 December 1941, quoted in Roosevelt, *War Report of the OSS*, 72.
85. Jakub, *Spies and Saboteurs*, 38.
86. Roosevelt, *War Report of the OSS*, 73; Dunlop, *Donovan*, 312. These branches were also known as SA/B and SA/G, respectively. The designations stand for "Special Activities" and reflect the initial leaders of each branch, David Kirkpatrick Este Bruce (SA/B) and M. Preston Goodfellow (SA/G).
87. Dunlop, *Donovan*, 350–54; Waller, *Wild Bill Donovan*, 115–16.
88. Mackenzie, *Secret History of SOE*, 389.
89. Roosevelt, *War Report of the OSS*, 84, 206–207.
90. Ellery Huntington, "SO Organization, Operations and Objectives, Based on London Trip, 9–27 September 194," Record Group 226, M 1642, Roll 111, National Archives (College Park, Md.), 24, quoted in Jakub, *Spies and Saboteurs*, 58.
91. "SOE and SO London (Operational Arrangements)," RG 226, M 1642, Roll 111, National Archives (College Park, Md.), quoted in Jakub, *Spies and Saboteurs*, 57. The agreements also generally divided the world into British and American spheres; although SOE and OSS would both operate in both areas, one or the other would take the lead. The British sphere included India, sub-Saharan Africa, western Europe, the Balkans, and the Middle East; the American sphere included China, Korea, Australia, Atlantic islands such as the Canaries, North Africa, and Finland. Cf. Stephenson, *British Security Coordination*, 29–30.
92. Roosevelt, *War Report*, 116; Ameringer, *U.S. Foreign Intelligence*, 159.
93. Cassidy, ed., *History of the Schools and Training Branch*, 37.
94. Forty, "History of the Training Section of S.O.E.," 75, TNA: PRO, HS 7/51; Stafford, *Camp X*, 31. The exchange was not entirely one-sided. While Britain shared its experience of clandestine warfare, the United States shared men, material, and contacts in countries, such as Vichy France, to which the United States had better access than Britain. See Mackenzie, *Secret History of SOE*, 390.
95. Rigden, *SOE Syllabus*, 11. There is also evidence that Americans were training in Britain around the time Camp X was established. In a memo to the president on 21 December, Donovan made reference to an American "who will be returning from England where I have had him at the guerrilla school" (Donovan, quoted in Dunlop, *Donovan*, 533). Americans were trained in Britain in larger numbers after the formal entry of the United States into the war. See Roosevelt, *War Report of the OSS*, 207. Gubbins recalled: "Immediately after Pearl Harbour, Donovan requested us to take some hundred of his Officers through our training courses, and they began streaming over [to Britain]. Other of them were given short courses at our training school near Toronto, a very popular event as by doing they qualified for a foreign service medal!" ("CG's Comments on Foot's Book," n.d., 3, Gubbins papers 3/2/57, IWM).
96. Stafford, *Camp X*, 12.

97. Col. Tommy Davies report on his U.S. visit, 15 October 1941, in the SOE Archives, quoted in Stafford, "Intrepid," 311.
98. Miller, *Behind the Lines*, 57, quoting a "secret assessment . . . written by a senior SOE officer after a visit to Washington in October 1942," in TNA: PRO, HS 7/283.
99. Stafford, *Camp X*, 90.
100. Ibid., 93. Part of Camp X's original purpose was also to give preliminary training to those SOE agents—generally French Canadians or recent immigrants from Europe—recruited in Canada, before attending finishing schools in Britain. This function tapered off both because the number of Canadian recruits dried up fairly quickly, the immigrant communities having been thoroughly canvassed, and because the American entry into the war accelerated the number of American students. See Rigden, *SOE Syllabus*, 11.
101. Stafford, *Camp X*, 92.
102. Stephenson, *British Security Coordination*, 423–24; Stafford, *Camp X*, 93–114.
103. Today Shangri-La is known by the name Pres. Dwight Eisenhower gave it: Camp David. Both Area B and Camp David are located within Catoctin Mountain Park.
104. Stafford, "Intrepid," 312–13.
105. Ibid., 314; Wheeler, "Resistance from Abroad," 108.
106. Stephenson, *British Security Coordination*, 424; Stafford, *Camp X*, xvi.
107. Roosevelt, *War Report of the OSS*, 81.
108. Wheeler, "Resistance from Abroad," 104.
109. O'Donnell, *Operatives, Spies and Saboteurs*, 4; cf. Cassidy, "Fairbairn in Shanghai," 71.
110. Stafford, *Camp X*, 10, 53; Rigden, *SOE Syllabus*, 13. Born in Paris on 23 September 1909, Brooker joined SOE's training section in March 1941. "Inside his large and powerful British frame," David Stafford writes, "was an American struggling to get out. . . . Lacking an Oxbridge education, and with a background in European commerce, he mixed uneasily with many of the City-bred executives and professional soldiers who staffed the upper reaches of the SOE" (Stafford, *Camp X*, 10–1). Perhaps reflecting a commonly held belief, Kim Philby writes, "As far as I am aware [Brooker] had never lived an underground life. But after a little research he could talk to trainees as if he had never lived otherwise" (*My Silent War*, 36). This is true in the sense that Brooker lacked a military background and had only brief experience in government secret service. However, he brought with him other kinds of useful experience. His father managed the Paris office of a travel agency and young Brooker learned French as his first language. In the 1930s he worked as a traveling export salesman for Nestlé; when the Spanish Civil War broke out he was in Barcelona and to him fell the task of getting the company's blocked currency to Switzerland. "We got [the Spanish pesetas] out through the Pyrenees, using couriers and

clandestine routes. . . . It took volumes of false papers and plenty of imagination" (quoted in Stafford, *Camp X*, 12). When World War II broke out he joined the Field Security Police and attended a course at the Intelligence Staff College at Matlock, "where his forthright and distinctly unmilitary attitudes to authority brought him into conflict with the commandant" (Stafford, *Camp X*, 12). This was followed by a stint at the rough Tyneside docks, where he learned about interrogating and searching suspects. Gubbins recognized in him a kindred spirit and recruited him into SOE.

111. Cassidy, *History of the Schools and Training Branch*, 73; Sweet-Escott, *Baker Street Irregular*, 143.
112. Cassidy, *History of the Schools and Training Branch*, 65.
113. "History of S&T" [draft], Record Group 226, Entry 146, Box 49, Folder 67, National Archives (College Park, Md.). This passage was adopted, with minor changes, for the S&T section of the *War Report of the OSS*. See Roosevelt, 232.
114. Roosevelt, *War Report of the OSS*, 81.
115. Cassidy, *History of the Schools and Training Branch*, 71. Cf. Forty, "History of the Training Section of S.O.E.," 75, TNA: PRO, HS 7/51. American instructors, as well as students, also studied at the SOE schools in Britain. See Jakub, *Spies and Saboteurs*, 58.
116. "Basic SI-SO Course of Instruction," Exhibit A, Cassidy, *History of the Schools and Training Branch*, 169–71; Rigden, *SOE Syllabus*, 31. The OSS Basic School covered nineteen topics, of which seventeen unambiguously corresponded to major topics of the SOE syllabus. Only one major section of the SOE syllabus—operations, including passive resistance and subversion of troops—was not covered by the OSS syllabus. The two topics in the OSS syllabus not directly paralleled in the SOE program were anonymous letter writing and map reading. Both SOE and OSS modified their training programs throughout the war; the SOE syllabus cited here is from February 1944, while the OSS syllabus is from March 1943. The comparison is imperfect but sufficient to demonstrate the substantial similarities.
117. See untitled notes, Record Group 226, Entry 146, Box 65, Folder 890, National Archives (College Park, Md.). The notes here unambiguously correspond to six British lectures: Rigden, *SOE Syllabus*, "Objects and Methods of Irregular Warfare" [A.1], 35–37, "Propaganda—Introductory" [C.1], 192–95, "Propaganda Presentation: Fundamental Principles" [C.3], 200–201, "Reproduction and Distribution—II" [C.6], 211–13, "Objects and Methods of Counter-Espionage" [A.6], 61–63, and "Appendix: Recruiting" [A.12.13.15], 96–97. There are no notes in this collection that do not correspond to a British lecture.
118. Stephenson, *British Security Coordination*, 425. Cf. Cassidy, *History of the Schools and Training Branch*, 71.
119. Roosevelt, *War Report of the OSS*, 231.
120. Archibald, *Blue Shirt and Khaki*, 125–26; Birtle *U.S. Army Counterinsurgency*; Johnston, "Investigation," 257–62; Linn, *Philippine War*;

Crane, "Paragraphs 93, 97 and 88," 254–56; Ameringer, *U.S. Foreign Intelligence*, 74–87; Stevens, *American Expansion*, 206–208, 214–24; U.S. Marine Corps, *Small Wars Manual*; Bickel, *Mars Learning*; Moon and Eifler, *Deadliest Colonel*, 2–14; Prince and Keller, *US Customs Service*, 213.
121. Jeffreys-Jones, "Role of British Intelligence," 9.
122. Ibid., 9; Wark, *Ultimate Enemy*, 240.
123. Memorandum No. 94, 22 December 1941, Donovan to Roosevelt, in Mattingly, *Herringbone Cloak*, appendix A, 236; *AGW*, 22 § 83; *PLH*, 4 § 6, 13 § 14. *The War Report of the OSS* comes to the same conclusion, using the phrase "small bands of local origin" when paraphrasing Donovan's proposal (Roosevelt, 80).
124. Memorandum No. 94, 22 December 1941, Donovan to Roosevelt, in Mattingly, *Herringbone Cloak* , 236.
125. Roosevelt, *War Report of the OSS*, 80; *AGW*, 22 § 83; *PLH*, 13 § 14. The remainder of Donovan's memo covered topics that, though not unique to Gubbins, also suggested his influence, particularly in light of Donovan's extensive contact with SOE. Among Donovan's themes were the vulnerability of communications, particularly to sabotage, and the importance of striking the enemy where he was weak.
126. Roosevelt, *War Report of the OSS*, 223.
127. "Outline of Training Programs at Areas 'A' and 'F' for Operational Groups," 1, Record Group 226, Entry 146, Box 264, National Archives (College Park, Md.), emphasis added.
128. Ibid., 1.
129. Roosevelt, *War Report of the OSS*, 81, 236–37.
130. History of S&T [draft], Record Group 226, Entry 146, Box 49, Folder 67, National Archives (College Park, Md.).
131. Wilkinson and Astley, *Gubbins and SOE*, 77, 113.
132. Dalton, *Second World War Diary*, 428 (10 May 1942).
133. Wilkinson and Astley, *Gubbins and SOE*, 113.
134. Dalton, *Second World War Diary*, 374–75 (21 February 1942); Wilkinson and Astley, *Gubbins and SOE*, 100. Pimlott suggests that Dalton was removed from his post largely because of his private campaign to acquire the PWE. See Pimlott, *Hugh Dalton*, 319. Dalton's diary, though certainly not explicit on this point, suggests the accusation may be true. On 4 February he alludes to his "M.P.E.W. [Ministry of Political and Economic Warfare] project," a plan to pull the PWE under his umbrella; as late as 19 February, two days before his reassignment, he recorded that he was still advocating for the idea.
135. Cadogan, *Diaries* , 437 (25 February 1942).
136. Wilkinson and Astley, *Gubbins and SOE*, 100.
137. Ibid., 112.
138. Gubbins to John Peart-Binns, n.d., c. April 1974, 1, Gubbins papers 3/2/76, IWM.
139. Dalton, *Second World War Diary*, 363 (6 February 1942).
140. Wilkinson and Astley, *Gubbins and SOE*, 120.

141. Foot, *SOE in France*, 16; Mackenzie, *Secret History of SOE*, 512; Stafford, *Britain and European Resistance*, 118; Wilkinson and Astley, *Gubbins and SOE*, 140–41.
142. Gladwyn, *Memoirs*, 101.
143. Mackenzie, *Secret History of SOE*, 512; Stafford, *Britain and European Resistance*, 118; Wilkinson and Astley, *Gubbins and SOE*, unpaginated introduction (i–ii).
144. Wheatley, *Deception Planners*, 134–35. Likewise, Wheatley observes that food and drink, paid for out of SOE's generous budget, were always in ample supply.
145. Wilkinson and Astley, *Gubbins and SOE*, 31, 241.
146. Foot, *SOE: An Outline History*, 60–62; Wilkinson and Astley, *Gubbins and SOE*, 96.
147. Gubbins to Donald Hamilton-Hill Esq., 13 December 1966, 1–2, Gubbins papers 3/2/58, IWM.
148. Ibid., 2.
149. Wilkinson and Astley, *Gubbins and SOE*, 96.

Chapter 7

1. Sacquety, *OSS in Burma*, 170.
2. "Special Operations, 1938–1945," part 2: Role of S.O., 3, TNA: PRO, HS 7/1.
3. "S.O.E. in Europe, 1938–1945," 12, 14d, TNA: PRO, HS 7/1.
4. Mackenzie, *Secret History of SOE*, 318–20, 519–20.
5. Ibid., 321.
6. Foot, *SOE: An Outline History*, 172.
7. Mackenzie, *Secret History of SOE*, 46; Anglim, *Orde Wingate and the British Army*, 107, 111.
8. Anglim, "Callwell versus Graziani," 602; Foot, *SOE: An Outline History*, 175–76, 185–89. Outside the Horn of Africa, G(R) also deployed Operational Centres in Vichy Lebanon.
9. Dodds-Parker, *Setting Europe Ablaze*, 72.
10. Foot, *SOE: An Outline History*, 190.
11. Charman, "Hugh Dalton, Poland and SOE," 64–65; Wilkinson and Astley, *Gubbins and SOE*, 81–82.
12. Foot, *SOE: An Outline History*, 191.
13. Gubbins, quoted in War Diary, "Survey of S.O.E. Activities, February 1941," 210–11, TNA: PRO, HS 7/213; Charman, "Hugh Dalton, Poland and SOE," 69; Mackenzie, *Secret History of SOE*, 313; Wilkinson and Astley, *Gubbins and SOE*, 81–82, 110.
14. Foot; *SOE: An Outline History*, 191; Wilkinson and Astley, *Gubbins and SOE*, 81–83.
15. Mackenzie, *Secret History of SOE*, 314, 516–18; Wilkinson and Astley, *Gubbins and SOE*, 88, 93, 97.
16. Foot, *SOE: An Outline History*, 191, 195; Mackenzie, *Secret History of SOE*, 524–25.
17. Howarth, *Undercover*, 40–41; Mackenzie, *Secret History of SOE*, 525.

18. Keegan, *Second World War*, 483–84.
19. Harrison, "British Special Operations Executive," 1071–91. Cf. Howarth, *Undercover*, 38; Mackenzie, *Secret History of SOE*, 521–22.
20. Gubbins, address to Anglo-Polish Society, 18 November 1972, 2, Gubbins papers 4/1/41, IWM.
21. Foot, *SOE: An Outline History*, 199.
22. Wilkinson and Astley, *Gubbins and SOE*, 83.
23. Foot, *SOE: An Outline History*, 201; Mackenzie, *Secret History of SOE*, 318–19; Wilkinson and Astley, *Gubbins and SOE*, 83.
24. Mackenzie, *Secret History of SOE*, 317–18.
25. Wilkinson and Astley, *Gubbins and SOE*, 107.
26. Foot, *SOE: An Outline History*, 200–201.
27. Mackenzie, *Secret History of SOE*, 320.
28. Foot, *SOE: An Outline History*, 201–202; Mackenzie, *Secret History of SOE*, 529–30.
29. Quoted in Foot, *SOE: An Outline History*, 174–75.
30. Mackenzie, *Secret History of SOE*, 537–38.
31. Ibid., 170.
32. *AGW*, 5 § 13.
33. Wilkinson and Astley, *Gubbins and SOE*, 168–69.
34. Foot, *SOE: An Outline History*, 229–30; Howarth, *Undercover*, 189; Mackenzie, *Secret History of SOE*, 542–45.
35. *AGW*, 18 § 66–67.
36. Foot, *SOE: An Outline History*, 230; Mackenzie, *Secret History of SOE*, 545–51, 557.
37. Howarth, *Undercover*, 191; Mackenzie, *Secret History of SOE*, 554–55.
38. Mackenzie, *Secret History of SOE*, 105–13.
39. Foot, *SOE: An Outline History*, 237; Wilkinson and Astley, *Gubbins and SOE*, 89.
40. War Diary, "Survey of S.O.E. Activities, October–December 1940," 14, TNA: PRO, HS 7/211.
41. Foot, *SOE: An Outline History*, 238; Mackenzie, *Secret History of SOE*, 117–18.
42. Gubbins to Sir Frank Nelson, 29 November 1941, quoted in Mackenzie, *Secret History of SOE*, 122. Cf. 119–22.
43. Mackenzie, *Secret History of SOE*, 122–23.
44. Ibid., 126–28, 423.
45. Ibid., 129–31, 423–25; Foot, *SOE: An Outline History*, 239.
46. Mackenzie, *Secret History of SOE*, 131–32, 423, 426–29, 433–37; Wilkinson and Astley, *Gubbins and SOE*, 133–36, 155–56, 162–63.
47. Mackenzie, *Secret History of SOE*, 431, 434. Among the British officers leading these missions was Fitzroy Maclean, whose memoirs, *Eastern Approaches* (London, 1949), gained wide readership. See also F. W. D. Deakin, *The Embattled Mountain* (London, 1971).
48. Mackenzie, *Secret History of SOE*, 439–40, 447.
49. "S.O.E. in Europe, 1938–1945," 18.ii, TNA: PRO, HS 7/1.
50. Mackenzie, *Secret History of SOE*, 44, 447.

51. Ibid., 140–41; Foot, *SOE: An Outline History*, 233–34.
52. Mackenzie, *Secret History of SOE*, 136.
53. Lord Selborne to Lord Glenconner, quoted in Mackenzie, *Secret History of SOE*, 157, from SOE Archives File (AD/S.1) HD/61.
54. No. 871, 18 March 1943 to the Minister of State as amended by No. 913, 20th March 1943, quoted in Mackenzie, *Secret History of SOE*, 462.
55. Foot, *SOE: An Outline History*, 234–35; Mackenzie, *Secret History of SOE*, 450–53. For a full account of the destruction of the Gorgopotamus bridge, see Denys Hamson, *We Fell among Greeks* (London, 1947). For the mission leaders' memoirs, see E. C. W. Myers, *Greek Entanglement* (London, 1955), and C. M. Woodhouse, *Apple of Discord* (London, 1948).
56. Foot, *SOE: An Outline History*, 235–36; Howarth, *Undercover*, 103–104.
57. Mackenzie, *Secret History of SOE*, 467, 482.
58. Ibid., 457–60, 469–72; Foot, *SOE: An Outline History*, 235–36.
59. Mackenzie, *Secret History of SOE*, 477–81; Wilkinson and Astley, *Gubbins and SOE*, 170–72.
60. Bailey, "SOE in Albania," 179–80; Mackenzie, *Secret History of SOE*, 488–90. See also the memoirs of Edmund Frank Davies, who oversaw much of this work: *Illyrian Venture* (London, 1952). For other accounts by SOE veterans of Albania, see Julian Amery, *Sons of the Eagle* (London, 1948); Peter Kemp, *No Colours or Crest* (London, 1958); and David Smiley, *Albanian Assignment* (London, 1984). Roderick Bailey persuasively argues that the decision to back the Communists was pragmatic, not ideological or driven by Soviet moles in SOE. See "SOE in Albania," 182–90.
61. Mackenzie, *Secret History of SOE*, 491–92. The Long Range Desert Group, formed in the summer of 1940 by Maj. Ralph Bagnold, conducted small, autonomous, long-range patrols in the Libyan desert for raiding and intelligence collection. See Hargreaves, *Special Operations*, 55–60.
62. Foot, *SOE: An Outline History*, 89; Wilkinson and Astley, *Gubbins and SOE*, 105. See also David Howarth, *The Shetland Bus* (London, 1951).
63. Mackenzie, *Secret History of SOE*, 192–95.
64. Ibid., 215–17, 648–49, 660; Cruickshank, *SOE in Scandinavia*, 3; Kraglund, "SOE and Milorg," 71–72.
65. Kraglund, "SOE and Milorg," 79–80; Mackenzie, *Secret History of SOE*, 201, 203, 649–53.
66. "Special Operations, 1938–1945," part 3: Special Operations in Europe, 11–12, TNA: PRO, HS 7/1; Cruickshank, *SOE in Scandinavia*, 198–202; Wilkinson and Astley, *Gubbins and SOE*, 106, 120. For a full account of the attack, see Knut Haukelid, *Skis against the Atom* (London, 1954).
67. Mackenzie, *Secret History of SOE*, 655–57, 671.
68. Ibid., 665.
69. Ibid., 665–67, 670.
70. "Brief History of S.O.E.," 18b, TNA: PRO, HS 7/1; Mackenzie, *Secret History of SOE*, 218–21.

71. Foot, *SOE: An Outline History*, 209; Mackenzie, *Secret History of SOE*, 679.
72. Foot, *SOE: An Outline History*, 209; Jespersen, "SOE and Denmark," 194–95, 199–200; Mackenzie, *Secret History of SOE*, 678–85.
73. Foot, "SOE in the Low Countries," 84; Mackenzie, *Secret History of SOE*, 295. See also Foot's longer treatment, *SOE in the Low Countries* (London, 2001).
74. Foot, "SOE in the Low Countries," 86; Wilkinson and Astley, *Gubbins and SOE*, 104.
75. Foot, "SOE in the Low Countries," 87; Mackenzie, *Secret History of SOE*, 628.
76. "S.O.E. in Europe, 1938–1945," 14a.iii.i, unpaginated postscript, TNA: PRO, HS 7/1; Foot, "SOE in the Low Countries," 88; Mackenzie, *Secret History of SOE*, 634–36. Resistance forces played a similar role in the preservation of facilities in Rotterdam.
77. Foot, "SOE in the Low Countries," 83–85.
78. Wilkinson and Astley, *Gubbins and SOE*, 84, 114. Even the Allies were willing to work with Vichy forces negotiating for their surrender in North Africa in 1942.
79. War Diary, "Survey of S.O.E. Activities, October—December 1940," 25, TNA: PRO, HS 7/211; Wilkinson and Astley, *Gubbins and SOE*, 84, 102.
80. War Diary, "Survey of S.O.E. Activities, March 1941," 365, 394, TNA: PRO, HS 7/214; "Survey of S.O.E. Activities, April 1941," part 2, 595, TNA: PRO, HS 7/215; "Survey of S.O.E. Activities, June 1941," 1101, TNA: PRO, HS 7/217; Foot, *SOE in France*, 152–59; Wilkinson and Astley, *Gubbins and SOE*, 84–85.
81. Foot, *SOE in France*, 161–62, 180–82; Wilkinson and Astley, *Gubbins and SOE*, 85, 102–103.
82. "S.O.E. in Europe, 1938–1945,"14a.ii, TNA: PRO, HS 7/1; "Special Operations, 1938–1945," part 3: Special Operations in Europe, 11–12, TNA: PRO, HS 7/1; Foot, *SOE in France*, 378–79.
83. "S.O.E. in Europe, 1938–1945," 14a.iv, TNA: PRO, HS 7/1.
84. Ibid., 18.iv; Foot, *SOE in France*, 362, 411.
85. Wilkinson and Astley, *Gubbins and SOE*, 121–22.
86. "S.O.E. in Europe, 1938–1945," 16, TNA: PRO, HS 7/1. In addition to SOE and OSS, SO(M) also coordinated the activities of SIS and MI9.
87. Gubbins to Foot, 31 January 1964, 1–2, Gubbins papers 3/2/57, IWM; Gubbins to Chief of SOE Security Section, 6 July 1942, quoted in the *War Diary of the Special Operations Branch of the Office of Strategic Services, London*, vol. 4, book 1, i, Record Group 226, National Archives (College Park, Md.), published in facsimile as Smith, *OSS Jedburgh Teams I*. David Stafford also attributes the concept of the JEDBURGHS to Gubbins. See *Secret Agent*, 212. Foot suggests that it owed something to GIDEON Force, commanded by Wingate in Abyssinia. See Foot, *SOE: An Outline History*, 190.
88. Mackenzie, *Secret History of SOE*, 603; *War Diary of the Special Operations Branch*, vol. 4, book 1, x–xii, published as Smith, *OSS Jedburgh Teams I*.

89. Roosevelt, *War Report of the OSS*, 210; "Personnel Rqmts SOE/ SO D-day Plan," 29 Sept. 1943, quoted in *War Diary of the Special Operations Branch*, vol. 4, book 1, xviii, published as Smith, *OSS Jedburgh Teams I*; Schoenbrun, *Soldiers of the Night*, 331. While seventy-five teams were designated for France, six teams each were also created for the Netherlands and Belgium, with personnel from those countries participating. As it turned out, events in Belgium moved too quickly to drop any teams there, though seven were dropped into the Netherlands. See Makenzie, *Secret History of SOE*, 604.
90. *AGW*, 1 § 4.
91. Brown, *Secret War Report of the OSS*, 389. Cf. Stafford, *Secret Agent*, 213. The JEDBURGH syllabus elaborates somewhat upon this description of the mission, explaining that JEDBURGHS "can fill any one of the following roles:—(a) Organise and lead raiding parties varying in size from 5 to 10 men up to a maximum of 100. (b) Organise the reception of stores and equipment for the personnel they recruit. (c) Organise acts of sabotage by small bodies of men working independently. (d) Secure and pass on information about enemy troop movements, location of vital points, etc. (e) Spreading of rumor, and fifth column work. (f) Preparing the civilian population for the arrival of Allied forces" (Forty, "History of the Training Section of S.O.E.," 196, TNA: PRO, HS 7/51).
92. *AGW*, 7 § 18.
93. Brown, *Secret War Report of the OSS*, 403.
94. État-Major des Forces Françaises de l'Intérieur or EMFFI. Mackenzie, *Secret History of SOE*, 605; Foot, *SOE in France*, 33.
95. "Preliminary Proposals for 'Jedburgh' Training," 21 July 1942, Record Group 225, Entry 146, Box 266, Folder 3656, National Archives (College Park, Md.). Cf. Forty, "History of the Training Section of S.O.E.," 59–60, 196, TNA: PRO, HS 7/51; *War Diary of the Special Operations Branch*, vol. 4, book 1, xxiii, published as Smith, *OSS Jedburgh Teams I*.
96. Forty, "History of the Training Section of S.O.E.," 59, TNA: PRO, HS 7/51; Mackenzie, *Secret History of SOE*, 604; *War Diary of the Special Operations Branch*, vol. 4, book 1, 1–3, published as Smith, *OSS Jedburgh Teams I*. Prior to the completion of this facility, JEDBURGH personnel began their training at regular SOE schools. Parachute training was conducted at STS 51, the SOE Parachute Training School at RAF Ringway, outside Manchester.
97. Brown, *Secret War Report of the OSS*, 403; Mackenzie, *Secret History of SOE*, 604; Foot, *Resistance*, 247. *The Secret War Report of the OSS* places the total figure at ninety-two.
98. Dunlop, *Donovan*, 438; Weale, *Secret War*, 75–76.
99. Dunlop, *Donovan*, 439.
100. Foot, *European Resistance*, 315. Foot argues that the French resistance was of far greater value in stopping German movements than were bombing raids. While air attacks destroyed all but one bridge across the Seine below Paris in May and early June 1944 and all but one across the Loire below Gien, German forces had learned from

their experience in Russia to always have field bridging equipment on hand. It was because of attacks by French partisans that the Germans were unable to use it to good effect.
101. Stafford places the number at a minimum of two thousand rail lines cut; SOE claimed upwards of three thousand confirmed cuts. See "S.O.E. in Europe, 1938–1945,"14c.i, TNA: PRO, HS 7/1; Stafford, *Britain and European Resistance*, 154–55.
102. "Numbers of Germans Tied Down by the Action of Resistance in Europe," 1–2, TNA: PRO, HS 7/1; "S.O.E. in Europe, 1938–1945," 14c.i-ii, TNA: PRO, HS 7/1; SHAEF, "The Value of SOE Operations in the Supreme Commander's Sphere," 13 July 1945, 1, Gubbins papers 3/2/36, IWM; Foot, *SOE in France*, 440–41.
103. Keegan, *Second World War*, 484.
104. "S.O.E. in Europe, 1938–1945,"14c.ii, TNA: PRO, HS 7/1; "Numbers of Germans Tied Down by the Action of Resistance in Europe," 1–2, TNA: PRO, HS 7/1. Although not quoting directly, the latter document cites Chiefs of Staff (45) 146.
105. A sample of JEDBURGH literature includes: Colin Beavan, *Operation Jedburgh* (New York, 2006); Roger Ford, *Steel from the Sky* (London, 2004); Will Irwin, *The Jedburghs* (New York, 2005); Tommy Macpherson, *Behind Enemy Lines* (Edinburgh, 2010); and John K. Singlaub, *Hazardous Duty* (New York, 1991). The debate about whether they were parachuted into France too late was well known in the decades after the war. Gubbins wrote to Foot in 1964, "I am in entire agreement with what most of the Jedburghs said, that they were dropped too late, or could anyway have been dropped more quickly early after D Day. Unfortunately these operations went out of my control, as you know, when [French general Marie-Pierre] Koenig took over Emffi about 1st July. . . . My pet project, the Jedburghs[,] had been absolutely wasted by not being pushed in at once. . . . I do not mind your criticism in the slightest except that I did my best to get them in long before they actually went" (Gubbins to Foot, 31 January 1964, 1–2, Gubbins papers 3/2/57, IWM).
106. Mackenzie, *Secret History of SOE*, 606.
107. SHAEF, "The Value of SOE Operations in the Supreme Commander's Sphere," 13 July 1945, 1–2, Gubbins papers 3/2/36, IWM. Similar assessments of resistance value were made for other campaigns in France. Gen. Sir Henry Maitland Wilson, who commanded the invasion of southern France, Operation DRAGOON, estimated that the German army operated at only 40 percent of its full fighting efficiency due to resistance attacks. See Foot, *SOE in France*, 442.
108. SHAEF, "The Value of SOE Operations in the Supreme Commander's Sphere," 13 July 1945, 1–2, Gubbins papers 3/2/36, IWM. Assassinations by Communist partisans in France resulted in horrific reprisals against civilians, reprisals that the Communists dismissed as "precipitating a revolutionary situation." In contrast, "many of SOE's sabotage coups were unnerving to German morale in a more sophisticated way, less prodigal of lives" (Foot, *SOE in France*, 439).

109. The economic damage caused by sabotage in the occupied countries—as distinct from the specific sabotage focused on military goals related to invasion and liberation—remains open to discussion. See Foot, *European Resistance*, 312–13; *SOE in France*, 434–35.
110. Dwight Eisenhower to Gubbins, 31 May 1945, Gubbins papers 3/2/36, IWM.
111. Cruickshank, *SOE in the Far East*, 83; Foot, *SOE: An Outline History*, 41–42.
112. Smith, "SOE in Afghanistan," 141–42.
113. Cruickshank, *SOE in the Far East*, 83.
114. Ibid., 16.
115. Ibid., 61–65; Foot, *SOE: An Outline History*, 242–43.
116. Cruickshank, *SOE in the Far East*, 77–79, 151–52.
117. Foot, *SOE: An Outline History*, 243–44.
118. Wilkinson and Astley, *Gubbins and SOE*, 186–89.
119. Cruickshank, *SOE in the Far East*, 96–98.
120. Ibid., 98–100.
121. "SOE in the Far East, 1941–1945," 2, TNA: PRO, HS 7/1; Slim, *Defeat into Victory*, 119. Guerrilla warfare came easily to the Karens, whose traditional methods of fighting involved "forays secretly organized and carefully executed against their enemies. . . . The warriors so timed their march as to reach the vicinity of the foe's village after dark, distributed their force around the unsuspecting inhabitants before dawn, and sallied forth with a great shout as soon as it was light" (Marshall, *Karen People of Burma*, 152, 156).
122. Astor, *Jungle War*, 231, 233.
123. Allen, *Burma*, 575.
124. "SOE in the Far East, 1941–1945," 5, TNA: PRO, HS 7/1; Allen, *Burma*, 576–77; Cruickshank, *SOE in the Far East*, 166; Hickey, *Unforgettable Army*, 150–51; Morrison, *Grandfather Longlegs*, 74–159. In 1945 the Burma National Army switched sides.
125. Wilkinson and Astley, *Gubbins and SOE*, 183–85.
126. Cruickshank, *SOE in the Far East*, 174.
127. Slim, *Defeat into Victory*, 485.
128. "SOE in the Far East, 1941–1945," 5, TNA: PRO, HS 7/1; Allen, *Burma*, 578–79; Lewin, *Slim*, 253; Morrison, *Grandfather Longlegs*, 193–201. Guerrillas were raised by SOE Special Groups, "patrols of twenty to twenty-five men . . . trained for offensive action" and supported by JEDBURGH teams (Cruickshank, *SOE in the Far East*, 20, 175n, 186).
129. Cruickshank, *SOE in the Far East*, 188.
130. Slim, *Defeat into Victory*, 485.
131. Lt. Col. J. R. Gardiner, "Consolidated Report and Maps on Burma Operations, 1941–1945," 23 December 1945, chapter 7, 5, TNA: PRO, HS 7/104; Cruickshank, *SOE in the Far East*, 189–90. Operation CHARACTER accounted for the bulk of casualties inflicted by SOE in Burma: 16,879 killed (65 percent), 995 wounded (65 percent), and 285 captured (6 percent). For similar figures from a slightly different period, see "SOE in the Far East, 1941–1945," 5, TNA: PRO, HS 7/1.

132. Gardiner, "Consolidated Report and Maps on Burma Operations," chapter 7, 4–5, TNA: PRO, HS 7/104; Cruickshank, *SOE in the Far East*, 190. Although SOE's primary mission was not intelligence, at its height it supplied 80 percent of the intelligence on Japanese-occupied Burma. In the Malaya invasion plans, an entire squadron was set aside for the sole purpose of hitting mobile targets reported by SOE.
133. Astor, *Jungle War*, 231–33; Slim, *Defeat into Victory*, 119.
134. Dunlop, *Behind Japanese Lines*, 34.
135. Astor, *Jungle War*, 231.
136. "SOE in the Far East, 1941–1945," 5, TNA: PRO, HS 7/1; Peers and Brelis, *Behind the Burma Road*, 60.
137. Cruickshank, *SOE in the Far East*, 164–65, 172–73; Slim, *Defeat into Victory*, 261.
138. Untitled history of OSS in the Far East, 5, 12, Record Group 226, Entry 146, Box 48, Folder 670, National Archives (College Park, Md.); Astor, *Jungle War*, 141–42. It was the guarantee of rescuing downed crews that led the Air Transport Command to agree to drop members of Detachment 101 and their equipment into the Kachin Hills.
139. Peers and Brelis, *Behind the Burma Road*, 184.
140. Ibid., 26, 138; Astor, *Jungle War*, 176.
141. Peers and Brelis, *Behind the Burma Road*, 63–64.
142. Untitled history of OSS in the Far East, 5, 12, 19–21, Record Group 226, Entry 146, Box 48, Folder 670, National Archives (College Park, Md.); Peers and Brelis, *Behind the Burma Road*, 141, 184.
143. Slim, *Defeat into Victory*, 548. The Chindits appear to be the primary object of criticism.
144. General Slim, "Account of Operations of Fourteenth Army 1944–1945," 29, TNA: PRO, CAB 106/48, quoted in Cruickshank, *SOE in the Far East*, 257.
145. Keegan, *Second World War*, 483–85.
146. Brown, introduction to *The Secret War Report of the OSS*, 7.
147. Chiefs of Staff (45) 665 (o), quoted in "Numbers of Germans Tied Down by the Action of Resistance in Europe," 1, TNA: PRO, HS 7/1.
148. SHAEF, "The Value of SOE Operations in the Supreme Commander's Sphere," 13 July 1945, 1, Gubbins papers 3/2/36, IWM.
149. "S.O.E. in Europe, 1938–1945,"14c.i, TNA: PRO, HS 7/1.
150. Parker, *Second World War*, 281–85. Cf. Dupuy and Dupuy, *Encyclopedia of Military History*, 1198.
151. "Personnel Employed by S.O.E.," table 2: British Officer and O.R. Personnel in Occupied Territories, TNA: PRO, HS 7/1. The entire force of SOE on that date consisted of 1,847 officers, 6,471 other ranks and 1,558 FANYs, a total of 9,876 men and women. See "Personnel Employed by S.O.E.," table 1: Home and Overseas Establishments, TNA: PRO, HS 7/1.
152. Stafford, *Britain and European Resistance*, 197.
153. Foot, *SOE in France*, 436, 505–17.

154. Table 1: "Comparison of Total R.A.F. Bomber Command Sorties from U.K. with Those Carried Out for S.O.E.," TNA: PRO, HS 7/1.
155. Foot, *European Resistance*, 313–14. Cf. SHAEF, "Development of Resistance in France," 4 July 1944, TNA: PRO, AIR 20/8945, quoted in Hargreaves, *Special Operations*, 250.
156. Keegan, *Second World War*, 483–84.
157. "Objects and Methods of Irregular Warfare" (A.1), Rigden, *SOE Syllabus*, 37.
158. *AGW*, 1 § 1, 1 § 4; Foot, *SOE in France*, 16; Mackenzie, *Secret History of SOE*, 512; Stafford, *Britain and European Resistance*, 118; Wilkinson and Astley, *Gubbins and SOE*, 140–41.
159. Foot, *SOE: An Outline History*, 197; Harrison, "British Special Operations Executive," 1079–88; Keegan, *Second World War*, 488.

Epilogue

1. Foot, *SOE in France*, ix, 524; Stafford, *Britain and European Resistance*, 202–203; Wilkinson and Astley, *Gubbins and SOE*, 231–37.
2. Wilkinson and Astley, *Gubbins and SOE*, 238.
3. Gubbins to Selborne, Friday 1 February 1946, 1–2, Papers of Roundell C. Palmer, 3rd Earl Selborne, MS Eng. Hist. c. 1002, fol. 48, Bodleian Library, Oxford University.
4. Wilkinson and Astley, *Gubbins and SOE*, 238.
5. Philip Rea to Selborne, 30 May 1946, Papers of 3rd Earl Selborne, MS Eng. Hist. c. 1002, fol. 48, Bodleian Library; Wilkinson and Astley, *Gubbins and SOE*, 238.
6. Wilkinson and Astley, *Gubbins and SOE*, 238–39, 241.
7. Gubbins papers 3/2, IWM.
8. Home Office to Lady Gubbins, 23 February 1951, Gubbins papers 3/4/9, IWM.
9. Wilkinson and Astley, *Gubbins and SOE*, 242–43.
10. Selborne to the Rt. Hon. J. J. Lawson, PC, MP, 17 October 1945, 1, Papers of 3rd Earl Selborne, MS Eng. Hist. c. 1002, fol. 10, Bodleian Library.

Bibliography

Archival Papers and Records

National Archives, College Park, Maryland
Private Papers of Major General Sir Colin M. Gubbins, KCMG, DSO, MC, Imperial War Museum, London, UK
Private Papers of Roundell C. Palmer, 3rd Earl Selborne, MS Eng. Hist. c. 1002, fol. 10, Bodleian Library, Oxford University
Public Record Office, The National Archives, Kew, UK

Newspapers

Independent
London Gazette
Times of London

Published Works by Colin Gubbins

The Art of Guerilla Warfare. Introduction by William Cassidy. San Francisco, 1981.
"Guerrilla." *Chamber's Encyclopedia*. London, 1968.
"SOE and the Co-Ordination of Regular and Irregular War." *The Fourth Dimension of Warfare*. Vol. I, *Intelligence, Subversion, Resistance*. Edited by Michael Elliott-Bateman, 83–110. Manchester, 1970.

Official Histories

Brown, Anthony Cave, ed. *The Secret War Report of the OSS*. New York, 1976.
Cassidy, William L., ed. *History of the Schools and Training Branch, Office of Strategic Services*. San Francisco, 1983.
Cruickshank, Charles. *SOE in the Far East*. Oxford, 1983.
———. *SOE in Scandinavia*. Oxford, 1986.
Government of India. *The Army in India and Its Evolution, Including an Account of the Establishment of the Royal Air Force in India*. Calcutta, 1924.
Mackenzie, W. J. M. *The Secret History of SOE: The Special Operations Executive, 1940–1945*. London, 2000.
Ministry of Information. *Combined Operations: The Official Story of the Commandos*. Forward by Lord Louis Mountbatten. New York, 1943.
Roosevelt, Kermit, ed. *War Report of the OSS*. New York, 1976.
Smith, Bradley F., ed. *OSS Jedburgh Teams I*. New York, 1989.
Stephenson, William Samuel, ed. *British Security Coordination:*

The Secret History of British Intelligence in the Americas, 1940–1945. New York, 1999.

Published Reports and Documents

de Fremery, Henri Johan Diederick. *A Dutch Spy in China: Reports on the First Phase of the Sino-Japanese War (1937–1939).* Edited by Ger Teitler and Kurt W. Radtke. Leiden, 1999.

Hart, Peter. *British Intelligence in Ireland, 1920–1921: The Final Reports.* Cork, 2002.

Johnston, W. T. "Investigation into the Methods Adopted by the Insurgents for Organizing and Maintaining a Guerrilla Force." War Department. *Annual Reports of the War Department for the Fiscal Year Ending June 30, 1900.* Vol. 7:257–62. Washington, D.C., 1900.

Scott, James Brown, ed. *The Hague Conventions and Declarations of 1899 and 1907.* New York, 1915.

Sheehan, William. *A Hard Local War: The British Army and the Guerrilla War in Cork, 1919–1921.* Stroud, UK, 2011.

———. *Hearts & Mines: The British 5th Division, Ireland, 1920–1922.* Cork, 2009.

War Department. *Annual Reports of the War Department for the Fiscal Year Ended June 30, 1899.* Washington, D.C., 1899.

Published Manuals and Statements of Doctrine

Callwell, C. E. *Small Wars: Their Principles and Practice.* 3rd ed. Introduction by Douglas Porch. Lincoln, Neb., 1996.

Fairbairn, W. E. *Scientific Self-Defence.* London, 1931.

Lawrence, T. E. "Guerrilla." *Encyclopædia Britannica.* London, 1929.

Mao Tse-tung. *On Guerrilla Warfare.* Translated by Samuel B. Griffith. New York, 1961.

Rigden, Denis, ed. *SOE Syllabus: Lessons in Ungentlemanly Warfare, World War II.* Kew, UK, 2004.

U.S. Marine Corps. *Small Wars Manual.* Washington, D.C., 1940.

Memoirs and Published Diaries

Astley, Joan Bright. *The Inner Circle: A View of War at the Top.* Durham, 2007.

Bickers, Robert. *Empire Made Me: An Englishman Adrift in Shanghai.* New York, 2003.

Booker, Edna Lee. *News Is My Job: A Correspondent in War-Torn China.* New York, 1941.

Cadogan, Alexander. *The Diaries of Sir Alexander Cadogan, O.M., 1938–1945.* Edited by David Dilks. New York, 1972.

Calvert, Michael. *Fighting Mad.* London, 1964.

Carlson, Evans Fordyce. *Twin Stars of China: A Behind-the-Scenes Story of China's Valiant Struggle for Existence by a U.S. Marine Who Lived & Moved with the People.* New York, 1940.

Carton de Wiart, Adrian. *Happy Odyssey*. London, 1950.
Dalton, Hugh Dalton, Baron. *The Fateful Years*. London, 1953.
———. *The Second World War Diary of Hugh Dalton, 1940–1945*. Edited by Ben Pimlott. London, 1986.
de Wet, Christiaan Rudolf. *Three Years' War*. New York, 1902.
Dodds-Parker, Douglas. *Setting Europe Ablaze*. London, 1983.
Foot, M. R. D. *Memories of an SOE Historian*. Barnsley, UK, 2009.
Gladwyn, Hubert Miles Gladwyn Jebb, Baron. *The Memoirs of Lord Gladwyn*. London, 1972.
Hiley, Alan R. I., and John A. Hassell. *The Mobile Boer: Being the Record of the Observations of Two Burgher Officers*. New York, 1902.
Ironside, Edmund Ironside, Baron. *Archangel, 1918–1919*. London, 1953.
Langelaan, George. *Knights of the Floating Silk*. London, 1959.
Lawrence, T. E. "The Evolution of a Revolt." *Army Quarterly* 1 (Winter 1920/21): 55–69.
———. *The Seven Pillars of Wisdom*. New York, 1962.
Lettow-Vorbeck, Paul von. *Mein Leben*. Biberach an der Riss, 1957.
———. *My Reminiscences of East Africa*. Introduction by Thomas P. Ofcansky. Nashville, 1990.
Lockhart, Robert Bruce. *The Diaries of Sir Robert Bruce Lockhart*. Vol II, *1939–1965*. Edited by Kenneth Young. London, 1980.
Marks, Leo. *Between Silk and Cyanide: A Codemaker's War, 1941–1945*. New York, 1998.
Marling, Percival Scrope. *Rifleman and Hussar*. London, 1931.
Moon, Thomas N., and Carl F. Eifler. *The Deadliest Colonel*. New York: 1975.
Nankivell, Joice M., and Sydney Loch. *Ireland in Travail*. London, 1922.
Peers, William R., and Dean Brelis. *Behind the Burma Road*. London, 1963.
Perham, Frank. *The Kimberley Flying Column: Being Reminiscences of Service in the South African War of 1899–1903*. New Zealand, n.d.
Philby, Kim. *My Silent War*. New York, 1968.
Pownall, Sir Henry. *Chief of Staff: The Diaries of Lieutenant-General Sir Henry Pownall*. 2 vols. Edited by Brian Bond. London, 1972.
Slim, William Joseph Slim, Viscount. *Defeat into Victory*. London, 1957.
Smuts, Jan. *Selections from the Smuts Papers*. Edited by W. K. Hancock and Jean van der Poel. Vol. I. Cambridge, 1966.
Snow, Edgar. *Red Star over China*. New York, 1938.
Soutar, Andrew. *With Ironside in North Russia*. London, 1940.
Strong, Kenneth. *Intelligence at the Top: The Recollections of an Intelligence Officer*. London, 1968.
Sweet-Escott, Bickham. *Baker Street Irregular*. London, 1965.
Wheatley, Dennis. *The Deception Planners: My Secret War*. London, 1980.
———. *Stranger than Fiction*. London, 1959.
Wilkinson, Peter. *Foreign Fields: The Story of an SOE Operative*. London, 1997.

Secondary Sources

Adams, Jack. *The Doomed Expedition: The Norwegian Campaign of 1940.* London, 1989.
Adams, R. J. Q. *British Foreign Policy in the Age of Appeasement, 1935–1939.* Stanford, 1993.
Albertson, Ralph. *Fighting without a War: An Account of Military Intervention in North Russia.* New York, 1920.
Allen, Louis. *Burma: The Longest War, 1941–1945.* New York, 1984.
Ameringer, Charles D. *U.S. Foreign Intelligence: The Secret Side of American History.* Lexington, Mass., 1990.
Andrew, Christopher M. "British-Polish Intelligence Collaboration during the Second World War in Historical Perspective." *Intelligence Co-operation between Poland and Great Britain during World War II.* Vol. 1, *The Report of the Anglo-Polish Historical Committee.* Edited by Tessa Stirling, Daria Nałęcz, and Tadeusz Dubicki, 54–59. London, 2005.
———. *Her Majesty's Secret Service: The Making of the British Intelligence Community.* London, 1985.
Anglim, Simon. "Callwell versus Graziani: How the British Army Applied 'Small Wars' Techniques in Major Operations in Africa and the Middle East, 1940–41." *Small Wars & Insurgencies* 19, no. 4 (December 2008): 588–608.
———. *Orde Wingate and the British Army, 1922–1944.* London, 2010.
Archibald, James F. J. *Blue Shirt and Khaki: A Comparison.* New York, 1901.
Arthur, George. *Life of Lord Kitchener.* 2 vols. London, 1920.
Aster, Sidney. *1939: The Making of the Second World War.* London, 1973.
Astor, Gerald. *The Jungle War: Mavericks, Marauders, and Madmen in the China-Burma-India Theater of World War II.* Hoboken, N.J., 2004.
Bailey, Roderick. "SOE in Albania: 'The Conspiracy Theory Reassessed.'" *Special Operations Executive.* Edited by Mark Seaman, 179–92. London, 2006.
Barnett, Correlli. *The Collapse of British Power.* London, 1972.
Baron, Nick. *The King of Karelia: Colonel P. J. Woods and the British Intervention in North Russia 1918–1919: A History and Memoir.* London, 2007.
Beckett, Ian F. W. *Modern Insurgencies and Counterinsurgencies: Guerillas and Their Opponents since 1750.* London, 2001.
Beevor, Antony. *The Battle for Spain: The Spanish Civil War, 1936–1939.* New York, 2006.
Bell, P. M. H. *A Certain Eventuality: Britain and the Fall of France.* Farnborough, UK, 1974.
Bennett, Gill. "Polish-British Intelligence Co-operation." *Intelligence Co-operation between Poland and Great Britain during World War II.* Vol. 1, *The Report of the Anglo-Polish Historical Committee.* Edited by Tessa Stirling, Daria Nałęcz and Tadeusz Dubicki, 159–68. London, 2005.

Bethell, Nicholas. *The War Hitler Won: The Fall of Poland, September 1939*. New York, 1972.
Bickel, Keith B. *Mars Learning: The Marine Corps' Development of Small Wars Doctrine, 1915–1940*. Boulder, Colo., 2001.
Bierman, John, and Colin Smith. *Fire in the Night: Wingate of Burma, Ethiopia and Zion*. New York, 1999.
Birtle, Andrew J. *U.S. Army Counterinsurgency and Contingency Operations Doctrine, 1860–1941*. Washington, D.C., 2009.
Blandford, Edmund L. *SS Intelligence: The Nazi Secret Service*. Edison, N.J., 2000.
Bond, Brian. *British Military Policy between the Two World Wars*. Oxford, 1980.
———. "Leslie Hore-Belisha at the War Office." *Politicians and Defence: Studies in the Formulation of British Defence Policy, 1845–1970*. Edited by Ian Beckett and John Gooch, 110–31. Manchester, 1981.
Bowden, Tom. *The Breakdown of Public Security: The Case of Ireland, 1916–1921, and Palestine, 1936–1939*. London, 1977.
Bowyer, Chaz. *RAF Operations, 1918–1938*. London, 1988.
Brown, Anthony Cave. *The Last Hero: Wild Bill Donovan*. New York, 1982.
Cakars, Janis. "Koos de la Rey in the Transvaal." *Great Raids in History: From Drake to Desert One*. Edited by Samuel A. Southworth, 127–45. New York, 1997.
Cassidy, William L. "Fairbairn in Shanghai: Profile of SWAT Pioneer." *Soldier of Fortune* 23 (September 1979): 66–71.
Charman, Terry. "Hugh Dalton, Poland and SOE, 1940–42." *Special Operations Executive: A New Instrument of War*. Edited by Mark Seaman, 61–70. London, 2006.
Cookridge, E. H. *Set Europe Ablaze*. New York, 1967.
Corum, James S. *The Luftwaffe: Creating the Operational Air War, 1918–1940*. Lawrence, 1997.
Costello, Francis. *The Irish Revolution and its Aftermath, 1916–1923*. Dublin, 2003.
Crane, Charles J. "Paragraphs 93, 97 and 88 of General Orders 100." *Journal of the Military Service Institution of the United States* 32 (March/April 1903): 254–56.
Crowe, J. H. V. *General Smuts' Campaign in East Africa*. Introduction by J. C. Smuts. London, 1918.
Cruickshank, Charles. *The Fourth Arm: Psychological Warfare, 1938–1945*. London, 1977.
de Jong, Louis. *The German Fifth Column in the Second World War*. Translated by C. M. Geyl. New York, 1973.
Dekel, Efraim. *Shai: Exploits of Haganah Intelligence*. New York, 1959.
D'Este, Carlo. *Warlord: A Life of Winston Churchill at War, 1874–1945*. New York, 2008.
Diez, Emeterio. "La censura radiofónica en la España nacional (1936–1939)." *Zer: Revista de Estudios de Comunicacion* 13, no. 24 (May 2008): 103–24.

Dong, Stella. *Shanghai: The Rise and Fall of a Decadent City*. New York, 2000.
Donovan, William and Edgar Mowrer. *Fifth Column Lessons for America*. Washington, D.C., n.d.
Dreyer, Edward L. *China at War, 1901–1949*. London, 1995.
Dunlop, Richard. *Behind Japanese Lines with the OSS in Burma*. Chicago, 1979.
———. *Donovan: American's Master Spy*. New York: 1982.
Dupuy, R. Ernest, and Trevor N. Dupuy. *The Encyclopedia of Military History from 3500 B.C. to the Present*. 2nd edition. New York, 1986.
Edwards, Roger. *Panzer: A Revolution in Warfare, 1939–1945*. London, 1998.
Engle, Eloise, and Lauri Paananen. *The Winter War: The Soviet Attack on Finland, 1939–1940*. Mechanicsburg, Penn., 1973.
Farwell, Byron. *The Great Anglo-Boer War*. New York, 1976.
———. *The Great War in Africa, 1914–1918*. New York, 1986.
Fisk, Robert. *In Time of War: Ireland, Ulster and the Price of Neutrality, 1939–45*. Dublin, 1983.
Fitzpatrick, David. *The Two Irelands, 1912–1939*. Oxford, 1998.
Fleming, Peter. *Operation Sea Lion: The Projected Invasion of England in 1940—An Account of the German Preparations and the British Countermeasures*. New York, 1957.
Foot, M. R. D. "The IRA and the Origins of SOE." *War and Society: Historical Essays in Honour and Memory of J. R. Western, 1928–1971*. Edited by M. R. D. Foot, 57–69. New York, 1973.
———. *Resistance: European Resistance to Nazism, 1940–1945*. New York, 1977.
———. *SOE: An Outline History of the Special Operations Executive, 1940–1946*. London, 1984.
———. *SOE in France: An Account of the Work of the British Special Operations Executive in France, 1940–1944*. London, 1966.
———. "SOE in the Low Countries." *Special Operations Executive*. Edited by Mark Seaman, 83–90. London, 2006.
———. "Was SOE Any Good?" *Journal of Contemporary History* 16, no. 1 (January 1981): 167–81.
Foot, M. R. D., and J. M. Langley. *MI9: The British Secret Service That Fostered Escape and Evasion, 1939–1945, and Its American Counterpart*. London, 1979.
Garliński, Józef. *Poland, SOE and the Allies*. Translated by Paul Stevenson. London, 1969.
Garnett, David. *The Secret History of PWE: The Political Warfare Executive, 1939–1945*. London, 2002.
Gibbs, Norman. "British Strategic Doctrine, 1918–1939." *The Theory and Practice of War*. Edited by Michael Howard, 185–212. London, 1965.
Gilbert, Martin. *Churchill: A Life*. New York, 1991.
Grew, E. S. *Field-Marshal Lord Kitchener: His Life and Work for the Empire*. Vol. 2. London, 1916.

Grob-Fitzgibbon, Benjamin. "Intelligence and Counter-Insurgency: Case Studies from Ireland, Malaya and the Empire." *RUSI Journal* 156, no. 1 (February/March 2011): 72–79.
Gwynn, Charles W. *Imperial Policing*. London, 1934.
Haarr, Geirr H. *The Battle for Norway: April–June 1940*. Annapolis, Md., 2010.
Hargreaves, Andrew L. *Special Operations in World War II: British and American Irregular Warfare*. Norman, Okla., 2013.
Harris, Stephen L. *Duffy's War: Fr. Francis Duffy, Wild Bill Donovan, and the Irish Fighting 69th in World War I*. Washington, 2006.
Harrison, E. D. R. "The British Special Operations Executive and Poland." *Historical Journal* 43, no. 4 (December 2000): 1071–91.
Hart, Peter. *The IRA and Its Enemies: Violence and Community in Cork, 1916–1923*. Oxford, 1998.
Hart-Davis, Duff. *Peter Fleming: A Biography*. London, 1974.
Harvey, Maurice. *Scandinavian Misadventure*. Tunbridge Wells, UK, 1990.
Heilbrunn, Otto. *Warfare in the Enemy's Rear*. New York, 1963.
Hickey, Michael. *The Unforgettable Army: Slim's XIVth Army in Burma*. Tunbridge Wells, UK, 1992.
Hinsley, F. H., E. E. Thomas, C. F. G. Ransom, and R. C. Knight. *British Intelligence in the Second World War: Its Influence on Strategy and Operations*. Vol. 1. London, 1979.
"Holland, Major-General John Charles Francis." *Who Was Who, 1951–1960*. London, 1961.
Horne, Edward P. *A Job Well Done, Being a History of the Palestine Police Force, 1920–1948*. Sussex, 2003.
Hopkirk, Peter. *Setting the East Ablaze: Lenin's Dream of an Empire in Asia*. Oxford, 1986.
Howarth, Patrick. *Undercover: The Men and Women of the Special Operations Executive*. London, 1980.
Howard, Michael. *The Continental Commitment: The Dilemma of British Defence Policy in the Era of the Two World Wars*. London, 1972.
Hoyt, Edwin P. *Guerilla: Colonel von Lettow-Vorbeck and Germany's East African Empire*. New York, 1981.
Hu Pu-yu. *A Brief History of the Sino-Japanese War, 1937–1945*. Taipei, Taiwan, 1974.
Hughes, Matthew. "Lawlessness Was the Law: British Armed Forces, the Legal System and the Repression of the Arab Revolt in Palestine, 1936–1939." *Britain, Palestine and Empire: The Mandate Years*. Edited by Rory Miller, 141–56. Farnham, UK, 2010.
Hyde, Montgomery. *The Quiet Canadian: The Secret Service Story of Sir William Stephenson*. London, 1962.
Jakub, Jay. *Spies and Saboteurs: Anglo-American Collaboration and Rivalry in Human Intelligence Collection and Special Operations, 1940–1945*. London, 1999.
Jeffery, Keith. *The Secret History of MI6*. New York, 2010.
Jeffreys-Jones, Rhondri. "The Role of British Intelligence in the Mythologies Underpinning the OSS and Early CIA."

American-British-Canadian Intelligence Relations. Edited by David Stafford and Rhodri Jeffreys-Jones, 5–19. London, 2000.
Jespersen, Knud J. V. "SOE and Denmark." *Special Operations Executive: A New Instrument of War.* Edited by Mark Seaman, 193–200. London, 2006.
Johnsen, Julia E., ed. *Chinese-Japanese War, 1937.* New York, 1938.
Judd, Denis, and Keith Surridge. *The Boer War.* New York, 2002.
Kahn, David. *Hitler's Spies: German Military Intelligence in World War II.* New York, 1978.
Keegan, John. *Intelligence in War: Knowledge of the Enemy from Napoleon to al-Qaeda.* New York, 2003.
———. *The Second World War.* London, 1989.
Kinvig, Clifford. *Churchill's Crusade: The British Invasion of Russia, 1918–1920.* London, 2006.
Kraglund, Ivar. "SOE and Milorg: 'Thieves on the Same Market.'" *Special Operations Executive: A New Instrument of War.* Edited by Mark Seaman, 71–82. London, 2006.
Kurowski, Franz. *The Brandenburger Commandos: Germany's Elite Warrior Spies in World War II.* Translated by David Johnston. Mechanicsburg, Pa., 2005.
Lampe, David *The Last Ditch.* New York, 1968.
Laqueur, Walter. *Guerrilla Warfare: A Historical and Critical Study.* London, 2006.
Lewin, Ronald. *Slim: The Standardbearer.* Hamden, Conn., 1976.
Liddell Hart, B. H. *T. E. Lawrence: In Arabia and After.* Westport, Conn., 1979.
Linderman, A. R. B. "Afrikaner Influence on the IRA and SOE." *Securing Africa: Local Crises and Foreign Interventions.* Edited by Toyin Falola and Charles Thomas, 33–63. New York, 2014.
Linn, Brian McAllister. *The Philippine War, 1899–1902.* Lawrence, Kans., 2000.
Lloyd, T. O. *The British Empire, 1588–1995.* 2nd ed. Oxford, 1996.
Macksey, Kenneth. *Commando: Hit-and-Run Combat in World War II.* Chelsea, Mich., 1990.
Maresch, Eugenia. "SOE and Polish Aspirations." *Intelligence Co-operation between Poland and Great Britain during World War II.* Vol. I, *The Report of the Anglo-Polish Historical Committee.* Edited by Tessa Stirling, Daria Nałęcz, and Tadeusz Dubicki, 198–215. London, 2005.
Marlow, Ann. *David Galula: His Life and Intellectual Context.* Carlisle, Pa., 2010.
Marshall, Harry Ignatius. *The Karen People of Burma: A Study in Anthropology and Ethnology.* Columbus, Ohio, 1922.
Mattingly, Robert E. *Herringbone Cloak—GI Dagger: Marines of the OSS.* Quantico, Va., 1979.
Middlemas, Keith. *Diplomacy of Illusion: The British Government and Germany, 1937–39.* London, 1972.

Miller, Rory. "'An Oriental Ireland': Thinking about Palestine in Terms of the Irish Question during the Mandatory Era." *Britain, Palestine and Empire*. Edited by Rory Miller, 157–76. Farnham, UK, 2010.

Miller, Russell. *Behind the Lines: The Oral History of Special Operations in World War II*. New York, 2002.

Mockaitis, Thomas R. *British Counterinsurgency, 1919–60*. New York, 1990.

Moreman, T. R. *The Army in India and the Development of Frontier Warfare, 1849–1947*. London, 1998.

———. "'Small Wars' and Imperial Policing: The British Army and the Theory and Practice of Colonial Warfare in the British Empire, 1919–1939." *Military Power: Land Warfare in Theory and Practice*. Edited by Brian Holden Reid, 105–31. London, 1997.

Morris, Eric. *Churchill's Private Armies*. London, 1986.

Morrison, Ian. *Grandfather Longlegs: The Life and Gallant Death of Major H. P. Seagrim, G.C., D.S.O., M.B.E.* London, 1947.

Occleshaw, Michael. *Dances in Deep Shadows: Britain's Clandestine War in Russia, 1917–20*. London, 2006.

O'Donnell, Patrick K. *Operatives, Spies and Saboteurs: The Unknown Story of the Men and Women of World War II's OSS*. New York, 2004.

O'Halpin, Eunan. "The Irish Experience of Insurgency and Counter-Insurgency since 1919." *An Art in Itself: The Theory and Conduct of Small Wars and Insurgencies*. Edited by Peter Dennis and Jeffrey Grey, 53–72. Canberra, 2006.

———. *Spying on Ireland: British Intelligence and Irish Neutrality during the Second World War*. Oxford, 2008.

Paddock, Alfred H. *U.S. Army Special Warfare: Its Origins*. Lawrence, Kans., 2002.

Pakenham, Thomas. *The Boer War*. New York, 1979.

Parker, R. A. C. *The Second World War*. Oxford, 1989.

Parritt, B. A. H. *The Intelligencers: The Story of British Military Intelligence up to 1914*. Ashford, UK, 1972.

Peattie, Mark R. "The Dragon's Seed: Origins of the War." *The Battle for China: Essays on the Military History of the Sino-Japanese War of 1937–1945*. Edited by Mark Peattie, Edward J. Drea, and Hans van de Ven, 48–80. Stanford, 2011.

Pepłoński, Andrzej, and Andrzej Suchcitz. "Organisation and Operations of the II Bureau of the Polish General Staff (PGS)." *Intelligence Co-operation between Poland and Great Britain during World War II*. Vol. I, *The Report of the Anglo-Polish Historical Committee*. Edited by Tessa Stirling, Daria Nałęcz, and Tadeusz Dubicki, 81–107. London, 2005.

Pepłoński, Andrzej, Andrzej Suchcitz, and Jacek Tebinka. "Intelligence Co-operation during the Second Half of the 1930s." *Intelligence Co-operation between Poland and Great Britain during World War II*. Vol. I, *The Report of the Anglo-Polish Historical Committee*. Edited by Tessa Stirling, Daria Nałęcz, and Tadeusz Dubicki, 169–80. London, 2005.

Pimlott, Ben. *Hugh Dalton*. London, 1985.
Popplewell, Richard J. *Intelligence and Imperial Defence: British Intelligence and the Defence of the Indian Empire, 1904–1924*. London, 1995.
Preston, Paul. *The Spanish Civil War: Reaction, Revolution, and Revenge*. New York, 2006.
Prince, Carl E., and Mollie Keller. *The U.S. Customs Service: A Bicentennial History*. Washington, D.C., 1989.
Rhodes, Benjamin. *The Anglo-American Winter War with Russia: 1918–1919: A Diplomatic and Military Tragicomedy*. Westport, Conn., 1988.
Robins, Peter. *The Legend of W. E. Fairbairn, Gentleman and Warrior: The Shanghai Years*. Harlow, UK, 2004.
Rose, R. S., and Gordon D. Scott. *Johnny: A Spy's Life*. University Park, Pa., 2010.
Roskill, Stephen. *Hankey: Man of Secrets*. New York, 1974.
Rowan, Richard Wilmer. *The Story of Secret Service*. New York, 1937.
Sacquety, Troy. *The OSS in Burma: Jungle War against the Japanese*. Lawrence, Kans., 2013.
Schoenbrun, David. *Soldiers of the Night: The Story of the French Resistance*. New York, 1980.
Seaman, Mark. "A New Instrument of War." *Special Operations Executive: A New Instrument of War*. Edited by Mark Seaman, 7–21. London, 2006.
Segev, Tom. *One Palestine, Complete: Jews and Arabs under the British Mandate*. Translated by Haim Watzman. London, 2000.
Silverlight, John. *The Victor's Dilemma: Allied Intervention in the Russian Civil War*. London, 1970.
Simson, H. J. *British Rule, and Rebellion*. Edinburgh, 1938.
Smith, Adrian. *Mountbatten: Apprentice War Lord*. London, 2010.
Smith, Bradley F. "SOE in Afghanistan during the Second World War." *Special Operations Executive: A New Instrument of War*. Edited by Mark Seaman, 137–47. London, 2006.
Spiers, Edward M. *The Victorian Soldier in Africa*. Manchester, 2004.
Stafford, David. *Britain and European Resistance, 1940–1945: A Survey of the Special Operations Executive, with Documents*. Toronto, 1980.
———. *Camp X: OSS, "Intrepid," and the Allies' North American Training Camp for Secret Agents, 1941–1945*. New York, 1986.
———. "Churchill and SOE." *Special Operations Executive: A New Instrument of War*. Edited by Mark Seaman, 47–60. London, 2006.
———. "'Intrepid': Myth and Reality." *Journal of Contemporary History* 22, no. 2 (April 1987): 303–17.
———. *Secret Agent: The True Story of the Covert War against Hitler*. New York, 2001.
Stevens, Sylvester K. *American Expansion in Hawaii, 1842–1898*. Harrisburg, Pa., 1945.
Stevenson, William. *A Man Called Intrepid: The Secret War*. New York, 1976.

Stuart, Duncan. "'Of Historical Interest Only': The Origins and Vicissitudes of the SOE Archives." *Special Operations Executive: A New Instrument of War.* Edited by Mark Seaman, 217–29. London, 2006.

Sweet-Escott, Bickham. "Nelson, Sir Frank." *Dictionary of National Biography.* Edited by H. C. G. Matthew and Brian Howard Harrison, 71. Vol. 40. Oxford, 2004.

Sykes, Christopher. *Orde Wingate: A Biography.* New York, 1959.

Taylor, A. J. P. *The Origins of the Second World War.* London, 1961.

Tegart, Charles. *Terrorism in India.* Calcutta, 1983.

Temperley, A. C. "Military Lessons of the Spanish War." *Foreign Affairs* 16, no. 1 (October 1937): 34–43.

Thomas, Hugh. *The Spanish Civil War.* New York, 2001.

Towle, Philip Anthony. *Pilots and Rebels: The Use of Aircraft in Unconventional Warfare, 1918–1988.* London, 1989.

Townshend, Charles. *Britain's Civil Wars: Counterinsurgency in the Twentieth Century.* London, 1986.

Trotter, William. *A Frozen Hell: The Russo-Finnish Winter War of 1939–1940.* Chapel Hill, 1991.

Waller, Douglas. *Wild Bill Donovan: The Spymaster Who Created the OSS and Modern American Espionage.* New York, 2011.

Wark, Wesley K. *The Ultimate Enemy: British Intelligence and Nazi Germany, 1933–1939.* Oxford, 1986.

Weale, Adrian. *Secret Warfare: Special Operations Forces from the Great Game to the SAS.* London, 1997.

West, W. J. *Truth Betrayed.* London, 1987.

Westwell, Ian. *Brandenburgers: The Third Reich's Special Forces.* Surrey, 2003.

Wheeler, Mark. "Resistance from Abroad: Anglo-Soviet Efforts to Coordinate Yugoslav Resistance, 1941–1942." *Special Operations Executive: A New Instrument of War.* Edited by Mark Seaman, 103–15. London, 2006.

White, Ralph. "Teaching the Free Man How to Praise: Michael Foot on SOE and Resistance in Europe." *War, Resistance and Intelligence: Essays in Honour of M. R. D. Foot.* Edited by K. G. Robertson, 105–18. Barnsley, UK, 1999.

Wilkinson, Peter, and Joan Bright Astley. *Gubbins and SOE.* London, 1997.

Wilson, Dick. *When Tigers Fight: The Story of the Sino-Japanese War, 1937–1945.* New York, 1982.

Wilson, Jeremy. *Lawrence of Arabia: The Authorized Biography of T. E. Lawrence.* New York, 1990.

Wilson, John S. *Scouting Round the World.* London, 1959.

Yang Kuisong. "Nationalist and Communist Guerrilla Warfare in North China." *The Battle for China: Essays on the Military History of the Sino-Japanese War of 1937–1945.* Edited by Mark Peattie, Edward J. Drea, and Hans van de Ven, 308–27. Stanford, 2011.

Yu Shen. "Juntong, SACO, and the Nationalist Guerrilla Effort." *China in the Anti-Japanese War, 1937–1945: Politics, Culture, and Society.* Edited by David P. Barrett and Larry N. Shyu, 135–54. New York, 2001.

Zarrow, Peter. *China in War and Revolution, 1895–1949.* London, 2005.

Ziegler, Philip. *Mountbatten.* New York, 1985.

Index

2nd SS Panzer Division (Germany), 168
Fourth Army, 13
4th Infantry Division, 40
5th Infantry Division, 23, 24; Guerrilla Warfare Class, 27, 29
5 Light Brigade, 40
8th Infantry Division, 82, 87
Eighth Route Army (China), 88, 171, 216n148
XII Corps, 113
Fourteenth Army, 172–73
17th Battery RFA, 26
24th (Guards) Infantry Brigade, 111
52nd (Lowland) Infantry Division, 109
69th Infantry Regiment (U.S.), 134

Abwehr, 97, 98, 99
Abyssinia, 48, 74, 82–83, 85, 86, 134, 150, 152
aerial bombing, 35, 36–37, 161, 165, 176; comparative value, 157, 241n100; fear of, 105
Afghan Wars. *See* Anglo-Afghan Wars
African soldiers ("askaris"). *See* "askaris"
agents provocateurs, 91
AGW. *See* The Art of Guerilla Warfare (Gubbins) (*AGW*)
air drops. *See* parachute drops
airpower, 34–37, 80, 86, 101, 115, 133
Air Transport Command, 244n138
Albania, 151, 160–61
alcohol, 125–26, 144
Allen, Louis, 172
Allenby, Edmund, 217n165
Allied Inter-Service Planning Staff. *See* Inter-Service Planning Staff

ambushes, 22, 29, 56, 78, 79–80, 173, 189n128; training, 27
Anglim, Simon, 4, 22, 37, 67, 83, 85, 212n98
Anglo-Afghan Wars, 18, 32, 34, 36
Anglo-Boer Wars. *See* First Anglo-Boer War; Second Anglo-Boer War
Anglo-Irish Treaty, 24
Anglo-Irish War. *See* Irish Revolution
Anglo-Norwegian Coordinating Committee, 161
Anglo-Russian Convention of 1907, 33
anticommunism, 16, 33, 94
Anzio, 156
Arab Bureau, 31
Arab Revolt (1916–18), 31, 61–67, 203n165, 203n171, 204n172
Arab Revolt in Palestine (1936–39), 31, 36, 47, 77–87, 128, 203n165
Archangel Expedition, 14–19, 34–35, 185n44, 186n56
The Art of Guerilla Warfare (Gubbins) (*AGW*), 5, 28, 37, 51–53, 62, 69, 218n170; ambushes in, 29; flying columns in, 21; Irish influence on, 30; leadership in, 71; Mackenzie view, 197n55; on "moral factor," 20; omissions, 101; physical description, 181n9; in SOE training syllabus, 130, 131–32, 133; training in, 84
"askaris," 69–70
assassination: Arab Revolt in Palestine, 78, 80, 81, 210n68; of Henry Wilson, 25; Spanish Civil War, 75; World War II, 97, 154–55, 242n108

259

260 INDEX

Astley, Joan Bright, 4, 23, 47, 49, 112, 197n58; on Grand and Holland, 198n75; on Gubbins, 9, 24, 120–21, 148; on Jebb, 120; on Jefferis, 46
Attlee, Clement, 117
Auchinleck, Claude, 111
Australia, 96, 171
Austria, 96, 97, 99–100
Auxiliary Units, 102, 103, 111–14, 121, 122

Baden-Powell, Robert, 128
Badoglio, Pietro, 156
Bagnold, Ralph A., 10
Baker, Kenneth, 138
Balkans, 44, 51, 107, 115, 140, 150, 157. *See also* Greece; Romania; Turkey; Yugoslavia
Baltic States, 51, 99, 104
Battle of Blood River Poort (1901), 56–57
Battle of Dabburiya (1938), 83
Battle of Elands River (1901), 58
Battle of Jassini (1915), 68
Battle of the Somme (1918), 13
bayonets and bayonet fighting, 95, 128–29
BBC. *See* British Broadcasting Corporation (BBC)
BEARSKIN. *See* Operation BEARSKIN
Beaumont-Nesbitt, Frederick George, 48, 116, 118
Belgium, 70, 163, 179
Beneš, Edvard, 154
Bingham, Phyllis, 148
Birdwood, Ian, 34
Blamey, Thomas, 171
blockading of roads, 79
Blood River Poort, Battle of. *See* Battle of Blood River Poort (1901)
Bloody Sunday (1920), 29–30
Bodø, Norway, 110, 111
Boer Wars. *See* First Anglo-Boer War; Second Anglo-Boer War

Bolshevik Revolution, 14–19, 31, 32, 185n43
bombing, 84, 86, 92, 216n150. *See also* aerial bombing
Bond, Brian, 41
boots, rubber-soled. *See* footwear, rubber-soled
Botha, Louis, 56, 68
Bourne, A. G. B., 116
Bowden, Tom, 78
Bowyer, Chaz, 33
Boy Scout Training Centre, 128
Brandenburg Regiment, 98
Bright, Joan. *See* Astley, Joan Bright
British air force. *See* Royal Air Force (RAF)
British Army, 40, 83, 109, 113, 166, 178; 5th Infantry, 23, 24, 27, 29; interwar period, 41–42; World War I, 61. *See also* British Expeditionary Force (World War II); Scots Guards
British Broadcasting Corporation (BBC), 44, 168
British Commandos. *See* Commandos
British Dominions. *See* Dominions
British Expeditionary Force (World War II), 105, 106, 116
British expedition to Archangel, Russia. *See* Archangel Expedition
British expedition to China (proposed), 95–96
British Foreign Office. *See* Foreign Office (UK)
British navy. *See* Royal Navy
British Security Coordination (BSC), 136
British War Office. *See* War Office (UK)
Brook, Robin, 6
Brooke, Alan, 40
Brooker, Richard M., 139–40, 141, 234n110
Brown, Anthony Cave, 175, 231n61

Bulgaria, 157
Burgess, Guy, 125, 228n1
Burma, 150–51, 170, 171–75
Burma Rifles, 171
Burnett-Stuart, John, 42

Cadogan, Alexander, 48, 115–17, 145
Callwell, Charles E., *Small Wars*, 18–22, 38
Calvert, Mike, 113
camp followers, 28, 189n133
Camp X (Canada), 124, 138–41, 234n100
Canada, 140, 234n100
Carlson, Evans Fordyce, 217n160
Carton de Wiart, Adrian, 12, 13–14, 103, 104, 105, 106, 220n5
Casablanca Conference, 155
Cassidy, William, 24, 130
casualties, World War II. *See under* World War II
cavalry, 22, 24, 56, 96, 134
Caxton Hall, 50, 122, 125
Chamberlain, Neville, 46, 48, 117, 226n121
Chaplin, Georgi, 15
Chapman-Walker, John, 171
CHARACTER. *See* Operation CHARACTER
Chiang Kai-shek, 88–89, 93, 170–71, 217n165
children. *See under* civilians
China, 46, 47, 72, 87–96, 118, 170–71; Eighth Route Army, 88, 171, 216n148; Lettow-Vorbeck in, 68; Red Army, 214n125, 217n164. *See also* First Sino-Japanese War; Second Sino-Japanese War; Shanghai
Chinese Civil War, 31, 35
Churchill, Winston, 98, 115, 116, 117, 118, 121, 146, 181n11; Norway, 161
cinemas, attacks on (and in), 63, 80
civilians, 29; Arab Revolt in Palestine, 81, 82, 84; Boer Wars, 57–58, 60, 61; bombing by, 92; Britain, 50, 112, 114, 117; children, 28, 59, 60, 92; concentration camp internment, 59; Gubbins's views, 28, 29, 50, 55, 63, 66–67, 90, 132, 147; as information source, 28, 42–43, 59–60, 63, 81; Ireland, 28; Lithuania, 99; Mao view, 94; Netherlands, 98, 99; Norway, 110; reprisals against, 101, 114, 242n108; Second Sino-Japanese War, 90, 91, 92; Spanish Civil War, 74, 75, 76; whispering campaigns, 34; women, 59, 60, 82, 85, 92, 189n133, 202n146
civil wars. *See* Chinese Civil War; Greek Civil War; Irish Civil War; Russian Civil War; Spanish Civil War
Clarke, Dudley, 10
codes and code-breaking, 33–34, 40, 132
collaboration with the enemy, 57, 58, 162–63
Collins, Michael, 26
Combined Operations, 116, 161, 162, 172
Commandos (UK), 10, 116, 125, 129, 130, 137, 158
commandos, 86; Boer, 54, 55, 58, 60; German, 98
Committee of Imperial Defence, 43
concentration camps, civilian internment, 59
Coon, Carleton, 136
Coordinator of Information (COI) (U.S.), 133–34, 136–38, 144
Corps of Royal Engineers. *See* Royal Engineers
coups and coup attempts, 84; Archangel, Russia, 15, 183n19; Italy, 156; Spain, 73
Crockett, Norman, 106
Croft, Andrew, 222n54
Cruickshank, Charles, 172, 194n23
cryptography. *See* codes and code-breaking

Cuban War of Independence, 118
Cutsem, W. E. van, 47, 48
Czechoslovakia, 40, 44, 45, 48, 66, 85, 151; Donovan in, 134–35; Gubbins award, 179; World War I, 14; World War II, 96, 97, 103, 107–108, 133, 153, 154–55. *See also* Sudetenland

Dabburiya, Battle of. *See* Battle of Dabburiya (1938)
Dalton, Hugh, 5, 77, 97, 115–16, 117–20, 123, 135, 145–47, 176; Gubbins's view, 225n98; PWE aspirations of, 236n134
Davies, Tommy, 104
deception, 56–57, 68, 72, 98, 147, 152, 201n132. *See also* disguise
Defence Requirements Committee, 42
De Fremery, Henri, 90, 92, 93, 214n131
DeGaulle, Charles, 164–65
De Jong, Louis, 99–100
De la Rey, Koos, 56, 57–58
demolition, 46, 86, 92, 109–10, 163; Burma, 174; Greece, 159, 160; maritime, 171; prevention, 167; training, 218n174. *See also* sabotage
Denmark, 98, 99, 108, 151, 162–63, 175; Gubbins's award, 179
Department of Propaganda in Enemy Countries. *See* Electra House (EH)
deportation, 86, 99
deserters and desertion, 17, 57, 185n48
destruction. *See* demolition
Deuxième Bureau, 107
De Valera, Éamon, 98
De Wet, Christiaan, 56, 57
Dewing, R. H., 48
disguise, 59, 60, 97, 98, 99, 126, 131
D/M Section, 48
Dollfuss, Engelbert, 97
Dominions, 42, 96

Donovan, William, 124, 133–38, 143, 231n64, 231n71, 232n77, 233n95, 236n125; *Fifth Column Lessons for America*, 99, 135; SIS view, 175
DRAGOON. *See* Operation DRAGOON
Dreyer, Edward, 214n132
Dublin, 23, 24, 25
Dunkirk, 105, 116
Dunlop, Richard, 173, 231n64
Dyer's Battalion, 185n48

EAM. *See* National Liberation Front (EAM) (Greece)
East Africa campaign (World War I), 39, 47, 67–71
East Africa campaign (World War II), 152
Eisenhower, Dwight, 156, 169, 234n103
Economic Warfare. *See* Ministry of Economic Warfare (MEW)
Elands River, Battle of. *See* Battle of Elands River (1901)
Electra House (EH), 43, 47, 116, 118, 119, 194n23
Englandspiel, Das. See Operation NORDPOL
escape and evasion service. *See* MI9
espionage. *See* spies and spying
esprit de corps. *See* morale
Ethiopia, 106
Ethiopian Empire. *See* Abyssinia
Ethnikón Apeleftherotikón Métopon. *See* National Liberation Front (EAM) (Greece)
execution and executions, 58, 75, 76, 172, 189n130. *See also* assassination

Fairbairn, William E., 10, 128–30, 141, 229n29, 229n32, 230n37. *See also* Sykes-Fairburn fighting knife
FANY. *See* First Aid Nursing Yeomanry (FANY)

Farwell, Byron, 55, 60, 202n146
Federal Bureau of Investigation (FBI), 137, 140
Fenian Brotherhood, 231n62
Field Service Regulations (FSR), 22, 192n180
"fifth column" (term), 74
Fifth Column Lessons for America (Donovan and Mowrer), 99, 135
film theater attacks. *See* cinemas, attacks on (and in)
Finland, 14, 106, 199n92, 233n91
firing squads. *See* execution and executions
First Aid Nursing Yeomanry (FANY), 147–48
First Anglo-Boer War, 18
First Sino-Japanese War, 88
First World War. *See* World War I
Fitzpatrick, David, 23
Fleming, Peter, 49, 95–96, 109, 113, 114, 155, 159
flying columns, 21, 23, 30, 64, 190n151
Foot, M. R. D., 4, 8, 9, 46, 49, 53, 116, 186n69; *SOE in France*, 4, 181n4; view of French resistance, 241n100
footwear, rubber-soled, 74, 83, 114, 212n97
Foreign Office (UK), 6, 43, 116, 117, 119, 135, 146; China policy, 96; Greece policy, 159; Jebb in, 115–16. *See also* Secret Intelligence Service (SIS or MI6)
France, 96, 97, 98, 121, 123, 151; German invasion, 114–15; Gubbins's awards, 179; Gubbins in, 106–107; Spanish Civil War, 92; World War I, 13, 134; World War II, 164–69, 175, 176, 218n170, 241n100. *See also* Dunkirk; Normandy; Paris
Franco, Francisco, 75
freedom of movement, restrictions on, 55, 65, 132

Freemasonry, 191n164
Frythe (residential hotel), 105–106, 125
Fuller, J. F. C., 75, 76

Gano, Stanislav, 51, 107, 199n92
Gardiner, John, 172
Garliński, Józef, 5
General Headquarters Auxiliary Units. *See* Auxiliary Units
General Staff (Research) (GS[R]), 4, 7, 10, 39, 45–50, 53–54, 68; on Arab Revolt, 77; China and, 89; Holland in, 30, 46–47, 48, 72; Jeffreys-Jones's view, 143; spirit of irregularity, 122
Geneva Convention of 1864, 202n146
"gentlemanly" behavior, 70, 206n234
German South-West Africa, 68
Germany, 12; East Africa campaign (World War I), 39, 47, 67–71; in Greece, 160; interwar years, 40, 41, 43, 44, 47, 48, 72, 73, 78, 134–35; interwar years (subversive forces), 96–100, 118, 219n185; invasion and occupation of Denmark, 98, 108, 174; invasion and occupation of France and Low Countries, 98, 114–15, 165, 167, 168; invasion of Britain (contingency), 102, 111–14; invasion of Norway, 98, 108, 109–11, 162; invasion of Poland, 103–104, 105; Irish Revolution and, 92; Italy occupation, 156; nuclear weapon project, 162; in Yugoslavia, 158
Gideon Force, 152
Gladwyn, Lord. *See* Jebb, Gladwyn
gold, 55
Goodfellow, Preston, 137
Gort, John Vereker, Viscount, 48
Gough, Hubert, 56–57

264 INDEX

governments-in-exile, 147, 151; Czechoslovakia, 107, 147, 151, 154; France, 150; Netherlands, 147, 164; Poland, 102, 107, 147, 151, 153, 199n92; Yugoslavia, 157, 158
G(R), 152
Grand, Douglas, 43, 44, 47–50, 93, 106, 107, 118, 119–20; Astley on, 198n75
Great Game, 33, 170, 193n179
Greece, 18, 151, 152, 155, 157, 159–60
Greek Civil War, 160
Grey, Robin, 35
Griffith, Samuel, 93
Grob-Fitzgibbon, Benjamin, 182n20
GSI(k), 170
GS(R). *See* General Staff (Research) (GS[R])
Gubbins, Colin, 3–14, 37–38, 143–44, 175, 176–77; on Americans training in Britain, 233n95; anticommunism, 16, 33, 94; Arab Revolt in Palestine, 78, 79, 80, 81, 84–86, 87; Auxiliary Units, 102, 103, 111–14, 122; Boer Wars, 54–61; childhood and family of origin, 8; China, 72; citizenship, 179; Czechoslovakia, 154–55; denial of document destruction, 7; Donovan relations, 135; foreign language study and ability, 12, 31–32, 33, 34, 184n29; on German subversive forces, 96, 100; GS(R), 39, 46–47, 49–51; Independent Companies, 102, 103, 108–11, 122; India, 31–34; Ireland, 23–31; on Joan Bright, 197n58; Lawrence and, 61, 62–67; as lecturer, 199n87; Lettow-Vorbeck and, 67–71; Mao and, 93–95; as Mason, 191n164; medals and honors, 178–79; Morris's view, 223n55; Norway, 102, 108–11, 122; No.

4 Military Mission, 103–108; Poland, 102, 103–108, 153, 154; postwar and death, 178–79; Russia, 14–17, 30; Scots Guards reputation, 223n61; *Small Wars* (Callwell) and, 19–23, 38; SOE creation and, 102–103, 118, 120–23; SOE directorship, 145–49; Spanish Civil War, 74, 76–77; view of Dalton, 225n98; view of over-organization, 94, 138, 204n192; view of people's will, 156, 186n68, 218n170; in War Office, 39–40; World War I, 12–14; Yugoslavia, 157. *See also The Art of Guerilla Warfare* (Gubbins) (*AGW*); *The Partisan Leader's Handbook* (Gubbins) (*PLH*)
Gubbins, John (father), 8, 179
Gubbins, Martin (grandfather), 8
Gubbins, Michael (son), 156
Gubbins, Norah (first wife), 147
"Guerrilla Warfare" (Lawrence). *See* "The Science of Guerrilla Warfare" (Lawrence)
Guerrilla Warfare (Mao). *See On Guerrilla Warfare* (Mao)
GUNNERSIDE. *See* Operation GUNNERSIDE

Haganah, 83
Hague Convention, 131, 202n146
Halifax, Edward Wood, Earl of, 48, 97, 117, 118
Hambro, Charles, 123, 138, 145, 146
Hamilton-Hill, Donald, 148
Hanbury-Williams, John, 146
hand-to-hand fighting, 128–29, 140
Hankey, Maurice, 225n103
Hargreaves, Andrew, 3, 19
Harrison, E. D. R., 153
Hart, Peter, 24, 30, 189n135
Hayden, J. R., 138
Henlein, Konrad, 97
Heydrich, Reinhard, 154–55

INDEX   265

Hillyard, Reginald, 33
Hippel, Theodor von, 98
Hitler, Adolf, 219n185
Holland, J. C. F., 31, 46–53, 72, 143; on Arab Revolt in Palestine, 79; Astley on, 198n75; China, 89; Ireland, 30, 31, 196n47; reading of Lettow-Vorbeck, 67–68; Second Anglo-Boer War, 54, 55; Spanish Civil War, 72, 74, 76, 83; World War II, 103, 106, 108, 109, 116, 118, 120
Home Forces, 112, 113
Home Office, 179
Hopkirk, Peter, 33
hostages, 86
How to Use High Explosives, 52, 130
Hudson, D. T., 157
hunger strikes, 24
Hu Pu-yu, 214n128, 215n137
HUSKY. *See* Operation HUSKY
Husseini, Amin al-, Grand Mufti of Palestine, 78, 79

identity cards, 55
ideology, 94, 187n87. *See also* anticommunism
Imperial General Staff, 40, 45–46, 48, 50, 54, 103, 104, 108
Independent Companies, 102, 103, 108–11, 114, 122, 125, 128, 162, 222n54, 223n55
India, 12, 31–34, 40, 96, 128, 170, 179. *See also* North-West Frontier, India
Indian Army, 110, 113
industrial sabotage, 127, 144, 160, 153, 165, 176
informers and informants, 27, 28, 42–43, 59–60, 63, 69–70, 81
insurance companies, 127, 133
Inter-Service Planning Staff, 166
Inter-Service Security Board, 201n132
Inter-Services Projects Board, 112
Iraq, 36, 42, 47, 87

Ireland, in World War II, 98, 118
Irish Civil War, 26, 181n6
Irish Republican Army (IRA), 10, 24, 25, 28, 29, 31, 49, 76, 92
Irish Republican Brotherhood, 231n62
Irish Revolution, 21, 23–31, 46, 47, 55, 57, 66, 78; Arab Revolt in Palestine compared, 79, 86; East African parallels, 70; executions, 189n130; punishment of collaborators, 58; RAF role, 35; South African parallels, 79; Spanish parallels, 76; women, 92, 211n85. *See also Record of the Rebellion in Ireland*
Ironside, Edmund, 15–16, 17, 18, 35, 41, 112, 224n71; memoirs, 183n19, 184n43, 185n51; Wingate meeting, 213n111
Italian Socialist Republic, 156
Italy: in Africa, 48, 152, 155; fascist era (pre–World War II), 72, 73, 78, 106, 115, 134; Military Intelligence Service, 156; World War II, 133, 140, 152, 155–56, 157, 158, 160

Jackson, Margaret, 121
Jackson, Robert, 136
Jaffa, 79, 86, 209n34, 213n115
Jakub, Jay, 136
Japan, 134; British relations, 128–29; Special Service Section, 91; World War II, 170, 171–75. *See also* First Sino-Japanese War; Second Sino-Japanese War
Jassini, Battle of. *See* Battle of Jassini (1915)
JAYWICK. *See* Operation JAYWICK
Jebb, Gladwyn, 115–16, 119, 120, 145, 146, 228n1
JEDBURGH teams, 141, 166–67, 168–69, 241n91, 241n96, 242n105
Jefferis, Millis, 46, 52, 109–10, 197n53

Jeffreys-Jones, Rhodri, 143
Jewish-Arab relations, 77, 80, 209n34
Jewish Supernumerary Police, 83

Kachin people, 171, 173–74
Karen people, 171–73, 243n121
Keegan, John, 8, 118, 175, 176, 182n20
Keyes, Roger, 116
Khartoum, 152
Kildare, Ireland, 23, 25
Killery, Valentine, 170
King Peter II of Yugoslavia. See Peter II of Yugoslavia
Kitchener, Horatio Herbert Kitchener, Earl, 55
Knox, Frank, 135, 136
Koenig, Marie-Pierre, 242n105
Korea, 88, 128, 233n91

Lampe, David, 112, 114, 224n71
Latin America, 136, 140
Lawrence, T. E., 22, 39, 47, 61–67, 82, 199n87, 203n166, 217n165
Leeper, Rex, 119
Lenin, Vladimir, 33
Lettow-Vorbeck, Paul von, 47, 67–71, 98, 206nn222–23
Libya, 48
Liddell, Guy, 31
Liddell-Hart, B. H., 42, 203n166, 203n172
Lillehammer, Norway, 109–10
Lindsay, Martin, 96
Lithuania, 99
local populations. See civilians
locomotives, attacks on, 160, 165–66
logistics, 58, 69
Long Range Desert Group, 10
looting, 23, 58, 59
Lord Halifax. See Halifax, Edward Wood, Earl of
Lord Kitchener. See Kitchener, Horatio Herbert Kitchener, Earl
Lord Lothian. See Lothian, Philip Henry Kerr, Marquis of

Lord Rawlinson. See Rawlinson, Henry Seymour Rawlinson, Baron
Lord Roberts. See Roberts, Frederick Sleigh Roberts, Earl
Lord Selborne. See Selborne, Roundell Cecil Palmer, Earl of
Lothian, Philip Henry Kerr, Marquis of, 135
Low Countries, 115, 133, 151, 163–64; German invasion, 98, 114. See also Belgium; Netherlands

MacArthur, Douglas, 171
Mackenzie, Colin, 170
Mackenzie, William, 4, 47, 67, 101, 151–52, 194n23, 196n45, 197n55; on Greek politics, 159; on JEDBURGHS, 169
MacLeish, Archibald, 137
"Mad Mullah of Somaliland." See Mohammed Abdullah Hassan
Mahmud Barzanji, 3
mail, 45, 55, 64, 91, 132, 204n176
Malaya, 170, 244n132
Manchukuo, 88
Mao Tse-tung, 72, 93–95, 171, 214n125, 217n160, 217n164
Marks, Leo, 9
Marshall, Harry Ignatius, 243n121
martial arts, 129
Masons. See Freemasonry
Massy, Hugh, 110, 111
McVean, Helen, 8
Menzies, Stewart, 48
MEW. See Ministry of Economic Warfare (MEW)
MI3(a), 74
MI3(c), 40
MI5. See Security Service (MI5)
MI9, 106, 129
Mihailović, Draža, 157, 158
Military Intelligence, 40, 47, 73, 76, 89, 91, 93, 103; SOE creation, 116. See also MI3(a); MI3(c); MI9; MI(R); Security Service (MI5)

The Military Lessons of the Arab Rebellion, 79–80, 81, 86–87, 213n116
Military Training Directorate (MTI), 40
Miller, Roy, 78
Ministry of Economic Warfare (MEW), 5, 6, 77, 97, 102, 115, 117, 119, 145
Ministry of Information, 43, 117, 118, 119
MI(R) (Military Intelligence [Research]), 48–50, 73, 77, 100, 101, 198n73; and Arab Revolt in Palestine, 79, 85, 86, 87; Auxiliary Units, 112, 114; China, 72, 88, 89, 93, 95, 96; G(R), 152; Greece, 159; incorporation into SOE, 102, 103, 116, 117, 119, 120, 124; Jack Wilson in, 128; Middle East, 85, 152; Norway, 108–11; Poland (No. 4 Military Mission), 103–105; training, 103, 122, 129; World War II, 106, 107, 114–15
Mockaitis, Thomas, 190n149, 211n91
Mockler-Ferryman, Eric, 197n58
Mohammed Abdullah Hassan, 35
Mola, Emilio, 74
Montgomery, Bernard, 87
morale, 19, 20, 21, 52–53, 59, 62–63, 66–67; assassination and, 210n68; Gubbins's view, 156; Independent Companies, 108–109; Spanish Civil War, 75–76; World War II, 115, 122, 131, 169, 242n108
Moravec, František, 108, 154, 155
Morris, Eric, 109, 223n55
Morris, Roland, 231n64
Moulin, Jean, 164, 165
Mountbatten, Louis Mountbatten, Earl, 172
movie theater attacks. *See* cinemas, attacks on (and in)
Mowrer, Edgar, 99, 135

MTI. *See* Military Training Directorate (MTI)
Mufti of Palestine Amin al-Husseini. *See* Husseini, Amin al-, Grand Mufti of Palestine
Mukden Incident, 88, 134
Mussolini, Benito, 134, 156
mutinies, 17, 90, 185n48
My Reminiscences in East Africa (Lettow-Vorbeck), 67, 68, 70–71

National Liberation Front (EAM) (Greece), 159, 160
Nelson, Frank, 9, 119, 123, 135, 145–46, 227n137
Netherlands, 74, 98, 99, 115, 163–64, 175, 179
neutrality, 139
neutral territory, 92, 216n152
New Zealand, 42
Nicholls, Frederick William "Nick," 34
night operations, 68, 79–80, 88, 210n51, 243n121; training, 109, 114. *See also* Special Night Squads (SNS) (Palestine)
NOAH'S ARK. *See* Operation NOAH'S ARK
NORDPOL. *See* Operation NORDPOL
Normandy, 115, 150; Allied landings, 163, 165, 166, 168
North-West Frontier, India, 32–33, 36, 37, 46, 74, 86–87, 110, 192n180
Norway, 100, 120, 150, 161–62, 223n55; Fleming in, 113; German invasion, 98, 99, 106, 108, 109–11; Gubbins's award, 179; Independent Companies in, 102, 108–11, 122, 123, 162; MI(R) scouting in, 106
Notes on Guerrilla Warfare in Ireland, 27, 29, 30, 37
Notes on the Sino-Japanese War, 89

O'Connor, Rory, 25, 26

Office of Strategic Services
(OSS), 124, 130, 135, 137–45,
235n116; France, 166–67, 168,
169; international sphere of
operation, 233n91; Norway,
161. See also *War Report of the OSS*
Office of War Information (OWI),
137
Officers' Emergency Reserve, 48, 50
O'Halpin, Eunan, 31
oil, 44, 78, 115
On Guerrilla Warfare (Mao), 93,
217n164, 218n170
Operation BEARSKIN, 158
Operation CHARACTER, 173, 243n131
Operation DRAGOON, 242n107
Operation GUNNERSIDE, 162
Operation HUSKY, 133, 156
Operation JAYWICK, 171
Operation NOAH'S ARK, 160, 161
Operation NORDPOL, 163
Operation OVERLORD, 158, 166
Operation RIMAU, 171
Orange Free State. See Second Anglo-Boer War
organization of forces, 94, 131, 151, 204n192
OSS. See Office of Strategic Services (OSS)
OVERLORD. See Operation OVERLORD
Oxford Group, 45

Pakenham, Thomas, 59
Palestine, 77, 98, 209n34. See also Arab Revolt in Palestine, 1936–39
Palestinian Arabs, British opinion of, 86–87
Palmer, Roundell. See Selborne, Roundell Cecil Palmer, Earl of
parachute drops, 101, 121, 153, 154; Albania, 161; France, 168, 242n105; Greece, 159–60; Norway, 162
parachute training, 126, 144

Paris, 75; Brandenburgers in, 98; Brooker roots in, 234n110; Czechs in, 108, 154, 155; Gubbins in, 106–107, 108; Wilkinson in, 108, 155
parties, 147, 148
The Partisan Leader's Handbook (Gubbins) (*PLH*), 5, 19, 28–29, 30, 51–53, 77, 101, 189n133; physical description, 18n9; in SOE training syllabus, 130, 131–33
Paul, Prince of Yugoslavia, 157
Peers, William, 174
Peninsular War, 118
Perkins, H. B., 227n161
Persia, 197n55
Peter II of Yugoslavia, 157
petroleum. See oil
Philby, Kim, 125, 195n35, 234n110
Piggott, F. S. G., 91, 92
Pimlott, Ben, 115, 236n134
Pink's War, 32, 36
Poland, 48, 51, 66, 85, 102, 108, 122, 150, 153–54; air support, 133; Auxiliary Units and, 113; Carton de Wiart in, 14; General Staff in Paris, 107; German subversive operations in, 97–98, 99; Gubbins's award, 178; Home Army, 107, 153–54, 177; intelligence, 114, 199n92; No. 4 Military Mission, 100, 103–105; in SOE's "Force 139," 151. See also Warsaw Uprising
police, 81, 83, 126, 127, 131; Burma, 172; India, 128; Shanghai, 129, 229n32, 230n37. See also Royal Irish Constabulary
Political Warfare Executive (PWE), 43, 119, 137, 236n134
Poole, Frederick, 15, 183n19
Porch, Douglas, 22
postal communications. See mail
Prendergast, J. H., 110
Prince, Tom von, 70
Prince Paul of Yugoslavia. See Paul, Prince of Yugoslavia

prisoners, 55, 64, 106, 118, 129, 155–56, 163
propaganda, 17, 43, 44, 93; anti-Japanese, 96; Arab Revolt in Palestine, 78; assassination as, 155; Bolshevik, 185n43; leaflet drops, 35, 36, 75–76; SOE section on, 119; Spanish Civil War, 75–76; World War II, 115
PWE. *See* Political Warfare Executive (PWE)

Qawuqji, Fawzi al-, 87

radio, 44, 75, 78, 192n175
RAF. *See* Royal Air Force (RAF)
railways, 69, 78, 79, 84, 88, 90, 91, 92; defense 56, 68, 79; Norway, 161; sabotage training, 126. *See also* locomotives
Rawlinson, Henry Seymour Rawlinson, Baron, 16
Read, Conyers, 135
reconnaissance. *See* scouts and scouting (reconnaissance)
Record of the Rebellion in Ireland, 25, 28, 189n35
reserve forces, British. *See* Officers' Emergency Reserve; Territorial Army (TA)
Riley, Quintin, 222n54
RIMAU. *See* Operation RIMAU
road blockading. *See* blockading of roads
Roberts, Frederick Sleigh Roberts, Earl, 55–56
Romania, 44, 48, 51, 103, 105, 157, 189n130
Roosevelt, Franklin, 135, 136, 137, 138, 143
Roosevelt, Kermit, 223n54, 231n61
Royal Air Force (RAF), 34–37, 41, 65, 105; Bomber Command, 176; France, 168; Norway, 161; parachute training, 126; Pink's War, 32, 36; Poland, 151, 153; Yugoslavia, 158

Royal Artillery (RA), 14, 23, 32, 40
Royal Artillery Mounted Rifles, 24
Royal Canadian Mounted Police, 140
Royal Engineers, 43, 46, 86
Royal Field Artillery (RFA), 24, 25, 32, 26
Royal Irish Constabulary, 26, 27, 81
Royal Marines, 128–29
Royal Military Academy, Woolwich, 12–13, 46, 49, 82
Royal Navy, 34, 41, 110, 141
Russia, 14–19, 30, 31, 32, 34–35, 47, 49, 134. *See also* Bolshevik Revolution
Russian Civil War, 47, 92, 229n32. *See also* White Russians
Russo-Japanese War, 128

sabotage, 44–45, 48, 50, 165; Auxiliary Units, 102; nighttime, 210n51; Philby on, 195n35; Second Sino-Japanese War, 216n150; Spanish Civil War, 74; training, 126, 127, 144; World War II, 115, 122, 160, 162, 163, 168. *See also* industrial sabotage
Sandford, D. A., 152
Schutzstaffel (SS), 98, 164, 168
Schutztruppe, 10, 67–71, 206n222
"The Science of Guerrilla Warfare" (Lawrence), 61, 64, 67
SCISSORSFORCE, 110–11, 222n54
Scotland: Gubbins retirement in, 179; training in, 125–26
Scotland Yard, 125
Scots Guards, 111, 223n54, 223n61
Scouting for Boys (Baden-Powell), 128
scouts and scouting (reconnaissance), 57, 58
Seagrim, Hugh, 172
Seaman, Mark, 4, 49
Second Anglo-Boer War, 10, 31, 39, 53, 54–61, 76, 90; Callwell in, 18; cavalry, 22; Churchill in, 118; international law, 202n146

Second Sino-Japanese War, 72, 87–92, 129, 214n132, 215n137, 215–16nn148–50, 216n156
Second World War. *See* World War II
The Secret History of SOE (Mackenzie), 194n23, 196n45, 197n55
Secret Intelligence Service (SIS or MI6), 4, 7, 48, 116, 117, 119, 145, 226n116; Czechoslovakia, 108; Denmark, 162; Donovan briefing, 135; Foreign Office relationship, 107; Inter-Services Projects Board, 112; SOE disbanding, 178; U.S. relations, 136, 137, 138, 175. *See also* Section D
Secret War Report of the OSS, 231n61
Section D, 7, 10, 31, 43–45, 47–50, 198n73; Auxiliary Units, 112, 113; incorporation into SOE, 102, 116, 117, 119, 120, 124; Jeffreys-Jones's view, 143; Philby in, 195n35; World War II, 105, 106, 107, 114–15, 159, 225n95
Security Service (MI5), 31, 45, 116, 126, 135
Segev, Tom, 211n91
Selborne, Roundell Cecil Palmer, Earl of, 6, 9, 145, 146, 149, 159, 178, 180
Seyss-Inquart, Arthur, 97
SHAEF. *See* Supreme Headquarters Allied Expeditionary Force (SHAEF)
Shanghai, 91, 129, 216n149, 229n32, 230n37
Sheehan, William, 189n135
Sherman, William T., 59
Sherwood, Bob, 232n83
"Shetland Bus," 161
shoes, rubber-soled. *See* footwear, rubber-soled
Siberia, 134, 231n64
Sicily, 133, 140, 156, 158, 160

Sinclair, Hugh, 194n23
Singapore, 170
Sino-Japanese War, 1894–95. *See* First Sino-Japanese War
Sino-Japanese War, 1937–45. *See* Second Sino-Japanese War
SIS. *See* Secret Intelligence Service (SIS or MI6)
Skinnarland, Einar, 162
Slavo-British Legion, 185n48
Slim, William, 173, 174–75
Slovakia, 176
Small Wars: Their Principles and Practice (Callwell), 18–22
smuggling, 59, 78, 115, 121, 160, 208n34
Smuts, Jan, 58, 59, 69, 201n122
Snow, Edgar, 89, 217n164
SNS. *See* Special Night Squads (SNS) (Palestine)
SOE in France (Foot), 4, 181n4
Solborg, Robert, 137
Somaliland, 13, 35
Somme Offensive. *See* Battle of the Somme (1918)
South African Air Force, 153
South African Republic. *See* Second Anglo-Boer War
Soviet Union, 33, 39, 40; German invasion, 153; German spies in, 99; Spanish Civil War, 73, 74–75; World War II, 155, 157, 158, 160
Spanish Civil War, 31, 35, 46, 72, 73–77, 83, 89, 92; international participation, 207n4; Brooker experience, 234n110
"sparrow war," 88
SPARTAN war games, 166
Special Air Service, 127, 130, 186n69
Special Forces Club, 179
Special Night Squads (SNS) (Palestine), 72, 82, 83–85, 211n91, 213n111
Special Operations (Australia) (SOA), 171

spies and spying, 58, 64, 70, 125, 142, 195n35; COI mission, 133; Donovan predilection, 124; German, 98, 99; Russia, 16; training, 125, 131, 138
SS. See *Schutzstaffel* (SS)
Stachiewicz, Wacław, 105
Stafford, David, 139, 226n128, 234n110
Stephenson, William, 136
Stevenson, Noel, 172
Stilwell, Joseph, 174
Stimson, Henry, 136, 232n77
Strange, William, 6
street fighting, 110
Strong, Kenneth, 188n101
Stuart, Campbell, 43, 194n23
Stuart, Duncan, 7
Sudetenland, 39, 40, 97, 124, 134–35, 219n181
Supreme Headquarters Allied Expeditionary Force (SHAEF), 166, 169, 175
Sweden, 44, 106, 109, 161
Switzerland, 97, 119, 234n110
Sykes, Alan, 130
Sykes, Christopher, 82, 84, 212n91
Sykes-Fairburn fighting knife, 130, 230n39

Taylor, A. J. P., 219n185
Taylor, George, 121
Tegart, Charles, 79, 98, 128, 229n24
Territorial Army (TA), 40, 48, 108, 109, 113
Thorne, Andrew, 113
Tiberias, 213n111
Tientsin, 91
"time-pencil," 51
Tito, Josip, 157, 158
torture, 211n91
Towle, Philip Anthony, 78
Townshend, Charles, 82
training, 70, 84–85, 122, 124–49; Auxiliary Units, 113; Independent Companies, 109; JEDBURGHS, 167, 241n96; jungle, 150; OSS, 235n116

Trappes-Lomax, T. B., 111
Turkey: Chanak crisis, 42; Greco-Turkish War, 18. *See also* Arab Revolt, 1916–18

uniforms, 58, 68, 131, 167; use in disguise, 59, 60, 97, 98, 126, 202n146
United States, 99, 232n78, 232n83; British role in training, 5–6, 124, 133–45, 233n95; in Burma, 174; Civil War, 59; Department of War, 137; German spies in, 99; Gubbins's award, 179; in Inter-Service Planning Staff, 166; Irish Revolution and, 92; JEDBURGHS role, 167; SIS relations, 136, 137, 138, 175; World War II casualties, 176. *See also* Office of Strategic Services (OSS)
U.S. Army Air Forces, 153. *See also* Air Transport Command
U.S. Marine Corps, 93, 217n160

van Cutsem, W. E. See Cutsem, W. E. van
Vereker, John. See Gort, John Vereker, Viscount
volunteers: British, 109; Dutch, 98; French, 164; Spanish Civil War, 73, 76

Waller, Douglas, 231n64
War Cabinet, 7, 115, 117–18, 121, 123, 226n116
War Office (UK), 4, 49, 89, 124; Anglo-Irish War, 25; Brooke in, 40; Gubbins in, 39–40; Inter-Services Projects Board, 112; Ireland, 190n149; SOE creation, 116–17. *See also* British Army; Combined Operations; General Staff (Research) (GS[R]); Home Forces; Military Intelligence
War Report of the OSS, 135–36, 142, 143, 231n61

Warsaw Uprising, 153, 176
Wassmuss, Wilhelm, 197n55
Waziristan, 32, 36–37
Weale, Adrian, 192n179
Westwell, Ian, 219n185
Wheatley, Dennis, 47, 74, 147–48, 208n16
Wheeler, Mark, 141
whispering campaigns, 34, 112, 184n43
White, Ralph, 186n69
White Russians, 15, 134, 178, 229n32, 231n64
Whitney, William, 232n83
Wilkinson, Peter, 4, 23, 24, 26, 106, 112, 120–21, 221n24; Czechoslovakia, 155; on first MI(R) courses, 199n87; in MI(R) training school, 61; Poland, 105; in Section D Balkan unit, 107, 221n24; in SOE, 121
Williams, Garland, 140
Willoughby, Charles, 171
Wilson, Henry, 25, 146, 242n107
Wilson, Jack S., 128, 227n161
Wilson, Woodrow, 134, 231n64
Wingate, Orde, 82–86, 152, 212n91, 212n98, 213n111
Wogan Browne, J. H., 25
women civilians. *See under* civilians
women SOE staffers, 147–48
Woolwich. *See* Royal Military Academy, Woolwich
World War I, 12–14, 15, 34, 41, 42; Dalton in, 123; Donovan in, 134; East Africa campaign, 39, 47, 67–71; Ministry of Blockade, 115
World War II, 3, 65, 66, 72, 100, 101, 102–23, 149, 175–77; Abwehr subversion in, 97–98; casualties, 176, 243n131; OSS report on, 135–36; SOE training in, 130–31; Spanish Civil War as testing ground, 73; United States, 136, 137–45

Yugoslavia, 151, 152, 155, 157–58
Yu Shen, 216n156

Zionists, 77

www.ingramcontent.com/pod-product-compliance
Lightning Source LLC
Chambersburg PA
CBHW022107150426
43195CB00008B/307